CompTIA®
Network+®
Review Guide
Exam N10-007
Fourth Edition

CompTIA®
Network+®
Review Guide
Exam N10-007
Fourth Edition

Jon Buhagiar

A Wiley Brand

Senior Acquisitions Editor: Kenyon Brown
Development Editor: David Clark
Technical Editor: Wynn D. Smith, Brent Hamilton
Copy Editor: Elizabeth Welch
Editorial Manager: Pete Gaughan
Production Manager: Kathleen Wisor
Executive Editor: Jim Minatel
Proofreader: Kim Wimpsett
Indexer: John Sleeva
Project Coordinator, Cover: Brent Savage
Cover Designer: Wiley
Cover Image: ©Getty Images, Inc./Jeremy Woodhouse

Copyright © 2019 by John Wiley & Sons, Inc., Indianapolis, Indiana

Published simultaneously in Canada

ISBN: 978-1-119-51954-6
ISBN: 978-1-119-51956-0 (ebk.)

Manufactured in the United States of America

For general information on our other products and services or to obtain technical support, please contact
our Customer Care Department within the U.S. at (877) 762-2974, outside the U.S. at (317) 572-3993 or
fax (317) 572-4002.

Wiley publishes in a variety of print and electronic formats and by print-on-demand. Some material
included with standard print versions of this book may not be included in e-books or in print-on-demand.
If this book refers to media such as a CD or DVD that is not included in the version you purchased, you
may download this material at http://booksupport.wiley.com. For more information about Wiley products, visit www.wiley.com.

Library of Congress Control Number: 2018946243

C10005056_110218

I dedicate this book to my wife Teresa and my son Joseph. I love you both.
—JAB

Acknowledgments

I'd like to thank the many people who made this book possible. Thanks to: Kenyon Brown at Wiley Publishing, for giving me the opportunity to write this book. David Clark, for working with me as the developmental editor and making the entire process seamless. Wynn D. Smith and Brent Hamilton, working as the technical editors on this book to ensure I didn't miss any details. Liz Welch, for her many edits that helped make this book a polished product. And the many other people I've never met who worked behind the scenes to make this book a success.

About the Author

Jon Buhagiar, BS/ITM, MCSE, CCNA is an information technology professional with two decades of experience in higher education and the private sector.

Jon currently serves as Supervisor of Network Operations at Pittsburgh Technical College. In this role, he manages datacenter and network infrastructure operations and IT operations and is involved in strategic planning of IT projects supporting the quality of education at the college. He also serves as an adjunct instructor in the college's School of Information Technology department, where he teaches certification courses for Microsoft and Cisco certifications. Jon has taught as an instructor for 18 years with several colleges in the Pittsburgh area, since the introduction of the Windows NT MCSE in 1998.

Jon earned his BS in Information Technology Management from Western Governors University. He also achieved an Associates in Business Management from Pittsburgh Technical College. He has recently earned his Windows Server 2012 R2 MCSE as well as Cisco CCNA Routing & Switching certification. Other certifications include CompTIA Network+, A+, and Project+.

In addition to his professional and teaching roles, he has authored *CCNA Routing and Switching Practice Tests: Exam 100-105, Exam 200-105, and Exam 200-125* (Sybex, 2016). He has also served as the technical editor for the second edition of the *CompTIA Cloud+ Study Guide* (Sybex, 2016), *CCNA Security Study Guide: Exam 210-260* (Sybex, 2018), and *CCNA Cloud Complete Study Guide: Exam 210-451 and Exam 210-455* (Sybex, 2018). He has spoken at several conferences about spam and email systems. He is an active radio electronics hobbyist and has held a ham radio license for the past 16 years (KB3KGS). He experiments with electronics and has a strong focus on the Internet of Things (IoT).

Contents at a Glance

Contents

xviii Contents

Chapter 3

CompTIA.

Becoming a CompTIA Certified IT Professional is Easy

It's also the best way to reach greater professional opportunities and rewards.

Why Get CompTIA Certified?

Growing Demand

Labor estimates predict some technology fields will experience growth of over 20% by the year 2020.* CompTIA certification qualifies the skills required to join this workforce.

Higher Salaries

IT professionals with certifications on their resume command better jobs, earn higher salaries and have more doors open to new multi-industry opportunities.

Verified Strengths

91% of hiring managers indicate CompTIA certifications are valuable in validating IT expertise, making certification the best way to demonstrate your competency and knowledge to employers.**

Universal Skills

CompTIA certifications are vendor neutral—which means that certified professionals can proficiently work with an extensive variety of hardware and software found in most organizations.

 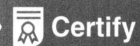 

Learn more about what the exam covers by reviewing the following:

- Exam objectives for key study points.

- Sample questions for a general overview of what to expect on the exam and examples of question format.

- Visit online forums, like LinkedIn, to see what other IT professionals say about CompTIA exams.

Purchase a voucher at a Pearson VUE testing center or at CompTIAstore.com.

- Register for your exam at a Pearson VUE testing center:

- Visit pearsonvue.com/CompTIA to find the closest testing center to you.

- Schedule the exam online. You will be required to enter your voucher number or provide payment information at registration.

- Take your certification exam.

Congratulations on your CompTIA certification!

- Make sure to add your certification to your resume.

- Check out the CompTIA Certification Roadmap to plan your next career move.

Learn more: Certification.CompTIA.org

* Source: CompTIA 9th Annual Information Security Trends study: 500 U.S. IT and Business Executives Responsible for Security
** Source: CompTIA Employer Perceptions of IT Training and Certification

Introduction

You may be new to the field of computer networking, or perhaps you are in pursuit of proving your knowledge and understanding of computer networking. In either case, the CompTIA Network+ certification exam is a great start to your professional development. The Network+ certification is considered by employers industry-wide to be proof of the knowledge of networking theory, skill, and systems. The Network+ certification is granted to those individuals who have attained this information and show a basic competency for meeting the needs of both personal and organization computing environments.

The CompTIA Network+ objectives have changed with the introduction of the CompTIA Network+ N10-007 certification exam. This change in objectives and topics from the prior exam was necessary to keep up with the latest technologies used in networks today. The foundation of networking concepts have remained relatively similar, despite the introduction of more advanced technologies. This is one of the reasons the CompTIA Network+ exam is so widely valued by employers. As of this writing, the objectives are current for the Network+ N10-007 certification exam as stated by CompTIA (https://www.comptia.org).

What Is Network+ Certification?

The Computing Technology Industry Association (CompTIA) developed the Network+ certification to be vendor neutral and recognized industry-wide. The Network+ certification is considered the benchmark of networking theory. Candidates who earn the Network+ certification have knowledge of the design, operation, maintenance, security, and trouble-shooting of networks. Employers worldwide recognize Network+ certified individuals as having a basic vendor-agnostic networking theory that can be applied to any specific system.

The Network+ certification was originally sponsored by IT industry leaders like IBM, Microsoft, and Compaq, among others. The goal was to create a certification that would give recognition of individuals with a basic theory of networking. Today, more complex networking theory is required by employers, and Network+ has evolved into a comprehensive exam. The CompTIA Network+ Exam N10-007 tests five domains of network theory:

- Network Concepts
- Infrastructure
- Network Operations
- Network Security
- Network Troubleshooting and Tools

For the latest pricing on the exam and updates to the registration procedures, go to www.vue.com. You can register online for the exam. If you have further questions about the scope of the exam or related CompTIA programs, refer to the CompTIA website at www.comptia.org.

Is This Book for You?

The *CompTIA Network+ Review Guide: Exam N10-007, Fourth Edition* is designed to be a complete, portable exam review guide that can be used either in conjunction with a more complete study program (such as Sybex's *CompTIA Network+ Study Guide: Exam N10-007*, computer-based training courseware, or a classroom/lab environment) or as an exam review for those who don't need more extensive test preparation. The goal of this book to thoroughly cover those topics you can expect to be tested on.

Perhaps you've been working with information technologies for many years. The thought of paying lots of money for a specialized IT exam preparation course probably doesn't sound too appealing. What can they teach you that you don't already know, right? Be careful, though—many experienced network administrators have walked confidently into the test center only to walk sheepishly out of it after failing an IT exam. I've run across many of these network administrators throughout my 20 years of teaching networking. After you've finished reading this book, you should have a clear idea of how your understanding of networking technologies matches up with the expectations of the Network+ test writers.

> The goal of the Review Guide series is to help Network+ candidates brush up on the subjects on which they can expect to be tested on the Network+ exam. For complete in-depth coverage of the technologies and topics involved, we recommend *CompTIA Network+ Study Guide* from Sybex.

How Is This Book Organized?

This book is organized according to the official objectives list prepared by CompTIA for the Network+ Exam N10-007. The chapters correspond to the five major domains of objective and topic groupings. The exam is weighted across these five domains:

- Domain 1.0 Network Concepts (23 percent)
- Domain 2.0 Infrastructure (18 percent)
- Domain 3.0 Network Operations (17 percent)
- Domain 4.0 Network Security (20 percent)
- Domain 5.0 Network Troubleshooting and Tools (22 percent)

In each chapter, the top-level exam objective from each domain is addressed in turn. This discussion also contains an Exam Essentials section. Here you are given a short list of topics that you should explore fully before taking the test. Included in the Exam Essentials are notations on key pieces of information you should have gleaned from *CompTIA Network+ Review Guide: Exam N10-007, Fourth Edition*. At the end of each chapter you'll find the "Review Questions" section. These questions are designed to help you gauge your mastery of the content in the chapter.

Tips for Taking the Network+ Exam

Here are some general tips for taking your exams successfully:

- Bring two forms of ID with you. One must be a photo ID, such as a driver's license. The other can be a major credit card or a passport. Both forms must include a signature.

- Arrive early at the exam center so you can relax and review your study materials, particularly tables and lists of exam-related information.

- Read the questions carefully. Don't be tempted to jump to an early conclusion. Make sure you know exactly what the question is asking.

- Don't leave any unanswered questions. Unanswered questions give you no opportunity for guessing correctly and scoring more points.

- There will be questions with multiple correct responses. When there is more than one correct answer, a message on the screen will prompt you to either "Choose two" or "Choose all that apply." Be sure to read the messages displayed so that you know how many correct answers you must choose.

- Questions needing only a single correct answer will use radio buttons for selecting an answer, whereas those needing two or more answers will use checkboxes.

- When answering multiple-choice questions you're not sure about, use a process of elimination to get rid of the obviously incorrect answers first. Doing so will improve your odds if you need to make an educated guess.

- On form-based tests (nonadaptive), because the hard questions will eat up the most time, save them for last. You can move forward and backward through the exam.

- For the latest pricing on the exams and updates to the registration procedures, visit CompTIA's website at www.comptia.org.

How to Contact the Publisher

Sybex welcomes feedback on all of its titles. Visit the Sybex website at www.sybex.com for book updates and additional certification information. You'll also find forms you can use to submit comments or suggestions regarding this or any other Sybex titles.

The Exam Objectives

The following are the areas (referred to as domains by CompTIA) in which you must be proficient in order to pass the Network+ exam:

Domain 1.0: Network Concepts   This domain begins with the descriptions of several protocols you will encounter as a network professional. The OSI layers and their specific function and purpose are then covered. The domain explores the basic concepts and characteristics of routing and switching. IP addressing, subnetting, and VLSM are covered to support routing and efficient network design. The domain also describes the various network topologies for both wired and wireless networking, as well as the technologies that support the Internet of Things (IoT). The domain also explores wireless technologies, their characteristics, and various configurations. Cloud computing concepts according to the NIST definitions are covered. The domain concludes with various network services that support IP addressing and name resolution.

Domain 2.0: Infrastructure   This domain covers the various cabling media, specifications, standards, connectors, and transceivers that you will encounter in network infrastructure. The domain explores the basic building blocks of network devices, such as firewalls, routers, switches, and more. The domain then covers more advanced network devices, such as wireless controllers, multilayer switches, VPN concentrators, and more. The domain also explores virtualization and network storage concepts found in many networks today to support private cloud computing. The domain concludes with the coverage of various WAN technologies that are used today, along with their characteristics and common media.

Domain 3.0: Network Operations   This domain covers the various diagram and documentation components so that network operations can be documented properly. The domain then explores availability concepts such as high availability and fault tolerance to support the network and its components. Recovery of sites and data are also covered to support the concepts of recovery from failure. The topics of scanning, monitoring, and patching are examined to support the concepts of secure operations and overall monitoring. The topic of remote access methods is also explored so you can understand how network operations are supported remotely. This domain concludes with the coverage of policies and best practices to support network operations.

Domain 4.0: Network Security   This domain focuses on security for both the physical and nonphysical aspects of network design and operations. This domain covers the various detection and prevention methods of security. It then explores authorization, authentication, and accounting theory and practice, along with the various factors of security and access control systems. Wireless security is also covered in its entirety to support secure wireless communications. The domain examines the various network attacks that you may encounter in a network. The domain concludes with hardening techniques and mitigation techniques so that security problems can be avoided.

Domain 5.0: Network Troubleshooting and Tools   This domain covers the various troubleshooting methodologies used to diagnose problems in a network. It then explores the various hardware and software tools that you will use to diagnose problems in both wired and wireless networks. The domain covers both wired and wireless connectivity issues and performance-related issues that you may encounter in your daily operations. The domain concludes with real-world application of the tools and troubleshooting methodologies used to diagnose problems in a network.

The Network+ Exam Objectives

At the beginning of each chapter, I have included a complete listing of the topics that will be covered in that chapter. These topic selections are developed straight from the test objectives listed on CompTIA's website. They are provided for easy reference and to assure you that you are on track with learning the objectives. Note that exam objectives are subject to change at any time without prior notice and at CompTIA's sole discretion. Please visit the Network+ Certification page of CompTIA's website (https://certification.comptia.org/certifications/network) for the most current listing of exam objectives.

Chapter 1: Domain 1.0: Networking Concepts

1.1 Explain the purposes and uses of ports and protocols.

- Protocols and ports
  - SSH 22
  - DNS 53
  - SMTP 25
  - SFTP 22
  - FTP 20, 21
  - TFTP 69
  - TELNET 23
  - DHCP 67, 68
  - HTTP 80
  - HTTPS 443
  - SNMP 161
  - RDP 3389
  - NTP 123
  - SIP 5060, 5061
  - SMB 445
  - POP 110
  - IMAP 143
  - LDAP 389
  - LDAPS 636
  - H.323 1720
- Protocol types
  - ICMP
  - UDP
  - TCP
  - IP
- Connection-oriented vs. connectionless

1.2 Explain devices, applications, protocols and services at their appropriate OSI layers.

- Layer 7 – Application
- Layer 6 – Presentation

- Layer 5 – Session
- Layer 4 – Transport
- Layer 3 – Network
- Layer 2 – Data link
- Layer 1 – Physical

1.3 Explain the concepts and characteristics of routing and switching.

- Properties of network traffic
  - Collision domains
  - Broadcast domains
  - CSMA/CD
  - CSMA/CA
  - Protocol data units
  - MTU
  - Broadcast
  - Multicast
  - Unicast
- Segmentation and interface properties
  - VLANs
  - Trunking (802.1Q)
  - Tagging and untagging ports
  - Port mirroring
  - Switching loops/spanning tree
  - PoE and PoE+ (802.3af, 802.3at)
  - DMZ
  - MAC address table
  - ARP table
- Routing
  - Routing types
    - Static
    - Dynamic
    - Default

- Routing protocols (IPv4 and IPv6)
    - Distance-vector routing protocols
        - RIP
        - EIGRP
    - Link-state routing protocols
        - OSPF
    - Hybrid
        - BGP
- IPv6 concepts
    - Addressing
    - Tunneling
    - Dual stack
    - Router advertisement
    - Neighbor discovery
- Performance concepts
    - Traffic shaping
    - QoS
    - Diffserv
    - CoS
- NAT/PAT
- Port forwarding
- Access control list
- Distributed switching
- Packet-switched vs. circuit-switched network
- Software-defined networking

1.4 Given a scenario, configure the appropriate IP addressing components.

- Private vs. public
- Loopback and reserved
- Default gateway
- Virtual IP
- Subnet mask
- Subnetting
    - Classful
        - Classes A, B, C, D, and E

- Classless
    - VLSM
    - CIDR notation (IPv4 vs. IPv6)
- Address assignments
    - DHCP
    - DHCPv6
    - Static
    - APIPA
    - EUI64
    - IP reservations

1.5 Compare and contrast the characteristics of network topologies, types, and technologies.

- Wired topologies
    - Logical vs. physical
    - Star
    - Ring
    - Mesh
    - Bus
- Wireless topologies
    - Ad-hoc
    - Infrastructure
    - Mesh
- Types
    - LAN
    - WLAN
    - WAN
    - MAN
    - CAN
    - SAN
    - PAN
- Technologies that facilitate the Internet of Things (IoT)
    - Z-Wave
    - Ant+
    - Bluetooth

- NFC
- IR
- RFID
- 802.11

1.6 Given a scenario, implement the appropriate wireless technologies and configurations.

- 802.11 standards
  - b
  - a
  - g
  - n
  - ac
- Cellular
  - TDMA
  - CDMA
  - GSM
- Frequencies
  - 2.4GHz
  - 5.0GHz
- Speed and distance requirements
- Channel bandwidth
- Channel bonding
- MIMO/MU-MIMO
- Unidirectional/omnidirectional
- Site surveys

1.7 Summarize cloud concepts and their purposes.

- Types of services
  - SaaS
  - PaaS
  - IaaS
- Cloud delivery models
  - Private
  - Public
  - Hybrid

- Connectivity methods
- Security implications/considerations
- Relationship between local and cloud resources

1.8 Explain the functions of network services.

- DNS service
  - Record types
    - A, AAAA
    - TXT (SPF, DKIM)
    - SRV
    - MX
    - CNAME
    - NS
    - PTR
  - Internal vs. external DNS
  - Third-party/cloud-hosted DNS
  - Hierarchy
  - Forward vs. reverse zone
- DHCP service
  - MAC reservations
  - Pools
  - IP exclusions
  - Scope options
  - Lease time
  - TTL
  - DHCP relay/IP helper
- NTP
- IPAM

Chapter 2: Domain 2.0: Infrastructure

2.1 Given a scenario, deploy the appropriate cabling solution.

- Media types
  - Copper
    - UTP

- STP
- Coaxial
  - Fiber
    - Single-mode
    - Multimode
- Plenum vs. PVC
- Connector types
  - Copper
    - RJ-45
    - RJ-11
    - BNC
    - DB-9
    - DB-25
    - F-type
  - Fiber
    - LC
    - ST
    - SC
      - APC
      - UPC
      - MTRJ
- Transceivers
  - SFP
  - GBIC
  - SFP+
  - QSFP
  - Characteristics of fiber transceivers
    - Bidirectional
    - Duplex
- Termination points
  - 66 block
  - 110 block
  - Patch panel
  - Fiber distribution panel

- Copper cable standards
  - Cat 3
  - Cat 5
  - Cat 5e
  - Cat 6
  - Cat 6a
  - Cat 7
  - RG-6
  - RG-59
- Copper termination standards
  - TIA/EIA 568A
  - TIA/EIA 568B
  - Crossover
  - Straight-through
- Ethernet deployment standards
  - 100BaseT
  - 1000BaseT
  - 1000BaseLX
  - 1000BaseSX
  - 10GBaseT

2.2 Given a scenario, determine the appropriate placement of networking devices on a network and install/configure them.

- Firewall
- Router
- Switch
- Hub
- Bridge
- Modems
- Wireless access point
- Media converter
- Wireless range extender
- VoIP endpoint

2.3 Explain the purposes and use cases for advanced networking devices.

- Multilayer switch
- Wireless controller
- Load balancer
- IDS/IPS
- Proxy server
- VPN concentrator
- AAA/RADIUS server
- UTM appliance
- NGFW/Layer 7 firewall
- VoIP PBX
- VoIP gateway
- Content filter

2.4 Explain the purposes of virtualization and network storage technologies.

- Virtual networking components
    - Virtual switch
    - Virtual firewall
    - Virtual NIC
    - Virtual router
    - Hypervisor
- Network storage types
    - NAS
    - SAN
- Connection type
    - FCoE
    - Fibre Channel
    - iSCSI
    - InfiniBand
- Jumbo frame

2.5 Compare and contrast WAN technologies.

- Service type
    - ISDN
    - T1/T3

- E1/E3
- OC-3 – OC-192
- DSL
- Metropolitan Ethernet
- Cable broadband
- Dial-up
- PRI
- Transmission mediums
  - Satellite
  - Copper
  - Fiber
  - Wireless
- Characteristics of service
  - MPLS
  - ATM
  - Frame relay
  - PPPoE
  - PPP
  - DMVPN
  - SIP trunk
- Termination
  - Demarcation point
  - CSU/DSU
  - Smart jack

Chapter 3: Domain 3.0: Network Operations

3.1 Given a scenario, use appropriate documentation and diagrams to manage the network.

- Diagram symbols
- Standard operating procedures/work instructions
- Logical vs. physical diagrams
- Rack diagrams
- Change management documentation
- Wiring and port locations

- IDF/MDF documentation
- Labeling
- Network configuration and performance baselines
- Inventory management

3.2 Compare and contrast business continuity and disaster recovery concepts.

- Availability concepts
  - Fault tolerance
  - High availability
  - Load balancing
  - NIC teaming
  - Port aggregation
  - Clustering
  - Power management
    - Battery backups/UPS
    - Power generators
    - Dual power supplies
    - Redundant circuits
- Recovery
  - Cold sites
  - Warm sites
  - Hot sites
  - Backups
    - Full
    - Differential
    - Incremental
- Snapshots
- MTTR
- MTBF
- SLA requirements

3.3 Explain common scanning, monitoring and patching processes and summarize their expected outputs.

- Processes
  - Log reviewing
  - Port scanning

- - Vulnerability scanning
  - Patch management
    - Rollback
  - Reviewing baselines
  - Packet/traffic analysis
- Event management
  - Notifications
  - Alerts
  - SIEM
- SNMP monitors
  - MIB
- Metrics
  - Error rate
  - Utilization
  - Packet drops
  - Bandwidth/throughput

3.4 Given a scenario, use remote access methods.

- VPN
  - IPSec
  - SSL/TLS/DTLS
  - Site-to-site
  - Client-to-site
- RDP
- SSH
- VNC
- Telnet
- HTTPS/management URL
- Remote fie access
  - FTP/FTPS
  - SFTP
  - TFTP
- Out-of-band management
  - Modem
  - Console router

3.5 Identify policies and best practices.

- Privileged user agreement
- Password policy
- On-boarding/off-boarding procedures
- Licensing restrictions
- International export controls
- Data loss prevention
- Remote access policies
- Incident response policies
- BYOD
- AUP
- NDA
- System life cycle
  - Asset disposal
- Safety procedures and policies

Chapter 4: Domain 4.0: Network Security

4.1 Summarize the purposes of physical security devices.

- Detection
  - Motion detection
  - Video surveillance
  - Asset tracking tags
  - Tamper detection
- Prevention
  - Badges
  - Biometrics
  - Smart cards
  - Key fob
  - Locks

4.2 Explain authentication and access controls.

- Authentication, authorization, and accounting
  - RADIUS
  - TACACS+

4.4 Summarize common networking attacks.

- DoS
  - Reflective
  - Amplified
  - Distributed
- Social engineering
- Insider threat
- Logic bomb
- Rogue access point
- Evil twin
- War-driving
- Phishing
- Ransomware
- DNS poisoning
- ARP poisoning
- Spoofing
- Deauthentication
- Brute force
- VLAN hopping
- Man-in-the-middle
- Exploits vs. vulnerabilities

4.5 Given a scenario, implement network device hardening.

- Changing default credentials
- Avoiding common passwords
- Upgrading firmware
- Patching and updates
- File hashing
- Disabling unnecessary services
- Using secure protocols
- Generating new keys
- Disabling unused ports
  - IP ports
  - Device ports (physical and virtual)

4.6 Explain common mitigation techniques and their purposes.

- Signature management
- Device hardening
- Change native VLAN
- Switch port protection
    - Spanning tree
    - Flood guard
    - BPDU guard
    - Root guard
    - DHCP snooping
- Network segmentation
    - DMZ
    - VLAN
- Privileged user account
- File integrity monitoring
- Role separation
- Restricting access via ACLs
- Honeypot/honeynet
- Penetration testing

Chapter 5: Domain 5.0: Network Troubleshooting and Tools

5.1 Explain the network troubleshooting methodology.

- Identify the problem
    - Gather information
    - Duplicate the problem, if possible
    - Question users
    - Identify symptoms
    - Determine if anything has changed
    - Approach multiple problems individually
- Establish a theory of probable cause
    - Question the obvious
    - Consider multiple approaches
    - Top-to-bottom/bottom-to-top OSI model
    - Divide and conquer

- Test the theory to determine the cause
    - Once the theory is confirmed, determine the next steps to resolve the problem
    - If the theory is not confirmed, reestablish a new theory or escalate
- Establish a plan of action to resolve the problem and identify potential effects
- Implement the solution or escalate as necessary
- Verify full system functionality and, if applicable, implement preventive measures
- Document findings, actions, and outcomes

5.2 Given a scenario, use the appropriate tool.

- Hardware tools
    - Crimper
    - Cable tester
    - Punchdown tool
    - OTDR
    - Light meter
    - Tone generator
    - Loopback adapter
    - Multimeter
    - Spectrum analyzer
- Software tools
    - Packet sniffer
    - Port scanner
    - Protocol analyzer
    - Wi-Fi analyzer
    - Bandwidth speed tester
    - Command line
        - ping
        - tracert, traceroute
        - nslookup
        - ipconfig
        - ipconfig
        - iptables
        - netstat
        - tcpdump
        - pathping
        - nmap

- route
- arp
- dig

5.3 Given a scenario, troubleshoot common wired connectivity and performance issues.

- Attenuation
- Latency
- Jitter
- Crosstalk
- EMI
- Open/short
- Incorrect pin-out
- Incorrect cable type
- Bad port
- Transceiver mismatch
- TX/RX reverse
- Duplex/speed mismatch
- Damaged cables
- Bent pins
- Bottlenecks
- VLAN mismatch
- Network connection LED status indicators

5.4 Given a scenario, troubleshoot common wireless connectivity and performance issues.

- Reflection
- Refraction
- Absorption
- Latency
- Jitter
- Attenuation
- Incorrect antenna type
- Interference
- Incorrect antenna placement
- Channel overlap
- Overcapacity

- Distance limitations
- Frequency mismatch
- Wrong SSID
- Wrong passphrase
- Security type mismatch
- Power levels
- Signal-to-noise ratio

5.5 Given a scenario, troubleshoot common network service issues.

- Names not resolving
- Incorrect gateway
- Incorrect netmask
- Duplicate IP addresses
- Duplicate MAC addresses
- Expired IP address
- Rogue DHCP server
- Untrusted SSL certificate
- Incorrect time
- Exhausted DHCP scope
- Blocked TCP/UDP ports
- Incorrect host-based firewall settings
- Incorrect ACL settings
- Unresponsive service
- Hardware failure

Network+ Acronyms

Here are the acronyms of security terms that CompTIA deems important enough that they're included in the objectives list for the exam. We've repeated them here exactly as listed by CompTIA.

AAA   Authentication Authorization and Accounting

AAAA   Authentication, Authorization, Accounting and Auditing

ACL   Access Control List

ADSL   Asymmetric Digital Subscriber Line

AES   Advanced Encryption Standard

AH   Authentication Header

AP   Access Point

APC   Angle Polished Connector

APIPA   Automatic Private Internet Protocol Addressing

APT   Advanced Persistent Tool

ARIN   American Registry for Internet Numbers

ARP   Address Resolution Protocol

AS   Autonomous System

ASIC   Application Specific Integrated Circuit

ASP   Application Service Provider

ATM   Asynchronous Transfer Mode

AUP   Acceptable Use Policy

BCP   Business Continuity Plan

BERT   Bit-Error Rate Test

BGP   Border Gateway Protocol

BLE   Bluetooth Low Energy

BNC   British Naval Connector/Bayonet Neill-Concelman

BootP   Boot Protocol/Bootstrap Protocol

BPDU   Bridge Protocol Data Unit

BRI   Basic Rate Interface

BSSID   Basic Service Set Identifier

BYOD   Bring Your Own Device

CaaS   Communication as a Service

CAM   Content Addressable Memory

CAN   Campus Area Network

CARP   Common Address Redundancy Protocol

CASB   Cloud Access Security Broker

CAT   Category

CCTV   Closed Circuit TV

CDMA   Code Division Multiple Access

CSMA/CD   Carrier Sense Multiple Access/Collision Detection

CHAP   Challenge Handshake Authentication Protocol

CIDR   Classless Inter-Domain Routing

CNAME   Canonical Name

CoS   Class of Service

CPU   Central Processing Unit

CRAM-MD5   Challenge-Response Authentication Mechanism–Message Digest 5

CRC   Cyclic Redundancy Checking

CSMA/CA   Carrier Sense Multiple Access/Collision Avoidance

CSU   Channel Service Unit

CVW   Collaborative Virtual Workspace

CWDM   Course Wave Division Multiplexing

DaaS   Desktop as a Service

dB   Decibel

DCS   Distributed Computer System

DDoS   Distributed Denial of Service

DHCP   Dynamic Host Configuration Protocol

DLC   Data Link Control

DLP   Data Loss Prevention

DLR   Device Level Ring

DMZ   Demilitarized Zone

DNAT   Destination Network Address Translation

DNS   Domain Name Service/Domain Name Server/Domain Name System

DOCSIS   Data-Over-Cable Service Interface Specification

DoS   Denial of Service

DR   Designated Router

DSCP   Differentiated Services Code Point

DSL   Digital Subscriber Line

DSSS   Direct Sequence Spread Spectrum

DSU   Data Service Unit

DWDM   Dense Wavelength Division Multiplexing

E1   E-Carrier Level 1

EAP   Extensible Authentication Protocol

EDNS   Extension Mechanisms for DNS

EGP   Exterior Gateway Protocol

EIA/TIA   Electronic Industries Alliance/Telecommunication Industries Association

EMI   Electromagnetic Interference

ESD   Electrostatic Discharge

ESP   Encapsulated Security Payload

ESSID   Extended Service Set Identifier

EUI   Extended Unique Identifier

FC   Fibre Channel

FCoE   Fibre Channel over Ethernet

FCS   Frame Check Sequence

FDM   Frequency Division Multiplexing

FHSS   Frequency Hopping Spread Spectrum

FM   Frequency Modulation

FQDN   Fully Qualified Domain Name

FTP   File Transfer Protocol

FTPS   File Transfer Protocol Security

GBIC   Gigabit Interface Converter

Gbps   Gigabits per second

GLBP   Gateway Load Balancing Protocol

GPG   GNU Privacy Guard

GRE   Generic Routing Encapsulation

GSM   Global System for Mobile Communications

HA   High Availability

HDLC   High-Level Data Link Control

HDMI   High-Definition Multimedia Interface

HIDS   Host Intrusion Detection System

HIPS   Host Intrusion Prevention System

HSPA   High-Speed Packet Access

HSRP   Hot Standby Router Protocol

HT   High Throughput

HTTP   Hypertext Transfer Protocol

HTTPS   Hypertext Transfer Protocol Secure

HVAC   Heating, Ventilation and Air Conditioning

Hz   Hertz

IaaS   Infrastructure as a Service

IANA   Internet Assigned Numbers Authority

ICA   Independent Computer Architecture

ICANN   Internet Corporation for Assigned Names and Numbers

ICMP   Internet Control Message Protocol

ICS   Internet Connection Sharing/Industrial Control System

IDF   Intermediate Distribution Frame

IDS   Intrusion Detection System

IEEE   Institute of Electrical and Electronics Engineers

IGMP   Internet Group Message Protocol

IGP   Interior Gateway Protocol

IGRP   Interior Gateway Routing Protocol

IKE   Internet Key Exchange

IMAP4   Internet Message Access Protocol version 4

InterNIC   Internet Network Information Center

IoT   Internet of Things

IP   Internet Protocol

IPS   Intrusion Prevention System

IPSec   Internet Protocol Security

IPv4   Internet Protocol version 4

IPv6   Internet Protocol version 6

ISAKMP   Internet Security Association and Key Management Protocol

ISDN   Integrated Services Digital Network

IS-IS   Intermediate System to Intermediate System

ISP   Internet Service Provider

IT   Information Technology

ITS   Intelligent Transportation System

IV   Initialization Vector

Kbps   Kilobits per second

KVM   Keyboard Video Mouse

L2TP   Layer 2 Tunneling Protocol

LACP   Link Aggregation Control Protocol

LAN   Local Area Network

LC   Local Connector

LDAP   Lightweight Directory Access Protocol

LEC   Local Exchange Carrier

LED   Light Emitting Diode

LLC   Logical Link Control

LLDP   Link Layer Discovery Protocol

LSA   Link State Advertisements

LTE   Long Term Evolution

LWAPP   Light Weight Access Point Protocol

MaaS   Mobility as a Service

MAC   Media Access Control/Medium Access Control

MAN   Metropolitan Area Network

Mbps   Megabits per second

MBps   Megabytes per second

MDF   Main Distribution Frame

MDI   Media Dependent Interface

MDIX   Media Dependent Interface Crossover

MGCP   Media Gateway Control Protocol

MIB   Management Information Base

MIMO   Multiple Input, Multiple Output

MLA   Master License Agreement/Multilateral Agreement

MMF   Multimode Fiber

MOA   Memorandum of Agreement

MOU   Memorandum of Understanding

MPLS   Multiprotocol Label Switching

MS-CHAP   Microsoft Challenge Handshake Authentication Protocol

MSA   Master Service Agreement

MSDS   Material Safety Data Sheet

MT-RJ   Mechanical Transfer-Registered Jack

MTU   Maximum Transmission Unit

MTTR   Mean Time To Recovery

MTBF   Mean Time Between Failures

MU-MIMO   Multiuser Multiple Input, Multiple Output

MX   Mail Exchanger

NAC   Network Access Control

NAS   Network Attached Storage

NAT   Network Address Translation

NCP   Network Control Protocol

NDR   Non-Delivery Receipt

NetBEUI   Network Basic Input/Output Extended User Interface

NetBIOS   Network Basic Input/Output System

NFC   Near Field Communication

NFS   Network File Service

NGFW   Next-Generation Firewall

NIC   Network Interface Card

NIDS   Network Intrusion Detection System

NIPS   Network Intrusion Prevention System

NIU   Network Interface Unit

nm   Nanometer

NNTP   Network News Transport Protocol

NTP   Network Time Protocol

OCSP   Online Certificate Status Protocol

OCx   Optical Carrier

OS   Operating System

OSI   Open Systems Interconnect

OSPF   Open Shortest Path First

OTDR   Optical Time Domain Reflectometer

OUI   Organizationally Unique Identifier

PaaS   Platform as a Service

PAN   Personal Area Network

PAP   Password Authentication Protocol

PAT   Port Address Translation

PC   Personal Computer

PCM   Phase-Change Memory

PDoS   Permanent Denial of Service

PDU   Protocol Data Unit

PGP   Pretty Good Privacy

PKI   Public Key Infrastructure

PoE   Power over Ethernet

POP   Post Office Protocol

POP3   Post Office Protocol version 3

POTS   Plain Old Telephone Service

PPP   Point-to-Point Protocol

PPPoE   Point-to-Point Protocol over Ethernet

PPTP   Point-to-Point Tunneling Protocol

PRI   Primary Rate Interface

PSK   Pre-Shared Key

PSTN   Public Switched Telephone Network

PTP   Point-to-Point

PTR   Pointer

PUA   Privileged User Agreement

PVC   Permanent Virtual Circuit

QoS   Quality of Service

QSFP   Quad Small Form-Factor Pluggable

RADIUS   Remote Authentication Dial-In User Service

RARP   Reverse Address Resolution Protocol

RAS   Remote Access Service

RDP   Remote Desktop Protocol

RF   Radio Frequency

RFI   Radio Frequency Interference

RFP   Request for Proposal

RG   Radio Guide

RIP   Routing Internet Protocol

RJ   Registered Jack

RPO   Recovery Point Objective

RSA   Rivest, Shamir, Adelman

RSH   Remote Shell

RSTP   Rapid Spanning Tree Protocol

RTO   Recovery Time Objective

RTP   Real-Time Protocol

RTSP   Real-Time Streaming Protocol

RTT   Round Trip Time or Real Transfer Time

SA   Security Association

SaaS   Software as a Service

SC   Standard Connector/Subscriber Connector

SCADA   Supervisory Control and Data Acquisition

SCP   Secure Copy Protocol

SDLC   Software Development Life Cycle

SDN   Software Defined Network

SDP   Session Description Protocol

SDSL   Symmetrical Digital Subscriber Line

SFP   Small Form-factor Pluggable

SFTP   Secure File Transfer Protocol

SGCP   Simple Gateway Control Protocol

SHA   Secure Hash Algorithm

SIEM   Security Information and Event Management

SIP   Session Initiation Protocol

SLA   Service Level Agreement

SLAAC   Stateless Address Auto Configuration

SLIP   Serial Line Internet Protocol

SMB   Server Message Block

SMF   Single-Mode Fiber

SMS   Short Message Service

SMTP   Simple Mail Transfer Protocol

SNAT   Static Network Address Translation/Source Network Address Translation

SNMP   Simple Network Management Protocol

SNTP   Simple Network Time Protocol

SOA   Start of Authority

SOHO   Small Office Home Office

SONET   Synchronous Optical Network

SOP   Standard Operating Procedure

SOW   Statement of Work

SPB   Shortest Path Bridging

SPI   Stateful Packet Inspection

SPS   Standby Power Supply

SSH   Secure Shell

SSID   Service Set Identifier

SSL   Secure Sockets Layer

ST   Straight Tip or Snap Twist

STP   Spanning Tree Protocol/Shielded Twisted Pair

SVC   Switched Virtual Circuit

SYSLOG   System Log

T1   Terrestrial Carrier Level 1

TA   Terminal Adaptor

TACACS   Terminal Access Control Access Control System

TACACS+   Terminal Access Control Access Control System+

TCP   Transmission Control Protocol

TCP/IP   Transmission Control Protocol/Internet Protocol

TDM   Time Division Multiplexing

TDR   Time Domain Reflectometer

Telco   Telecommunications Company

TFTP   Trivial File Transfer Protocol

TKIP   Temporal Key Integrity Protocol

TLS   Transport Layer Security

TMS   Transportation Management System
TOS   Type of Service
TPM   Trusted Platform Module
TTL   Time to Live
TTLS   Tunneled Transport Layer Security
UC   Unified Communications
UDP   User Datagram Protocol
UNC   Universal Naming Convention
UPC   Ultra Polished Connector
UPS   Uninterruptible Power Supply
URL   Uniform Resource Locator
USB   Universal Serial Bus
UTM   Unified Threat Management
UTP   Unshielded Twisted Pair
VDSL   Variable Digital Subscriber Line
VLAN   Virtual Local Area Network
VNC   Virtual Network Connection
VoIP   Voice over IP
VPN   Virtual Private Network
VRF   Virtual Routing Forwarding
VRRP   Virtual Router Redundancy Protocol
VTC   Video Teleconference
VTP   VLAN Trunk Protocol
WAF   Web Application Firewall
WAN   Wide Area Network
WAP   Wireless Application Protocol/Wireless Access Point
WEP   Wired Equivalent Privacy
WLAN   Wireless Local Area Network
WMS   Warehouse Management System
WPA   Wi-Fi Protected Access
WPS   Wi-Fi Protected Setup
WWN   World Wide Name
XDSL   Extended Digital Subscriber Line
XML   eXtensible Markup Language
Zeroconf   Zero Configuration

CompTIA®
Network+®
Review Guide
Exam N10-007
Fourth Edition

Chapter

1

Domain 1.0: Networking Concepts

THE FOLLOWING COMPTIA NETWORK+ OBJECTIVES ARE COVERED IN THIS CHAPTER:

✓ **1.1 Explain the purposes and uses of ports and protocols.**

- Protocols and ports
    - SSH 22
    - DNS 53
    - SMTP 25
    - SFTP 22
    - FTP 20, 21
    - TFTP 69
    - TELNET 23
    - DHCP 67, 68
    - HTTP 80
    - HTTPS 443
    - SNMP 161
    - RDP 3389
    - NTP 123
    - SIP 5060, 5061
    - SMB 445
    - POP 110
    - IMAP 143
    - LDAP 389
    - LDAPS 636
    - H.323 1720

- Protocol types
  - ICMP
  - UDP
  - TCP
  - IP
- Connection-oriented vs. connectionless

✓ **1.2 Explain devices, applications, protocols and services at their appropriate OSI layers.**

- Layer 7 – Application
- Layer 6 – Presentation
- Layer 5 – Session
- Layer 4 – Transport
- Layer 3 – Network
- Layer 2 – Data link
- Layer 1 – Physical

✓ **1.3 Explain the concepts and characteristics of routing and switching.**

- Properties of network traffic
  - Collision domains
  - Broadcast domains
  - CSMA/CD
  - CSMA/CA
  - Protocol data units
  - MTU
  - Broadcast
  - Multicast
  - Unicast
- Segmentation and interface properties
  - VLANs
  - Trunking (802.1Q)
  - Tagging and untagging ports

- NAT/PAT
- Port forwarding
- Access control list
- Distributed switching
- Packet-switched vs. circuit-switched network
- Software-defined networking

✓ **1.4 Given a scenario, configure the appropriate IP addressing components.**

- Private vs. public
- Loopback and reserved
- Default gateway
- Virtual IP
- Subnet mask
- Subnetting
  - Classful
    - Classes A, B, C, D, and E
  - Classless
    - VLSM
    - CIDR notation (IPv4 vs. IPv6)
- Address assignments
  - DHCP
  - DHCPv6
  - Static
  - APIPA
  - EUI64
  - IP reservations

✓ **1.5 Compare and contrast the characteristics of network topologies, types and technologies.**

- Wired topologies
  - Logical vs. physical
  - Star

- Ring
- Mesh
- Bus
- Wireless topologies
  - Ad-hoc
  - Infrastructure
  - Mesh
- Types
  - LAN
  - WLAN
  - WAN
  - MAN
  - CAN
  - SAN
  - PAN
- Technologies that facilitate the Internet of Things (IoT)
  - Z-Wave
  - Ant+
  - Bluetooth
  - NFC
  - IR
  - RFID
  - 802.11

✓ **1.6 Given a scenario, implement the appropriate wireless technologies and configurations.**

- 802.11 standards
  - b
  - a
  - g
  - n
  - ac

- Cellular
    - TDMA
    - CDMA
    - GSM
- Frequencies
    - 2.4GHz
    - 5.0GHz
- Speed and distance requirements
- Channel bandwidth
- Channel bonding
- MIMO/MU-MIMO
- Unidirectional/omnidirectional
- Site surveys

✓ **1.7 Summarize cloud concepts and their purposes.**

- Types of services
    - SaaS
    - PaaS
    - IaaS
- Cloud delivery models
    - Private
    - Public
    - Hybrid
- Connectivity methods
- Security implications/considerations
- Relationship between local and cloud resources

✓ **1.8 Explain the functions of network services.**

- DNS service
    - Record types
        - A, AAAA
        - TXT (SPF, DKIM)

When I first started on my career path as a network professional 25 years ago, I began by learning the basic concepts of networking by reading a book similar to this one. The original networking concepts have not really changed all that much. Some concepts have been replaced by new ones, and some have just become obsolete. This is because networks have evolved and networking needs have changed over the years. Over the course of your career, you too will see similar changes. However, most of the concepts you learn for this objective will become your basis for understanding current and future networks.

When learning network concepts, you might feel you need to know everything before you can learn one thing. This can be an overwhelming feeling for anyone. However, I recommend that you review the sections again once you've read the entire chapter. Not only does this help with review and memorization, but the pieces will make more sense once you see the entire picture.

For more detailed information on Domain 1's topics, please see *CompTIA Network+ Study Guide,* 4th ed. (978-1-119-43225-8) or *CompTIA Network+ Certification Kit,* 5th ed. (978-1-119-43228-9) published by Sybex.

1.1 Explain the purposes and uses of ports and protocols.

As a network professional, you will be expected to be fluent in acronyms. You'll run across lots and lots of acronyms, and knowing their definitions is going to be the easy part. Understanding the practical application of these protocols will be what defines your knowledge of networking concepts.

Protocols and Ports

In this section I will introduce numerous protocols that are used to support network communications and administer networking components, as well as configure and troubleshoot networking components. The following are associated with each of these protocols:

- A transport layer protocol in which it operates
- A port number where it listens for requests

I will cover the transport layer protocols as well as the entire Open Systems Interconnection (OSI) model in the section "Explain devices, applications, protocols and services at their appropriate OSI layers."

SSH (22)

Secure Shell (SSH) is a cryptographic protocol that is used to remotely administer Linux server and network equipment through a text console. The SSH protocol uses public key cryptology to authenticate and encrypt network access from the remote computer. This allows the user to securely log in without risk of the password being transmitted in clear text. Once the user is authenticated, all network transmissions are uniquely encrypted. The SSH protocol listens for incoming requests on TCP port 22. It is common practice for cloud providers to use SSH for authentication of administrators. They do this by providing the private key of the key pair to the administrator. I will cover key pairs in Chapter 4, "Domain 4: Network Security."

DNS (53)

Domain Name Services (DNS) is a distributed directory of domain resource records. The resource records are primarily used in translating *fully qualified domain names (FQDNs)* to IP addresses, such as www.sybex.com to an IP address of 208.215.179.132. DNS can also be used for other lookups such as IP addresses to FQDNs (called reverse DNS lookups) and for locating services such as Lightweight Directory Access Protocol (LDAP) servers. I will cover DNS in more depth in the section "Explain the functions of network services." DNS resolvers operate on UDP port 53 for simple lookups. DNS servers also use TCP port 53 (called the zone transfer) for data replication.

SMTP (25)

Simple Mail Transport Protocol (SMTP) is a protocol used by *mail transfer agents (MTAs)* to deliver emails to a destination email server. The protocol is used only in the process of delivering the email to the email server. Other protocols (such as Internet Message Access Protocol [IMAP] and Post Office Protocol [POP]) on the email server are responsible for client access. I will cover both of these protocols later in this section. SMTP operates on TCP port 25, where the server awaits an incoming delivery of email from the MTA.

SFTP (22)

Secure File Transfer Protocol (SFTP) is a file transfer protocol that uses the SSH inner workings. When SSH is installed on a system such as Linux, SFTP is automatically enabled to transfer files. The command used on many of these systems is scp, which stands for Secure Copy Protocol. Since SFTP is used with the SSH protocol, the server awaits an incoming connection on TCP port 22.

FTP (20, 21)

File Transfer Protocol (FTP) is a legacy file-sharing protocol that is still commonly used on the Internet. The FTP protocol is slowly being replaced with the SFTP protocol, because

SFTP offers encryption and doesn't have the firewall issues FTP has. FTP is an odd protocol; it consists of a control channel and a data channel. The FTP protocol also operates in two modes: active and passive. In both modes, the command channel, also known as the control channel, listens for requests on TCP port 21 on the FTP server. This is generally why we associate FTP with port 21. The control channel is responsible for receiving commands from the FTP client and processing those commands.

The data channel works differently in active mode than it does in passive mode, as shown in Figure 1.1. In active mode, when a server needs to transfer a file or information (such as a directory listing) to the client, the information comes from TCP port 20 on the server and is sent to a destination port above TCP 1023 directed to the client; this port is communicated through the control channel. This behavior creates a problem on firewalled networks and networks that use network address translation (NAT), because the client awaits the incoming request from the server on a different port than it initially communicated on. Passive mode was created to address this problem; in passive mode, the client initiates the data channel from a port above TCP 1023 and sends it to a waiting port on the server above TCP 1023. The behavior of the client initiating the transmission to the server for the data channel is what firewalled and NAT networks expect as a dataflow.

FIGURE 1.1   FTP active and passive modes

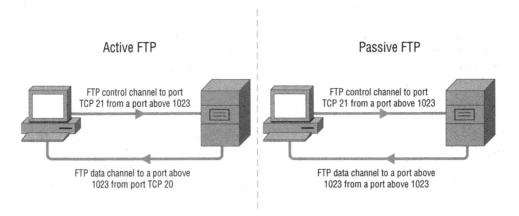

TFTP (69)

Trivial File Transfer Protocol (TFTP) is a handy protocol because it provides no security and is simplistic in its operation. The TFTP protocol is used to boot computers over the network with the Preboot Execution Environment (PXE). It is also used to transfer software images for network devices such as routers and switches during software upgrades. Network devices also use TFTP to back up and restore configurations. The TFTP server listens for requests on UDP port 69. It is often used during upgrades and configuration backup/restores, and the network administrator starts the TFTP server on his or her workstation. The network administrator can then copy the file(s) to or from the TFTP server to complete the task.

Telnet (23)

Telnet is another legacy protocol slowly being replaced by the SSH protocol. The Telnet protocol allows remote administration of network devices through a text-based console. One major disadvantage of Telnet is its lack of encryption compared to SSH. A Telnet server or device will await connection on TCP port 23.

DHCP (67, 68)

Dynamic Host Configuration Protocol (DHCP) is a protocol that provides automatic configuration of IP addresses, subnet masks, and options such as Domain Name Server (DNS) servers and the remote gateway to network devices. DHCP operates in a connectionless state, because during the process the client does not yet have an established IP address. During the configuration process, the DHCP server waits for a request from clients on UDP port 67. Clients will send the initial request from UDP port 68, as shown in Figure 1.2. When the server responds to the client, it responds to UDP port 68 from UDP port 67. The DHCP process is discussed in further detail in the section "Explain the functions of network services." You will find DHCP in use in everything from small home networks to large enterprise networks.

FIGURE 1.2　An overview of the DHCP process

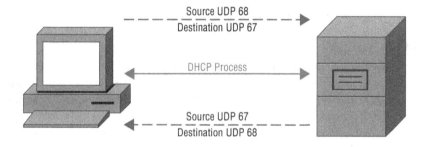

HTTP (80)

Hypertext Transfer Protocol (HTTP) is an application protocol for web data communications. When a web page is requested from a web server, an HTTP request is made for the Hypertext Markup Language (HTML) page. When the page is returned to the web browser, subsequent requests are made for the elements in the HTML page (such as images and JavaScript); all of this is done via the HTTP protocol. Web browsers are only one type of user agent (UA) that can request objects via the HTTP protocol. Many other UAs exist, including web crawlers and mobile apps. The server listens for incoming requests on TCP port 80.

HTTPS (443)

Hypertext Transfer Protocol over SSL (HTTPS) is also an application for web data communications. It provides the same functionality as HTTP but also allows for the encryption of these transfers via a Secure Socket Layer (SSL). SSL is a cryptographic protocol that uses

Public Key Infrastructure (PKI). I will cover PKI in greater detail in Chapter 4. The web server listens for requests on TCP port 443. A private key must be imported into the web server from a mutually trusted source to allow SSL to properly work.

SNMP (161)

Simple Network Management Protocol (SNMP) is a protocol used for the management of servers and network devices. SNMP can be used to collect data from servers and network devices such as memory, CPU, and bandwidth. When used in this way, the data is read from a centralized network management station (NMS). The NMS is then responsible for arranging the data into an acceptable display such as a graph; this allows an administrator to create a baseline of performance.

SNMP can also be used in a trap configuration. If a certain variable such as CPU usage crosses a threshold the administrator has set, the SNMP agent can send a trap message to the NMS. The NMS will then notify an administrator that something is wrong using a text message or email.

SNMP can also be used in a writable mode. This is often done with network equipment, because SNMP requests can be sent to reconfigure the equipment. An example of reconfiguration is changing a port on a switch to another virtual local area network (VLAN). SNMP agents and servers listen for requests on UDP port 161. I will cover SNMP further in Chapter 3, "Domain 3: Network Operations."

RDP (3389)

Remote Desktop Protocol (RDP) is a Microsoft protocol used for connecting to another Microsoft computer or server for remote administration. RDP has been built into the Microsoft operating systems since Windows 2003. Prior to Windows 2003, it was called Terminal Services. The RDP client built into the Microsoft operating system is mstsc.exe (the Microsoft Terminal Services Client). The operating system listens for requests on TCP port 3389.

NTP (123)

Network Time Protocol (NTP) is a network protocol that is optimized for synchronizing clocks between computers over the Internet. Because there is a round-trip delay in requesting time over the Internet, the NTP protocol uses an algorithm for calculating the precise time accounting for this delay. NTP listens for requests on UDP port 123. The requesting host will send requests from UDP port 123 as well. The NTP protocol is a rare protocol that uses a symmetrical port for both the request and reply of the NTP packet.

SIP (5060, 5061)

Session Initiation Protocol (SIP) is a communication protocol for the setup and signaling of Voice over IP (VoIP) calls. The SIP protocol does not transport the media stream—it only assists in setting up the media stream for the communication session. The SIP protocol is a text-based protocol developed by the *Internet Engineering Task Force (IETF)*. It is extremely extensible, so new functionality can be added. You will find that many VoIP private branch exchange (PBX) manufacturers add functionality to SIP. These proprietary functions add functionality to the vendors' SIP phones while providing basic backward compatibility with other SIP phones. The SIP protocol functions on UDP port 5060, although TCP can be used as well. SIP can also use encryption via *Transport Layer Security (TLS)* on UDP port 5061 and can be changed to TCP if needed.

A VoIP PBX will communicate with VoIP phones and the SIP provider via the SIP protocol. When a VoIP phone joins the VoIP PBX, a SIP registration is exchanged and authentication occurs. Once the VoIP phone is registered to the VoIP PBX, SIP notifications occur that act as a keepalive and register the state of the VoIP phone. Information transmitted in the notify packets can include line events and message-waiting indicator status and do not disturb status. During a call setup, the VoIP phone will communicate with the VoIP PBX to negotiate codecs for the call and the IP address and port number that the Real-time Transport Protocol (RTP) will use to transport the voice data.

In addition to VoIP phones, the SIP protocol is used for the SIP trunk. The SIP trunk connects the VoIP PBX to the public switched telephone network (PSTN). Chapter 2, "Domain 2.0: Infrastructure," covers the SIP trunk.

SMB (445)

The Server Message Block (SMB) protocol is a common network file and printer sharing protocol that is used with Microsoft products. It is also referred to as the Common Internet File System (CIFS). However, when referring to SMB as CIFS, it is implied that SMB 1.*x* is in use. Many network attached storage (NAS) units support the SMB protocol as the filer protocol. I cover storage technologies in Chapter 2. Linux also has an SMB filer called Samba that is compatible with the SMB file protocol for file and printer sharing. The SMB protocol is enabled on every server and client in a Microsoft network. The SMB protocol waits for a connection on TCP port 445.

Over the years Microsoft has updated the SMB protocol to overcome security issues, speed, negotiation, and failover. The current specification of SMB is 3.1.1. SMB 3.1.1 is used for database and virtual machine storage over the network. It now supports many features of block-level storage protocols, such as remote direct memory access (RDMA), failover, and *Advanced Encryption Standard (AES) encryption.*

 The term *filer* is used to describe the function of file sharing with high-level protocols, such as Server Message Blocks (SMBs) and Network File System (NFS). You find the term used throughout this book.

POP (110)

The Post Office Protocol (POP) is a legacy protocol, but it's still used on the Internet today. The POP protocol is slowly being replaced with the IMAP protocol.

POP allows email clients, also called *mail user agents (MUAs)*, to log in and retrieve email. Common email clients are Microsoft Outlook and Mozilla Thunderbird. POP listens for requests to the server on TCP port 110. When an email client initially connects to the POP server, it will download the mail from the server. This creates a problem when multiple email clients are used because only the last email client to access the POP server will have the latest mail.

IMAP (143)

Internet Message Access Protocol (IMAP) is used to allow email clients to retrieve and read email on the email server. The IMAP protocol allows for multiple email clients to access the same email box simultaneously. This multi-email client access is one of the reasons IMAP is so popular and POP is becoming outdated. IMAP also uses flags on the messages so that email clients can keep track of which emails are read and unread. The IMAP protocol listens for incoming connections on the email server from email clients on TCP port 143, and IMAP over SSL operates on TCP port 993.

LDAP (389)

Lightweight Directory Access Protocol (LDAP) is an application protocol that can search a directory service for objects. Microsoft Active Directory (AD) is an example of a directory service that uses LDAP to locate objects. AD uses directory services to locate objects such as domain controllers (DCs) and user objects for Group Policy (GP) application. An LDAP client communicates to LDAP servers on TCP port 389; it can also use UDP port 389.

LDAPS (636)

Lightweight Directory Access Protocol over SSL (LDAPS) is the application protocol of LDAP when SSL is configured. By default, on Microsoft networks LDAP traffic is unencrypted. However, by installing an SSL certificate into AD, you enable the LDAPS protocol. Any open source versions of LDAP also allow for LDAPS to be enabled with the same process of installing an SSL certificate. LDAPS operates on TCP port 636 and can also use UDP port 636.

H.323 (1720)

H.323 is a recommendation by the ITU Telecommunication Standardization Sector (ITU-T) for communications over the Internet. The H.323 protocol is similar to the SIP protocol, but different in the respect that it encompasses all of the communications technologies used by VoIP and videoconferencing. The H.323 protocol performs call setup on TCP port 1720.

The H.323 protocol has four main functionality areas:

- Terminal control, which provides endpoint signaling such as the VoIP phone itself

- Gateway services that provide transcoding functionality as well as communications with circuit-switched and packet-switched networks

- Gatekeeper services that provide admission control (authentication and authorization), bandwidth control, and management of endpoints (also known as zone management)

- The multipoint control unit (MCU), which provides conference call capabilities and call control of data, voice, and video for future in-call conferencing

Protocol Types

We just finished a review of several different protocols at the upper layers of TCP/IP. During the review of these protocols, I made several references to TCP and UDP. Both of these protocols are part of the TCP/IP protocol stack and provide support for the application and application protocols you just learned. In the following section, I will take a closer look at the protocols that make up the TCP/IP stack.

ICMP

Internet Control Message Protocol (ICMP) is a support protocol for TCP/IP that operates alongside of the IP protocol on the network layer. It is used by networking devices such as routers to identify operation problems, such as a gateway that is no longer responsive. A router will create an ICMP packet back to the originating host of network traffic if the destination network is unreachable.

The ping and traceroute commands also use ICMP to help technicians perform troubleshooting of the network. The ICMP protocol operates at layer 3 of the OSI (which will be discussed in the section "Explain devices, applications, protocols and services at their appropriate OSI layers.").

In IPv6, the ICMP protocol has a much larger role than it does in IPv4. ICMP in IPv6 is responsible for the Neighbor Discovery Protocol (NDP), which is the equivalent of the Address Resolution Protocol (ARP) in IPv4. ICMP in IPv6 is also responsible for the discovery of the network gateway(s) with ICMP *Router Solicitation (RS)* and *Router Advertisement (RA)* packets so that hosts can find a way out of the network. In addition, ICMP in IPv6 performs duplicate address detection (DAD) so that hosts do not duplicate IPv6 addressing. I will cover IPv6 in greater detail in the section "Explain the concepts and characteristics of routing and switching."

UDP

The User Datagram Protocol (UDP) is a transport protocol for TCP/IP. UDP is one of two protocols at the transport layer that connect network applications to the network. When application developers choose to use UDP as the protocol their application will work with, they must take several considerations into account.

UDP is connectionless, which means that data is simply passed from one IP address over the network to the other IP address. The sending computer won't know if the destination computer is even listening. The receipt of the data is not acknowledged by the destination computer. In addition, the data blocks sent are not sequenced in any way for the receiving computer to put them back together. In Figure 1.3 you can see a UDP segment; the header has only a source port, destination port, length of data, and checksum field.

FIGURE 1.3 UDP segment

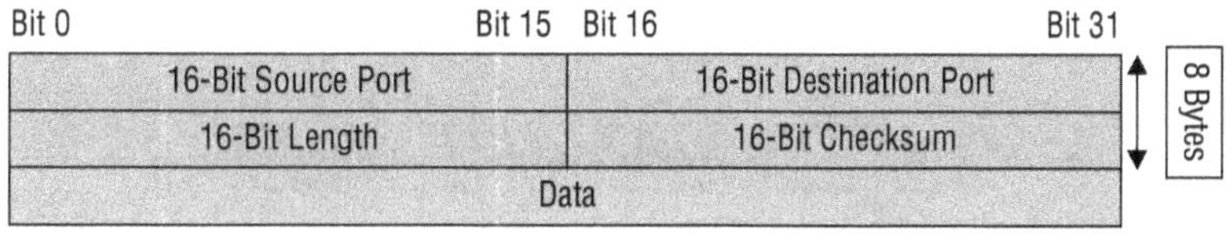

Bit 0	Bit 15	Bit 16	Bit 31	
16-Bit Source Port		16-Bit Destination Port		8 Bytes
16-Bit Length		16-Bit Checksum		
Data				

You may be wondering at this point why you would ever use UDP. We use UDP because it is faster than TCP. The application developer must make the application responsible for the connection, acknowledgment, and sequencing of data if needed. As an example, an NTP client uses UDP to send short questions to the NTP server, such as "What is the time?" We don't need a large amount of overhead at the transport layer to ask a simple question like that. Other protocols, such as the Real-time Transport Protocol (RTP) VoIP protocol, don't care to acknowledge segments or retransmit segments. If a segment of data doesn't make it to the destination, RTP will just keep moving along with the voice data in real time.

TCP

Transmission Control Protocol (TCP) is another transport protocol for TCP/IP. Just like the UDP protocol, TCP is a protocol at the transport layer that connects network applications to the network. When application developers choose to use TCP as the protocol their applications will work with, the protocol is responsible for all data delivery.

The TCP protocol has all the bells and whistles for a developer. TCP is a connection-oriented protocol. During the transmission of information, both ends create a virtual circuit over the network. All data segments transmitted are then sequenced, acknowledged, and retransmitted if lost in transit. The TCP protocol is extremely reliable, but it is slower than UDP.

When the sending computer transmits data to a receiving computer, a virtual connection is created using a three-way handshake, as shown in Figure 1.4. During the three-way handshake, the window buffer size on each side is negotiated with the SYN and ACK flags in the TCP header. When both the sender and receiver acknowledge the window's size, the connection is considered established, and data can be transferred. When the data transfer is completed, the sender can issue a FIN flag in the TCP header to tear down the virtual connection.

FIGURE 1.4   TCP three-way handshake

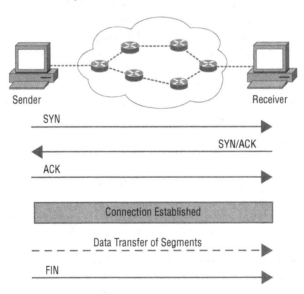

The buffer size negotiated in the three-way handshake determines the sliding TCP window for acknowledgment of segments during the transfer. As shown in Figure 1.5, the negotiated TCP sliding window size is 3. After three sequenced packets are delivered and put back in order on the receiving computer, the receiving computer sends an acknowledgment for the next segment it expects. If a segment is lost and the window cannot fill to the negotiated three segment window size to send the acknowledgment, the acknowledge timer will be triggered on the receiver, and the receiver will acknowledge the segments it currently has received. The sender's retransmit timer will also expire, and the lost segment will be retransmitted to the receiving computer. This is how the sequencing and acknowledgment of segments operate with the use of TCP sliding windows. In Figure 1.6, the TCP header is shown with all the fields just described.

FIGURE 1.5 TCP sliding window example

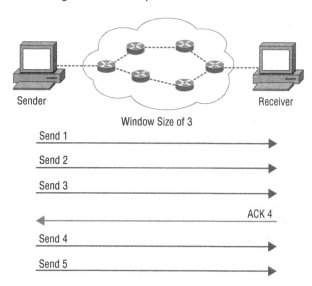

FIGURE 1.6 TCP segment

16-Bit Source Port			16-Bit Destination Port	
32-Bit Sequence Number				
32-Bit Acknowledgment Number				
4-Bit Header Length	Reserved	Flags	16-Bit Window Size	
16-Bit TCP Checksum			16-Bit Urgent Pointer	
Options				
Data				

IP

The Internet Protocol (IP) is a network layer protocol that allows for the logical addressing of networks and hosts. The addressing of networks is the mechanism that allows routing to be used. The addressing of the hosts within the networks is the mechanism that allows end-to-end connectivity to be achieved over the network.

The UDP and TCP protocols function on top of the IP protocol. UDP and TCP are protocols that handle the data for the applications. The IP protocol is responsible for encapsulating these protocols and delivering it to the appropriate addresses. At this point, you are probably imagining a letter that is folded and put into an envelope that is addressed from the sender to the destination. You would be correct—the IP protocol handles the delivery of data segments from applications in IP packets.

Figure 1.7 shows the fields that are contained in an IP packet header. I will cover the most important fields as they pertain to this exam. The first 4 bits contains the version of IP; this is how IPv4 and IPv6 packets are differentiated. The priority and type of service (ToS) fields are used for *quality of service (QoS)*; I will discuss this further in the section "Explain the concepts and characteristics of routing and switching." The time to live (TTL) field is used for routing so that packets are not endlessly routed on the Internet. The protocol field defines where to send the data next—UDP, TCP, ICMP, and so on. Then of course we have the source and destination IP address fields for routing to the destination computer and responding of the destination computer. Throughout this book, I will be covering TCP/IP in depth, because it is the predominant protocol in all networks today.

FIGURE 1.7   An IP packet

Bit 0			Bit 15	Bit 16		Bit 31
Version (4)	Header Length (4)	Priority and Type of Service (8)		Total Length (16)		
Identification (16)				Flags (3)	Fragmented Offset (13)	
Time to Live (8)		Protocol (8)		Header Checksum (16)		
Source IP Address (32)						
Destination IP Address (32)						
Options (0 or 32 If Any)						
Data (Varies If Any)						

Connection-Oriented vs. Connectionless

A connection-oriented protocol is the TCP protocol. During the conversation with the destination computer, both the source and destination share information about each other and the progress of the data transfer. The TCP protocol establishes a connection with the other computer using a three-way handshake. During the three-way handshake, information about both sides of the connection is shared, and the connection is established.

A connectionless protocol is the UDP protocol. During the transfer with the destination computer, neither the source nor the destination knows the progress of the data transfer.

That statement does not imply that the data transfer is unknown—it is only unknown at the transport layer. Upper-layer protocols that use UDP might keep track of the data transfer depending on the application. If the application is TFTP and you are transferring a file, the TFTP application is going to be responsible for retransmission of missing segments of data. I will be covering the OSI layers in the next chapter.

Because UDP and TCP are both used at the transport layer for the TCP/IP protocol, it is important to understand the differences between the two protocols. Both protocols are used to connect network applications to the network and provide flow control of the data. Both UDP and TCP are used differently by the developer of the application.

It is important to note that if an application solely uses either TCP or UDP, unless it is rewritten, you as the administrator cannot change the protocol. Table 1.1 shows a list of features for both UDP and TCP.

TABLE 1.1   Key features of UDP and TCP

TCP	UDP
Sequenced	Unsequenced
Reliable	Unreliable
Connection-oriented	Connectionless
Virtual circuit	Low overhead
Acknowledgments	No acknowledgments
Windowing flow control	No windowing or flow control of any type

Exam Essentials

Know the various application protocol and port numbers.   You should be able to define the various application protocols and their uses in the network. Along with each application protocol, you should be able to define the transport protocol and port number.

Understand the various protocol types.   ICMP is a protocol that helps with the notification of problems to the originating host in IPv4 networks. The ping and traceroute commands send and receive ICMP packets and are used for troubleshooting. In IPv6 networks, ICMP is an integral part of the IPv6 addressing and communications processes. UDP is a connectionless transport layer protocol; it is fast and normally used for question-and-answer type dialogues. TCP is a connection-oriented transport layer protocol; it is slower than UDP and more reliable. The TCP protocol uses a three-way handshake to establish the communications process. The IP protocol is a network layer protocol that allows for the routing and transportation of packets from host to host.

Know the differences between connection-oriented and connectionless protocols.
Connection-oriented protocols, such as the TCP protocol, create a virtual connection
between the two endpoints for data transfer. Connectionless protocols such as UDP do not
create connections at the transport layer. The applications are expected to create a connection between the endpoints if reliability of data is required. You should know the differences between the UDP and TCP protocols.

1.2 Explain devices, applications, protocols and services at their appropriate OSI layers.

The Open Systems Interconnection (OSI) reference model was created by the International
Organization for Standardization (ISO) to standardize network connectivity between appli-
cations, devices, and protocols. Before the OSI was created, every system was proprietary.
Of course, this was back in the days of mainframes and early microcomputers! Today, the
OSI layers are used to build standards that allow for interoperability between different
vendors.

Beside interoperability, the OSI layers have many other advantages. The following is a
list of the common networking advantages the OSI layers provide:

- The reference model helps facilitate communications between various types of hardware and software.

- The reference model prevents a change in one layer from affecting the other layers.

- The reference model allows for multivendor development of hardware and software
  based on network standards.

- The reference model encourages industry standardization because it defines functions
  of each layer of the OSI model.

- The reference model divides a complex communications process into smaller pieces to
  assist with design, development, and troubleshooting.

- Network protocols and connectivity options can be changed without affecting applications.

The last advantage is what I consider the most important for any network administrator.
The network communications process is a complicated process. However, when we break
the process down into smaller pieces, we can understand each piece as it relates to the
entire process.

When you understand what happens at each layer of the OSI, you will have a better
grasp of how to troubleshoot network applications and network problems. When I first
learned the OSI layers over 20 years ago, I never thought I would use this knowledge—but
I could not be as successful as I am without understanding this layered approach. When
we review the upper layers of the OSI (application, presentation, and session), you will not

have as deep an understanding as you do of the lower layers. The upper layers are generally where developers create applications, whereas the lower layers are where network administrators support the applications.

In Figure 1.8 you can see the seven layers of the OSI. The top three layers are where applications operate. The transport and network layers are where TCP/IP operates. The data link and physical layers are where connectivity technology, such as wireless or Ethernet, operates. These groupings are considered macro layers and will help you understand the OSI layers better as we progress through each individual layer.

FIGURE 1.8   The layers of the OSI

| Application |
| Presentation |
| Session |
| Transport |
| Network |
| Data Link |
| Physical |

Application Layer

The application layer (layer 7) is the highest layer of the communication process. It is the layer that provides the user interface to the user and often the beginning of the communication process. Although programs like Microsoft Word have an interface for the user, it is not considered a network application. Applications that do not communicate with the network are considered end-user application or stand-alone applications. There is a running joke in networking that some problems are layer 8 problems; that would be the user.

The application layer defines the role of the application, since all network applications are generally either client or server. A request for information is started at the application layer through one of three methods: a *graphical user interface (GUI)*, a console application, or an *application programming interface (API)*. These terms are synonymous with the application layer. A request for information can begin with a click of a mouse, a command in an application, or a request via API call.

The application layer also defines the purpose of the application. A file transfer application will differ significantly in design from an instant messaging application. When a programmer starts to design a network application, this is the layer the programmer begins with because it will interface with the user. As firewalls have advanced throughout the years, it is now common to find firewalls operating at layer 7. Chapter 2 covers next-generation firewall (NGFW) layer 7 firewalls that operate at these higher layers.

Many events begin at the application layer. The following are some common application layer events, but in no way is this a complete list. The list of application protocols—and the events that begin at this layer—grows by the minute.

- Sending email
- Remote access
- Web surfing
- File transfer
- Instant messenger
- VoIP calls

Presentation Layer

The presentation layer (layer 6) is the layer that presents data to the application layer. This layer is responsible for encryption/decryption, translation, and compression/decompression. When a stream of data comes from the lower layers, this layer is responsible for formatting the data and converting it back to the original intended application data.

An example is a web request to a web server for an encrypted web page via SSL. The web page is encrypted at the web server and sent to the client. When the client receives the page, it is decrypted and sent to the application layer as data. This process is bidirectional, and it is important to note that the presentation layer on both the client and server make a connection to each other. This is called peer-layer communications, and it happens at all layers of the OSI in different ways.

An example of translation services that are performed at this layer is converting Extended Binary Coded Decimal Interchange Code (EBCDIC) data to American Standard Code for Information Interchange (ASCII), or ASCII to Unicode.

Examples of compression and decompression, often referred to as codecs, are MP3 to network streaming protocols and H.264 video to streaming protocols. In addition, JPEG, GIF, PICT, and TIFF operate at the presentation layer by compressing and decompressing image formats, when used in conjunction with a network application.

Session Layer

The session layer (layer 5) is responsible for the setup, management, and teardown of a session between two computers. This layer is also responsible for dialogue control. Application developers must decide how their application will function with the network at this layer in respect to the network conversation. There are three basic forms of communications a network application can use at the session layer:

- *Half-duplex* is a two-way communications between two hosts where only one side can communicate at a time. This is similar to a walkie-talkie and is how many protocols operate. A web browser will request a page from the web server and the web server will return the page. Then the web browser asks for the other elements contained in the HTML web page. In recent years, web developers have made it seem like a full-duplex conversation with Ajax (Asynchronous JavaScript and XML) requests, by sending each keystroke and querying a response. However, it is still a half-duplex conversation.

- *Full-duplex* is two-way communications between two hosts, where both sides can communicate simultaneously. Not only is this type of communications similar to a telephone call, but it is used by VoIP to make telephone calls over a network. This type of dialogue control is extremely tough for programmers, since they must program for real-time events.

- *Simplex* is a one-way communication between two hosts. This type of communications is similar to tuning to a radio station—you do not have any control of the content or communications received.

Transport Layer

The transport layer (layer 4) is the first layer that we network administrators are responsible for maintaining. A good grasp of the upper three layers is important so that we can properly troubleshoot these lower layers.

The transport layer for TCP/IP contains two protocols that you learned about in the previous section "Protocol Types." TCP and UDP operate at this layer, and the programmer of the network application must decide which to program against. At this layer, the operating system presents the application with a socket to communicate with on the network. In the Windows operating system, it is called a *Winsock*; in other operating systems like Linux, it is called a *socket*. When we discuss the socket in the context of networking, it is called a *port*. All of these terms are basically interchangeable. I will refer to it as a port for the remainder of this section.

When a network server application starts up, it will bind to the port, as shown in Figure 1.9. The server application will then listen for requests on this port. The programmer will choose which port and protocol to use for their server application. Because UDP/TCP and the port number define the application, it is common to find firewalls operating at this layer to allow or block application access.

FIGURE 1.9   Transport server port binding

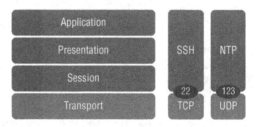

So far I have discussed how the server application listens for requests. Now I will explain how client applications use ports for requests. When a client needs to request information from a server, the client application will bind to a port dynamically available above 1023 as the source port. Port number 1023 and below are defined in RFC 3232 (or just see www.iana.org). These lower port numbers are called *well-known* port numbers, and they're reserved for servers. In the example in Figure 1.10, a web browser is creating a request for three elements on a web page to the server. The client will bind to ports 1024, 1025, and 1026 to the web browsers and send the request to the destination port of 80 on the web server. When the three requests return from the web server, they will be returning from the source port of 80 on the web server to the destination ports of 1024, 1025, and 1026 on the client. The client can then pass the proper element to the web page via the incoming data on the respective port. Once the client receives the information, both the client and server will close the session for the port and the port can be recycled. UDP ports will be recycled after a specific period of time, because the client and server do not communicate the state of the connection (UDP is connectionless).

FIGURE 1.10   Transport client requests

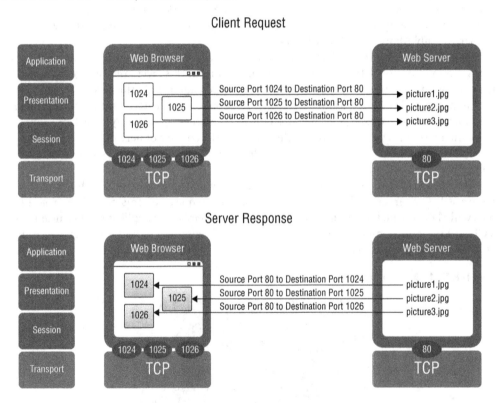

It is important to note a few concepts that are resonated throughout this section on the OSI layers. The first concept is each layer of the OSI communicates with the same layer on the other host—this is called *peer-layer communications*. The second concept is that every layer communicates with the layer above and the layer below. The transport layer performs this communication to the layer above with the use of a port number. The transport layer communicates with the layer below by moving information down to the network layer from either the TCP or UDP protocol. In the next section, you will learn how this information is conveyed and used by the network layer.

Network Layer

The network layer (layer 3) is responsible for the logical numbering of hosts and networks. The network layer is also responsible for transporting data between networks through the process of *routing*. Routers operate at the network layer to facilitate the movement of packets between networks; therefore, routers are considered layer 3 devices. Figure 1.11 details three networks that are logically numbered with IP addresses, each belonging to a unique network. We will explore network routing in the section "Explain the concepts and characteristics of routing and switching."

FIGURE 1.11   Logical network addressing

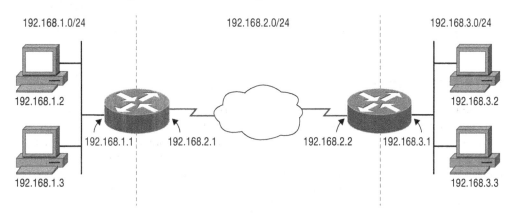

The IP protocol is not the only protocol that functions at this layer; ICMP also functions at the network layer. There are many other network layer protocols, but for the remainder of this section we will focus on the IP protocol.

The IP protocol at the network layer communicates with the layer above by using a protocol number. The protocol number at the network layer helps the IP protocol move the data to the next protocol. As you can see in Figure 1.12, when the protocol number is 6 the data is decapsulated and delivered to the TCP protocol at the transport layer. When the protocol number is 17, the data is delivered to the UDP protocol at the transport layer. Data does not always have to flow up to the transport layer. If the protocol number is 1, the data is moved laterally to the ICMP protocol.

FIGURE 1.12   Network layer protocol numbers

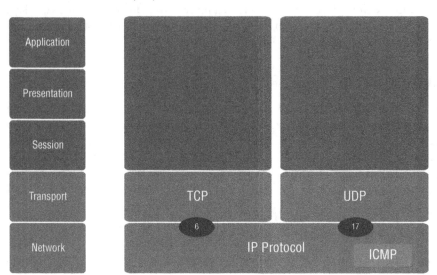

Data Link Layer

The data link layer (layer 2) is responsible for the framing of data for the physical layer or media as well as the static addressing of hosts. At the data link layer, unique MAC addresses are burned into the network cards (computers) and network interfaces (network devices). The data link layer is only concerned with the local delivery of frames in the same network. At the data link layer, there are many different frame types. Since we are focused on TCP/IP, the only frame types we will discuss are Ethernet II frame types. Switching of frames occurs at the data link layer; therefore, this layer is where switches operate.

As shown in Figure 1.13, the data link layer is divided into two sublayers: the logical link control (LLC) layer and the media access control (MAC) layer. The LLC layer is the sublayer responsible for communicating with the layer above (the network layer). This sublayer is where CPU cycles are consumed for the processing of data. The MAC layer is responsible for the hardware processing of frames and the error checking of frames. The MAC layer is where frames are checked for errors, and only relevant frames are passed to the LLC layer. The MAC layer saves CPU cycles by processing these checks independently from the CPU. The MAC layer is the layer responsible for the transmission of data on a physical level.

The LLC layer communicates with the network layer by coding a type of protocol field in the frame itself. This field is called the Ethernet type field, as shown in Figure 1.14. It carries the protocol number for which traffic is destined. You may ask whether IP is the only protocol used with TCP/IP, and the answer is no. Although TCP/IP uses the IP protocol, a helper protocol called the Address Resolution Protocol (ARP) is used to convert IP addresses into MAC addresses. Other protocols that can be found in this field are FCoE, 802.1Q, and PPPoE, just to name a few.

FIGURE 1.13   The data link layer and the sublayers within

FIGURE 1.14   The LLC sublayer and the network layer

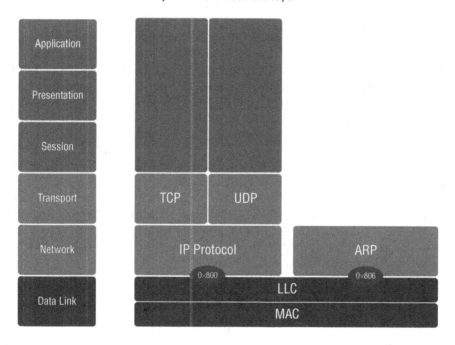

The MAC address layer is responsible for the synchronization, addressing, and error detection of the framing. In Figure 1.15 you can see the complete Ethernet II frame with the LLC layer (type field). The preamble is 7 bytes of alternating 1s and 0s at a synchronization frequency according to the speed of the connectivity method. The start frame delimiter (SFD) is a one-byte field and part of the preamble with an extra bit at the end to signal the start of the destination MAC address (10101011). The preamble and SFD help the receiving side form a time reference for the rest of the frame signaling; the SFD synchronizes the physical timing for both sides of the transmission. Hence, it is the way the data link layer communicates with the layer below. The destination MAC address is a 6-byte field and is the physical destination of the data. The source MAC address is a 6-byte field and is the physical source of the data. The type field is a 2-byte field, as described earlier, and is part of the LLC sublayer. The data field can vary between 46 bytes and a maximum of 1500 bytes. The frame checking sequence (FCS) is a *cyclical redundancy check (CRC)*, which is a calculation of the entire frames for error detection. If the CRC does not match the frame received, it is automatically discarded at the MAC address sublayer as invalid data.

FIGURE 1.15   An Ethernet II frame

A MAC address is a 48-bit (6-byte) physical address burned into the network controller of every network card and network device. The address is normally written as a hexadecimal expression such as 0D-54-0D-C0-10-52. The MAC address format is governed by, and partially administered by, the IEEE. In Figure 1.16 a MAC address is shown in bit form. The Individual Group (I/G) bit controls how the switch handles broadcast traffic or individual traffic for the MAC address. If the I/G bit in a MAC address is 0, then it is destined for an individual unicast network device. If the I/G bit in a MAC address is a 1, then the switch treats it as a broadcast or multicast frame. The Global/Local (G/L) bit signifies if the MAC address is globally governed by the IEEE. If the G/L bit in the MAC address is a 0, then the MAC address is globally unique because it has been governed by the IEEE. If the G/L bit in the MAC address is 1, then it is locally governed—that is, it is statically set by an administrator. The *organizationally unique identifier (OUI)* is governed by the IEEE for each vendor that applies to make networking equipment. The I/G bit, G/L bit, and the OUI make up the first 24 bits of a MAC address. The last 24 bits are assigned by the vendor for each network controller that is produced. This is how the IEEE achieves global uniqueness of every MAC address for networking equipment.

FIGURE 1.16   MAC address format

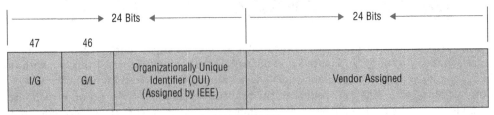

Example: 0000.0c12.3456

The IEEE publishes the list of OUIs that have been registered for network controller production. With this list, you can determine the manufacturer of the device from the first six hexadecimal digits of a MAC address. Many protocol analyzers use this same list to translate the source and destination fields in a frame to a friendly manufacturer ID. The complete list changes daily and can be found at https://regauth.standards.ieee .org/standards-ra-web/pub/view.html#registries. The site https://www.wireshark.org/tools/oui-lookup.html has a friendly search function for parsing this list and returning the vendor.

Physical Layer

The physical layer is responsible for transmitting the data of 1s and 0s from the data link layer. The data of 1s and 0s are modulated or encoded for transmission via radio waves, light, electricity, or any other physical method of transmitting data.

The physical layer is an integral component of many different types of transmission methods such as wireless (802.11), fiber optics, and Ethernet, just to name a few. In all cases, the physical layer is tied directly to the data link layer, so together the physical layer and the data link layer are considered a macro layer. This macro layer allows an application to transmit in the same way over an Ethernet connection as it does a wireless connection, such as when you disconnect and go wireless. Hubs and repeaters operate at the physical layer because they are not tied to the data link layer—they just repeat the electrical signals.

The physical layer also defines the connection types used with the various networking technologies. The physical layer is the most common place to find problems, such as a loose connection or bad connection. A list of the different connection types and transmission media can be found in Chapter 2.

Exam Essentials

Understand the various layers of the OSI and how they facilitate communications on each layer. The application layer is the beginning of the communication process with the user and is where applications are defined as client or server. The application layer is also where events, such as network requests, clicks on a GUI, or commands in a console application, are acted on. The presentation layer converts data formats, encrypts and decrypts, and provides compression and decompression of data. The session layer is responsible for setup, maintenance, and teardown of the communications for an application as well as dialogue control. The session layer has three main methods of communication for applications: half-duplex, full-duplex, and simplex communications. The transport layer is responsible for flow control of network segments from the upper layers. The two protocols for TCP/IP that operate at the transport layer are UDP and TCP. The network layer is responsible for the logical assignment and routing of network and host addresses. The network layer is where the IP protocol for the TCP/IP suite of protocols functions. The data link layer is the layer responsible for the framing of data for transmission via a physical media. The data link layer is composed of two sublayers: the LLC sublayer and the MAC sublayer. The LLC sublayer is responsible for communicating with the upper layers, and the MAC sublayer is responsible for synchronizing communications on the physical media, addressing transporting of data and error detection of the data received. The physical layer is the layer at which data is transmitted via air, light, or electricity. The physical layer is where connection types and media are defined.

Know the various devices that function at each layer of the OSI model.   Next-generation firewalls (layer 7) operate on the application layer of the OSI model. Traditional firewalls operate at the transport layer, because protocols and ports define the applications that operate at this layer. Therefore, we can allow or block applications by controlling access to these protocols and ports. Routers operate at the network layer by facilitating routing of networks and forwarding of information to hosts. Switches operate at the data link layer by forwarding frames to the ports with the respective destination MAC address. Hubs and repeaters operate at the physical layer. These devices retransmit the signals received at the physical layer without discrimination of data contained within the data link layer.

1.3 Explain the concepts and characteristics of routing and switching.

The topic of routing and switching of network traffic makes up a large portion of the CompTIA Network+ exam. This section will focus on Ethernet switching and TCP/IP network routing, and you'll find that the daily job of a network administrator will focus heavily on these subjects as well! You should be extremely proficient on the subject matter.

Properties of Network Traffic

In this section I will describe the properties of network traffic, in particular the properties of local area network (LAN) traffic. In a typical network, we should see a nominal amount of network traffic, but this does not necessarily mean we will see network congestion. Understanding the key topics in this section will help you identify and understand network congestion as well as nominal traffic in your network.

Collision Domains

A collision will occur when two nodes send a frame simultaneously on the same physical network or media. The key concept is that frame collisions happen at the physical layer. Collisions are common on networks that use hubs, because hubs communicate using half-duplex Ethernet. The same pair of wires used to transmit data is the same pair of wires used to receive data. Therefore, data could possibly be transmitted on the same pair simultaneously by two nodes, thus causing a collision.

When a collision occurs, all the nodes on the physical network must stop and wait for a random period of time via the CSMA/CD contention method. No data can be transmitted during this wait time. (I will explain CSMA/CD later in this section.) This wait time means that bandwidth is reduced as more collisions occur. A typical 10 Mbps connection with only two or three computers may be able to sustain a top speed of only 6 or 7 Mbps, due to collisions.

The best way to solve collisions is to replace all hubs with switches and verify full-duplex Ethernet connectivity. As shown in Figure 1.17, a switch will place each node in its own collision domain regardless of half-duplex or full-duplex operation. Full-duplex communications can only be achieved with switches. Switches reserve a pair for transmit and a pair for receive; this guarantees that collisions will not occur.

FIGURE 1.17   Hubs, switches, and collision domains

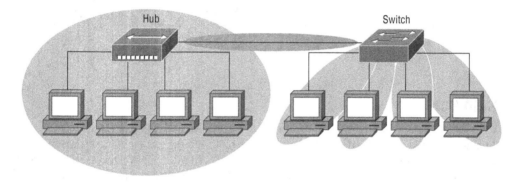

Broadcast Domains

The broadcast domain is defined as a group of devices on a network segment that hear all broadcasts transmitted on the network segment. These broadcasts are generally layer 2 broadcasts. I will discuss different types of broadcasts later in this section.

Excessive broadcast traffic in a network can create congestion for unicast network traffic. Some broadcast traffic in a network is considered a healthy portion of traffic. We can't totally get rid of broadcast traffic because many supporting protocols rely on it. As an example, you could try getting rid of DHCP by putting a static IP address on each computer. However, ARP is still required for resolving IPs to their associated MAC addresses. ARP is required for normal communications, and it is a broadcast-based protocol, just like DHCP.

As your network grows, the broadcast traffic required to support it also increases. To combat congestion that can be caused by broadcasts, we can simply create more broadcast domains and limit the number of devices affected. As we increase the number of broadcast domains, we reduce the number of computers affected by the broadcasts in each domain. This is commonly done by creating additional network segments and connecting the segments together with a router, because routers stop broadcasts. In Figure 1.18 you see two network segments with four computers in each broadcast domain. The broadcast traffic generated by the computers in the first segment will not affect computers in the second segment. However, the computers in the first segment can still communicate with the computers in the second segment via the router connecting the two segments.

FIGURE 1.18   Two broadcast domains connected with a router

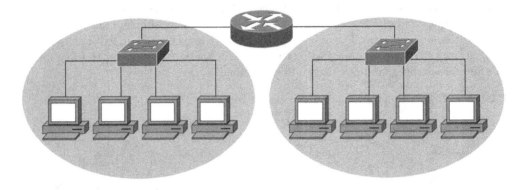

CSMA/CD

Carrier-sense multiple access with collision detection (CSMA/CD) is a wired Ethernet contention method. CSMA allows the network controller to sense a carrier to transmit data. CSMA also provides a path for multiple computers to talk or have access to the same network. I often use the example of a group of people meeting. All the people in the group have equal access to speak. Each person can also sense when they can speak by listening for silence in the group. Network nodes work the same way; when a node wants to talk, it will first check for the presence of a signal on the wire. If the wire is clear, the node can begin transmitting the data.

The CD, or collision detection, method is used to detect a collision of two nodes talking at the same time within the same collision domain. When a collision occurs, both nodes begin transmitting a temporary jam signal; this prevents any other nodes from creating additional collisions. All nodes that hear the jam signal use a back-off algorithm to determine a random amount of time before they can attempt to transmit again. The CD method is similar to two people in the group talking at the same time. They both stop and give courtesy to the other person, and then one of them starts the conversation again after a random amount of time. One difference is that after the back-off algorithm is triggered, all nodes have equal access to transmit.

CSMA/CA

Carrier-sense multiple access with collision avoidance (CSMA/CA) is another contention method that is commonly used with wireless Ethernet and token-based networks. The CSMA/CA contention method allows for multiple access by all nodes in the network, just like the CSMA/CD contention method. However, unlike the CSMA/CD contention method, CSMA/CA avoids collisions rather than dealing with them.

In token-based networks, a node cannot transmit until it obtains the token. This token passing allows for nodes to avoid collisions, because only one token is active at a time. Wireless Ethernet uses request to send (RTS) and clear to send (CTS) signaling. The RTS/CTS method also avoids collisions by only allowing one node at a time to transmit after it receives a CTS signal.

Protocol Data Units

Protocol data units (PDUs) is how we describe the type of data transferred at each layer of the OSI model. The layers of the OSI and their corresponding PDU can be seen in Figure 1.19. The first three layers of the OSI (application, presentation, and session) reference the components of an application. The PDU is considered user datagrams, or just datagrams. The datagrams are created by the application and passed to the transport layer. The transport layer is where segments are created from the datagrams, and then the segment is passed to the network layer. At the network layer, packets are created from the segments and the packet is passed to the data link layer. The data link layer creates frames for transmitting the data in bits at the physical layer.

FIGURE 1.19   OSI layers and PDUs

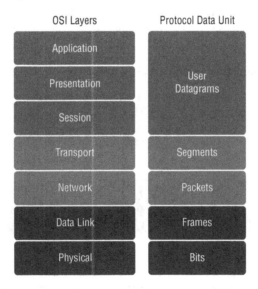

MTU

The *maximum transmission unit (MTU)* is the largest size of the data that can be transferred at the data link layer. The MTU for Ethernet is 1500 bytes. Including 12 bytes for the destination and source MAC address, a 2-byte type field, and 4 bytes for the frame checking sequence (FCS) brings the MTU to 1518 bytes. The smallest MTU is 46 bytes, or 64 bytes if including the frame fields.

The MTU is often referred to as a layer 3 data size. When data is passed down to the data link layer, the packet is sized to the MTU of the data link layer. Therefore, we can consider the MTU a constraint on the network layer. However, it is usually adjustable only at the data link layer, such as when you're configuring a switch port on a switch.

The Ethernet specification allows for either an MTU of 1500 bytes or an MTU of 9000. When the MTU is increased to 9000 bytes, the frame is considered a jumbo frame. I will discuss jumbo frames in greater detail in Chapter 2.

Broadcast

As discussed in the previous section, broadcasts are useful for IPv4 networking. Broadcasts are used for DHCP, ARP, and a multitude of other supporting protocols. Networks today would not function without broadcasts! However, when we use the term *broadcast*, it is used as a general term. Broadcasts exist at both the data link and network layers.

As shown in Figure 1.20, the data link layer can contain a broadcast frame. When the destination MAC address is FF:FF:FF:FF:FF:FF or all 1s, switches will forward the frame to all active network interfaces. When a network card (network interface) receives a broadcast frame, it will process the data to the network layer. The network layer protocol does not have to be the IP protocol shown in Figure 1.20; it can be ARP or DHCP. However, in Figure 1.20 we see an IP packet at the network layer with a destination address of 255.255.255.255. When the destination IP address is all 1s (or in this case, 255.255.255.255), the broadcast is considered a network layer broadcast. The operating system at this point processes the data within the packet when a network layer broadcast is received.

FIGURE 1.20   A broadcast frame and IP packet

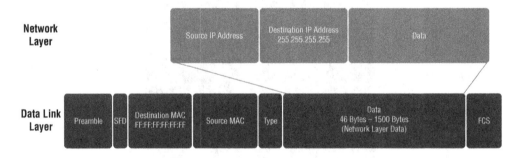

Not all data link layer broadcasts are forwarded to the network layer. Where a broadcast gets forwarded to next depends on the protocol type in the frame. It is safe to say that all network broadcasts are also data link layer broadcasts.

Multicast

Multicasts are similar to broadcasts in that communications is a one-to-many flow of information. This is sometimes referred to as point-to-multipoint communications. However, that is where the similarities end. Multicast is a smart type of broadcast controlled by the switch. Multicast traffic is delivered only to the devices participating in the multicast session. This multicast process helps reduce bandwidth usage for computers not participating in the multicast communications.

A special range of IP addresses is set aside for multicast addressing. The address range for multicast is 224.0.0.0 to 239.255.255.255. When a multicast session is created, the first host begins by registering a multicast IP address, and the port on the switch becomes part of the multicast group. When other hosts join the session, they register with the same IP address, and their ports are added to the multicast group; this process is called the *Internet Group Management Protocol (IGMP)* join.

When any host participating in the multicast group sends data to the switch with a specially crafted MAC address, the data will be forwarded to only the members of the multicast group. All multicast MAC addresses start with `01:00:5E`, the rest of the MAC address is a bitwise calculation of the multicast IP address.

Unicast

Unicast communications is a one-to-one conversation between two network devices. Unicast communications should make up 95 to 98 percent of the bandwidth in a typical network.

As you can see in Figure 1.21, the destination MAC address at the data link layer is a specific MAC address on the network. A switch will forward this frame only to the port associated with this MAC address. In Chapter 2, I will cover switching functions in more depth.

FIGURE 1.21 A unicast frame and packet

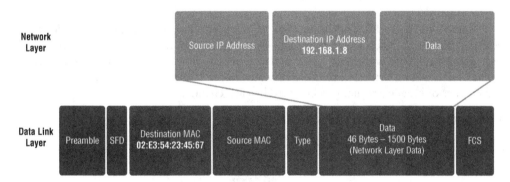

Once the frame is delivered to the host with the destination MAC address, the data is passed to the network layer. If the destination IP address matches the host, then the data is further processed.

Segmentation and Interface Properties

Segmentation of a network is necessary to control broadcast domains, as discussed in the prior section "Properties of Network Traffic." In this section, we will cover the mechanisms for segmenting a network such as VLANs, trunks, and tagging of frames. In addition, there are several properties of switched interfaces that will be covered in this section, such as the MAC address table, port mirroring, and the Spanning Tree Protocol (STP).

VLANs

Virtual local area networks (VLANs) are the primary mechanism to segment networks. However, before we can understand the need for VLANs, let's examine a network without VLANs. In Figure 1.22 you see one network segment connected with a switch; this is considered a flat network because there is no segmentation and all clients share the same broadcast domain. We can add additional switches, but that will only extend the broadcast domain further. Regardless of the job function, the hosts share the same switch; in the figure you can see Sales and HR on the same physical switch. It is important to note that VLANs are usually numbers from 1 to 4096, but for the remainder of this section we will use friendly names.

FIGURE 1.22   A flat switched network

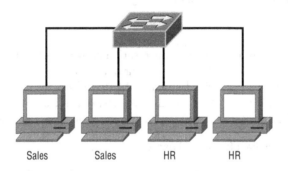

| Sales | Sales | HR | HR |

As shown in Figure 1.23, when we implement VLANs in a network, we can logically segment a network inside a physical switch. We can even connect switches together and extend the VLANs to additional switches (I will explain how later). The key point is that we have created two separate broadcast domains in the same physical switch, thus reducing the number of broadcasts that can be heard by each client.

FIGURE 1.23   A network using VLANs

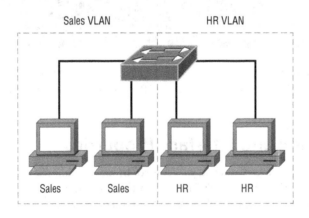

VLANs help control broadcasts by creating logical segmentation (logical switches) inside a switching infrastructure; these are virtual switches. When we create multiple logical segments inside the switch infrastructure, it allows the network to become scalable to thousands of hosts without repercussions for bandwidth from broadcasts. VLANs also help provide flexibility to the daily maintenance of adding and moving clients within a job function. If a salesperson were to move from one floor to another floor, we can simply reconfigure the switches with the appropriate VLANs, and the salesperson is within the same VLAN. VLANs are more commonly used today in conjunction with security. Because we can group users together inside a switch, we can apply access control lists (ACLs) to the VLANs and restrict traffic between them.

Here is a short list of benefits to implementing VLANs:

- Network adds, moves, and changes are achieved with ease by just configuring a port into the appropriate VLAN.

- A group of users that require a level of security can be put into a VLAN so that users outside of the VLAN can be prevented from accessing it.

- As a logical grouping of users by function, VLANs can be considered independent from their physical or geographic locations.

- VLANs greatly enhance network security if implemented correctly.

- VLANs increase the number of broadcast domains while decreasing their size.

When VLANs are implemented in our network, it will create a layer 2 segmentation. However, we still need to get unicast traffic to communicate between the two segments. This requires a router so that unicast traffic can be routed between the two segments. Additionally, we must provide a layer 3 logical address scheme for each of the VLANs. As shown in Figure 1.24, the Sales VLAN is assigned an IP address scheme of 192.168.1.0/24, and the HR VLAN is assigned an IP address scheme of 192.168.2.0/24. If the Sales VLAN needs to communicate with the HR VLAN, it must send the traffic to its default gateway (router), and the traffic will be routed to the appropriate VLAN and host. Routing between VLANs is required, even if the VLANs are all in the same physical switch.

FIGURE 1.24   Routed VLANs

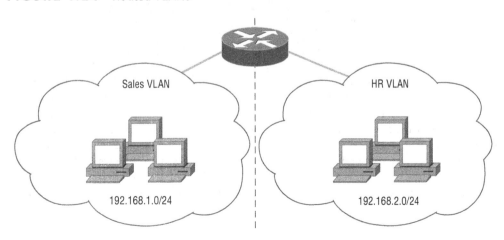

Sales VLAN

HR VLAN

192.168.1.0/24

192.168.2.0/24

Trunking (802.1Q)

Up to this point I have covered VLANs within the same switch. When we need to extend a VLAN infrastructure past a single switch, we use trunking. Trunking allows the VLAN information to be prepended to the switched frame as it traverses the switches. When the adjacent switch receives this frame, the trunking information is stripped off and the frame is forwarded to the appropriate port(s).

There are two main trunking protocols that are used today in switching. One is *Inter-Switch Link (ISL)*, which is proprietary to Cisco equipment. The other trunking protocol is *802.1Q*, which is an IEEE standard that is compliant with all switching equipment, including Cisco. The 802.1Q trunking protocol is nothing more than a prepended field on an Ethernet frame. As you can see in Figure 1.25, the top frame looks identical to a standard Ethernet II frame, with the exception of the 4 bytes for VLAN tagging. The EtherType field, or type field, contains the first 2 bytes that comprise a VLAN tag; the position of these first 2 bytes is what the LLC sublayer would expect for the position of a normal (non-802.1Q) frame. Since the type field is set to 0x8100 (802.1Q), this tells the device that the frame has tagging information inside. The original type field is still there—it is right before the data—and it will reflect the upper protocol the data is destined for after it is put on the proper VLAN. Inside the VLAN tag, a priority is embedded for a length of 3 bits; this is a QoS value that we will discuss later in this section. A discard eligibility indicator appears after the priority bits; it is normally not used for Ethernet. Then at the end we have the VLAN ID, for a total of 12 bits. Since we are using 4 bytes for this VLAN tag, we must subtract it from the data payload, so rather than being able to transmit 1500 bytes we can transmit only 1496 bytes.

FIGURE 1.25   An 802.1Q frame

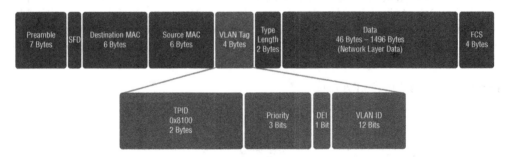

When we connect a switch to another switch and configure an 802.1Q trunk between them, we allow multiple VLANs to traverse the trunk link. The example in Figure 1.26 shows computer C in the HR VLAN sending a broadcast message. When the switch receives the broadcast, it forwards the broadcast to all other computers on the switch in the same VLAN. The switch also tags the frame and sends it across the 802.1Q trunk. When the frame is received at the adjacent switch, the tag is processed and the frame is forwarded to computer H because it is a member of the same HR VLAN. All other computers—A, B, E, F, and G—never see the frame because of their VLAN membership. In this example I've shown you a broadcast frame/packet and how it traverses the trunk link. Unicast frames use the MAC address table and are directed across the trunk link if the destination computer is on the other switch. We will cover MAC address tables later.

FIGURE 1.26 802.1Q trunk link and broadcasts

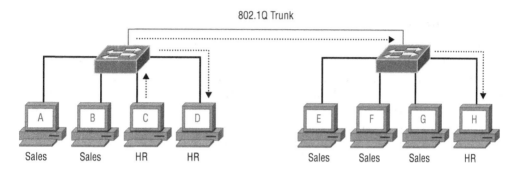

Tagging and Untagging Ports

As you know, 802.1Q trunks tag packets with VLAN tagging information; these ports are considered to be tagging ports. Normal network clients don't need to see the 802.1Q tagging information. For the most part, they never really know what VLAN they are in—it's the switches' job to put them in the respective VLAN.

In Figure 1.27 you can see a client and switch connected to another switch with an 802.1Q trunk link. When the frame leaves the PC, it is untagged as a normal Ethernet II frame. If the destination computer is on the far side switch, then it must traverse the 802.1Q trunk link. When it leaves this port, it receives the VLAN tagging information; therefore, the 802.1Q trunk port is considered a tagging port. When it is received on the adjacent switch, the tagging information is read and forwarded to the destination host. When the information comes back from the far side switch, it is again tagged as it leaves the far-side trunk port. It is then read by the adjacent switch and forwarded onto the respective VLAN/port. When it leaves the host port, the tagging information is removed; hence, this port is called an untagging port.

FIGURE 1.27 Untagging and tagging ports

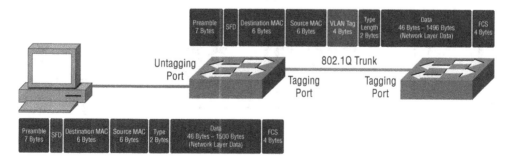

Many different switch vendors use different terminology for this functionality. Cisco calls an untagging port an *access port* and a tagging port a *trunk port*. There are also ports that listen for tagging information so that VoIP data can be switched properly; these are called *voice ports*. Many generic switch vendors will refer to these ports as tagging and untagging ports. The concept is identical between all vendors.

Port Mirroring

When we run into networking issues, we sometimes need to capture packets with a packet analyzer. However, switches isolate our conversation as you will learn in Chapter 2. We could put a hub in place and attach our packet capture host to the hub. However, doing so could create other problems such as bandwidth issues. Most managed switches allow for the mirroring of a port to another port; this functionality allows us to eavesdrop on a conversation and record it for analysis with a packet capture host. Cisco and many other vendors refer to port mirroring as the *Switched Port Analyzer (SPAN)* feature.

Switching Loops/Spanning Tree

Multiple paths between switching equipment in a network should exist for redundancy. However, multiple paths can also create switching loops, and these instantly kill bandwidth on a network. In Figure 1.28 you see an example of two switches with a redundant link between them. The unicast frames sent from host A will enter into the first switch, only to be forwarded out each link of the switch to the adjacent switch. The far side switch will then receive two frames, which it will forward to host B; this cuts the bandwidth in half. Although that is a problem, you could probably still function—that is, until a broadcast frame is introduced into the network. In Figure 1.29 you see host A send a broadcast frame to the first switch; this switch then forwards it to all ports. The adjacent switch does the same, and this begins what is called a broadcast storm. All hosts are instantly crushed with bandwidth, and the MAC address table is thrashed from multiple MAC address entries. The host's network cards accept the data and pass it to the layer above, so the hosts also see a spike in CPU utilization as the operating system processes the broadcast.

FIGURE 1.28 Duplicate unicast packets

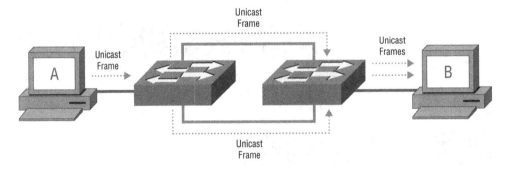

FIGURE 1.29   A broadcast storm

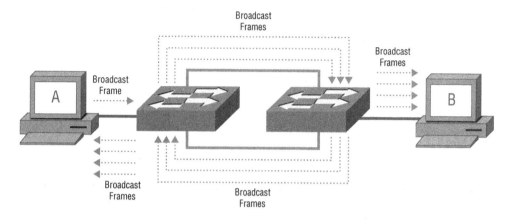

We can create redundant connections in our network for redundancy and avoid switching loops if we use the Spanning Tree Protocol (STP). STP will monitor redundant links and block data from being switched on a redundant link, to avoid the problems just mentioned. STP manages the redundant link and allows data to pass if the primary link goes down.

STP (802.1D)

The original STP protocol was developed by Digital Equipment Corporation (DEC) back in 1993. The IEEE later created its own version of STP called 802.1D (STP). The STP protocol uses the Spanning Tree Algorithm (STA) to block redundant links from causing a switching loop. The STP (802.1D) protocol is still used today because it manages redundant links very well, but it has its shortcomings, as you will see.

Before you begin learning how STP operates, here are a few terms you must learn:

Root Bridge   The root bridge is the switch with the lowest bridge ID. The switches participating in STP will elect a root bridge. The root bridge becomes the root of the network, and all redundancy is managed with the root as the focus of the network. All of the other switches must make a path to the root bridge. The root bridge is often where the servers are located.

Non-root Bridges   These are switches that are not the root bridge. Non-root bridges participate in STP by exchanging Bridge Protocol Data Units (BPDUs).

Bridge ID   The bridge ID is a calculation of the lowest MAC address on the switch and the priority. The default bridge priority is 32768 for most switches. The bridge priority can be adjusted in multiples of 4096 to force a switch to become the root bridge.

Port Cost   The port cost helps determine the fastest connection to the root bridge. When there is a redundant connection to an adjacent switch, the port cost determines which port is turned to a blocking mode. In Table 1.2 you can see the IEEE port cost for each link speed.

TABLE 1.2 IEEE STP link costs

Link speed	IEEE cost
10 Mbps	100
100 Mbps	19
1,000 Mbps	4
10,000 Mbps	2

Root Port   The root port is the port leading to the root bridge on the adjacent switch. If there is more than one from the same switch leading to the root bridge, the port with the lowest cost becomes the root port.

Forwarding Port   A forwarding port is a port that is allowed to forward frames. A forwarding port is marked as a designated port that assists in forwarding frames to a root bridge and has the lowest cost.

Blocking Port   A blocking port is a port that is not allowed to forward frames. It is the redundant link that has a higher cost to the root bridge. Although blocking ports will not forward data, they will forward BPDUs.

STP OPERATIONS

Now that you've learned some of the terminology, let's see how STP operates by blocking redundant links and avoids switching loops. Figure 1.30 shows three switches redundantly connected. All of the switches have the same default priority, so the lowest MAC address will win the election of the root bridge. All of the links between the switches also have the same cost.

FIGURE 1.30   Three switches with redundant links

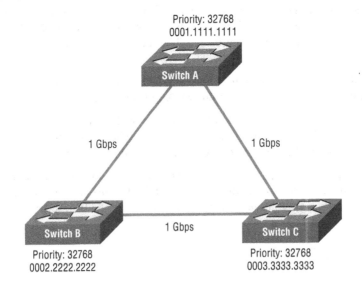

Once the root bridge is selected, as in Figure 1.31, we can label the forwarding ports on switch A. All ports on the root bridge will be in a forwarding mode. The root ports (RPs) can then be labeled on switches B and C, since they are the ports on the adjacent switches that lead back to the root bridge. Now the link between switch B and switch C is the remaining link that is redundant. The switch with the lower cost (switch B) will have its port put into a forwarding mode. The switch with the higher cost (switch C) will have its port put into a blocking mode. If anything in this network changes, STP will recalculate.

FIGURE 1.31   Three switches with STP calculated

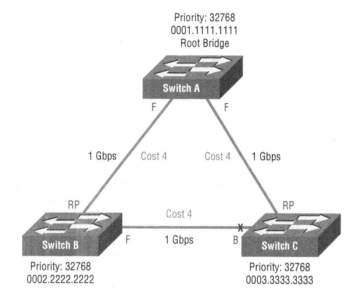

STP PORT STATES

When a port becomes active on a switch, the port transitions between several states before allowing frames to be forwarded. These port transitions are necessary to avoid switching loops in the network, but during this time we cannot forward traffic. The possible port states are as follows:

Disabled   This port state is not really an STP port state; it is just a state of any port that has been disabled by an administrator.

Blocking   This is the first state of any active port; it ensures that a loop will not occur. During the blocking mode, BPDUs are still transmitted so that STA can calculate redundant paths.

Listening   This port state allows the port to listen for BPDUs.

Learning   This mode port state works in conjunction with a listening port; it allows the switch to listen to BPDUs of other switches so that it can calculate its own STP database.

Forwarding   If the port does not have a redundant path or is the lowest cost port, it then transitions into the forwarding mode. In this mode, frames are allowed to be forwarded.

STP CONVERGENCE

STP convergence is the process of placing all ports on the switch into either a forwarding or blocking mode as they become active. The STP convergence time is 50 seconds; during this time no data is passed. If at any time an STP port needs to recalculate, it will block frames for a total of 50 seconds. This convergence time can cause a significant impact to a network. Simply unplugging a connection and plugging it back in can cause a 50-second wait for frames to be forwarded during this convergence period.

An active port will transition to blocking while listening and learning, it will then either remain blocking if it is the higher cost redundant link or transition to forwarding if it is the lower cost redundant link. This transition process can be modified for servers and clients when you can guarantee there are no redundant links in the network. Spanning Tree PortFast allows for forwarding, listening, and learning based on the convergence to either remain forwarding or blocking.

RSTP (802.1w)

The *Rapid Spanning Tree Protocol (RSTP)* is a newer IEEE standard of STP that fixes many of the issues with STP (802.1D). The first feature that RSTP has is fast convergence time, because RSTP is more proactive with calculations; it does not need the 50-second convergence time. RSTP is also backward compatible with STP and can be configured on a port-by-port basis on most switches. Some terminology has changed slightly with RSTP. For example, see the port states shown in Table 1.3. RSTP will transition from a discarding, to a learning, to a forwarding, or remain discarding if it is a higher cost redundant link.

TABLE 1.3   802.1D vs. 802.1w port states

802.1D state	802.1w state
Disabled	Discarding
Blocking	Discarding
Listening	Discarding
Learning	Learning
Forwarding	Forwarding

Another main difference with RSTP compared to STP is that path cost is taken into account when calculating forwarding ports. The entire path is calculated versus the individual port cost. RSTP introduces two other port modes of backup and alternate ports. In Figure 1.32 you see switch B connected to another segment of C; one port is placed into a designated port role, and the other redundant port is placed into a backup port role. On switch C there is an alternate path to the root bridge from the segment C if the designated port were to fail. The original STP specification would have just placed these ports into a blocking mode and treated convergence time the same.

FIGURE 1.32   Backup and alternate ports

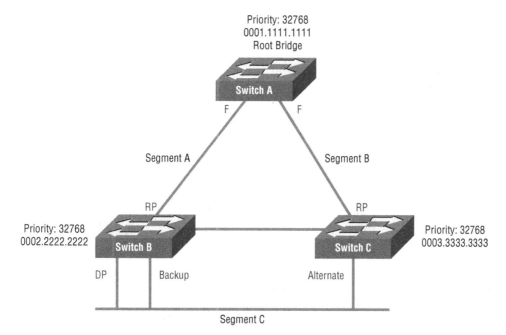

PoE and PoE+ (802.3af, 802.3at)

Power over Ethernet (PoE) allows for the both power and data to be transmitted on a standard Ethernet connection. This technology is what allows VoIP phones to be powered from the switching equipment without the need for power adapters. It is also used for devices, such as video surveillance cameras and wireless access points (WAPs), in remote locations that could not be powered otherwise.

Two standards for PoE exist: PoE (802.3af) and PoE+ (802.3at). The PoE (802.3af) standard is used to supply up to 15.4 watts of power and is commonly used with phone and video surveillance cameras. The PoE+ (802.3at) standard is used to supply up to 25.5 watts of power. PoE+ (802.3at) is sometimes required for the latest wireless standards on WAPs that require more power than PoE (802.3af).

It is important to note that identification protocols such as *Link Layer Discovery Protocol (LLDP)* and the *Cisco Discovery Protocol (CDP)* communicate power requirements to the switch. These power requirements conveyed to the switch lower the supply wattage of PoE and PoE+ at the switch. This allows for more efficient power usage of the end devices.

DMZ

The demilitarized zone (DMZ) is a physical or logical segmentation of a network that allows public access or external access to semi-internal resources. There are three main segments of a network in relation to security. The internal network segment is the innermost portion of your network; it contains your database servers, mailbox servers, and so on.

The external network segment is where the Internet or public network connects. The network that is positioned between the external and internal segments is the DMZ—the segment where you would install a public web server or email server.

It is common to have an internal firewall and an external firewall, as shown in Figure 1.33. The area between these two firewalls is considered the DMZ. An alternate deployment consists of a single firewall that sits between the external, internal, and DMZ segment, as shown in Figure 1.34.

FIGURE 1.33 Two firewalls connected to a DMZ

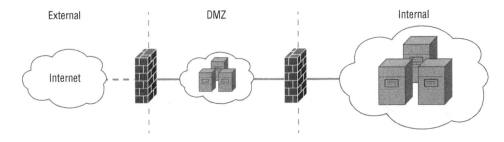

FIGURE 1.34 One firewall connected to a DMZ

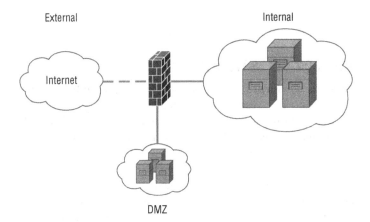

MAC Address Table

The MAC address table is responsible for associating a MAC address or multiple MAC addresses with a physical port on the switch. The MAC address table is sometimes referred to as content-addressable memory (CAM).

When a switch is first started, a table is created in memory, appropriately called the MAC address table. When Computer A sends a message to Computer D in Figure 1.35, a frame is created with the source MAC address of Computer A (Step 1). When the switch receives the frame, it inspects the source MAC address of the frame (Step 2) and records it in the MAC address table on the port it was received on. This is the MAC address learning function of a switch; more specifically, it is called source address learning. The switch then needs to forward the frame to the destination MAC address/port, but the table is empty other than Computer A's entry. So it floods the MAC address to all of the ports (Step 3). The process of deciding the destination port based on the MAC address table is the forward filtering function of the switch. However, since the switch was just started and the table is empty, it must flood the frame to all ports. When Computer D responds to Computer A (Step 4), a frame is received by the switch, and the source MAC address is entered in the MAC address table (Step 5). A forward filter decision can now be made based on the destination MAC address (Step 6). The frame is now delivered directly to Port 1 (Step 7). All communication between Computer A and Computer D will now be isolated to their respective ports based on the MAC address table.

FIGURE 1.35   The MAC address learning process

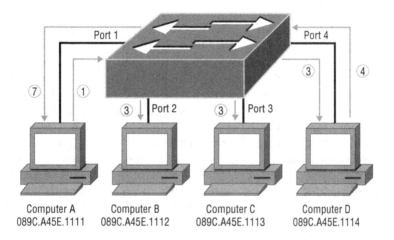

ARP Table

The ARP table is a temporary table in memory to reduce ARP requests for IP address–to–MAC address mappings. When a packet is created at the network layer, it is passed down to the data link layer for framing. The source MAC address is known because it is the host the data was initiated on. However, the destination MAC address is unknown, so the ARP protocol is used to find the MAC address for the destination IP address.

   The ARP protocol will send an ARP request to all listening hosts and devices on the network via a broadcast. An ARP reply is then sent from the matching hosts or device. The ARP reply will contain the MAC address of the IP address requested; the requesting host will then store the IP address and MAC address mapping in the ARP table and continue processing the frame at the data link layer. All consecutive requests for the MAC address will be resolved from the ARP table in memory, until the entry is expired from the ARP table.

Routing

So far you have learned several layer 2 (data link layer) concepts. We will now focus on layer 3 (network layer) routing. All network hosts are configured with a logical IP address. This IP address has two parts: a logical network and a logical host section. Routing is the process of moving data to the destination logical network that contains the logical host contained within it. Routers do not care about the host—routers base all routing decisions based on the destination network.

The process is similar to the post office with the use of zip codes. The mail is sent to your local town, and then the post office within your town is responsible for delivering the mail to your specific address.

Routers perform this critical decision making based on routing tables, which are statically entered or dynamically entered via routing protocols. Let's examine how routers make these decisions based off a static routing table for a simple network. In Figure 1.36 you see two networks separated by a router. Computer A sends a packet to the destination IP address of 192.168.2.2 (Step 1). The router receives the packet, looks at the destination IP address, and calculates the network it belongs to. The router then looks at its internal routing table (Step 2) and makes a decision on which interface to send the packet out for the destination IP address. Computer B then receives the packet (Step 3), and the process starts again in the opposite direction when Computer B responds. The source address in the packet is never relevant in this process—with the exception of Computer B so that it can respond to originating source.

FIGURE 1.36   The basic routing process

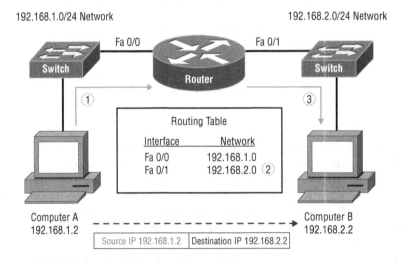

Routing Types

There are three basic type of routing that all routing processes and protocol fall into. Figure 1.36 shows a simple network with two networks containing one router. This example is extremely simple because only one router is used. Depending on the number of routers and where the routers are located, you will need to decide which routing type to use for the given scenario.

Static Routing

Static routing is the simplest of all the types of routing we can perform. It is generally used in small networks without much change, because it is time-consuming for the network administrator. However, the benefit of static routing is that it doesn't change!

In Figure 1.37 we have three networks with two routers. Below each of the routers we have a routing table. The routing table consists of the destination network, exit interface, and a metric. On router A, networks 192.168.1.0/24 and 192.168.2.0/24 are directly connected because an IP address belonging to those networks is configured on the respective interfaces. When an IP address is configured on a router's interface, an entry is automatically placed into the routing table for the network it belongs to. This is a form of static routing, because the IP address is statically configured; therefore, the routing entry is considered to be statically configured.

In Figure 1.37, we use the exit interface as the gateway, because it is a serial line and any packets that enter the serial line are transmitted to the other side. However, the exit interface can also be an IP address. For router A, we can substitute S0/0 for the gateway of 192.168.2.2, and for router B we can substitute S0/0 for 192.168.2.1. In Ethernet networks, you must specify the gateway by IP address, because the packets can take any path, unlike serial links in the figure.

FIGURE 1.37 Two-router network

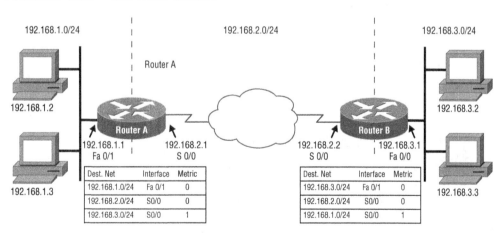

On router A, we can see that a third entry is configured for the 192.168.3.0/24 network. This entry was configured by an administrator because router A doesn't know about the third network of 192.168.3.0/24. We can also see the opposite exists for router B. If a third network was introduced, we would need to manually update both router A and router B with the new entry. If something changed in the network, we would need to manually update all the routers. So static routing is reserved for small networks with very little change.

Dynamic Routing

Dynamic routing reduces the amount of administrator intervention by automating the trading of routing tables or entries with the use of routing protocols. This allows routers to learn new routes to networks from other routers participating in the dynamic routing process.

Routing decisions are optimized with the use of routing protocols in the dynamic routing process. Multiple routes to the same destination network can exist; the routing protocol will select the best route based on the metric.

There are three types of dynamic routing protocols: distance-vector, link-state, and hybrid. I will cover dynamic routing protocols next.

Default Routing

Default routing is useful in stub networks, where all destination networks are reachable through a particular gateway or interface. An example of this is the Internet.

In Figure 1.38 we have two routers connecting two networks and the Internet. Router A is the stub of the network; therefore, we do not need an entry for 192.168.2.0/24. The default route of everything, 0.0.0.0/0, will push packets out of the S0/1 interface, and router B will route the packets to the appropriate destination. Router B is also a stub of the network in respect to the Internet; therefore, anything that is not matched in the routing table will be routed to the Internet router via the S0/1 interface.

FIGURE 1.38 Default routing example

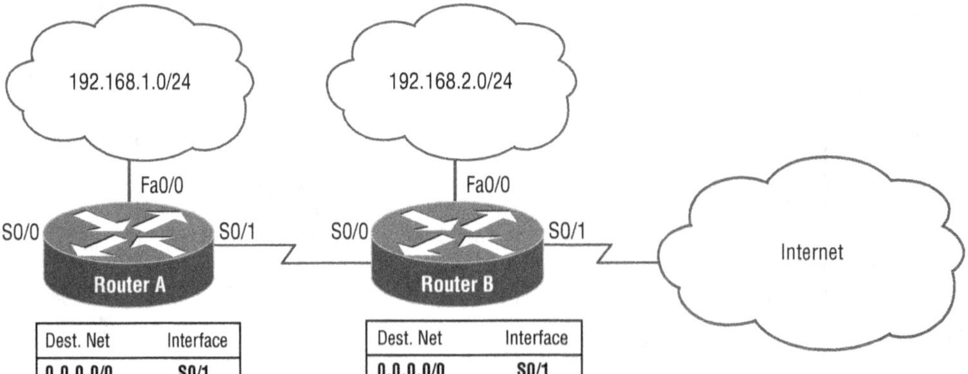

Dest. Net	Interface
0.0.0.0/0	**S0/1**
192.168.1.0/24	Fa0/1

Dest. Net	Interface
0.0.0.0/0	**S0/1**
192.168.2.0/24	Fa0/0
192.168.1.0/24	S0/0

Routing Protocols (IPv4 and IPv6)

Routing protocols have two responsibilities: dynamic routing updates, as discussed earlier, and optimized routing decisions. There are several different methods that routing protocols use to populate and update routes among the participating routers.

Each routing protocol also uses a different algorithm to calculate routing decisions from a set of metrics. Every router will trust a routing protocol over another routing protocol. Cisco calls these trust levels the administrative distance (AD). Table 1.4 is a list of the various ADs.

TABLE 1.4   Cisco administrative distances

Routing protocol	Administrative distance
Directly connected interface	0
Static route	1
EBGP	20
Internal EIGRP	90
OSPF	110
RIP	120
Internal BGP	200
Unknown	255

Distance-Vector Routing Protocols

Distance-vector routing protocols use the metric of distance to calculate routing decisions. The metric used is hop count, which is how many routers a packet must traverse to get to the destination network. Distance-vector routing protocols are susceptible to routing loops, because they only look at the number of hops and no other criteria.

RIP

The *Routing Information Protocol (RIP)* is a true distance-vector routing protocol. It is an older protocol used for dynamic routing in small networks. RIP sends the complete routing table to the neighboring router out all active interfaces every 30 seconds. RIP uses the hop count as a metric and the Bellman–Ford algorithm to calculate the routing decision.

RIP has a maximum hop count of 15. A destination network with a hop count of 16 is deemed unreachable. There are several versions of RIP:

RIP version 1 uses broadcasts to send routing updates and the initial routing table. RIP version 1 can only use classful routing, because the subnet mask is not transmitted in the routing updates. This means that all networks need to use the associated subnet mask and cannot be broken down into subnets.

RIP version 2 uses the multicast address of 224.0.0.9 to send routing updates and the initial table to participating routers. The use of multicast helps with bandwidth concerns of broadcasts, but the protocol still has the limitations of 15 hops. RIP version 2 also addresses the problem of using subnets in the network. RIP version 2 transmits the table with the subnet mask included; this is called classless routing.

RIPng (RIP next generation) is an IPv6 implementation of the RIP routing protocol. Like the IPv4 versions, RIPng uses hop count and the Bellman–Ford algorithm to calculate routing decisions and has a maximum hop count of 15. RIPng uses an IPv6 multicast address of FF02::9 to transmit route updates and the initial table every 30 seconds out of all active interfaces.

All versions of RIP have a slow convergence time because routers must pass the complete table around the network. A router four hops away might need to wait up to 90 seconds to obtain the full table. Because of the slow convergence time with RIP, it is susceptible to routing loops. A few techniques exist to prevent routing loops, such as the following:

Split horizons prevent routing updates from being received on the same interface that a route update was sent from stating that the destination network is down. This creates an artificial horizon where a router cannot be told a path to its own network is available via another router.

Poison reverse exploits the maximum hop count of 15 to stop routers from receiving an update to an alternate path to the same network. When a router detects a network that it manages is down, it will adjust the hop count to 16 and continue to populate the route entry. This will poison all the tables in the network for the affected network. When it comes back up, the route entry will be adjusted back.

Hold-downs are used to slow down routing updates for an affected network. It allows all the tables in the network to converge by holding down any updates for the affected network. The normal hold-down time is six times the update period of 30 seconds, for a total of 180 seconds.

EIGRP

The *Enhanced Interior Gateway Routing Protocol (EIGRP)* is a Cisco proprietary protocol and is only available on Cisco products. EIGRP is not a true distance-vector routing protocol. EIGRP has the characteristics of both distance-vector and link-state protocols.

EIGRP is a more modern protocol than RIP and therefore has many more features than RIP. EIGRP allows for scalability with the use of autonomous system (AS) numbers. This allows routers within an AS to participate in routing updates. EIGRP also has a default hop count of 100 and a maximum of 255; both of these features support scalability of the protocol so it can be used in large networks. EIGRP supports classless routing (subnets), variable-length subnet masking (VLSM), discontiguous networks, and summarization of networks.

EIGRP doesn't use hop count solely for routing decisions; it can use a combination of bandwidth, delay, load, reliability, and maximum transmission units (MTUs). By default, to compute routing decisions EIGRP uses a combination of bandwidth and delay called a composite metric. The algorithm EIGRP uses is the Diffusing Update Algorithm (DUAL). The algorithm make use of protocol-dependent modules (PDMs), which allows IPv4, IPv6, or any other protocol to be used with DUAL.

EIGRP uses three main tables: the neighbor table, the topology table, and the routing table (see Figure 1.39). EIGRP starts by associating with neighboring routers through a process called neighbor discovery. Router A will send a multicast Hello packet to 224.0.0.10; router B and router C will respond with a Hello/ACK packet. In the Hello packet the AS number and metrics (K values) will be sent. In order for EIGRP neighboring routers to be considered a neighbor, three pieces of information must be exchanged: Hello and ACK packets, matching AS numbers, and identical metrics. When this occurs, the neighboring router will be added to the neighbor table.

FIGURE 1.39   EIGRP tables

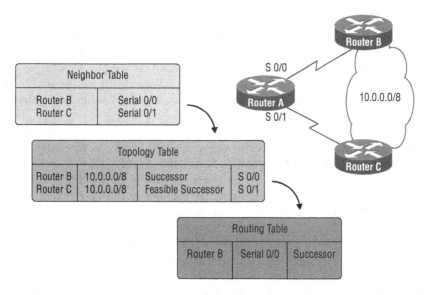

The topology table is populated by the DUAL algorithm. DUAL will inspect the neighbor table and calculate the metrics to the destination networks. In this case, two paths exist to the destination network of 10.0.0.0/8: one through S 0/0 (router B) and another through S 0/1 (router C). DUAL will choose a successor route and a feasible successor router to

10.0.0.0/8. The successor route will be sent to the routing table, and the feasible successor will remain in the topology table. If the successor route fails, then the feasible successor route will become the successor route and move to the routing table.

EIGRP maintains the neighbor table with the Reliable Transport Protocol (RTP). RTP will multicast Hello packets every 60 seconds to the multicast address of 224.0.0.10. RTP will maintain a list of neighbors who have responded and those who have not. If a neighbor does not respond to a multicast, RTP will unicast Hello packets to the neighbor. After 16 unicast attempts, the neighbor will be dropped out of the neighbor table and DUAL will recalculate. This is one of the reasons EIGRP is not considered a true distance-vector protocol!

EIGRPv6 is the IPv6 version of EIGRP and functions the same as EIRGP for IPv4. Since DUAL supports PDMs, IPv6 is treated the same as IPv4. There are a few minor differences, such as how it is configured. The IPv6 multicast address is FF02::A, which is easy to remember because A equals 10 in hex, and the IPv4 multicast address is 224.0.0.10.

Link-State Routing Protocols

Link-state routing protocols do exactly what their name says; they not only keep track of neighbors, but they also track the state of their neighbor's links. This is the main difference between distance-vector routing protocols and link-state routing protocols. Link-state routing protocols make independent decisions based on the links versus distance-vector protocols that can only make decisions based on what other routers preprocess.

OSPF

Open Shortest Path First (OSPF) is a true link-state protocol. It is an open standard, which means that it can be configured on any manufacturer router—that is, if it is included in the feature set. OSPF is extremely scalable and is used for very large networks. OSPF uses the Dijkstra algorithm to construct the initial shortest path tree and calculates routes based on the bandwidth metric. The hop count of OSPF is unlimited, unlike EIGRP and RIP.

OSPF uses the concept of areas to create a hierarchal routing structure. All OSPF configuration must start with an area of 0, sometimes referred to as the backbone area of 0.0.0.0. The use of areas allows the OSPF protocol to be scalable, because routing updates can be constrained to routers participating within the area to control bandwidth. Areas communicate with other areas to send summary route advertisements through routers called area border routers (ABRs). In addition, OSPF areas can connect other autonomous systems such as EIGRP, BGP, and so on. The routers that connect OSPF to other autonomous systems are called autonomous system boundary routers (ASBRs).

When the OSPF process starts on a router, it selects the highest IP address on the router and uses this IP address as the router ID (RID). The RID is how the routers are tracked by OSPF. The Hello protocol is used for neighbors to form on the multicast address of 224.0.0.5 and also used for link-state advertisements (LSAs). However, in order for routers to become neighbors, the same area IDs must match, the authentication password must match (if used), and Hello/Dead intervals must match.

OSPF will form an adjacency with neighboring routers; adjacent routers permit the direct exchange of route updates for OSPF route calculation. However, adjacencies are not formed with all neighbors—only with routers that share a direct link, such as a point-to-point connection. Adjacencies are also formed with designated routers (DRs). A router becomes the DR by having the highest RID in an election. The designated router is used in broadcast networks such as Ethernet and is allowed to form adjacencies with other routers in the same broadcast network. In broadcast networks, a multicast address of 224.0.0.6 is used for LSAs.

OSPF contains similar tables (databases) to the EIGRP protocol described in the previous section. It maintains a neighborship database, a topological database, and of course the routing table. The neighborship database is populated by the process described earlier. The topological database is built by the OSPF process and feeds the routing table with respective routes to destination networks.

OSPFv3 is the IPv6 version of OSPF version 2 (IPv4). In OSPF version 2, the RID is calculated on the router as the highest IP address. In OSPFv3, the RID is an IPv4 address configured on the router, because IPv6 addresses are too long and sometimes autoconfigured. OSPFv3 works similar to its IPv4 counterpart—it still requires the first area to be area 0.0.0.0. The multicast addresses used are FF02::5 for point-to-point routers and FF02::6 for broadcast routers.

Hybrid

Hybrid routing protocols are protocols that have characteristics of both a link-state routing protocol and a distance-vector routing protocol. EIGRP is the only hybrid routing protocol covered on the CompTIA Network+ exam objective, but it is the clearest example of a hybrid routing protocol.

BGP

Border Gateway Protocol (BGP) is a path-vector routing protocol. The protocol is most commonly used for Internet routing of IPv4 and IPv6. Although you could use it internally in your network, there are better protocols that are made for internal routing, such as OSPF. Path-vector routing protocols are classified as distance-vector routing protocols, because they listen to peer routers for their information. BGP uses a process called the BGP Best Path Selection algorithm for choosing the best route to the destination network.

BGP is often used by enterprises to either load-balance connections over two Internet providers or provide failover between two Internet service providers (ISPs). When it is used with a single connection to each ISP, it is considered a single multihomed connection. When an enterprise needs to populate the Internet with routes and a single ISP, it is considered a single-homed connection. There are other variations of the connection, but these two are the most common.

BGP is resource intensive on a router when used in a multihomed connection, because your router is processing the routes learned from the ISPs. Currently there are over 600,000 IPv4 routes for the Internet that your router must learn and process. The BGP routing tables are almost one gigabyte in size, and routers often need double that in RAM to process and function; this is just for IPv4.

The BGP routing protocols uses an autonomous system number (ASN) to allow routers inside an ASN to share internal routes. When the BGP peer (neighbor) routers are inside an ASN, the BGP process is considered Internal Border Gateway Protocol (iBGP). When the BGP peers are between two different ASNs, the BGP process is considered External Border Gateway Protocol (eBGP). Before you can use BGP to populate routes on the Internet, you must register for an ASN number from the *regional Internet registry (RIR)*—such as ARIN, RIPE, AFRINIC, LACNIC, and APNIC.

When BGP routers create a peering with another router, they transmit Network Layer Reachability Information (NLRI) between each other. This NLRI is composed of length and prefix. The length is the *classless interdomain routing (CIDR)* notation of the network mask, and the prefix is the network address. BGP peers send a keepalive every 60 seconds via a unicast message on TCP/179. BGP is a unique routing protocol because it uses a transport layer to communicate network layer information.

IPv6 Concepts

IPv6 was developed by the IETF and was published in 1998. It is now 20 years later and it is still slowly being adopted! The motivation for IPv6 was the exhaustion of the IPv4 address space; in the year 2000, half of the IPv4 addresses were allocated. Through the years since the IPv4 exhaustion was first forecasted, many technologies were developed to lessen the impact. One such technology was network address translation (NAT), covered later in this section. IPv6 has many unique features that you will learn.

Addressing

Before you learn about IPv6, let's compare it to IPv4. The IPv4 address consists of a 32-bit network and host address. A 32-bit address is capable of supplying 4.3 million IP addresses. However, with the classification of IP addresses, we really have only 3.7 million usable addresses. In comparison, there are 7.5 billion people on the planet. So I think you can see the problem? The IPv6 address consists of a 128-bit address and can supply 3.4×10^{38} usable addresses.

There is a learning curve to the IPv6 address, but it is actually easier than IPv4. No complicated binary math is involved with subnetting; the IETF built it into the IPv6 address. However, it is a really large number to notate compared to IPv4, and we must use hexadecimal in the addressing. This is probably the biggest intimidation factor for IPv6, but trust me, it is simple.

Figure 1.40 shows an IPv6 address. The first half (64 bits) is the network ID, and the second half (64 bits) is the interface ID—resulting in a 128-bit address. It is written in hexadecimal, so each digit represents 4 bits. There are 32 digits in an IPv6 address, each containing 4 bits of information, and 32 × 4 = 128 bits. The first 48 bits are called the global prefix and are assigned by the RIR, just like an IPv4 network address. The next 16 bits are the subnet bits, and although they comprise the network ID, they can be assigned by the organization assigned to the global prefix. The last 64 bits comprise the interface ID that we will discuss later in this section.

FIGURE 1.40   IPv6 address example

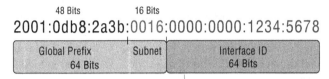

IPv6 Shorthand

Because the length of an IPv6 address is long, there are a few ways to shorten it. When you're shortening, you need to follow a few rules. Here is an example of an IPv6 address in its uncondensed form:

2001:0db8:0045:0000:0000:0056:0000:0012

We can condense it by first removing all of the leading zeros between the colons. The leading zeros need to be there for a complete IPv6 address, but the IETF has given us a shortcut. Consider this: We don't have $0010; we have $10. This is an easy way to remember the leading zero concept. When we are done, the IPv6 address will look like this:

2001:db8:45:0:0:56:0:12

We can condense it further by removing the zeros between the colons, but you can only do this once. So either IPv6 here is correct:

2001:db8:45:0:0:56::12
2001:db8:45::56:0:12

In the second IPv6 address we removed a colon completely. When the host puts the address back together for processing, it will first add the leading zeros back to the address (using the second example):

2001:0db8:0045::0056:0000:0012

The host will then add the zeros between the double colons to create a 128-bit address again. Here's another example:

2001:0db8:0000:0000:0000:0000:0001:0012
2001:db8::1:12

Address Types

There are many different IPv6 address types, and again they are not all that different than their IPv4 counterparts. *Internet Assigned Numbers Authority (IANA)* is responsible for mandating addressing of IPv6 prefixes. In the following definitions, I will compare the IPv4 counterpart:

> *Unicast* packets in IPv6 are the same as unicast packets IPv4. They are direct communications between two hosts. Just like in IPv4, there are public IP address and private IP addresses. The only things that change are the terminology and the address prefix.

Global unicast addresses (2000::/3) are the same as public IP addresses in IPv4. They are assigned by a regional Internet registry. The structure makes sense, because it has a logical hierarchy, as shown in Figure 1.41. The first 23 bits of the 64-bit network ID defines the RIR. The next 9 bits are assigned to an ISP, and the next 16 bits are assigned to a company. In other words, looking at the first 23 bits you can tell which registry assigned the network ID. Looking at the first 32 bits, you could tell which registry and ISP assigned the network ID. Finally, looking at the first 48 bits, you could tell the registry, ISP, and company the network ID was assigned to. The largest block an ISP can assign is a /48 block, because the final 16 bits are used by the company to subnet the address further.

FIGURE 1.41   Breakdown of an IPv6 global unicast address

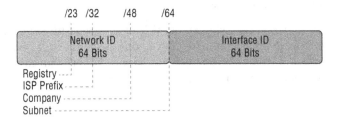

Link-Local addresses (FE80::/10) are the same as link-local addresses in IPv4. In IPv4 Microsoft calls a link-local address an *Automatic Private IP Address (APIPA)*. These addresses are used for local access on a network and are unrouteable. As shown in Figure 1.42, the first 10 bits will always start with 1111 1110 10, or written in hexadecimal, FE80. This might confuse you at first, because FE80 is actually 16 bits and I'm stating that the first 10 bits are mandated by IANA. It is true—the last 6 bits can be anything as long as the first 10 bits are FE8. IANA notates all prefixes as 16-bit hexadecimal addresses.

FIGURE 1.42   A link-local prefix

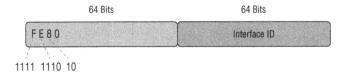

Unique local addresses (FC00::/7) are similar to private IP addresses in IPv4. The addresses are used for internal routing and not intended for Internet routing. The first 7 bits are mandated by IANA, and the other 57 bits can be assigned by the organization. Whenever you see FC00 as the prefix, it is a link-local address. Again, IANA only mandates the first 7 bits to be FC, but IANA notates all addresses in a 16-bit hexadecimal address.

Multicast addresses (FF00::/8) are similar to multicast addresses in IPv4. A multicast is a one-to-many address used in lieu of broadcasts in IPv6. In IPv6 broadcast addresses no longer exist. In lieu of broadcasts, IPv6 uses multicasting. IANA mandates that the first 8 bits are all 1s or FF. So whenever you see an address starting with FF, know that it is an IPv6 multicast address.

Anycast addresses are also similar to their IPv4 counterparts. Anycast addresses are used for a one-to-nearest connectivity. The address is a standard global unicast address, but it is populated in multiple routing tables. The root DNS servers function with this special address type. You should make note that although anycast addresses are global unicast addresses, the IETF has reserved the first 128 addresses for each /64 for use with anycast addressing.

Tunneling

Tunneling is used as a transition technology for IPv6 networking over an IPv4 network. There are several different technologies for achieving co-existence between an IPv6 network and an IPv4 network. These technologies are commonly used because an application must function with IPv6 or a particular service requires IPv6.

6to4 encapsulates IPv6 packets inside an IPv4 packet using network protocol 41. 6to4 can be used in two ways; the first is site-to-site over an IPv4 network such as the Internet. The 6to4 router will encapsulate an IPv6 packet over the IPv4 Internet to the destination 6to4 router, where it is decapsulated and routed on the IPv6 network. The second way 6to4 can be used is to allow an IPv6 network to communicate over the IPv4 Internet to the IPv6 Internet. When it is used in this scenario, your 6to4 router must be pointed to a 6to4 router connected to the IPv6 Internet. These 6to4 endpoint routers use an anycast address of 192.88.99.1 as the IPv4 destination network address.

Toredo tunneling is another IPv6 transitional technology. It is used when an IPv6 host is behind a network address translation (NAT). The IPv6 packets are sent as UDP/3544 IPv4 packets to a Toredo server that is connected to the IPv6 network. Many ISPs have Toredo servers for public use to the IPv6 Internet. A Toredo relay is a router that interacts with a Toredo server, to facilitate IPv4 client to IPv6 hosts.

Intra-Site Automatic Tunnel Addressing Protocol (ISATAP) allows dual-stack hosts to communicate on an IPv4 network to an IPv6 router. When a dual-stack host is configured for ISATAP, it will resolve the DNS ISATAP well-known entry. This request will resolve to an IPv4 ISATAP router that will allow the host to communicate to the IPv6 network. The client will then obtain an IPv6 network address and communicate with the IPv6 router by using IPv6-in-IPv4 encapsulation.

Dual Stack

When the IPv4 OSI layers work together, it is known as a network stack. The IPv6 OSI layers are similar to IPv4, with the exception of IPv6 at the network layer; IPv6 is also considered a network stack. A dual-stack router or host is considered to have both the IPv4 and IPv6 network stacks running simultaneously. This allows the router or host to communicate on both versions of the IP protocol.

Router Advertisements

When a host boots up in an IPv6 network, the host will configure itself with a link-local IPv6 network address starting with FE80. This IPv6 address is used to send a Router Solicitation (RS) request via a multicast address of FF02::2. RS packets use ICMP type 133. All routers in the network will respond with a Router Advertisement (RA) on a multicast address of FF02::1. RA packets use ICMP type 134. Inside this RA packet the network ID will be contained; the client will assume this network address and configure a host ID dynamically. The address received in the RA packet is now the host's default gateway out of the network. Over the host's lifetime in the network, it will continue to listen for RAs and refresh its internal routing table.

Neighbor Discovery

When an IPv4 host needs to communicate with another IPv4 IP address on the link-local network, it requires the MAC address. The process requires an ARP request and ARP reply, which is broadcast based. IPv6 has eliminated broadcasts, and the ARP protocol with the ICMPv6 protocol calls the Neighbor Discovery Protocol (NDP).

When an IPv6 host needs to communicate with another IPv6 host on the link-local network, it will multicast a Neighbor Solicitation (NS) called a solicited node multicast to a multicast address of FF02::1. The NS packets use ICMPv6 type 135. The neighbor will then reply with a Neighbor Advertisement (NA) with its MAC address. The NA packets use ICMPv6 type 136. The requestor will then cache this address in the neighbor cache, which is similar to the ARP cache in IPv4. This entire process is similar to IPv4 ARP requests and replies, but it uses multicast to facilitate the traffic and eliminate broadcasts.

Performance Concepts

Networks are used to transmit all sorts of data, from iSCSI to web surfing. Depending on which IP services you use in your network, some services should take priority over others. For example, VoIP should take a higher precedence in the network than simple web browsing or even file-based access, because it is a time-sensitive service. You will learn several techniques in this section to make VoIP or iSCSI take precedence over other non-time-sensitive network traffic.

Traffic Shaping

Traffic shaping is implemented on routers to shape traffic to the speed of the connection. If you had a 1 Gbps interface but pay for overages over 800 Mbps of traffic, you need to slow down the outgoing traffic. This is where traffic shaping comes in handy.

With traffic shaping, we allow the output queue to send data for a specific bit rate, and then we wait for the remainder of the cycle. In Figure 1.43 you see a time reference of one second on the bottom of the legend. If we were to transmit the full rate of the interface (which is 1 Gbps), then it would take an entire second. However, with traffic shaping we will transmit only 800 million bits in 800 milliseconds, and then we will wait the remainder of the cycle, or 200 milliseconds. We have effectively slowed the bit rate down to 800 Mbps!

FIGURE 1.43   A traffic shaping example

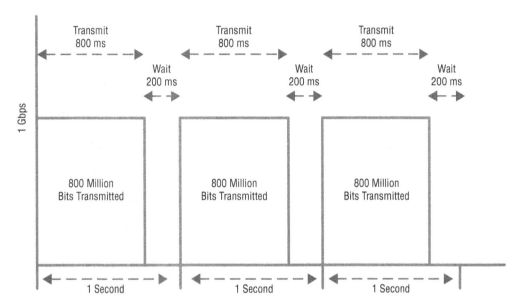

This example is exaggerated for explanation purposes. An interval of 200 ms is an eternity for data to wait for the next transmit cycle of data. Therefore, in practical application we would divide 1000 ms by 100 and use a cycle of 10 ms. We would transmit for 8 ms and wait 2 ms. The effect is the same because we have, over a one-second interval, shaped the data to 800 Mbps.

QoS

Quality of service (QoS) is the concept of the prioritization of protocols. You always want time-sensitive protocols like VoIP or iSCSI to have priority in networks over web surfing traffic or file access. QoS can be achieved at layer 3 and layer 2 of the OSI model. It is important to note that, although our internal routers and switches can be programmed to abide by the layer 3 and layer 2 QoS markings, Internet routers usually don't care.

Diffserv

Differentiated Services Code Point (DSCP), or DiffServ, is a 6-bit value contained in the 8-bit Type of Services (ToS) field of an IP header at layer 3. Before DiffServ was created, the first 3 bits in the 8-bit ToS field was used for IP Precedence (IPP) QoS markings. IPP is deprecated and no longer used (the DSCP markings are now used), but the IPP markings are still present for backward compatibility. So when you see the DSCP priorities in Table 1.5, the Class Selector (CS) values are there for backward compatibility with IPP.

TABLE 1.5 DSCP markings

DSCP binary value	Decimal value	Label	Drop probability	IPP equivalent
000 000	0	Best Effort	N/A	000 - Routine
001 010	10	AF11	Low	001 - Priority
001 100	12	AF12	Medium	001 - Priority
001 110	14	AF13	High	001 - Priority
010 010	18	AF21	Low	010 - Immediate
010 100	20	AF22	Medium	010 - Immediate
010 110	22	AF23	High	010 - Immediate
011 010	26	AF31	Low	011 - Flash
011 100	28	AF32	Medium	011 - Flash
011 110	30	AF33	High	011 - Flash
100 010	34	AF41	Low	100 - Flash Override
100 100	36	AF42	Medium	100 - Flash Override
100 110	38	AF43	High	100 - Flash Override
001 000	8	CS1		1
010 000	16	CS2		2
011 000	24	CS3		3
100 000	32	CS4		4
101 000	40	CS5		5
110 000	48	CS6		6
111 000	56	CS7		7
101 110	46	EF		Critical

The DSCP Assured Forwarding (AF) values are a combination of a two-digit value. The first digit identifies the queue, where 1 is worst and 4 is best. The second digit is the drop probability, where 1 is low and 3 is high. Traffic classified with a DSCP value of AF12 has a higher probability of being dropped and queued later than traffic classified with a DSCP marking of AF31.

CoS

Class of Service (CoS) is a 3-bit field in the layer 2 802.1Q frame. CoS is used for the prioritization of traffic between switches on 802.1Q trunk links. In Figure 1.44 you can see the 802.1Q frame and the 3-bit value for priority. The 3-bit value maps to a priority of eight possible queues (0 through 7), where 0 is best effort (worst) and 7 is the highest priority (best). VoIP traffic normally uses a priority value of 5, and web traffic normally uses a priority value of 0.

FIGURE 1.44   An 802.1Q frame

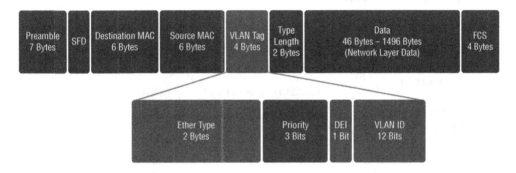

NAT/PAT

Network address translation (NAT) is used for translating one network address to another. This process is required when using a private IP address scheme and you want to request resources on the Internet. We call the device in our house a router, but in actuality it is a NAT device. There are other instances when we need NAT, such as when we have an overlapping IP address scheme. This normally happens when a company merges and you can't pick the IP address scheme, since it's already in use at the other company. There are several types of NAT, and I will cover them next.

Static NAT

Static network address translation (SNAT) is used for one-to-one mappings between local (private or inside) and global (Internet) addresses. This requires an IP address on the outside of the NAT process for each IP address inside your network.

In Figure 1.45 you see a group of internal computers on the left; these IP addresses are considered the inside local addresses. When a message is sent to the router from the host (packet A), the source IP address is 192.168.1.10, and the destination IP address is 208.215.179.146. When the packet arrives at the router, a table lookup is performed in the NAT table, and the source IP address is replaced with 24.20.1.2 from the table (packet B). This IP address is called the inside global IP address, since it is controlled (inside your network), but it is globally routed on the Internet. The packet is then sent on the Internet to the destination, called the outside global IP address (packet C), since it is outside of your network and control and it is globally routed on the Internet. The server then sends the packet back to a destination IP address of 24.20.1.2 (packet D). When it returns at the router performing NAT, it is looked up in the table, and the destination address is replaced with the inside local IP address (packet E). The router then sends it to the original requesting host (packet F). The host never knew that the packet's source and destination address were altered during the process.

FIGURE 1.45   The static NAT process

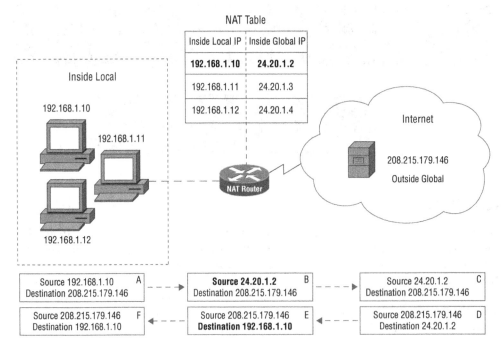

Dynamic NAT

Dynamic network address translation (DNAT) functions similar to static NAT, as shown in Figure 1.46. DNAT is a one-to-one mapping of IP addresses, with the difference that a pool of IP addresses is attached to the NAT process. When an internal host (inside local) is destined for the Internet through the NAT router, an IP address (inside global) is mapped dynamically from the pool to the inside local IP address, and the entry is added to the table. This dynamic mapping is allocated for a set period of time; after the time period is up, the IP address can then be recycled. This process still requires as many IP addresses on the inside global side as you have inside local IP addresses. The benefit is that each IP address does not require a static mapping.

FIGURE 1.46   Dynamic NAT process

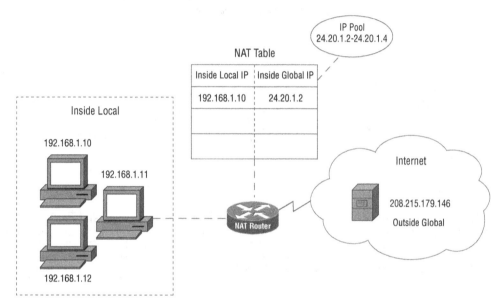

PAT

Port address translation (PAT) is a many-to-one mapping of IP addresses. It is basically what your home NAT router does. It uses a single public (inside global) IP address to translate all of the private (inside local) IP addresses, in your house or business. It performs this by adding the inside local (private) IP address and port number to the table. PAT then maps the inside global (public) IP address and port number. The important concept here is that the inside local port number does not need to be the same as the inside global port number, since it will be translated in the table. In Figure 1.47, I've purposely used a different port number to illustrate the NAT table lookup and this concept. You can see the translation of IP address and port number in packets B and E. Although I didn't include the outside global address in the table for simplicity, it's in there. PAT will include the outside global address in the table, since many requests from host(s) to the same server could exist and this will allow for proper translation.

FIGURE 1.47   Port address translation process

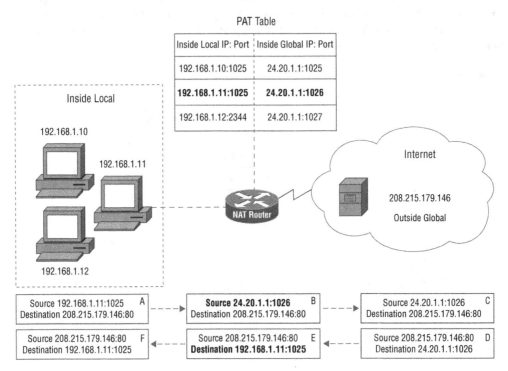

Port Forwarding

Port forwarding is a PAT concept, but for the remainder of this section I will refer to it as NAT. Port forwarding allows outside global (public Internet) hosts to contact services on an inside local (private) host in your network behind a NAT. It performs this function with a manual static entry mapping of the inside local IP address and port to an IP address on the public interface of the router. When a packet destined for the IP address and the port is remapped to the internal host IP address and port number, think of it as a reverse NAT entry. It allows the administrator to publish services on servers internally on the internal network. In Figure 1.48 you see a port forwarding entry for an internal web server with an IP address of 192.168.1.15. The entry is mapped to the outside IP address on the router of 209.160.245.2 and port 80. When a connection is made to the outside IP address, it is forwarded to the internal server.

FIGURE 1.48 Port forwarding example

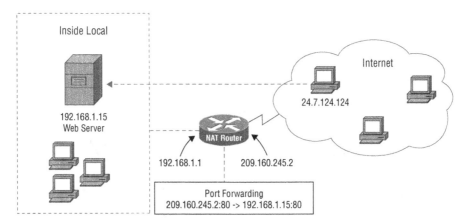

Access Control List

Access control lists (ACLs) are used for security on network firewalls, routers, and switches. ACLs consist of a list of conditions and actions. A typical condition might be if a packet matches a destination IP address and port number. If a particular condition matches, then the action configured with the condition is acted upon. Typical actions are deny, permit, or log (permit).

Every vendor will have their own formatting of an ACL and pattern of behavior. Figure 1.49 shows an ACL formatted for Cisco routers. The pattern of behavior for an ACL on a Cisco router is as follows:

- Only one ACL per interface, per direction, per protocol can be applied at one time.

- The ACL list is compared from top to bottom; when a condition is met, the processing of rules stops, and the action is acted upon.

- At the end of all ACLs is an implicit deny of all traffic, so an ACL list without one permit is a useless list.

In Figure 1.49 the ACL of 110 permits the host 192.168.1.2 (host A) from any port to the host 192.168.2.2 on port 80 (WWW). The ACL then denies host 192.168.1.4 from any port to the host 192.168.2.2 on port 80. Because there is an implicit deny any any at the end of all access lists on Cisco, we must specify the permit ip any any. The last statement will ensure that all other clients have access to all ports (applications).

You will also notice that the interface fa 0/2 has the access list applied to an outbound direction. Any packets leaving the interface of fa 0/2 will be checked against the ACL of 110. Only one ACL can be used per interface (fa 0/2), per protocol (IP), per direction (outbound) on a Cisco router.

FIGURE 1.49 ACL example

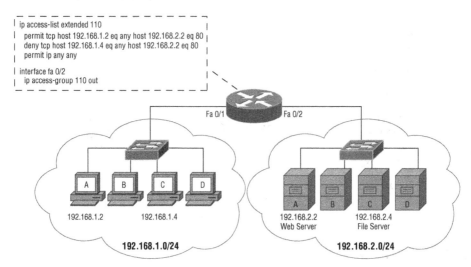

```
ip access-list extended 110
  permit tcp host 192.168.1.2 eq any host 192.168.2.2 eq 80
  deny tcp host 192.168.1.4 eq any host 192.168.2.2 eq 80
  permit ip any any

interface fa 0/2
  ip access-group 110 out
```

ACLs can be used to control users and application. Although the ACL in the figure is targeting a host, most ACLs target networks of users. This allows the administrator to control IP ranges from accessing applications. It is extremely common for VLANs to be created and assigned a network range. Then when the users are assigned to the VLAN, the ACL is automatically applied to the network used for the VLAN.

Distributed Switching

Distributed switching is the concept of a hierarchical network design. In large-scale networks it is common to see a three-tier network design. The access layer often referred to as edge switches, which connect the end-user hosts. The access layer provides local switching and the creation of collision domains. The distribution layer is often referred to as the workgroup layer. The distribution layer is where packet filtering, security policies, routing between VLANs, and defining of broadcast domains are performed. You can think of it as the distribution of switching from the core to the access layer. The core layer is designed for high availability and only provides routing and switching of the entire network. Nothing should be done at the core layer to slow it down!

In a perfect world, with unlimited budgets, the three-tier model should be implemented in every network. However, reality sets in and budgets are tight, so the collapsed core model has been adopted by mid-sized companies. The collapsed core model does not just make sense monetarily; it makes sense in a single campus network. Enterprise has adopted a model of the collapsed core design at each site. Both the three-tier model and the collapsed core model has its uses in enterprises. Figure 1.50 shows a side-by-side comparison of both models. The collapsed core design uses a single tier of switches to provide the core and distribution of switching.

FIGURE 1.50   Three-tier model vs. collapsed core model

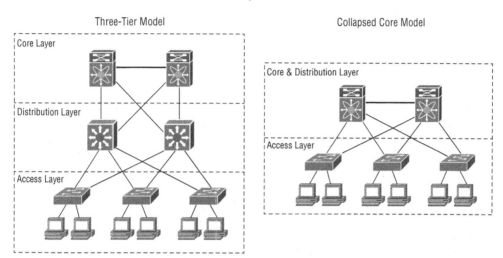

Packet Switched vs. Circuit-Switched Networks

Packet-switched networks divide data streams into packets, and the packets are routed through the internetwork. The packets do not necessarily take the same path to the destination. The packets can take multiple different paths to the same destination. TCP/IP is a packet-switched technology.

Circuit-switched networks connect two network hosts or nodes together to transmit information over a dedicated connection. WAN connections often use circuit-switched networks called point-to-point connections. These connections are often referred to as circuits, because they are dedicated communications between two routers.

Software-Defined Networking

Software-defined networking (SDN) is a broad term used by *virtualization* vendors, cloud providers, and network hardware vendors. Virtualization vendors and cloud providers often use it in context to describe the networking services provided at a software level of the *hypervisor.*

The term SDN is often used by virtualization and cloud vendors to describe the internal network service their hypervisor or cloud service can perform. Another definition of SDN used by network hardware vendors is to describe the control and programmability of network hardware from a centralized controller. The controller is the brains of the network that allows centralized control to all switching and routing in the network. The controller communicates with the network devices through the *southbound interface (SBI).* When an administrator wants to create a policy, they can program it into the controller. The controller will then program the network devices through the SBI, and the network equipment will adhere to the policy across the enterprise.

Exam Essentials

Understand the various properties of network traffic. A collision domain is a segment of the network where two or more nodes can send a frame simultaneously on the same physical network or media, which causes a collision. A broadcast domain is a segment of the network where all the hosts can see a broadcast. CSMA/CD is a contention method used with Ethernet. CSMA/CA is another contention method used with wireless and token ring. Protocol data units (PDUs) are labels we give to describe data at the various layers of the OSI. The maximum transmission unit (MTU) is the largest amount of data that can be transmitted at the data link layer. Broadcasts rob bandwidth and are present in all networks because of ARP and supporting protocols such as DHCP. Multicast is similar to broadcasts in the respect it is a one-to-many transmission. However, multicasts are sent only to ports participating in the multicast session. Unicast traffic is directed communications between two hosts and should make up 95–98 percent of all network communications.

Understand and be able to describe the segmentation of networks and interface properties. Virtual local area networks (VLANs) allow for the logical segmentation of a physical network. VLANs support segmentation of networks by creating broadcast domains. Trunking allows multiple VLANs to be transmitted between switches using a process of 802.1Q tagging. Tagging ports tag VLAN information on frames so that the frames can be transmitted across a trunk port. Untagging ports remove the VLAN information from frames before the traffic leaves the port. Port mirroring such as SPAN allows for a copy of the frames on one interface to be mirrored on another interface for packet capture. Switching loops rapidly degrade bandwidth and the network. Spanning Tree Protocol (STP) allows redundant links to be used in the network while avoiding switching loops. The original STP protocol of 802.1D was created in 1993, and although still useful, it has a lengthy convergence time of 50 seconds. Rapid Spanning Tree Protocol (RSTP) 802.1w was created as an update the 802.1D STP protocol and RSTP allows for rapid convergence time. The PoE (802.3af) standard is used to supply up to 15.4 watts of power and is commonly used with phone and video surveillance cameras. The PoE+ (802.3at) standard is used to supply up to 25.5 watts of power. The demilitarized zone (DMZ) is a physical or logical segmentation of a network that allows public access or external access to semi-internal resources. The MAC address table is used to associate MAC addresses with the ports of the switch the MAC address was learned on to provide forwarding filter decisions. The ARP table allows for the caching of IP addresses to MAC addresses for a defined period of time.

Understand the various concepts of routing and the supporting dynamic routing protocols. Routing allows for information to be passed between logical IP networks with the use of routing tables. Static routing requires administrator intervention to program the routes into the routing table. Dynamic routing allows for the routing tables to be exchanged automatically between routers. Default routing is used on stub networks, where all routes existing through a particular gateway. Distance-vector routing protocols exchange information about their routes and report the distance they calculated. BGP is a path-vector protocol and is used on the Internet for routing. Link-state routing protocols calculate their own costs from routes learned. Hybrid routing protocols contain characteristics of both distance-vector and link-state routing protocols.

Be able to articulate key concepts of IPv6.   IPv6 was created by the IETF to combat the problem of IPv4 address exhaustion. IPv6 is a 128-bit address written as hexadecimal. There are various ways to shorten the IPv6 address, such as by removing the leading zeros and multiple zeros between the colons in the address. Global unicast addresses (2000::/3) are the same as public IP addresses in IPv4. Link-local addresses (FE80::/10) are the same as link-local addresses in IPv4 and always start with FE80. Unique local addresses (FC00::/7) are similar to private IP addresses in IPv4 and always start with FC00. Multicast (FF00::/8) is similar to multicast addresses in IPv4 and always starts with FF00. Tunneling is a transitional technology between IPv4 and IPv6. Dual-stack network nodes have both an IPv4 and IPv6 network stack for dual communications between both IP protocols. Router Advertisement and Router Solicitation packets are ICMPv6 packets used to support IPv6 network assignment, gateway discovery, and neighbor discovery.

Know the various performance concepts used in a network.   Traffic shaping allows for the queuing and timing of packets to slow down traffic exiting an interface. The timing allows for a defined amount of bits to leave and interface for a specific amount of time before a waiting period during a time interval. Quality of service (QoS) is a concept in which protocols are prioritized so that time-sensitive protocols have higher priority. Differentiated Services Code Point (DSCP), or DiffServ, is a layer 3 QoS mechanism for layer 3 devices such as routers. Class of Service (CoS) is a layer 2 QoS mechanism used with 802.1Q frames for prioritization of frames.

Understand the concepts of NAT and PAT.   Network address translation (NAT) allows IP addresses to masquerade as different IP address on a network or the Internet. The translation between the two IP addresses allows for network address overlap and private IP addresses to be routed on the public Internet. Port address translation (PAT) allows for multiple IP addresses to use a single IP address. PAT creates a translation that includes the source and destination port of the packet.

Understand the concepts of port forwarding.   Port forwarding is used when a host is behind a NAT process. It allows for a specific destination port from the outside IP address to be translated to the inside IP address and destination port.

Understand how access control lists are used in a network.   Access control lists are used to secure traffic between a single host or multiple hosts (networks). Every vendor has a different ACL format. However, every vendor has a specific order in which the rules are applied; rules are compared, and the default rule is used if nothing matches.

Understand the concepts of distributed switching.   Two models of distributed switching are used for hierarchal design of networks. The three-tier network design consists of the core, distribution, and access layers. The core should only be used for routing and distribution to switching. The distribution layer is used to connect the access layer and the core layer, as well as to provide packet filtering and security policies. The access layer provides connectivity for edge network devices. The second model is the collapsed core design, where the core and distribution layer are a single switching layer.

Know the various methods of software-defined networking.   Cloud providers and virtualization vendors define SDN as software networking components at the hypervisor level. Hardware manufacturers define SDN as a software layer that programs and controls all hardware switching equipment.

1.4 Given a scenario, configure the appropriate IP addressing components.

When building networks, we must plan the logical IP address space for both the internal and external networks. We must also plan the default gateway and subnet mask and alter the subnet mask to accommodate subnetting.

In this section, we will explore several concepts, such as classful versus classless IP addresses, as well as how to use CIDR notation. These concepts will allow you to build logical networks for the flow of information. In addition, you must understand how IP addresses are assigned statically and dynamically. Several methods of dynamic IP address assignment are available such as DHCP, APIPA, and EUI64 for IPv6.

Private vs. public

When assigning addresses on an internal network, you should be familiar with RFC1918. It defines the private IPv4 address spaces that are reserved for internal networks. These addresses are non-Internet routable—as a matter of fact, Internet routers abide by RFC1918 and have no routes in their table for these addresses. RFC 1918 defines three categories of IP addresses for private assignment:

- Large networks—10.0.0.0/8 with a range of 10.0.0.0 to 10.255.255.255
- Medium networks—172.16.0.0/12 with a range of 172.16.0.0 to 172.31.255.255
- Small networks—192.168.0.0/16 with a range of 192.168.0.0 to 192.168.255.255.

It should be noted that small networks have a range of 192.168.0.0 to 192.168.255.255 using the /16 mask. The network IDs in this range are normally subnetted with a mask of /24 to provide a smaller range of 254 usable addresses. We will discuss subnetting later in this section.

Public IP addresses are Internet routable and used on the exterior of networks for Internet connectivity. Public IP addresses are coordinated by the Internet Assignment Numbers Authority (IANA). IANA assigns public blocks of IP addresses to private companies, government entities, and the Regional Internet Registry (RIR). Because of the shortage of IPv4 addresses, IANA no longer assigns IPv4 addresses to private companies and government entities. The RIR is the Internet registry in your region of the world:

- AFRINIC: Africa Region

- APNIC: Asia/Pacific Region

- ARIN: Canada, the United States, and some Caribbean Islands

- LACNIC: Latin America and some Caribbean Islands

- RIPE NCC: Europe, the Middle East, and Central Asia

The RIR for your region is responsible for the assignment of IPv4 address blocks to private companies. These blocks are much smaller than the legacy assignments of IANA, and often they are assigned to Internet service providers (ISPs). The ISPs are then responsible for the management and assignment of IP addresses to their customers.

IANA publishes the entire IPv4 address space at https://www.iana.org/ assignments/ipv4-address-space/ipv4-address-space.xhtml. Many of the IP addresses will still resolve to the address prefixes registered. For example, as of this writing, www.level3.net will resolve to 4.68.80.110, which is registered to Level 3 Communications, Inc.

Loopback and Reserved

Several reserved IPv4 addresses are used for special purposes. You should be familiar with RFC5735, which defines these special-use IP addresses. The loopback is one of these special IP addresses used as a "loopback" to the internal IPv4 address stack. The most important special use IP addresses are defined here:

- 0.0.0.0/8 addresses in this block refer to the source host on the immediate network. It can also be used to define all addresses by using 0.0.0.0/0 and is used in default routing statements.

- 10.0.0.0/8 addresses are defined as private IP addresses in RFC1918.

- 127.0.0.0/8 addresses are reserved for use as loopback addresses.

- 169.254.0.0/16 addresses are reserved for link-local addresses (APIPA).

- 172.16.0.0/12 addresses are defined as private IP addresses in RFC1918.

- 192.88.99.0/24 addresses are reserved for 6to4 relay anycast addresses.

- 192.168.0.0/16 addresses are defined as private IP addresses in RFC1918.

- 224.0.0.0/4 addresses are reserved for multicast IP address assignment.

- 240.0.0.0/4 addresses are reserved for future use and not assigned or used.
- The address of 255.255.255.255/32 is used for limited broadcasting for layer 3 broadcasts.

In this section, I will cover the special-use IP addresses listed here in further detail. You should commit this list to memory since these are the most common ones. IP addresses not mentioned here are used for documentation purposes and can be found in RFC5735.

Default Gateway

The default gateway is the IP address that provides routing out of the immediate network. The default gateway is an option for configuration of an IP address on a host, since leaving the network is optional. It is sometimes called the gateway of last resort when referring to the routing table. When there is no specific route in the routing table for the destination network, the packet will take the gateway of last resort to another router that can hopefully provide a route to the destination network. Hosts also contain a routing table; however, they usually have only the immediate network configured in the table along with the default gateway.

Virtual IP

The default gateway is the only way out of our network. However, if a router fails or needs to be serviced, the default gateway will become unavailable. This might not be a problem for average web surfing. However, if VoIP depends on the default gateway, we now have a bigger problem.

Since the default gateway is just an IP address configured on every host that responds to ARP requests, we can virtualize it using a *first hop redundancy protocol (FHRP)*. We can create a highly available default gateway by letting more than one router respond to an ARP request. As you can see in Figure 1.51, all we need to do is use a virtual IP address and virtual MAC address. No one router owns the virtual IP address or the virtual MAC address. However, they all respond to ARP requests with the configured virtual MAC address. Two protocols are used for creating highly available default gateways: *Virtual Router Redundancy Protocol (VRRP)* and *Hot Standby Router Protocol (HSRP)*.

VRRP is an open standard FHRP for creating highly available routers. VRRP functions in an active/passive configuration; only the active router will answer requests for ARP requests for the virtual IP address with associated virtual MAC address. If the active router fails, the passive router will become the new active router and start serving ARP requests for the virtual IP address and the associated virtual MAC address.

HSRP is a Cisco proprietary FHRP for creating highly available routers. HSRP also functions as an active/passive configuration. The operation of HSRP is identical to VRRP, except that all devices must be Cisco devices.

FIGURE 1.51 Typical FHRP setup

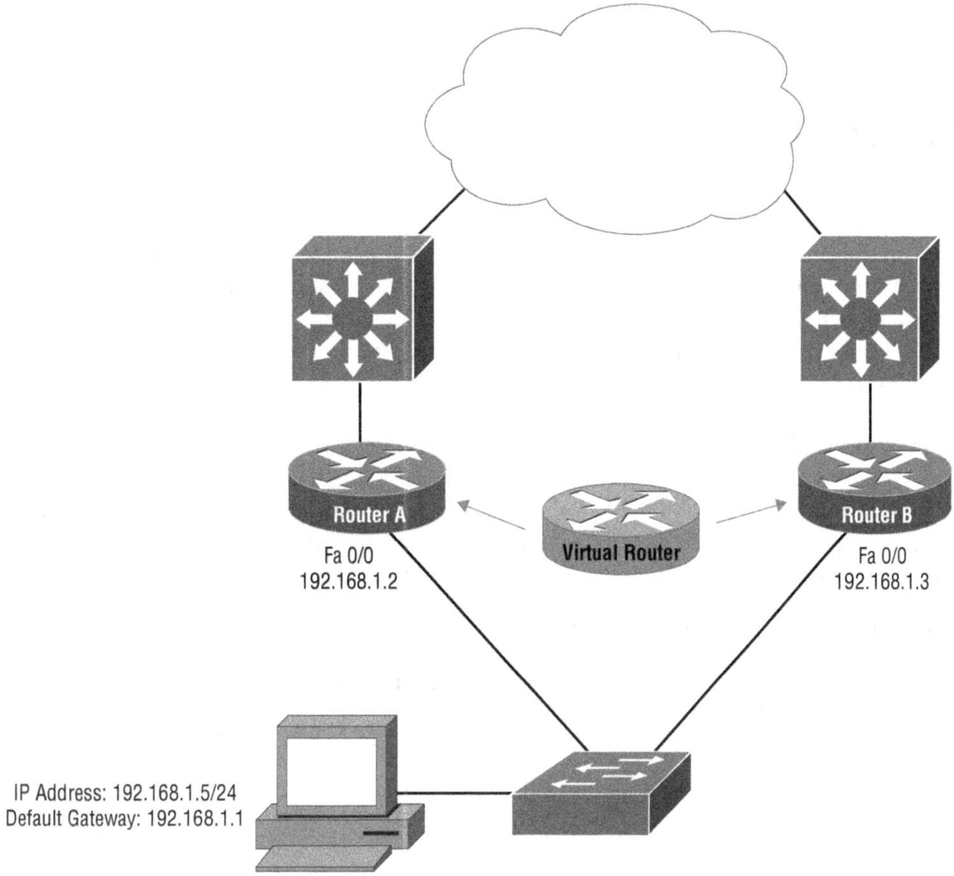

Subnet Mask

When a source host begins to send information to a destination host, it calculates the immediate network it belongs to. This is done by ANDing the subnet mask and its IP address; the result is the network that the source host belongs to. Next the source will calculate its subnet mask against the destination IP address; the result is the network that the source believes the destination host is a part of.

If both of these addresses match, then the traffic is deemed to be local on the immediate network. The source host will send an ARP request for the destination IP address to obtain the MAC address of the destination host. If the results are not equal, then the destination is deemed remote. The source host will send an ARP request for the default gateway IP address to obtain the MAC address of the default gateway.

When the source host calculates the immediate network and the destination network, the subnet mask is responsible for both of these calculations. It is the perception of the host's immediate network to the destination network that is the deciding factor of sending the traffic to the local host or the default gateway.

Subnetting

Subnetting is the process of changing the subnet mask to break a logical network into smaller logical networks. Subnetting is often used for addressing of physical locations, such as point-to-point WAN connections. Subnetting is also used for network segmentation—for example, to facilitate routing between VLANs. In all cases, subnetting changes the host's immediate network in which it is assigned.

Because of the ANDing process on the host, when the host calculates its immediate network and the destination network, the subnet mask is directly responsible for the results. If we change the subnet mask, we can change the results.

As shown in Figure 1.52, host A performs the ANDing process against its subnet mask to produce the network it belongs to. Then host A performs the ANDing process against the destination address and host A's subnet mask to produce the second result. This second result is the perceived distance of the destination host from host A's perspective, because host A must decide if the frame will go directly to the destination or be sent to a router.

FIGURE 1.52   The ANDing process

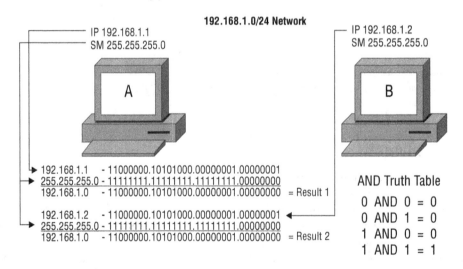

In Figure 1.53, an IP address is detailed in quad dotted decimal notation and its underlying binary equivalent. The IP address of 192.168.1.1 has a default subnet mask of 255.255.255.0. Therefore, the first three octets define the network ID, and the last octet of 8 bits defines the host ID. If we subnet this network ID further, we must borrow bits from the host section for the subnet ID. This borrowing of bits becomes part of the subnet mask, as seen in the figure. The new subnet mask would now be 255.255.255.224.

FIGURE 1.53   Subnetting of an IP address

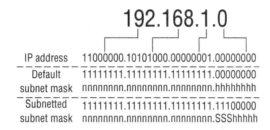

Figure 1.54 shows the eight different subnets that are created when we subnet the IP network from the previous example. As you can see, the last octet is written out, detailing the 3 bits we borrowed from the host section. As we count up in binary, the subnets identify themselves.

FIGURE 1.54   Subnet IDs

Subnet 1 – Subnet 0	**000**00000	192.168.1.0/27
Subnet 2 – Subnet 32	**001**00000	192.168.1.32/27
Subnet 3 – Subnet 64	**010**00000	192.168.1.64/27
Subnet 4 – Subnet 96	**011**00000	192.168.1.96/27
Subnet 5 – Subnet 128	**100**00000	192.168.1.128/27
Subnet 6 – Subnet 160	**101**00000	192.168.1.160/27
Subnet 7 – Subnet 192	**110**00000	192.168.1.192/27
Subnet 8 – Subnet 224	**111**00000	192.168.1.224/27

When calculating the host IDs, you must follow a few rules. The first rule is that all zeros in the host ID identify the network address and cannot be used as a host ID. The second rule is that all 1s in the host ID are the broadcast IP address for the immediate network. This address cannot be used to assign to a host. As shown in Figure 1.55, the last octet has been written out in binary format to show the mechanics of subnetting and calculating the valid host IDs.

Understanding the binary mechanics that are underlying in subnetting is useful. However, when we are subnetting, it is inefficient and confusing—mainly because our brains have a hard time switching between binary and decimal and applying artificial rules of subnetting to the mathematics. In Figure 1.56, I've detailed how to create a subnet calculator. This calculator is the fastest method for making subnetting calculations. Let's look at the two bottom lines; if we borrow 3 bits from the host ID, then we count from left to right and use the column with 224 and 32. The bottommost line is the subnet mask 255.255.255.224. The middle line is the subnet IDs; as in the previous example, we would count from 0 by 32. It's really that simple!

FIGURE 1.55   Host ID calculations

Subnet 1 – Subnet 0	**00000000** = 192.168.1.0	Network ID
	00000001 = 192.168.1.1	First Valid ID
	00011110 = 192.168.1.30	Last Valid ID
	00011111 = 192.168.1.31	Broadcast ID
Subnet 2 – Subnet 32	**00100001** = 192.168.1.33	First Valid ID
	00111110 = 192.168.1.62	Last Valid ID
Subnet 3 – Subnet 64	**01000001** = 192.168.1.65	First Valid ID
	01011110 = 192.168.1.94	Last Valid ID
Subnet 4 – Subnet 96	**01100001** = 192.168.1.97	First Valid ID
	01111110 = 192.168.1.126	Last Valid ID
Subnet 5 – Subnet 128	**10000001** = 192.168.1.129	First Valid ID
	10011110 = 192.168.1.158	Last Valid ID
Subnet 6 – Subnet 160	**10100001** = 192.168.1.161	First Valid ID
	10111110 = 192.168.1.190	Last Valid ID
Subnet 7 – Subnet 192	**11000001** = 192.168.1.193	First Valid ID
	11011110 = 192.168.1.222	Last Valid ID
Subnet 8 – Subnet 224	**11100001** = 192.168.1.225	First Valid ID
	11111110 = 192.168.1.254	Last Valid ID
	11111111 = 192.168.1.255	Broadcast ID

FIGURE 1.56   Creating a subnet calculator

Write out the place values of 2 staring with 1.

| 128 | 64 | 32 | 16 | 8 | 4 | 2 | 1 |

Write out the powers above the place values.

| 7 | 6 | 5 | 4 | 3 | 2 | 1 | 0 |
| 128 | 64 | 32 | 16 | 8 | 4 | 2 | 1 |

Write the subnet masks below the place values.

7	6	5	4	3	2	1	0
128	64	32	16	8	4	2	1
128	192	224	240	248	252	254	255

128 + 64
128 + 32   248 Should Always line up with 8.
224 + 16

Powers	7	6	5	4	3	2	1	0
Subnet	128	64	32	16	8	4	2	1
Subnet Mask	128	192	224	240	248	252	254	255

If we wanted to segment a network into four logical networks, we would use the formula of $2^x =$ or > 4, where x should be equal to or greater than 4. We can use the top line to calculate this formula. As seen in Figure 1.57, if we plug 2 into the formula, then we get 4 ($2^2 = 4$). The 2 represents the number of bits we are borrowing from the host ID for the network ID, just like in the previous example. So we count from left to right on the two bottom lines and circle them. We now have our subnet mask of 255.255.255.192 and the subnet IDs of 0, 64, 128, and 192. To calculate the host ID, we follow the +1 from the network ID and −2 from the next ID, so for the first IP address range it would be 192.168.1.1 to 192.168.1.62. The next range is 192.168.1.65 to 192.168.1.126, and so on. As you can see we have 62 valid IP addresses in each of the four network IDs. We use the calculation of $2^x - 2$ to equal the valid network IP addresses ($2^6 - 2 = 62$). So where did the 6 come from? We had 8 bits in the host ID and we used 2 for the network ID (subnet), leaving us with 6 bits for the host ID.

FIGURE 1.57   The subnet calculator

Powers	7	6	5	4	3	2	1	0
Subnet	128	64	32	16	8	4	2	1
Subnet Mask	128	192	224	240	248	252	254	255

We can switch the formulas to calculate a subnet that will accommodate x number of clients. However, you must pay close attention to the subnet ID. In Figure 1.58, if we need 6 clients per subnetwork, we can use the formula of $2^x - 2 =$ or > 6. When we use the calculation $2^3 - 2 = 6$, the 3 bits are now used for the host ID, and we must figure out the network bits (8 bits − 3 for the host = 5 for the network). We then use this 5 to count from left to right on the bottom two rows. Our subnet mask is 255.255.255.248, and our subnet IDs are 0, 8, 16, 24, 32, and so on.

FIGURE 1.58   Subnetting for hosts

Powers	7	6	5	4	3	2	1	0
Subnet	128	64	32	16	8	4	2	1
Subnet Mask	128	192	224	240	248	252	254	255

So far we have been subnetting the last 8 bits of an IP address. If we look at a larger address like 170.26.0.0, these addresses have a default subnet mask of 255.255.0.0. So we have 16 bits to subnet with in the last two octets. The same rules apply with larger numbers. For instance, if we needed 8 subnets, our network IDs would be 170.26.0.0, 170.26.32.0, and 170.26.64.0 to 170.26.224.0 for the last network ID. The subnet mask would be 255.255.224.0; this is derived by counting from the left for the number of subnet bits on the calculator. Just remember we are subnetting across 16 bits, so the 224 belongs to the third octet. This gives us a number of 32, which we use to calculate the subnets. The total number of networks would be $2^3 = 8$ subnetworks, each containing $2^{13} - 2 = 8190$ hosts each (3 + 13 = 16 bits). The host IDs are a bit different to calculate, because we have two octets to deal with, as shown in Figure 1.59.

FIGURE 1.59   Valid host IDs for a 13-bit host ID

Subnet 0	from	X.X.0.1	- +1	0.0	= 00000000.00000000	Cannot be used, it is the subnet number. See rule.
	to	X.X.31.254	- -2		= 00000000.00000001	
					= 00011111.11111110	
				31.255	= 00011111.11111111	
				32.0	= 00100000.00000000	Cannot be used, it is the broadcast address for the subnet.
Subnet 32	from	X.X.32.1	- +1		= 00100000.00000001	
	to	X.X.63.254	- -2		= 00111111.11111110	
Subnet 64	from	X.X.64.1	- +1		= 00100000.00000001	
	to	X.X.95.254	- -2		= 01011111.11111110	
Subnet 96	from	X.X.96.1	- +1		= 01100000.00000001	
	to	X.X.127.254	- -2		= 01111111.11111110	
Subnet 128	from	X.X.128.1	- +1		= 10000000.00000001	
	to	X.X.159.254	- -2		= 10011111.11111110	
Subnet 160	from	X.X.160.1	- +1		= 10100000.00000001	
	to	X.X.191.254	- -2		= 10111111.11111110	
Subnet 192	from	X.X.192.1	- +1		= 11000000.00000001	
	to	X.X.223.254	- -2		= 11011111.11111110	
Subnet 224	from	X.X.224.1	- +1		= 11100000.00000001	
	to	X.X.255.254	- -2		= 11111111.11111110	

Classful

When we discuss the default subnet mask a network ID has, we are talking about its IP class. Classful IP network addresses are addresses that follow this strict classification. We often use the term *classful* when describing routing protocols. A classful routing protocol is a routing protocol that does not abide by subnetting. As an example, if a network had the default subnet mask of 255.255.0.0 and we subnetted the network as 255.255.224.0, the routing protocol would treat all the network IDs the same under the classful assignment of 255.255.0.0. Fortunately, RIPv1 is the only routing protocol that does this; RIPv2 abides by the subnetted IDs.

The different IP classes were originally proposed and drafted by the Internet Engineering Task Force (IETF). They define large, medium, and small networks, along with specialized IP assignments. The class of an IP address is defined by the first octet of the IP address, as you'll see in the following section.

Class A

Class A network IDs have a defined range of 1 to 126 for the first octet and a default mask of 255.0.0.0. They are for really large networks with $2^{24} - 2 = 16,777,214$ hosts, although we would subnet this down further.

The leading bit in the 32-bit IP address is always a zero, so that defines a range of 0 to 127:

$\underline{0}$0000000.hhhhhhhh.hhhhhhhh.hhhhhhhh = 0

to

01111111.hhhhhhhh.hhhhhhhh.hhhhhhhh = 127

All zeros are reserved by RFC5735 for special use, and 127.0.0.0 is reserved for loopbacks.

Class B

Class B network IDs have a defined range of 128 to 191 for the first octet and a default mask of 255.255.0.0. They are for medium-sized networks with $2^{16} - 2 = 65,534$ hosts, although we would subnet this down further.

The leading bit in the 32 bit IP address is always a one and a zero, so that defines a range of 128 to 191:

10000000.nnnnnnnn.hhhhhhhh.hhhhhhhh = 128

to

10111111.nnnnnnnn.hhhhhhhh.hhhhhhhh = 191

Class C

Class C network IDs have a defined range of 192 to 223 for the first octet and a default mask of 255.255.255.0. They are for small networks with $2^8 - 2 = 254$ hosts.

The leading bit in the 32-bit IP address is always a one, a one, and a zero, so that defines a range of 192 to 223:

11000000.nnnnnnnn.nnnnnnnn.hhhhhhhh = 192

to

11011111.nnnnnnnn.nnnnnnnn.hhhhhhhh = 223

Class D

Class D network IDs are not used for individual networks. They are specialized IP addresses for multicasting purposes, as defined originally by the IETF and RFC5735. Just like Classes A, B, and C, they follow the same premise of leading bits. Class D IP addresses start with 1110 for a usable range of 224 to 239. Multicast IP addresses (class D) do not have a default subnet mask because of their specialized purpose.

Class E

Class E network IDs are not used at all—they are considered for experimental use only and were never used. A while back, the IETF investigated and allowed this range of unused IP addresses to be used again. However, it was found that all networking devices would have to be reprogrammed, mainly because they all follow classifications of IP addressing. The idea was scrapped, and the range from 240 to 254 is not used to this day. Class E defines the leading bits of the IP address starting with 1111.

Theoretically, there would have been a Class F and further classifications. Following the binary mechanics of classifications, we could have 248 to 254. However, all of these addresses are grouped into the Class E assignment.

Classless

The classless IP address category specifies that we do not adhere to the classful assignment of the IETF. With the scarcity of IPv4 addresses, we need to subnet! It also means that we can *supernet*, which is the opposite of subnetting. The RFC1918 address of 172.16.0.0/12 (255.240.0.0 mask) is supernetted. The 172 address falls between the Class B assignment range, but the mask is going the other way. We are mandated by Class B addressing to have a mask of /16 (255.255.0.0 mask), but we elect to group multiple /16 networks into a /12 network. This is supernetting, and it wouldn't be possible without classless IP addresses.

VLSM

In all our subnet examples, we've assumed that all the networks use the same subnet mask. However, this is extremely inefficient, because not all subnetworks require that same number of hosts. Luckily, every host makes the determination of where to forward the frame based on the destination network address. As long as we do not overlap addressing, we can vary the subnet mask. Figure 1.60 shows a small network requiring a different number of hosts. Router R1 has a routing table with a single entry point to router R2. Router R2 contains the routing table that will forward the packet to the appropriate subnet.

FIGURE 1.60   A variable-length subnet mask (VLSM) network

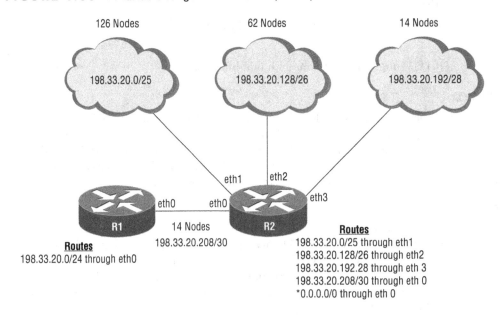

The smallest assignment of a network is a block of four addresses. Two of the four addresses will be used for the network ID and broadcast ID, which leaves us with two usable valid IP addresses. To calculate variable-length subnet mask (VLSM) networks, we simply create a spreadsheet or table using a block size of four. Inside the table we can allocate block sizes of 4, 8, 16, 32, 64, and 128, but the block must start on a multiple of those numbers. As shown in Figure 1.61, we calculated the four subnets used in the previous example without overlapping addresses.

FIGURE 1.61   VLSM worksheet

0		64		128		192	
4		68		132		196	
8		72		136		200	
12		76		140		204	
16		80		144		208	
20		84		148		212	
24		88		152		216	
28		92		156		220	
32		96		160		224	
36		100		164		228	
40		104		168		232	
44		108		172		236	
48		112		176		240	
52		116		180		244	
56		120		184		248	
60		124		188		252	

Subnet 1 - 198.33.20.0/25 Usable Range of 198.33.20.1 to 198.33.20.126
Subnet 2 - 198.33.20.128/26 Usable Range of 198.33.20.129 to 198.33.20.190
Subnet 3 - 198.33.20.192/28 Usable Range of 198.33.20.193 to 198.33.20.206
Subnet 4 - 198.33.20.208/30 Usable Range of 198.33.20.209 to 198.33.20.210

CIDR Notation (IPv4 vs. IPv6)

Classless interdomain routing (CIDR) notation is a network engineer's shorthand. It is just another way of writing out the network mask. We count the number of bits and represent it using a / and the number. So a subnet mask of 255.255.255.248 is 11111111.11111111.11111111.11111000 in binary, and in CIDR notation it is 8 + 8 + 8 + 5 = 29, or /29.

In Figure 1.62 you can see a simple CIDR calculator. I have something similar hanging by my desk for when I need to double-check a subnet mask or block size.

FIGURE 1.62   A CIDR calculator

Subnet	128	64	32	16	8	4	2	1
Subnet Mask	128	192	224	240	248	252	254	255
CIDR 4th Octet	/25	/26	/27	/28	/29	/30	/31	/32
CIDR 3rd Octet	/17	/18	/19	/20	/21	/22	/23	/24
CIDR 2nd Octet	/9	/10	/11	/12	/13	/14	/15	/16
CIDR 1st Octet	/1	/2	/3	/4	/5	/6	/7	/8

With IPv6, CIDR notation is the only way to notate the network ID. It really is, because the number is so large and it is in hexadecimal. So we always see CIDR notation with the 128-bit IPv6 addresses. As an example, 2001:db8:45:0/64 would represent our network ID in IPv6.

Address Assignments

We can assign IP addresses in one of three ways: auto-assignment, dynamic assignment, and static assignment. IPv6 operates with auto-assignment of IPv6 addressing, although we can use DHCPv6 for dynamic assignments. Dynamic assignment allows for centralized management of IP addresses. IPv4 supports both auto-assignment and dynamic assignment, but auto-assignment of IP addresses is nonroutable, as you will see later. We also always have the choice of statically assigning IP addresses for both IPv4 and IPv6.

DHCP

Dynamic Host Configuration Protocol (DHCP) is responsible for automatic configuration of IP addresses and subnet masks for hosts from a pool of IP addresses. It is also responsible for configuration of such options as default gateways, DNS server addresses, and many other IP-based servers. It performs configuration of the host in a series of network broadcasts and unicasts.

The process of DHCP for a client is called DORA—Discover, Offer, Request, Acknowledgment. In Figure 1.63 you see a DHCP client and a DHCP server. The client begins by sending a DHCP Discover broadcast packet to the network. The server hears the broadcast and processes the request based on the client's MAC address and IP address availability in the pool. The server sends a unicast frame back to the client with a DHCP Offer of an IP address, subnet mask, and any options. The client still doesn't have an IP address, so it broadcasts a DHCP Request for the IP address, subnet mask, and options. The request for the configuration is then acknowledged by the DHCP server with a DHCP Acknowledge unicast to the client. At this point, the client assumes the IP address, subnet mask, and options, and a lease timer starts. I will cover the DHCP lease period in the next section.

FIGURE 1.63   The DHCP DORA process

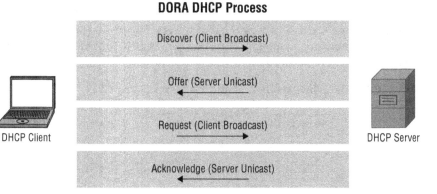

DORA DHCP Process

Discover (Client Broadcast)

Offer (Server Unicast)

Request (Client Broadcast)

Acknowledge (Server Unicast)

DHCP Client

DHCP Server

DHCPv6

Dynamic Host Configuration Protocol v6 (DHCPv6) is the IPv6 version of DHCP for IPv4. DHCP in IPv6 can be deployed in stateless mode and stateful mode. It is often deployed in stateless mode because IPv6 automatic address assignment is built into IPv6.

In stateless mode, DHCPv6 is only used for the assignment of DHCP options. In this mode, DHCPv6 does not fully function like its IPv4 counterpart. DHCPv6 doesn't assign IPv6 addresses in this mode. By default, an IPv6 host sends Router Solicitation (RS) packets when it requires an IPv6 address. The router will send back a Router Advertisement (RA) packet containing the network address. The host will then auto-assign the interface ID portion of the IPv6 address. However, throughout this process the DHCP options are never transmitted by the router. This is where stateless DHCPv6 service comes in—it provides the DHCP options for critical services such as DNS. These options are transmitted via an RA packet that has the O flag set to 1 for "other stateful configuration." This might be confusing because DHCPv6 in stateless mode has the "other stateful configuration" flag set! Keep in mind that we are forcing the client to take these options, so we are forcing the state—hence the name.

In stateful mode DHCPv6 is responsible for the assignment of IPv6 network addresses and interface IDs, similar to its IPv4 counterpart. In fact, it operates exactly like an IPv4 DHCP server; it will assign the IP address and keep the state of the IP address it has assigned the client, just as its mode states (no pun intended). The stateful DHCPv6 service operates similar to an IPv6 router, listening and responding to RS packets with RA packets. However, the RA packet contains an M flag set to 1 for "managed address configuration." This tells the client to accept both the network address and interface ID from the RA packet. The M and O flags can be set to provide both the IPv6 address and the options.

Static

Dynamic IP addressing is the standard in small-to-large networks when configuring client computers. Static IP addressing should only be used under certain circumstances for client computers, since it is not very scalable and a nightmare to keep track of manually. DHCP allows for a central management of the IP address space versus static assignment of individual hosts (which is decentralized). Static IP addressing should only be used on network resources such as routers, network printers, and servers. Figure 1.64 shows the IPv4 configuration page of a network adapter on Windows Server 2016, although the dialog box has not changed at all since Windows 95.

FIGURE 1.64   The Windows DHCP/static IP address dialog box

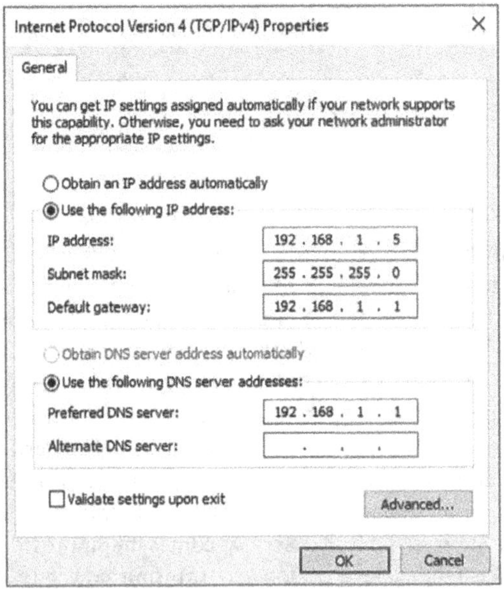

APIPA

Automatic Private IP Addressing (APIPA) is a Microsoft term for link-local addressing defined in RFC3927. This auto-assignment of IP address allows for multiple hosts to automatically obtain an IP address. Although the IP address is auto-assigned, the default gateway is not used. So APIPA allows for local network connectivity but not internetwork connectivity.

APIPA addressing always starts with 169.254.x.x, so it's easy to recognize. APIPA only auto-assigns the IP address if the DHCP server is unavailable. If you see an APIPA address on an interface adapter, it probably means that DHCP has failed or is unavailable. On Windows operating systems, the DHCP client will continue in the background to obtain an IP address if DHCP becomes available.

EUI-64

Extended Unique Identifier 64 (EUI-64) is used with IPv6 addressing. EUI-64 provides a mechanism for logical assignment of the host's MAC address in the interface ID of the host's

IPv6 address. By default with many operating systems, a random interface ID is created and checked for possible duplication. This is the default auto-assignment process for IPv6.

If EUI-64 is enabled, the MAC address of 48 bits will be padded and inserted into the 64-bit interface ID. The EUI-64 process is a two-step process. First, the MAC address is split into two 24 bit pieces and padded with FFFE, as shown in Figure 1.65. Anytime you see the FFFE in the middle of the interface ID, you can assume that the interface ID is a EUI-64 address.

FIGURE 1.65 Padding process of EUI-64 addresses

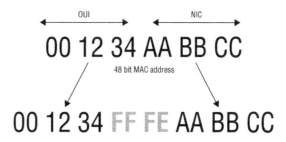

Next, we must flip the universal/local bit, which is the seventh bit from the left of the interface ID. This bit identifies whether this interface identifier is universally or locally administered. If the bit is 0, the address is locally administered; if the bit is 1, the address is globally unique. Although most of the time this bit will be a 1, you should know that RFC4291 recommends the bit be flipped. Flipped means that it will be the opposite of what it is—a 1 will become a 0 and a 0 will become a 1. So the next step is to flip the bit on our IPv6 address, as shown in Figure 1.66.

FIGURE 1.66 Bit flipping for EUI-64 addresses

Our interface ID is now complete as the address of 0212:34FF:FEAA:BBCC. The full address might look like 2001:0DB8:0045:0000:0212:34FF:FEAA:BBCC, with the first 64 bits being the network ID.

Reservations

When a client request an IP address from a DHCP via the DORA process, the client's MAC address is transmitted in the CHADDR DHCP packet. A rule on the DHCP server called a *DHCP reservation* can tie the client's MAC address to a particular IP address. When a reservation is created for a client, the client is guaranteed to obtain the same IP address every time the DHCP Discovery packet is received by the DHCP server. When a reservation is created on the DHCP server, no other hosts can obtain the reservation IP address unless they have the MAC address that matches the reservation. This type of assignment is considered a dynamically static-assigned IP address.

Reservations can be very handy when static IP addresses are too troublesome to configure, such as network printers with poor configuration options. I've been known to set a reservation on network printers and move on when faced with a finicky static IP address process. You too, can save an hour of busy work in the right situation. Reservations can also be useful when you need to make specific firewall rules for a client based on its IP address.

Exam Essentials

Know the various private and public IP address schemes.   RFC1918 defines the three private IP address schemes for Class A, Class B, and Class C networks of 10.0.0.0/8, 172.16.0.0/12, and 192.168.0.0/16. Public IP addresses are assigned by IANA and the RIR for your region.

Know the various special IP addresses that are considered reserved.   Several special IP addresses are reserved, as per RFC5735. The short list of special IP addresses discussed in the section "Loopback and Reserved" should be committed to memory; they are the most common reserved IP addresses.

Understand how the default gateway is used in networks for routing.   The default gateway is configured to the IP address of the router in the network. The router allows for hosts on the immediate network to be routed to the remote networks. It serves as a gateway out of the immediate network.

Understand how virtual IP addresses are used to create redundancy.   A virtual IP address and virtual MAC address are associated with a First Hop Router Protocol (FHRP). FHRPs used for redundancy are Virtual Router Redundancy Protocol (VRRP) and Hot Standby Router Protocol (HSRP).

Understand the relevance of the subnet mask and how it is used.   The subnet mask defines the network the host belongs to. Through the process of ANDing, the host calculates its immediate network. Then the host calculates the network of the destination address. These two calculations help the host decide if the traffic is local or remote.

Understand how subnetting is performed and how it is used.   Subnetting is the process of creating smaller logical networks from a larger logical network. This is performed for routing between VLANs and geographic use of IP networks for WAN connections, among other reasons. We subnet a logical network by using the bits from the host section of the IP address and changing its subnet mask. CIDR notation is the total number of bits used for the network address and is expressed with a slash after the network address, followed by the number of bits used.

VLSM is the process of breaking the logical network into small logical networks in blocks of 128, 64, 32, 16, 8, and 4.

Know the various methods of assigning IP addressing for hosts via auto-assignment, dynamic assignment, and static assignment.　Static assignment should be reserved only for servers and networking equipment that must always have the same IP address. DHCP is the most common method for assigning IP addressing to hosts because it is centrally administered. Auto-assignment is the method used with IPv6 because DHCPv6 can be used to assign options or addresses for IPv6. When auto-assignment is used with IPv4, it is non-routable and often called APIPA addressing.

1.5 Compare and contrast the characteristics of network topologies, types, and technologies.

The topology of a network defines the shape the network is connected in. Many of the topologies I will cover are no longer relevant for networking. However, you should understand how information moves within the topology, because you will see other technologies use these topologies.

The topology is a schematic of the overall network. Besides the topology of our network, sections of our network are defined by functional type such as local area network (LAN) and wide area network (WAN). In this section, you will learn about various functional types of networks.

A new emerging technology called the *Internet of Things (IoT)* is becoming the responsibility of the network administrator. There are several networking technologies that you must understand to support IoT devices. We will explore several common networking technologies used with IoT in this section.

Wired Topologies

I'll discuss several wired topologies that are no longer used for Ethernet networking. However, that doesn't mean that they are deprecated and no longer used. You will see many of these topologies in other areas of technology, such as storage area networks (SANs), industrial control systems, and WANs.

Logical vs. Physical

There are two main types of topologies: physical and logical. If you ever sit down to document a network and end up with a mess of lines and details, you are trying to display both the physical and logical in one drawing. The logical topology of a network should be a high-level view of the information flow through semi-generic components in your network. This shows how the network operates and should be your first drawing. The physical topology defines why it works, such as which port on the router is connected to which port on a switch, and so on.

Star

The star topology is currently used in networks today, and it's the main topology used to connect edge devices (end users). All network devices are wired back to a hub or switch. The computers can be next to each other or spread out across an office space, but all communication goes back to a central location. This topology has been widely adopted because it concentrates the failure and diagnostic points in a central location. Another added benefit is that we can swap out the edge switches all from the same location. A disadvantage is that if a switch fails, every device connected to the switch is affected. Many buildings will have multiple star topologies; as an example, the edge switch is wired back to a larger switch, sometimes called a core switch. In Figure 1.67, you see a typical example of a star topology.

FIGURE 1.67   A typical star topology

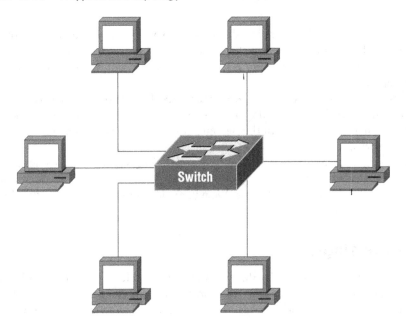

Ring

Ring topology was used over 20 years ago, and it was called token ring. IBM produced a lot of the hardware used in token ring networks, operating at a maximum speed of 4 Mbps and 16 Mbps. The networked devices would pass a token around the ring; any device that could seize the token could transmit a message around the ring. In Figure 1.68, you can see a logical ring topology. Physically the computers had one wire connected, similar to networks today. The wire consisted of a ring in pair and a ring out pair.

FIGURE 1.68   A logical ring topology

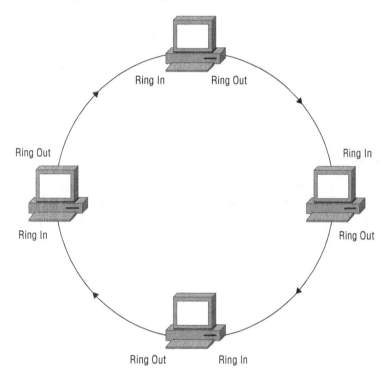

Token ring is now a deprecated technology for LAN connectivity. Token ring is not deprecated for WAN connectivity; it is used with *SONET rings* and *Fiber Distributed Data Interface (FDDI)* rings. I will cover LANs and WANs in this chapter. Token ring is still popular because of its resiliency when a fault occurs.

Mesh

The full mesh is a topology often used in datacenters, because it allows for redundant connection in the event of a component failure. Cloud computing uses a lot of mesh type connectivity, because a failure should not hinder the customer(s). You will not see this used at the edge of a network where end-user computers connect to the network, mainly because it is too costly. If you wanted to calculate how many connections between four switches you would need to achieve a full mesh, you would use the following formula:

$$[n(n - 1)]/2 = \text{total number of connections}$$

$$[4(4 - 1)]/2 =$$

$$[4(3)]/2 =$$

$$12/2 = 6 \text{ cable connections}$$

In this example, you would need six cable connections between the switches using the formula. More importantly, you would need to have three switch ports available on each switch, because each cable has two ends (6 ÷ 2 = 3). In Figure 1.69, you can see a full mesh between four network switches. If you have a failure on any cable or switch, the network will continue to function. If a switch were to go down, the failure would be isolated to the failed switch.

FIGURE 1.69 A physical topology of a full mesh

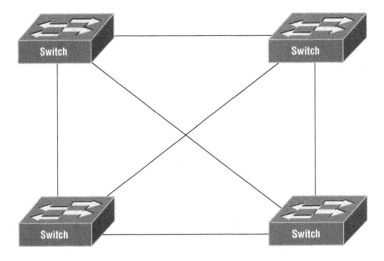

The Internet is not really a full mesh; it is a partial mesh. This is due to the costs of running cables to every provider on the Internet. So providers have partial meshes connecting them to upstream providers. When there is a failure on the Internet, it is usually localized to the path to the provider. Many providers have their own redundancy internally in their networks and use full meshes internally.

Bus

The bus concept is the most important networking concepts to understand. It established the baseline for nearly all networking concepts and improvements that followed. The bus topology was common in networks 25 years ago; it is now considered legacy in its design. It used coaxial cables joining computers with BNC connectors. The reason it is deprecated is that a failure on the bus would affect all the computers on the bus. These networks also required external terminators on the ends of the bus segment. They are basically resistors; terminators stopped the reflection of electrical signals reflecting back in the direction it came from. So why are we talking about bus networks? Bus networks are how SCSI, RS-422 (industrial serial), and many other types of technologies work. It is important to understand how they work so that you can diagnose problems in these other technologies. When a computer wants to communicate on a bus network, it sends the signal out and all other computers see the message. Only the computer it is destined for by its destination MAC address processes the message and responds. SCSI disk networks use a device ID similar to how the MAC address is used on computer bus type networks. You can see this comparison in Figure 1.70.

FIGURE 1.70 A comparison of bus networks to SCSI disk networks

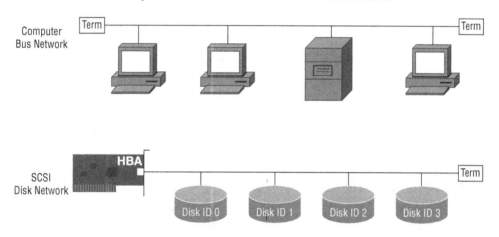

Hybrid

The hybrid topology is more representative of internal networks today. Hybrid topology design combines multiple topologies for resiliency, load balancing, and connectivity. In Figure 1.71, you can see several different topologies being used to effectively create redundancy and connectivity. You can also see several types of topologies. The edge switches are connected in a star topology, the distribution switches are connected in a partial mesh, and the core and distribution are connected in a full mesh. Also notice that the WAN connectivity is being supplied by a SONET ring topology.

FIGURE 1.71 A hybrid topology

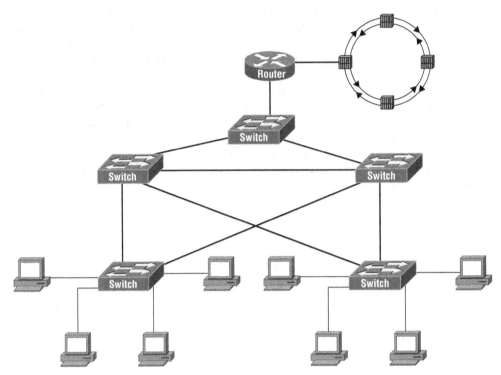

Wireless Topologies

The concept of wireless topologies is very similar to that of wired topologies. The various topologies define how the infrastructure is logically connected. With wireless, we are creating logical connections between wireless infrastructure and wireless clients via radio frequency (RF).

Ad Hoc

Most wireless devices that we use daily function in infrastructure mode. Even when connecting to another wireless device, we use a wireless access point (WAP) to connect. However, when we need to connect two wireless devices and don't have any wireless infrastructure, ad hoc networks can be created. Ad hoc wireless networks are impromptu networks that do not require any infrastructure at all. They are peer-to-peer network connections between two or more devices over 802.11 wireless (although other wireless technologies have ad hoc modes as well).

A disadvantage to ad hoc mode is that we can normally connect only two devices together. WAPs arbitrate wireless communications between devices with request-to-send and clear-to-send (RTS/CTS) signaling. When we use ad hoc mode, both clients must arbitrate the RTS/CTS signaling, which limits the connection to usually two devices—although it is possible to have as many wireless clients connected in ad hoc mode as wireless bandwidth will allow or the operating system.

Another disadvantage is the distance at which two devices can communicate. Normally we would have a WAP between two clients, allowing an average range of 100 feet. This would enable two clients to have a maximum distance between them of 200 feet, assuming the WAP is in the middle. When we use ad hoc mode, the distance is usually less than 100 feet. This is because of the transmitting power of the client wireless adapters, which is normally lower than that of WAPs on average. Also the client's antenna is smaller in size than WAP antennas.

Infrastructure

Infrastructure mode extends the wired network to a wireless network, with the use of a wireless access point (WAP). Wireless devices communicate directly to the WAP, even if the devices are communicating with each other and right next to each other. The WAP arbitrates connections with request-to-send and clear-to-send (RTS/CTS) signaling, which is a carrier-sense multiple access with collision avoidance (CSMA/CA) contention method.

Basic service set (BSS) is the simplest building block for designing 802.11 wireless networks. A BSS consists of a single WAP wired to a network that provides access to a group of devices, as shown in Figure 1.72. If this sounds familiar, it should be, since it is probably how you have your wireless set up at home.

FIGURE 1.72   Basic service set example

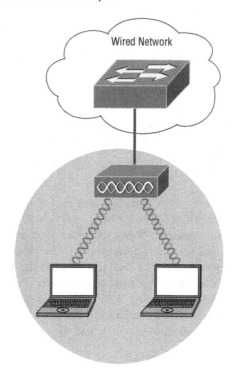

Extended service set (ESS) is a grouping of basic service sets to serve a common group of wireless devices. An ESS allows us to cover greater distances and enables wireless device to roam between WAPs. Figure 1.73 shows an example of a typical ESS. Because wireless clients can roam between WAPs, we should implement a *wireless LAN controller (WLC)* to coordinate channels between WAPs, authentication of the client, security credentials, and overall roaming. However, a WLC is not required to create an ESS. The ESS consists of multiple BSSs with the same SSID and security settings.

FIGURE 1.73 Extended service set example

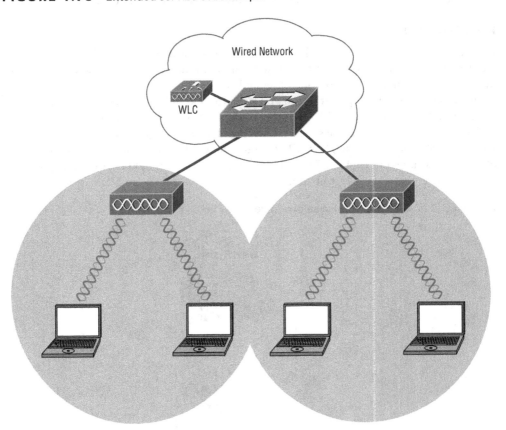

I often find that people purchase two WAPs and place them at far ends of their house for extended coverage, only to find that their devices suffer disconnects and poor performance. This is because there is no coordination of channels between the WAPs. Both WAPs could use the same channel, which will limit bandwidth. Also, clients would connect to the first WAP and never be told to roam to the other WAP. When WAPs are used without a WLC, they are considered autonomous WAPs. An ESS can be created without the use of a WLC; however, each BSS cell will operate autonomously and could be problematic.

Mesh

In a wired mesh network, each switch is connected to the other switches in a mesh-type fabric of redundant connections. In a wireless mesh, each WAP can wirelessly connect to the other WAPs over RF.

The running joke is, wireless is not wireless—meaning that we still need to wire the WAPs back to the wired network. We have to wire WAPs back to the physical network for power (POE) and data. However, in many cases we cannot wire the WAPs back to the network because of cabling costs or the installation location. This is where mesh wireless networks come in.

Let's examine the use case of a 100,000-square-foot warehouse that requires wireless coverage throughout. WAPs are mounted on ceilings, and the cable runs in the middle would be too long to use Ethernet cabling. As shown in Figure 1.74, if we use mesh WAPs we can wire in the WAPs closest to the switching equipment and allow the other WAPs to mesh together. All we need to do is supply power!

FIGURE 1.74   Mesh WAP example

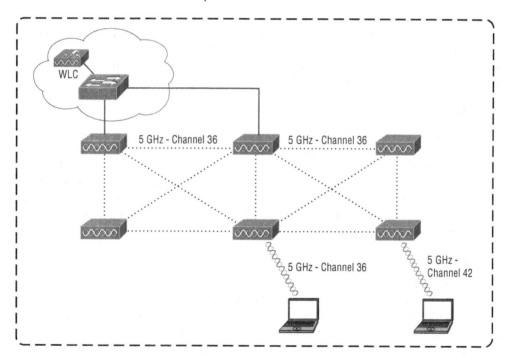

Mesh requires a wireless LAN controller for the coordination of channel assignment and forwarding traffic between WAPs. Mesh WAPs will use one channel for backhaul data (between WAPs) and other channels for serving the wireless clients.

Recently, many consumer networking equipment vendors started selling mesh WAP systems under $500 that can cover an average house of 2000 square feet. In residential houses, we have only one centralized spot where our Internet comes in and the first WAP is located. However, it is rarely in the middle of the house! These consumer-grade WAPs have a built-in WLC that allows meshing of the other WAPs to cover the entire house, and all you need is power for the other locations.

Types

When we refer to parts of our network, we classify the section of network with a type. This designation of type helps us generalize its use and function. Consider your property; you have inside doors, outside doors, and storm doors. The inside doors serve the function of privacy. The outside doors function the same but add security. The storm doors are used for security and safety. Our network has different areas that we label with these types so that we can quickly identify the area's purpose. The type of network also helps us plan for infrastructure that the network will serve.

LAN

A local area network (LAN) defines the company's internal network. As its name infers, it is the "local area" of your network that is locally managed. As it pertains to infrastructure implementation, there should be little or no consideration for the placement of resources within the LAN. LAN speeds "should" always be the fastest within your network design and can be internally upgraded as needed.

WLAN

A wireless local area network (WLAN) defines the company's internal wireless network. As LAN infers, it is the "local area" that is locally managed. The WLAN is a wireless extension of our wired local area network. As it pertains to infrastructure, we should always design the wireless network for the wireless client density it could serve. Although wireless networks are upgradable, because of the physical location of WAPs such upgrades are usually costly. When designing WLANs, we should always start with a site survey to estimate the best placement of WAPs.

WAN

A wide area network (WAN) is a network that interconnects your network location together via a provider, and as the acronym infers, it is over a "wide area." These locations could be within the region or different regions of the world. An example of this is two locations that are connected with a point-to-point leased line within the state. As is pertains to your infrastructure implementation, a consideration is the placement of your resource within your various networks that are interconnected. This is mainly due to the fact that WAN connections usually operate at lower speeds than your internal networks. So resources should be placed closest to the users. They also could use different protocols than your internal networks do, so certain broadcast-based technologies might not work.

MAN

A metropolitan area network (MAN) is a type of WAN. It is connected over a defined geographical area and has a higher connection speed between network locations via a provider. The area could be a city or a few-block radius or region of a state. The infrastructure implementation is similar to a WAN; the difference is the speed of the connection, because a MAN is built out by the provider as the backbone for your network locations. As it pertains to your infrastructure implementation, the placement of resources is less of a concern because of the higher speeds between the locations. An example of this is a company that has a branch office in the next town. You may have no administrators at that location, so centralizing the server at the primary location is the design goal. This requires a higher speed and reliable backbone between the locations.

CAN

A campus area network (CAN) defines multiple buildings (LANs) that are connected together, all of which are locally managed by your company. As long as you locally manage the connections between the buildings, it is considered to be a campus area network. The CAN connects multiple LANs with a private communications infrastructure. You should always take the speed between LANs into consideration for the placement of resources. As an example, file servers should always be placed closest to the majority of users.

SAN

A storage area network (SAN) defines the network reserved for storage access. SANs often use dedicated switching equipment to provide low latency and lossless connectivity. SANs often use redundant connections in the form of a partial-mesh for fault tolerance. Because this switching equipment is dedicated, it is usually found only in the datacenter and is used for connecting servers to the storage. A common SAN technology found in datacenters is Fibre Channel (FC). However, SANs can be any technology as long as the infrastructure is dedicated for storage access. I cover SANs and SAN technologies in Chapter 2 in more detail.

PAN

A personal area network (PAN) defines an ultra-small network for personal use. If you have a smartphone that is paired to your vehicle, you probably have a PAN. Many people walk around using a PAN every day: smart watches, smartphones, and personal fitness devices transmit data back and forth. A protocol often used with PANs is Bluetooth. However, PANs can use any protocol and any media. They can be wired or wireless, as long as they enable communications for devices near the person and are used for personal access.

Technologies That Facilitate the Internet of Things (IoT)

The Internet of Things (IoT) is not just a buzzword. IoT enables the collection of large amounts of data for analysis and machine learning. An example of IoT is a deployment of temperature sensors in a large building. The sensors read the temperature in spots of the building and report them back to a cloud service. The data is then analyzed for efficient cooling and heating. This will ultimately save money by helping tune schedules of cooling and heating intervals. Other examples can be applied to safety, product testing, productivity, and performance; the possibilities are endless!

IoT doesn't always need to be on a grand scale. We can find IoT in our homes today. Many examples are thermostats that learn, automated lighting, Internet-enabled security systems—again, the possibilities are limitless!

IoT can help solve all types of problems, because the hardware is relatively inexpensive and it's connected wirelessly. These devices don't need local storage as long as they have connectivity—and this is where our responsibilities begins. The network professional's job is to support the technologies that enable IoT to communicate to the Internet and communicate between each other. We must understand the technologies that help facilitate the Internet of Things.

Z-Wave

Z-wave is a wireless communication protocol that is used in home automation and residential controls. Z-wave can be found in home cinema automation, security systems, lighting controls, and home access controls. There are many other products Z-wave can be found in. Z-wave was originally developed to be a cheaper alternative to *Zigbee*.

Z-wave operates on the 900 MHz *industrial, scientific, and medical (ISM)* radio band. In the United States, Z-wave operates on 908.42, and in Europe, it operates on 868.42 MHz. Z-wave functions in a mesh network topology and can have a maximum of 232 nodes. It requires one primary controller, and secondary controllers are optional. The addressing for Z-wave consists of a network ID containing 4 bytes, and the node ID is 1 byte.

ANT+

ANT+ is a wireless communication protocol that is used in health, sports, and fitness equipment. ANT+ is ultra-low power in design that is well suited to PANs. ANT+ is owned and licensed by Garmin, and it was originally based on the ANT communication protocol.

ANT+ operates on the 2.4 GHz ISM radio band. ANT+ can be used in a wide range of topologies, such as peer-to-peer, star, and mesh topologies, just to name a few. Addressing of ANT+ uses an 8-bit device type and a 16-bit device number.

Bluetooth

Bluetooth is a very popular wireless communication protocol that is used for all types of products. It enables wireless PANs, and as of 2002, is ratified by the IEEE 802.15.1 working group.

Bluetooth operates on the 2.4 GHz ISM radio band using 40 different channels, each 2 MHz wide. Throughout the years since its introduction in 2000, Bluetooth undergone many different versions. Addressing for Bluetooth is identical to Ethernet MAC addressing. Each device has a 48-bit MAC address consisting of a 24-bit organization unique identifier (OUI) and a 24-bit unique address.

Bluetooth version 4.0 is a popular standard used today. Bluetooth version 4.0 has a maximum speed of 25 Mbps and a maximum distance of 200 feet—although as distance increases the speed diminishes.

Bluetooth 4.0 Low Energy (LE) is also called Bluetooth Smart and BLE. It has a lower bandwidth and lower maximum distance than version 4.0. However, it requires milliamps to operate and is used in many wearable devices.

Bluetooth 5.0 is the current version (released in 2016). Version 5.0 is focused on IoT support, which is touted to be as fast as 802.11 wireless. Bluetooth 5.0 has a maximum speed of four times the 4.0 specification and a maximum range of 800 feet. Although similar to version 4.0, as distance increases the speed diminishes.

Bluetooth version 4.0 supports both point-to-point and star topologies. Version 5.0 supports everything that version 4.0 supports and includes support for mesh routing topologies.

NFC

Near-field communication (NFC) is a short-distance wireless communication protocol. NFC is built into many mobile devices for the application of payment systems, such as Android Pay and Apple Pay. In addition, NFC is used for data exchange between mobile devices. A use case for this application is the transfer process when a new mobile device is purchased. You can simply tap the two devices together, and the new mobile device pulls the information from the existing mobile device.

NFC nominally requires a distance of 4 centimeters or less to operate. NFC operates in a point-to-point topology and has a maximum bandwidth of 424 Kbps. NFC does not use addressing as other technologies do; the NFC protocol uses NFC tags, or a string of numbers.

IR

Infrared (IR) is a wireless communication protocol that uses the infrared spectrum of light (850 to 900 nanometers). Infrared is typically used to control home electronics such as TVs, stereos, and set-top boxes (STBs). Infrared has not taken off as a communication protocol because of privacy concerns.

The IR protocol has speeds ranging from 2.4 Kbps to 1 Gbps, although Gigabit IR (GigaIR) is still in development and not widely adopted. IR operates in a point-to-point topology.

RFID

Radio Frequency Identification (RFID) is a wireless communication protocol. It is used for identification, tracking, payment systems, and access control applications. RFID tags, which are also called RFID transponders, work in two different ways.

Active RFID tags (also called RFID beacons) have an internal power source. These RFID tags are mainly used in asset tracking and constantly broadcast their ID to an RFID scanner. Because active RFID contains its own internal power source, the distance of these beacons is normally 1000 meters (3,281 feet).

Passive RFID tags have no internal power source. Passive RFID works by using the signal the reader sends out to power and respond. A passive RFID tag consists of a large antenna wire wound around the transponder chip. The average distance of a passive RFID is 10 feet.

However, with the proper antennas on the RFID reader, distances of 600 feet or more can be achieved.

RFID operates in a point-to-point topology and has a data rate in kilobits. The RFID transponders do not use a formal addressing since they only transmit tag numbers, similar to NFC. RFID can operate on a number of different frequencies, depending on the application and region of the world. Lower frequency transponders are used for tattle tapes used to prevent theft in retail stores and payment systems. Super-high frequency transponders are used for asset tracking.

- Low frequency (LF) of 125 kHz to 134.2 kHz
- High frequency (HF) of 13.56 MHz
- Ultra-high frequency (UHF) of 860 MHz to 960 MHz
- Super-high frequency (SHF) of 2.45 GHz

802.11

The IEEE 802.11 wireless specification is the most popular for IoT applications. It has become the standard of IoT communications, because it is already supported by networking professionals. 802.11 is used when devices need to communicate to the Internet or an internal IP resource. The applications for IoT with wireless are being invented every day, and the possibilities are endless! The next section, "Given a scenario, implement the appropriate wireless technologies and configurations." covers the 802.11 standards in depth.

Exam Essentials

Know the various wired topologies.   Logical topologies are a high-level overview of the network and how it operates. The physical topology is a more detailed view of the network and why it can operate. Star topologies are used for Ethernet networks and the most common topology. Ring topologies are used for WAN connectivity because they are resilient to faults, but they are not used internally in networks. Mesh topologies are commonly found in the core of the network and are often used for SAN connectivity. Bus topologies are no longer used for Ethernet, but bus topologies can be found in many other technologies.

Know the various wireless topologies.   Ad hoc wireless topologies are normally point-to-point connections between two wireless devices, without the use of a wireless access point. Infrastructure wireless topologies can be basic service sets (BSSs) or extended service sets (ESSs). A BSS is a wireless access point (WAP) connected to a wireless network providing service to a common group of computers. An ESS is several WAPs working together to extend wireless coverage for a wired network. Mesh wireless topologies allow for WAPs to extend coverage by connecting to neighboring WAPs via another wireless channel.

Know the various types of networks.   A local area network (LAN) is the locally managed network. The wireless local area network (WLAN) is the wireless network that connects back to the LAN. The WLAN extends the LAN for wireless capabilities. The wide area network (WAN) defines the provider's network that allows a site to get access to another site or Internet access. The metropolitan area network (MAN) is a type of WAN that is constrained to a town or metropolitan area. The campus area network (CAN) defines multiple buildings connected together in a relatively small area that is locally managed. The storage area network (SAN) is exclusively used for connecting to storage such as Fibre Channel (FC) or InfiniBand networks. The personal area network (PAN) is a network that is for personal use; it can be wired or wireless.

Know the various technologies that facilitate the Internet of Things (IoT). The Z-wave protocol is a cheaper alternative to Zigbee operating on the 900 MHz ISM radio band. Z-wave can have 232 nodes and requires a primary controller. ANT+ is a wireless protocol used for health, sports, and fitness equipment. Bluetooth version 4.0 has a maximum speed of 25 Mbps and operates on the 2.4 GHz ISM radio band. Bluetooth version 5.0 has a maximum speed of four times Bluetooth 4.0 and was created to support IoT. Near-field communication (NFC) is a wireless protocol that is used in 4 centimeters or less and transmits a string of numbers or small amounts of data. Infrared (IR) is used as a wireless protocol for the control of consumer electronics via infrared light. Radio Frequency Identification (RFID) is used for identification systems via four possible frequency bands. RFID transponders can be active or passive. Active RFID transponders have greater distances than passive and are internally powered. Passive RFID transponders are not internally powered; they are powered from the RF of the RFID reader. 802.11 is the most common wireless protocol for IoT, when the device must connect to an IP network.

1.6 Given a scenario, implement the appropriate wireless technologies and configurations.

Wireless technologies are useful in the two main scenarios of mobility and ease of access. In the past 20 years, mobile computing has become expected in society and networks. The expansive growth of mobile computing has required more bandwidth and better wireless coverage, which has led to steady advancements in wireless hardware and protocols. Ease of access is another scenario in which wireless has become a required technology. When network access is too expensive or logistically impossible to wire, wireless technologies come to the rescue.

This section covers both the mobility and ease of access for wireless technologies. We will first explore the various 802.11 standards, and then we will cover cellular technologies, along with the supporting technologies from almost two decades of enhancements.

802.11 Standards

Wireless standards are developed the Institute of Electrical and Electronics Engineers (IEEE) 802.11 working group. The original 802.11 wireless standard was ratified in 1997. The original specification had a maximum bandwidth of 1 and 2 Mbps.

Over the past 20 years, new standards have been ratified by various 802.11 working subgroups. When we discuss 802.11a, the "a" stands for the working subgroup of the IEEE, and it also represents the ratified standard.

Wireless equipment vendors will adhere to these standards when producing new wireless hardware. However, when new standards are to be ratified soon, vendors will often prerelease standards hardware. This allows the vendor to get a jump on the market, and when the specification is formally ratified, the vendors will release firmware for the ratified standard.

802.11b

The 802.11b standard was ratified in 1999. It was the first wireless protocol to become popular with wireless networks and was responsible for the expansive growth of wireless in the following years.

The 802.11b standard operates on the 2.4 GHz frequencies in the industrial, scientific, and medical (ISM) radio band. It can use 11 frequency channels in North America and only 3 of the 11 channels are nonoverlapping. The standard uses *direct-sequence spread spectrum (DSSS)* modulation. It is capable of a maximum speed of 11 Mbps and a maximum distance of 350 feet. As the signal gets weaker, the speed drops at these intervals: 11, 5.5, 2, and 1 Mbps.

The 802.11b standard is considered legacy, because it requires the channel it's operating on to shift from newer modulation techniques to DSSS. When an 802.11b client enters the network, all other devices on the network must shift back to 802.11b for backward compatibility since the WAP is now operating with this older modulation. Most administrators completely turn off 802.11b functionality for this reason.

802.11a

The 802.11a standard was ratified in 1999 alongside of 802.11b. The 802.11a standard was mainly used in corporate networks for bridging between buildings via wireless. In the early 2000s, 802.11a was not as popular as 802.11b, and the equipment was more expensive.

The 802.11a standard operates on the 5 GHz frequencies in the *Unlicensed National Information Infrastructure (U-NII)* radio band. The standard can use 12 frequencies of nonoverlapping channels. It uses *orthogonal frequency-division multiplexing (OFDM)* modulation, which has become the standard for all subsequent wireless standards. 802.11a is capable of a maximum speed of 54 Mbps and a maximum distance of 190 feet. As the signal gets weaker, the speed drops at these intervals: 54, 48, 36, 24, 18, 12, 9, and 6 Mbps.

The 802.11a standard is also considered legacy, because the 802.11n standard can access 23 nonoverlapping frequency channels. The *Federal Communications Commission (FCC)* released an additional 11 channels in 2004 and 2008.

802.11g

The 802.11g standard was ratified in 2003 and served as an updated standard for 802.11b. This new standard became very popular, because the cost was about the same and the standard introduced newer features.

The 802.11g standard operates on the 2.4 GHz frequencies in the ISM radio band. It can use 11 frequency channels in North America and only 3 of the 11 channels are nonoverlapping. The 802.11g standard is capable of a maximum speed of 54 Mbps and a maximum distance of 310 feet. Just like other standards, as the signal gets weaker, the speed drops at these intervals: 54, 48, 36, 24, 18, 12, 9, and 6 Mbps.

The updated standard switched to the OFDM modulation and was backward compatible with the DSSS modulation (802.11b). This backward compatibility comes with a cost to all other clients on the WAP: everyone will be switched back to a maximum of 11 Mbps!

802.11n

The 802.11n standard was ratified in 2009 and introduced faster speeds, more channels, and longer distances. I would consider the 802.11n standard to be the best advancement in wireless since wireless was first introduced. The standard introduced many features that newer standards have built upon.

The 802.11n standard operates on the 2.4 GHz frequencies in the ISM radio band and the 5 GHz frequencies U-NII radio band. The standard can use 23 frequencies of non-overlapping channels in the 5 GHz radio band and can use all 11 of the channels in the 2.4 GHz radio band in North America. It allows for bonding of up to two 20 MHz channels, to provide a single 40 MHz channel for higher speeds. However, bonding of channels should be avoided on 2.4 GHz, because of limited number of nonoverlapping channels. I will cover channel bonding later in this section.

The 802.11n standard is backward compatible with 802.11g and 802.11a by working in a mixed mode and reading the preamble of the wireless frame. It is also backward compatible with 802.11b at the cost of everyone's speed, because 802.11b uses a different modulation.

The 802.11n standard uses OFDM modulation along with multiple input, multiple output (MIMO), called MIMO-OFDM. The standard will allow up to four spatial streams of MIMO. I will cover MIMO later in this section. The 802.11n standard is capable of a maximum speed of 600 Mbps, with 4×4 MIMO and a 40 MHz channel. However, it is not common to find a WAP that supports 4×4 MIMO and the nominal maximum bandwidth is found to be 450 Mbps with 3×3 MIMO. The maximum distance for 802.11n is 230 feet.

802.11ac

The 802.11ac standard was ratified in 2013 and is the current gold standard for wireless. This standard built upon many of the new technologies that 802.11n introduced to produce fast speeds.

The 802.11ac standard operates on the 5 GHz frequencies U-NII radio band. The standard can use 24 frequencies of nonoverlapping channels. It allows for bonding of up to eight 20 MHz channels, to provide a single 160 MHz channel for higher speeds. The 802.11ac standard is backward compatible with all previous 5GHz wireless standards.

The 802.11ac standard uses MIMO-OFDM modulation and will support up to eight spatial streams of MIMO. A theoretical maximum speed of 6.93 Gbps is possible with *802.11ac Wave 2*. The 802.11ac standard allows for 160 MHz channel bonding. However, there are only 23 nonoverlapping channels and bonding of 8 channels diminishes usable channels to two 160 MHz channels, so it is not commonly done in enterprise networks. It is common to bond channels into 80 MHz channels and use 3×3 MIMO to provide 1.3 Gbps.

The 802.11ac standard supports 1.3 Gbps at a maximum distance of 90 feet. However, 802.11ac allows for a greater distance at slower than 1.3 Gbps speeds, so distance is a trade-off for top speed.

Cellular

Cellular connectivity methods are typically not used for connecting our businesses to the Internet, since most data usage is metered by the provider on a monthly basis. Where this technology excels is for the mobility of workers with a laptop and cell card. This connectivity is also used in remote equipment locations that don't need a constant stream of data, such as digital signage, equipment monitoring, and even payphones in remote locations.

TDMA

Time-division multiple access (TDMA) is a legacy cellular network protocol that is no longer used by carriers. TDMA provided 2G network services and has been incorporated into GSM cellular network protocols. The bandwidth of TDMA was 14.4 Kbps to 64 Kbps.

CDMA

Code Division Multiple Access (CDMA) was originally designed by Qualcomm in the United States as a competitor to GSM networks. Several cellular providers still use CDMA as their 3G cellular network protocol. Sprint, Verizon Wireless, and Virgin Mobile are just a few that used CDMA.

CDMA cellular phones and equipment are not compatible with GSM networks. Although CDMA cell equipment contains a subscriber identification module (SIM) card, the cell equipment retrieves the subscriber information from the provider's servers.

CDMA-2000 is a 3G protocol used by many of the providers that support CDMA. The protocols can deliver a maximum of 3 Mbps for data. Evolution-Data Optimized (EV-DO) CDMA will not allow simultaneous voice and data, but Simultaneous Voice and EV-DO data (SV-DO) allows simultaneous voice and data. The more common CDMA protocol is EV-DO, because North American carriers have not adopted SV-DO.

GSM

Global System for Mobile communications (GSM) is a standard developed by the *European Telecommunications Standards Institute (ETSI)*. GSM is a global standard used around the world. It is not compatible with CDMA equipment. AT&T and T-Mobile are among the providers that use GSM networks. Several carrier technologies are built upon GSM:

> *Enhanced Data Rates for GSM Evolution (Edge)* is used as a connectivity method for cellular data on 2G networks. It has a maximum data speed of 1 Mbps but is normally limited to 500 Kbps. It can provide backward compatibility with GSM networks, which operate at 43.2 Kbps. Many providers have moved away from Edge to the current standards of LTE.

Third-Generation (3G) operates on GSM networks worldwide and CDMA networks in the United States and limited areas. When 3G was first introduced, it had a maximum speed of 200 Kbps, but with a number of variations on 3G from providers, it can deliver up to 4 Mbps. The speed depends on whether the receiving object is stationary or moving.

High-Speed Packet Access Plus (HSPA+) is a variation of third-generation cellular that uses GSM networks. It has a theoretical speed of 168 Mbps download and 23 Mbps upload, but it is often limited by the carrier since it requires enormous RF bandwidth to achieve those speeds. Typical speeds are around 42 Mbps download and 11 Mbps upload. It is still supported with 3G phones and devices for certain carriers.

LTE/4G

Long-Term Evolution (LTE) fourth-generation (4G) is the current standard of cellular data today that is based on GSM/EDGE and HSPA technologies. LTE/4G is not a CDMA technology; it uses orthogonal frequency-division multiple access (OFDMA).

The current maximum data for LTE/4G throughput is 299 Mbps download and 75.4 Mbps upload, although typical consumer bandwidth is much lower at 12 Mbps download with a peak of 50 Mbps and 5 Mbps upload. LTE Advanced is proposed to support 1 Gbps download and 500 Mbps upload speed.

Frequencies

The frequencies used with wireless local area networks (WLANs) vary by standard. The two main frequencies used are 2.4 GHz and 5 GHz. The 2.4 GHz frequencies are governed by the industrial, scientific, and medical (ISM) radio bands. The 5 GHz frequencies are governed by the Unlicensed National Information Infrastructure (U-NII) radio band.

2.4 GHz

The 2.4 GHz spectrum is governed by the ISM radio band. The 802.11b/g/n standards operate on 2.4 GHz frequencies. The band consists of 14 channels 22 MHz wide. In North America only the first 11 of the channels can be used for wireless. In Japan all 14 channels can be used, and almost everywhere else in the world the first 13 channels can be used.

Only 3 of the 14 channels are considered nonoverlapping, as seen in Figure 1.75. The channels of 1, 6, and 11 are considered prime channels for WLAN because they do not overlap with the other channels in the channel plan. Therefore, three WAPs can function in an extended service set (ESS), without experiencing interference from each other.

FIGURE 1.75   The 2.4 GHz channel plan

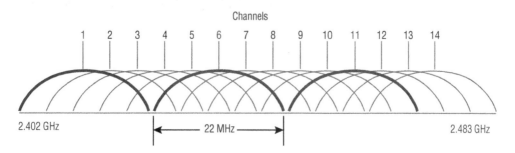

The 2.4 GHz ISM radio band is nearing the end of its life because of the limited number of channels and nonoverlapping channels. The latest standard of 802.11ac does not support 2.4 GHz. WAPs that support 802.11ac and allow 2.4 GHz connection have dual radios built in and use 802.11 b/g/n for the 2.4 GHz radio.

5 GHz

The 5 GHz frequencies are governed by the Unlicensed National Information Infrastructure (U-NII) radio band. The 802.11 a/n/ac standards operate on 5 GHz frequency spectrum.

As seen in Figure 1.76, the band consists of 24 nonoverlapping channels. In North America the 802.11a standard can function on 12 channels consisting of 36, 40, 44, 48, 52, 56, 60, 64, 149, 153, 157, and 161. Each regulatory domain restricts the number of channels and specific channels for the region.

In North America, the 802.11ac standard can use 24 of the nonoverlapping channels as seen in Figure 1.76. In Europe and Japan the channels are limited to the U-NII 1, U-NII 2, and U-NII2e list of channels. The 802.11n standard only allowed the first 23 channels in North America, because channel 165 was in the ISM band.

FIGURE 1.76   The 5 GHz channel plan

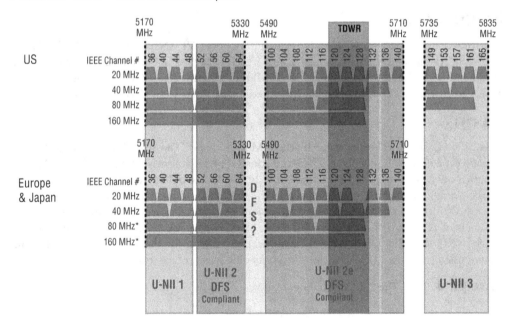

Speed and Distance Requirements

The distance of wireless outdoors will always be better than wireless indoors. Wireless outdoors has the advantages of an open space environment, which reduces the backscatter and absorptions of wireless signals.

Wireless signals bounce off any surface and create this backscatter of RF that attributes to *wireless multipath* interference, thus reducing the overall signal quality. We can see this effect in a room that has an audible echo. The echo can sometimes be so extreme it drowns out a conversation. Wireless signals experience this same effect when backscatter is severe.

Wireless signals also suffer from absorption into materials. In a house or commercial building we generally have sheetrock and wood. These materials tend to absorb the signal, which lowers the strength of the signal on the other side. Although backscatter and absorption are only two of the many problems we can have with wireless signals, they are the two most common.

Speeds will always be higher on 5 GHz wireless, such as the 802.11 a/n/ac standards. The 802.11ac standard can use a maximum of 24 nonoverlapping channels. However, the 802.11 b/g/n standards are restricted to the 2.4 GHz wireless band with three nonoverlapping channels. To future-proof new installations of wireless, focus on 5 GHz coverage and hardware. The 802.11ac standard exclusively covers 5 GHz.

Regardless of the standard used, there is a relationship between distance and speed. As the client station moves further away from the WAP, the speed is automatically reduced for a reduced error rate and maximum throughput. As we see in Figure 1.77, the maximum speed of 1.3 Gbps at 90 feet can be achieved. However, as the client station moves away from the WAP, the bandwidth is reduced significantly.

FIGURE 1.77   802.11ac data rates vs. distance

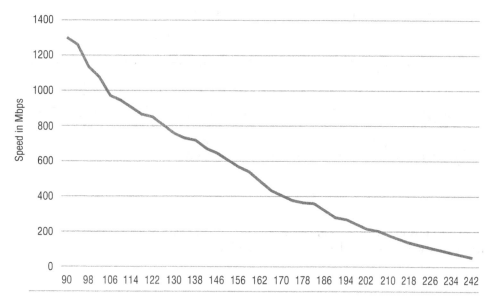

Distance in Feet

Channel Bandwidth

The channel bandwidth of a 2.4 GHz channel is 22 MHz and a 5 GHz channel has a bandwidth of 20 MHz. When speaking in radio frequency (RF) terms, bandwidth is the width of the channel hertz or how many bits can be transmitted per second (per cycles).

In RF terms, bandwidth is different from throughput because of modulation and coding techniques. Each new standard has improved the throughput of wireless by using more advanced modulation and coding techniques. As network professionals we use the term bandwidth in relation to throughput.

Channel Bonding

With the introduction of the 802.11n wireless standard, bonding adjacent channels together became possible. When channels are bonded together, we gain increased throughput for the combined channels. With the introduction of 802.11ac, we can now bond eight 20 MHz channels together for a 160 MHz of bandwidth. With modern modulation and coding techniques, we can obtain the throughput of 6.93 Gbps over these bonded channels!

Bonding can create bonded channels of 20, 40, 80, and 160 MHz, as detailed in Figure 1.78. One of the problems with channel bonding is the reduction of channels that are nonoverlapping. With 24 nonoverlapping channels, we can have twelve 40 MHz channels, six 80 MHz channels, or two 160 MHz channels. This limits the number of nonoverlapping channels and the complexity of your design for maximum throughput.

FIGURE 1.78   Channel bonding in the 5GHz radio band

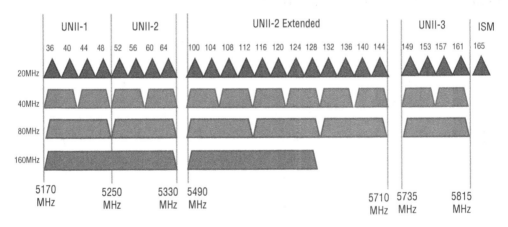

It is also possible to bond channels with the 2.4 GHz radio band. However, because there are only three nonoverlapping channels, it is not practical.

MIMO/MU-MIMO

Multiple input, multiple output (MIMO) technology allows for wireless devices to transmit and receive the same signal across multiple antennas. These signals are called spatial streams and are often referred to as 2×2, 3×3, 4×4, and 8×8. The 2×2 designation means that two antennas on the WAP are used and two antennas on the client are used; 3×3 means that three antennas on the WAP are used and three antennas on the client are used. I think you see where this is going.

You may wonder, why would we transmit and receive the same signal? MIMO is a radio frequency (RF) technique of using multipath transmissions to boost overall signal quality. Multipath happens when a wireless device transmits in a room or area that has RF reflective surfaces. The signal bounces off these surfaces and arrives at the destination in several different paths. In most cases the multipath transmissions degrade the signal. However, in 802.11n and 802.11ac, digital signal processing (DSP) allows for several streams to be compared and combined to simultaneously boost the signal, as seen in Figure 1.79.

FIGURE 1.79   MIMO wireless example

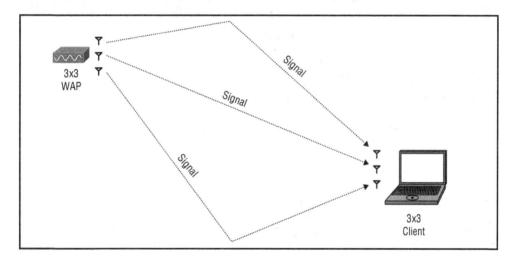

MIMO only really works in closed areas that propagate RF multipath. When wireless devices are used in open spaces such as outdoors and multipath does not exist, MIMO is automatically turned off.

Multiuser multiple-input, multiple-output (MU-MIMO) technology was released in 802.11ac Wave 2, as an extension to the 802.11ac standard. It allows for spatial streams to be transmitted simultaneously to multiple users. In standard MIMO, streams are time-shared between the various clients. Each client would need to wait their turn, until the time slice was round-robin shared with them. With advancements in DSP chips, the wireless clients can separate their signal out from the multiple streams being transmitted simultaneously.

Unidirectional/Omnidirectional

Wireless antennas can be purchased in many different functional designs. Each design of antenna produces gain with a certain pattern. The patterns along with the gain information are often found on the wireless vendor's website in the section typically referred to as the ordering guide.

In Figure 1.80, we see a unidirectional antenna called a *Yagi antenna*. It has a decibel gain of 13.5 dBi and operates on the 2.4 GHz radio frequency band. As we can see in the figure, there is an *azimuth plane* radiation pattern and an *elevation plane* radiation pattern. The azimuth plane is the radiation pattern left to right. The elevation plane is the radiation pattern from top to bottom. With these two patterns, we can effectively cover an area, depending on the application. In the case of the Yagi antenna design (unidirectional) in Figure 1.80, the shape would look like a blunt cone emanating from the antenna.

FIGURE 1.80   A Yagi antenna radiation pattern example

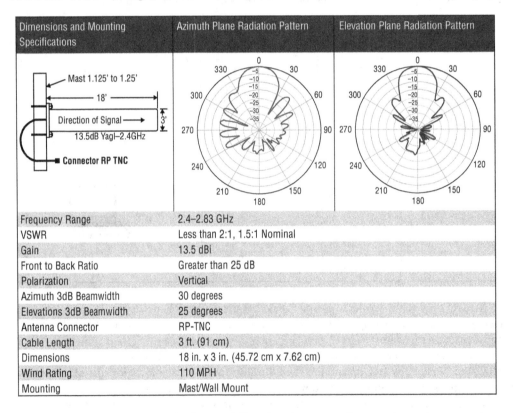

Dimensions and Mounting Specifications	Azimuth Plane Radiation Pattern	Elevation Plane Radiation Pattern

Frequency Range	2.4–2.83 GHz
VSWR	Less than 2:1, 1.5:1 Nominal
Gain	13.5 dBi
Front to Back Ratio	Greater than 25 dB
Polarization	Vertical
Azimuth 3dB Beamwidth	30 degrees
Elevations 3dB Beamwidth	25 degrees
Antenna Connector	RP-TNC
Cable Length	3 ft. (91 cm)
Dimensions	18 in. x 3 in. (45.72 cm x 7.62 cm)
Wind Rating	110 MPH
Mounting	Mast/Wall Mount

The most common antenna is the omnidirectional antenna, because it produces a uniform radiation pattern. The radiation pattern of the azimuth plane (left to right) is uniform in all directions. The elevation will vary from antenna to antenna, but it will be somewhat uniform. If we were to image the 360-degree view, it would look like a giant doughnut around the antenna. An example of an omnidirectional antenna can be seen in Figure 1.81.

FIGURE 1.81   An omnidirectional antenna radiation pattern example

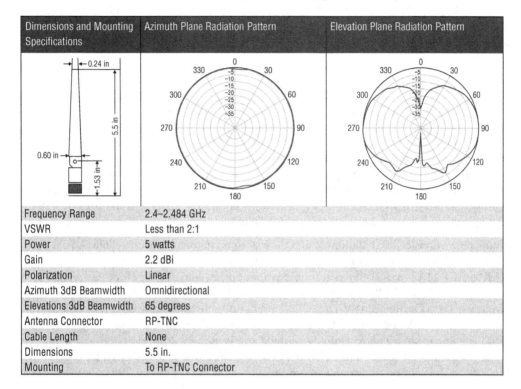

Dimensions and Mounting Specifications	Azimuth Plane Radiation Pattern	Elevation Plane Radiation Pattern
Frequency Range	2.4–2.484 GHz	
VSWR	Less than 2:1	
Power	5 watts	
Gain	2.2 dBi	
Polarization	Linear	
Azimuth 3dB Beamwidth	Omnidirectional	
Elevations 3dB Beamwidth	65 degrees	
Antenna Connector	RP-TNC	
Cable Length	None	
Dimensions	5.5 in.	
Mounting	To RP-TNC Connector	

Site Surveys

Carpenters have a saying: "measure twice, cut once." When we are designing a wireless network the placement of the WAPs is critical, for both cost and coverage. Often we need to mount these WAPs on a high ceiling and run the wiring in conduit for fire code reasons. So the carpenter's saying holds very true in these situations. Before ordering WAPs we should have a good understanding of where they are going to be mounted and what the coverage is going to look like.

Fortunately, site surveys can help us future-proof the wireless design. During a site survey, the equipment is temporarily positioned in the estimated location. This positioning can be done with a special tripod with extensions that allow for high elevation, or it can just be zip-tied to the spot. The key is that it is temporary so that we can take measurements. The equipment should be the exact model, firmware, and antenna so that our readings are as close to the future design as possible.

Once the equipment is temporally mounted, we can take our readings around the expected coverage area. Software like Netscout AirMagnet allows for a drawing of the coverage area to be imported, then we can simply click the spot we are standing in and the software will register: signal strength, *signal-to-noise ratio (SNR)*, and various other metrics from the laptop's wireless card. After several points are registered, the software can create a heat map of the coverage area.

Because of the cost and acquisition of the wireless equipment and software for a site survey, it is general practice to purchase these services from the reseller. The reseller can then be the single point of contact when the coverage is not as expected or needs expanded upon. If you contract these services, be careful to scrutinize the *scope of work (SOW)*.

Exam Essentials

Know the various 802.11 standards and features for each standard.   802.11b operates on 2.4 GHz and can supply a maximum bandwidth of 11 Mbps. 802.11a operates on 5.0 GHz and can supply a maximum bandwidth of 54 Mbps. 802.11a can use a maximum of 12 nonoverlapping frequency channels. 802.11g operates on 2.4 GHz and can supply a maximum bandwidth of 54 Mbps. 802.11n operates on 2.4 and 5.0 GHz and is possible of supplying a maximum bandwidth of 600 Mbps. 802.11n introduced multiple-input, multiple-output (MIMO) technology and channel bonding. 802.11ac is the latest standard and operates solely on 5.0 GHz to supply 1.3 Gbps.

Know the various cellular standards and their accompanying features.   TDMA is a legacy cellular standard that provided 2G cellular; it has a bandwidth of 14.4 Kbps to 64 Kbps. CDMA is a 3G cellular technology that Sprint, Verizon Wireless, and Virgin Mobile use. CDMA-2000 can supply a maximum of 3 Mbps of bandwidth per subscriber. Evolution-Data Optimized (EV-DO) CDMA will not allow simultaneous voice and data, but Simultaneous Voice and EV-DO data (SV-DO) will allow simultaneous voice and data. GSM is a European standard globally adopted and is used by 2G and 3G cellular standards. High-Speed Packet Access Plus (HSPA+) is a variation of 3G cellular. LTE/4G is the latest 4G cellular standard capable of a maximum data throughput of 299 Mbps download and 75.4 upload.

Know the two standard wireless frequencies used with 802.11.   2.4 GHz consists of 14 channels 22 MHz wide. Only channels 1, 6, and 11 of the 14 channels are nonoverlapping. The 2.4 GHz wireless frequencies are part of the industrial, scientific, and medical (ISM) band. 5.0 GHz consists of 24 nonoverlapping channels 20 MHz wide; only 23 are usable in North America. The 5.0 GHz wireless frequencies are governed by the Unlicensed National Information Infrastructure (U-NII) radio band.

Understand the concepts of speed and distance with 802.11 wireless.   Wireless speed on 5.0 GHz wireless will always be higher than 5.0 GHz wireless, because of the number of nonoverlapping channels available. Wireless in outdoor settings has better distance capabilities, because there is less reflection and absorption of the wireless signal.

Understand the concept of channel bandwidth vs. throughput.   A 2.4 GHz wireless radio channel has a bandwidth of 22 MHz, and a 5.0 GHz wireless radio channel has a bandwidth of 20 MHz. The channel bandwidth is the capability of signals per second (cycle). The throughput can be higher because of modulation and encoding techniques.

Understand the concept of channel bonding for wireless.   Channel bonding is the ability to join two adjacent nonoverlapping to function as one operational channel. Bonding can create bonded channels of 20, 40, 80, and 160 MHz.

Understand the concept and functionality of MIMO and MU-MIMO.   Multiple-input, multiple-output (MIMO) technology allows wireless devices to transmit and receive on multiple antennas. MIMO helps produce more usable bandwidth by using the multipath bounce of a wireless signal to increase the usable throughput.

Understand the concepts of unidirectional and omnidirectional antennas.   Unidirectional antennas focus the signal in one general direction both up and down (elevation) and left to right (azimuth). Omnidirectional antennas focus the signal in all directions for elevation and azimuth.

Understand the concept of a wireless site survey.   The wireless site survey helps to validate coverage for a wireless design. The importance of the wireless site survey is to limit the need for additional WAPs. It also limits the added labor to move the WAP after installation, if coverage is not as expected.

1.7 Summarize cloud concepts and their purposes.

The traditional compute model was based on a one-to-one relation of application-to-server. However, most applications only use a fraction of the compute resources during idle periods, and all applications collectively seldom use all of the compute resources at the same time.

Virtualization allows us to partition compute resources for each guest operating system (OS) supporting an application running on the host hardware. The hypervisor allows the partitioning of compute resources, which I will cover in Chapter 2. The partitioning of virtualization allows each OS to operate as if it had exclusive control of the host hardware. Compute resources consist of central processing unit (CPU), memory, and devices related to a physical server.

Cloud services allow us to pool the resources together collectively for each host server providing virtualization. When the resources of computer, network, and storage are pooled together, the cloud gains fault tolerance and scale. This allows us to lose a host and still maintain the ability to compute the workload of the guest operating systems supporting our applications. It also allows us to add resources of compute, network, and storage to scale the cloud out for additional workloads. The scale of workloads is referred to as elasticity.

The cloud model is based on a many-to-many model where the exact location of the resources doesn't matter to the end user. We can create an application by allocating available resources to a guest OS from a pool of resources. The guest OS will then gain the fault tolerance of the cloud along with the added benefit of elasticity of the cloud.

The National Institute of Standards and Technology (NIST) defines cloud computing with five attributes: on-demand self-service, broad network access, resource pooling, rapid elasticity, and measured service. Earlier I described resource pooling, rapid elasticity, and on-demand self-service. Broad network access means the capabilities are accessible over a network and are not a contrived system like the old mainframe systems. Measured service means that a provider or private entity can meter and control bandwidth, storage, processing, and accounts.

Types of Services

The term *cloud* has become a ubiquitous buzzword in IT, applied to anything involving hosted services. However, the *National Institute of Standards and Technology (NIST)* has defined three service types for cloud computing: Software as a Service (SaaS), Platform as a Service (PaaS), and Infrastructure as a Service (IaaS).

There are many more service types than the three mentioned, but they are not defined by the NIST standards for cloud computing. That doesn't mean they are just buzzwords; it just means that NIST believes that they fit into one of the three categories already. An example of this is a cloud provider that offers Disaster Recovery as a Service (DRaaS); this service would fit into the IaaS service type.

SaaS

Software as a Service (SaaS) is one of the oldest models of cloud computing, before the term was created. It dates back to the dialup services of the 1980s and 1990s like CompuServe, AOL, and the Dow Jones stock service. Today, SaaS providers are accessed through a web browser, such as the services of Twitter, Facebook, and Gmail.

SaaS is any application that you use but do not own or maintain. The application is the provided service and is maintained by the service provider on their cloud. Facebook and Gmail are popular examples; you use their services and never have to worry about the underlying infrastructure.

Social media and email are not the only examples of SaaS. There are many others that you might not even think of, such as WebEx by Cisco and GitHub. The provider extends these services to you as either a pay-as-you-go, contract, or free service.

PaaS

Platform as a Service (PaaS) is another model of cloud computing. PaaS allows a customer to generate code on the provider's platform that can be executed. Web hosting providers like GoDaddy and A Small Orange are examples of PaaS. You can purchase web hosting from these providers and set up a WordPress or custom web application using PHP or ASP.Net.

Web hosting is not the only example of PaaS. Google App Engine is a platform that allows an application to be coded in Java, Python, or PHP. The application then is executed on Google's PaaS cloud; they can even provide storage like SQL.

SaaS applications can be produced on a PaaS platform. Evernote is hosted as of this writing on Google's cloud platform. Evernote is a SaaS application that allows collecting and sharing of ideas across various mobile and desktop devices.

Google App engine is not the only PaaS provider—there are countless other providers. Amazon Web Services (AWS) and Microsoft Azure are other examples, and countless other providers have begun to offer PaaS as well.

Applications are isolated between customers. The processes are allotted resources by the customer and can scale out for demand. PaaS providers generally charge the customer according to CPU cycles used.

IaaS

Infrastructure as a Service (IaaS) is the established model of computing that we generally associate with cloud computing. Amazon Web Services (AWS), Microsoft Azure, and Rackspace are just a few providers. These providers allow the customer to use the provider's infrastructure of compute, network, and storage.

When the customer needs IaaS, it is as simple as purchasing an instance of compute resources and then choosing an operating system and region of the world for the instance and connecting to it. The customer will not know the exact host server, network equipment, or storage the guest VM is running upon. All of the worries of the infrastructure are left up to the provider.

Computing resources are not the only services that you can purchase from a cloud provider. For example, Amazon Web Services and Microsoft Azure offer backup services. You can purchase space on the provider's cloud and back up straight to it.

Any infrastructure that you would normally purchase as a capital expense (lease or own) can be converted into an operational expense (rent) via services from the provider. Whenever I am looking to purchase physical infrastructure, I incorporate IaaS into my cost analysis. However, you must also weigh the nonmonetary saving such as infrastructure maintenance and overall administration of the infrastructure. You must ask yourself, is it better to own this infrastructure or rent this infrastructure long term?

Cloud Delivery Models

When we discuss the cloud, names like Amazon AWS and Microsoft Azure come to mind. However, anyone can own their own cloud as long as the resources meet the criteria of the NIST standard for cloud computing. We can classify the ownership of these models within the three main categories of public, private, and hybrid.

I often find that companies will begin entering into the cloud via a public cloud provider. These public clouds, as discussed in the previous section, are like renting compute power. The charges are charged to an operational expense budget, because there is no equity in the service, much like renting a house. Once companies realize the saving of virtualization, they often purchase the equipment to transform into a private cloud. The purchase of this equipment is a capital investment, because we have equity in the equipment, much like owning a house.

Private

The private cloud model is defined as cloud infrastructure that is provisioned for exclusive use by a single organization. It can be owned, managed, and operated by the organization, a third party, or a combination of both. The infrastructure can also be located on or off premise. This makes the cloud resources exclusive to the owner.

There are several reasons to move to a private cloud deployment, such as regulatory, privacy, monetary, budgetary impact, and overall control. Private clouds give the owner ultimate control of the cloud and its design. Sometimes the public cloud may not offer certain features or hardware that a private cloud can be built to support. The creation of the private cloud might not be for purposes of new technology; it could be designed to support legacy systems that may not be compatible with public cloud offerings.

The private cloud model has the advantage of ultimate control, with a price that is not immediately evident. When equipment is purchased such as compute, network, and storage, the company must forecast growth over a nominal 5- to 7-year period. In a public cloud, resources can be purchased on demand and relinquished when not needed, but in the private cloud model we must acquire these additional resources and are burdened with the ownership.

Obsolescence of the equipment must also be considered, because the average expected life of compute, network, and storage resources is usually 5 to 7 years. Private clouds often need hardware refreshes every 5 to 7 years because of newer features or end-of-life warranties.

Public

The public cloud model is defined as infrastructure that is provisioned for open use by the general public. It can be owned, managed, and operated by a business academic, government organization, or a combination thereof. However, the infrastructure exists on the premise of the cloud provider.

The public cloud is often a public market place for compute, network, and storage in which you can rent or lease compute time. This compute time, of course, is segregated from other customers, so there is a level of isolation between customers on the same infrastructure. Examples of public cloud providers are Amazon Web Services (AWS), Microsoft Azure, and Google Cloud; these are just a few providers, and the list grows every day.

A benefit of the public cloud is the pay-as-you-go utility model. You can purchase the compute power you need for a period of time. You are charged only for the compute time that you use or purchase, and there is no initial capital investment on the part of the customer.

Another benefit to the public cloud is the elasticity of compute, network, and storage resources. If a customer is an online retailer and needs extra compute power for the holiday season, the customer can purchase more scale-out, and when the busy period is over, they can relinquish the resources.

A disadvantage to the public cloud is the lack of control and hardware configuration. If custom hardware is required, then the public cloud is not an option. Heavily regulated industries might not be able to use the public cloud because of restrictions on where data can be stored and who can access it.

Hybrid

The hybrid cloud model is a combination of both the private and public cloud models. It is the most popular model, because many businesses leverage public cloud providers while maintaining their own infrastructure.

Many cloud providers now offer integration for private cloud software, such as Microsoft Hyper-V and VMware vSphere. This integration allows private clouds to gain the on-demand elasticity of the public cloud. When a private cloud uses the public cloud for elasticity of resources or additional capacity, it is called cloud bursting.

Connectivity Methods

Before public clouds, the applications, authentication, and users were all within a local area network (LAN) or the organization's network. Public clouds allow us to host our application in datacenters located in the public cloud. However, users still need to access these applications, and the applications still need to access authentication systems in our datacenter. Because cloud providers offer broad network access, the Internet is usually the way we access these applications located in the public cloud.

There are two main ways to we can provide access to applications hosted in the public cloud. Cloud providers often sell virtual private network (VPN) virtual appliances that can create a VPN tunnel back to our datacenter. Although you don't necessarily need the provider's virtual appliance, you can always install your own in the public cloud if there is a particular VPN package you elect to use. These VPN virtual appliances allow for data to be transmitted over the Internet in an encrypted tunnel.

The other method of connectivity is to build out a private WAN to the public cloud, with the help of a WAN provider or Internet service provider (ISP). This method requires planning and often ties you to a particular datacenter location, because dedicated fiber-optic lines run directly from your location to the cloud provider.

Security Implications/Considerations

When using cloud providers, keep in mind several security implications. When applications are moved to the provider's cloud, we give up the control of the hardware and data running on it. We trust that the provider takes proper precaution to protect our data, but we cannot rely on it. Another consideration is connectivity to the applications and data. Most of the time it is across the Internet, where *man-in-the-middle (MitM)* attacks and eavesdropping can occur.

When data is transmitted or accessed to or from the public cloud, the data should be encrypted in transit. The protocol used to encrypt the data during transit should allow for authentication of the data and strong encryption, to prevent replay attacks, MitM attacks, and interception of the data. Application authentication should also be encrypted to prevent theft of identity of services running the application and users accessing the application.

When data is at rest on the storage of the public cloud, the data should also be encrypted. This restful encryption will ensure that our data residing on the hardware at the provider is safe in the event of theft, misplacement, or any other circumstance out of our control.

In addition to security, identity management must be considered. When applications are moved to the public cloud, we should ensure that we maintain *single sign-on (SSO)*. It is common practice to create a VPN tunnel to the cloud resources we have purchased so that we can allow for native authentication back to our identity systems.

SSO can also be in the form of a federated identity solutions such as Microsoft Federated Services or Shibboleth federated service. Federated services allow for the authentication of users and computers on our immediate network. We then provide the application with a response-token guarantee that we have authenticated the user or computer.

Relationship between Local and Cloud Resources

It is common for most enterprise networks to be built on a hybrid cloud model. There are many applications that should be hosted locally in the company's private cloud, such as file services. Then there are applications that should be hosted remotely in the public cloud, such as external websites.

When looking at the resources we can host locally and remotely, we must consider how to leverage the public cloud to our advantage. When we back up our local server farm, we want to do it locally because the resources we are backing up are local. However, if we leverage cloud storage and transmit the month-end backups to the public cloud, we can guarantee that if we have a local disaster the data will still be available.

Compute power is another resource I touched on briefly when discussing the hybrid cloud. We can burst our local cloud and bring on resources from the public cloud to scale out our service. One use of cloud bursting might be to scale out our intranet web servers or a particular application that was in high demand but that didn't warrant purchasing of more equipment. Cloud bursting is also used when the equipment will take too long to acquire.

There are countless other examples of augmenting the local private cloud with public cloud resources. When making these decisions, we should consider where our user base is located, consider how long the resources will be needed, perform a cost analysis between purchasing the equipment and using the public cloud, and of course calculate what the potential savings will be to our company.

Exam Essentials

Know and understand the various type of cloud services.   Software as a Service (SaaS) allows us to use an application provided and maintained by the service provider. Platform as a Service (PaaS) is a platform for designing applications that are compiled and executed in the cloud. Infrastructure as a Service (IaaS) allows the customer to rent the infrastructure of compute, network, and storage from the cloud provider.

Know and understand the various cloud delivery models.   The private cloud defines that the resources are owned by the organization and exclusively used by the organization. The public cloud defines that the resources at the provider are provisioned and used by the general public. The public cloud allows a pay-as-you-go strategy that is similar to renting the equipment rather than owning it. A hybrid model is a blend of both the public cloud and private cloud within an organization.

Understand common connectivity methods to the public cloud.   When we host resources in the public cloud we need local resources such as authentication. Virtual private networks (VPNs) are used to allow an encrypted tunnel to be built across the public Internet. VPNs allow for the agility of change, such as switching datacenters. Public wide area networks (WANs) can be built out from the customer to the public cloud provider; these connections are exclusive for the customer.

Understand security implications and considerations for public cloud applications. Data should be transmitted with encryptions to prevent eavesdropping of the data. When data lands on the public cloud, it should be encrypted at rest on the disk. In addition to encryption of data, we should consider identity management and maintaining a single sign-on (SSO) environment for our users.

Understand the relationship between local and cloud resources. There are several different ways to augment the local resources of compute and storage with the public cloud. An example of using the public cloud for local compute resources is cloud bursting, when purchasing the equipment is too expensive or will take too long to acquire. Storage resources can be used for month-end backups of our local server farm; this moves the backups away from our physical location in the event of disaster.

1.8 Explain the functions of network services.

When we are building networks, there are essential services that all networks require to operate: name resolution, dynamic assignment of IP addresses, synchronization of time, and management of IP address resources. As networks scale out, these essential services help manage and maintain the network and are usually centrally managed.

DNS

The hosts file is a static file that was originally used for translation of hosts to IP addresses. It was centrally managed and used in the early days of the ARPANET, when there was a limited number of hosts. However, as the ARPANET expanded into the Internet back in 1983, DNS was proposed and created to decentralize the name resolution process. The hosts file still exists today locally on operating systems as an override to DNS.

Domain Name System (DNS) is a decentralized hierarchical database used for resolving fully qualified domain names (FQDNs) to IP addresses. An FQDN is a name that has been registered with a name authority and resolves to an IP address. An example of an FQDN is www.wiley.com, which resolves to 208.215.179.146. Computers need the numeric IP address to retrieve our data, but as humans we have a hard time remembering phone numbers let alone IP addresses. We also use DNS to resolve for other name resolution situations, as I will discuss in this section.

DNS Records

DNS is decentralized technology using zone files to partition the domain namespace. This partitioning allows for the namespace to be delegated, and I will discuss it in detail later in this section. The zone file contains resource records, such as FQDN-to-IP address records.

These resource records allow DNS to perform more than just IP address lookups. In the following examples, I will use the *Berkeley Internet Name Domain (BIND)* file convention. The most common records you will encounter on a DNS server are as follows.

A (Address Record)

A records allow a host to resolve an FQDN to an IPv4 address, also called a forward DNS query. We use these records every time we visit an address like www.wiley.com or www.sybex.com; they resolve to an IP address.

```
; host   class  record   IP address
  ns1    IN     A        192.168.1.1
  ns2    IN     A        192.168.1.2
  www    IN     A        192.168.1.3
```

AAAA (Quad A Record)

AAAA records are the IPv6 equivalent of an A record. It allows a host to resolve an FDQN to an IPv6 IP address.

```
; host      class  record   IP address
  mail      IN     AAAA     2001:db8::1
  www       IN     AAAA     2001:db8::2
  terminal  IN     AAAA     2001:db8::3
```

TXT (SPF, DKIM)

TXT records allow for text to be queried from DNS. TXT records are often used for proof of ownership of a domain name, such as management of search engine crawling. Mail servers use TXT records for identifying the authorized IP addresses of originating mail server. The Sender Policy Framework (SPF) record is used to define these IP addresses so that other mail servers can combat spam. Domain Keys Identified Mail (DKIM) records allow for organizations to authenticate messages sent through a cryptographic key stored in the TXT record.

```
; SPF Record
@        IN TXT "v=spf1 mx a ptr ip4:208.215.179.0/24"

; DKIM Record
1500514958.wiley._domainkey.www.wiley.com. IN TXT (
"v=DKIM1;t=s;p=MIGfMA0GCSqGSIb3DQEBAQUAA4GNADCBiQKBgQC3pAs2gR+4d0Bjl9nE7n20LJyY"
        "XcabqzpAgsjquwf73TOoNJKto/adyB3zHGAriQWAWja8hBdrlFX28Q8vG/11F0nu"
        "/xda3KcdNWIHC71oKkY3WNAEOTj3ofXJ7w4R/lucZGh5+fr1PCU2Ym0x6w5ZOO+0"
        "e6LKFS64pVRRM3OLpQIDAQAB")
```

SRV (Service Locator Records)

SRV records are used for locating services such as LDAP, which is used by Active Directory and Linux for login services. The SRV record is formatted with the service name and protocol followed by the TTL, class (Internet), SRV, priority, weight, port number, and target FQDN. The lowest priority gets used first and the weight helps the client decide if multiple entries for the same service exist.

```
; _service._proto.name.    TTL   class record  priority  weight  port  target
  _ldap._tcp.example.com. 86400 IN    SRV      10        50      389   ldap.example.com.
  _sip._tcp.example.com.  86400 IN    SRV      10        50      5060  sip.example.com.
```

MX (Mail Exchanger)

MX records assist a mail server in identifying the mail server for your domain. You must publish an MX record for your mail server if you want to receive mail from other mail servers. The @ symbol refers to the domain the zone file belongs to, and the priority is how the sending server picks the host to send mail to; the lowest priority is chosen first.

```
;    class record  priority  target
@    IN    MX       10        mail1.example.com.
@    IN    MX       20        mail2.example.com.
@    IN    MX       30        mail3.example.com.
```

CNAME (Canonical Name)

CNAME records allow an FQDN to resolve to an A record. This is quite handy when you have one host that has multiple names. Although multiple A records could be created if you every change the IP address, all of them would need to be updated. With a CNAME record that points to a single A record, only the A record's IP address would need to be changed.

```
; host  class  record  target
  sftp  IN     CNAME   www.example.com.
  ftp   IN     CNAME   www.example.com.
  www   IN     A       192.168.1.3
```

NS (Name Server)

NS records contain all the servers responsible for a particular zone file. If a DNS server does not have an NS record, it is not allowed to perform a zone transfer (copying the zone).

```
;    class  record  target
@    IN     NS      192.168.1.1
@    IN     NS      192.168.1.2
```

SOA (Start of Authority)

SOA records define a zone file and allow secondary DNS servers to know when the zone file has changed via the serial number, using a reverse date code; how often to check the primary zone file for changes via the refresh interval; how often to keep checking if it becomes unavailable via the retry interval; and what the default TTL (Time To Live) is for caching

via the TTL. The NS records and their corresponding A records always follow the SOA
record.

```
@  1D  IN  SOA ns1.example.com. hostmaster.example.com. (
                         2017071901 ; serial yyyymmddss
                         1H ; refresh
                         15 ; retry
                         1w ; expire
                         1h ; ttl
                         )
;    class  record  target
@    IN     NS      192.168.1.1
@    IN     NS      192.168.1.2
; host  class  record   IP address
  ns1   IN     A        192.168.1.1
  ns1   IN     A        192.168.1.2
```

PTR (Pointer Record)

PTR records allow a client to resolve an IP address to an FQDN. PTR record queries are
called reverse lookups. This is useful for learning the name of a host and are mainly used
by administrators.

```
; 1.168.192.IN-ADDR.ARPA. zone file
; host  class  record   FQDN
  1     IN     PTR      ns1.example.com.
  2     IN     PTR      ns2.example.com.
  3     IN     PTR      www.example.com.
```

Dynamic DNS

Dynamic DNS allows hosts to add and update their own A records. These records are normally only edited manually. However, when we use dynamic updates, we allow the hosts to
maintain these records for us. Dynamic updates can also add and update PTR records by
the host or with the assistance of a DHCP server. This allows reverse lookups PTR records
to be automatically maintained as well. Dynamic updates help automate the entries into
DNS and maintain the entries thereafter; they provide consistency for the administrator
and services dependent on DNS.

Windows Server and Active Directory add an extra layer of protection with Active
Directory integrated zones. The protection is provided to the entries by adding security
information to the record when the host adds the record, and therefore only the host can
modify or delete it. You can even prevent non-domain members from adding entries into
DNS with the use of Secure Updates.

Internal vs. External DNS

Name authorities can be public, such as the root servers and registrar server, or they can be an internal DNS zone file (database), in which all the clients are pointed to a particular DNS server for name resolution.

It is common to have DNS servers dedicated to resolution of hosts on the Internet and DNS servers dedicated to resolution of hosts on the interior of our network. The two servers must be managed separately; this is called a *split-brain DNS* model. We need to do this because the DNS we provide for internal clients will resolve to private IP addresses, such as www.wiley.com to 192.168.1.1. Public DNS will resolve to a public IP address, such as www.wiley.com to 208.215.179.146.

It is best practice to separate out the internal DNS servers from external DNS servers. We can always use a different namespace outside versus inside, such as wiley.com and wiley.local. However, if the same server is used for both internal and external DNS, a malicious user can try to query internal names from the DNS and gain internal information.

Third-Party/Cloud-Hosted DNS

It is common practice as described in the prior section to use separate DNS servers for internal and external queries. We do a good job as administrators of securing and operating internal DNS, but sometimes it is easier to outsource the external DNS.

When a public domain name (FQDN) is registered, it is common that the registrar will provide DNS for you. This solves the dilemma for the administrator of setting up an external DNS server. The registrar will often provide a simple web page to configure the DNS records for the FQDN.

If the number of records and maintenance of the external DNS is large, then we can always use IaaS. Many cloud providers, such as Amazon Web Servers (AWS), will provide cloud-based DNS. AWS offers a service called Route 53 that allows administrators to host DNS in the cloud. This service offers many features; one such feature allows a DNS record to be queried differently from a different region of the world via a route policy. Another unique feature allows for a DNS client to receive the lowest latency IP for servers hosted in the AWS cloud. Each provider will have unique features that average administrators would be hard pressed to support themselves.

Hierarchy

DNS is a distributed hierarchy; think of it as a directory of directories where you will eventually resolve the FQDN to a resource record (IP address). In Figure 1.82 we see this distributed hierarchy.

When FQDNs are resolved, they are resolved from right to left with a dot at the end; this signifies the root of all DNS resolution. The root DNS servers point to the registrars of com, net, and gov, and the registrars point to the owner's DNS server, which keeps a database of resource records. In Figure 1.82 we see an example of two resource records for www and ftp for wiley.com.

FIGURE 1.82   DNS hierarchy

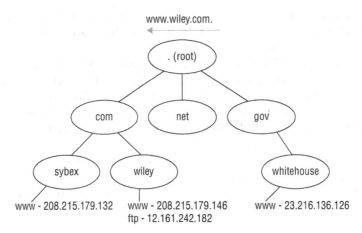

In the prior example, I explained the hierarchy of the DNS as it pertains to the Internet. Internal DNS environments also have a hierarchy. However, the internal domain is the starting zone record in lieu of the root domain. An example of this is wiley.local., which would be hosted as a zone on the DNS server that all clients are pointed to for resolution.

In the following I will cover the most common types of DNS server configurations. A DNS server's job is either to resolve DNS on behalf of the client or to host a DNS zone, which can be considered a database of records. A DNS server can do both jobs, resolving clients and hosting zone files, or they can be specific purposed.

Primary DNS Server

A primary DNS server's job is to host a domain's zone file. When the primary zone is hosted on the DNS server, the DNS server is considered the primary DNS server when referring to that particular zone. A zone must have at least one primary DNS server, which hosts the primary zone. This special primary zone is the only writable copy of the DNS zone file.

Secondary DNS Server

A secondary DNS server is not required, but it's a good idea to have one, since it is the backup copy of the zone file. The secondary zone file is updated through a zone transfer from the primary zone file. The server hosting the secondary zone is considered the secondary DNS server for that zone. A DNS server can both be a primary and secondary server, depending on which domain DNS zone file you are speaking about.

In Figure 1.83 we have two DNS servers hosting two different DNS zones. Server A is the primary DNS server for sybex.com and the secondary DNS server for wiley.com. Server B is the primary DNS server for wiley.com and the secondary DNS server for sybex.com. Server A and server B are both a primary and secondary DNS server, when speaking in the context of the zone file.

FIGURE 1.83 Primary and secondary DNS servers

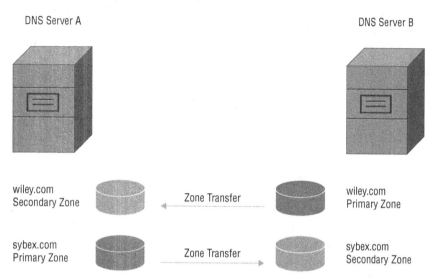

Forwarding/Caching DNS Server

A forwarding DNS server is a server that forwards requests for DNS to another server such as an Internet service provider (ISP) DNS server. The server saves bandwidth by caching the answers, so the server does not need to make another request to the ISP's DNS server for the same request. A forwarding/caching DNS server can also maintain a primary or secondary zone file.

Forward vs. Reverse Zone

In the prior section, I covered the various DNS server types. You learned that primary DNS servers host the editable copy of the DNS zone file and the secondary DNS server is a read-only copy. When we host a zone file on the DNS server, there are two different types of zone files: forward and reverse zones.

Understanding the differences between forward and reverse zone types is easier once we know what a reverse zone is used for. Reverse zone types are used for reverse IP address resolution. This is handy when we are troubleshooting and we want to know the host-name an IP address belongs to. We can use reverse DNS with a reverse zone type and PTR records to reverse the IP to an FQDN.

Reverse zone files are named in reverse of the IP address. Let's use an IP address of 192.168.1.3 as an example. When we look at the IP address, the least specific portion starts with 192 and the most specific is the end of 3. However, when we look at a DNS FQDN of www.example.com., the least specific is the root at the far right of the FQDN. The most specific portion is the www portion of the FQDN at the far left. Therefore, when hosting a reverse zone, we must reverse the IP address. In the example of 192.168.1.3, it would be reversed as shown here. The 3 is the PTR record that is mapped to the FQDN of www.example.com. The complete zone file with the SOA record is detailed here so that you can see a working reverse zone file. It should be noted that the semicolon is nothing more than a comment line. It allows you to create sections in a zone file for readability purposes.

```
; 1.168.192.IN-ADDR.ARPA. zone file example
@ 1D     IN   SOA ns1.example.com. hostmaster.example.com. (
                    2017071901 ; serial yyyymmddss
                    1H ; refresh
                    15 ; retry
                    1w ; expire
                    1h ; ttl
                    )

; PTR records
1        IN   PTR     ns1.example.com.
2        IN   PTR     ns2.example.com.
3        IN   PTR     www.example.com.
4        IN   PTR     sip.example.com.
```

Forward zone files are used for lookups by DNS clients for destination and informational purposes. So, basically all other queries other than reverse queries are forward queries. I've shared a complete zone file example from the individual examples covered earlier in this section.

```
; example.com. zone file example
@ 1D     IN   SOA ns1.example.com. hostmaster.example.com. (
                    2017071901 ; serial yyyymmddss
                    1H ; refresh
                    15 ; retry
                    1w ; expire
                    1h ; ttl
                    )
; name servers
@        IN   NS      192.168.1.1
@        IN   NS      192.168.1.2
; SPF Record
@        IN   TXT "v=spf1 mx a ptr ip4:208.215.179.0/24"
; mail servers
@        IN   MX 10   mail1.example.com.
@        IN   MX 20   mail2.example.com.
@        IN   MX 30   mail3.example.com.
; host records
```

```
sftp      IN    CNAME    www.example.com.
ftp       IN    CNAME    www.example.com.
ns1       IN    A        192.168.1.1
ns2       IN    A        192.168.1.2
www       IN    A        192.168.1.3
sip       IN    A        192.168.1.4
mail      IN    AAAA     2001:db8::1
www       IN    AAAA     2001:db8::2
terminal  IN    AAAA     2001:db8::3
; SRV records
_sip._tcp 86400 IN SRV 10 50 5060  sip.example.com.
```

DHCP Service

The purpose of the DHCP service is to assign an IPv4 address to clients dynamically as they join the network. Figure 1.84 shows the Windows Server 2016 DHCP server management console. This dialog box has not changed much since Windows NT 4.0, although new features have been added throughout the years, such as fault tolerance and load balancing. Microsoft server operating systems have supported DHCP since the NT product line was launched.

FIGURE 1.84   The Windows DHCP management console

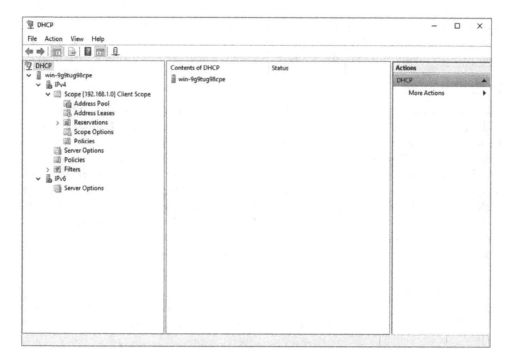

This is only one example of DHCP services. Linux and Unix operating systems also support DHCP services. They are just as common in networks as Microsoft DHCP servers. Router operating systems also support DHCP services. Most routers have a built-in process, and many default to serving out DHCP IP addresses. You more than likely have one in your home today.

MAC Reservations

Dynamic assignment is preferable in networks via DHCP, because we have centralized management of the IP addresses and associated options. We can change options such as DNS servers, and the DHCP clients will receive the changes next time they boot or renew their lease. However, sometimes we need a DHCP client to receive a specific IP address or the same address all the time. If we statically changed the IP address, we would be burdened with manually changing the DNS server if it ever changed.

Nearly all DHCP services allow for MAC address reservations. We can enter the MAC address of the DHCP client into the DHCP service and specify the desired IP address in the DHCP pool. In Microsoft DHCP services, we can right-click a current lease and convert it to a MAC reservation as well. When we add a reservation, the client will behave as if it is a DHCP client, but it will receive the same IP address every time.

Pools

DHCP pools are a logical grouping of consecutive IP addresses a DHCP server can serve out to clients. DHCP pools are called DHCP scopes in Microsoft terminology; both terms mean the same thing. You can have several DHCP scopes on the DHCP server. It is best practice to organize DHCP scopes for each subnet that is configured on the DHCP server. If possible, the DHCP scopes should be labeled with a description so that the purpose is clear to other administrators. Microsoft DHCP and most servers allow for a description.

IP Exclusions

As you learned in the previous section, IP pools, also called scopes, are consecutive IP addresses. An example of a consecutive range is 192.168.1.1 to 192.168.1.254. However, we need some reserved IP addresses for the gateway and possible servers in the range.

IP exclusions allow us to exclude a range of these IP addresses for service use. When we add an exclusion range, the DHCP server will exclude this range from the IP addresses served out. It is typical to reserve the lower portion of an address space for IP services. An exclusion example would be 192.168.1.1 to 192.168.1.10, using the earlier scope example.

It is also important to note that most DHCP servers will allow you to simply exclude ranges by entering only the range of IP addresses you want to serve to clients. An example would be to enter a range of 192.168.1.11 to 192.168.1.254, using the previous examples.

Scope Options

A DHCP server at a bare minimum will only serve out an IP address and subnet mask to clients. Although this is enough for a client to function on the local network, we need extra configuration called DHCP options. These options allow the client to leave the network, obtain name resolution, and obtain the DNS name they are a part of. You can even extend functionality of options via custom user-specific parameters.

The most important DHCP option is the router option. The router option configures a default gateway IP address on the client computer. This default gateway is how the client can leave the network through a router, so you can communicate with other subnets or the Internet. Another vital DHCP option is the DNS server IP address. Without DNS we would need to memorize IP addresses; going to www.sybex.com would look like http://208.215.179.132. So a DNS server IP address configured on the client is also a bare necessity. We can configure another DHCP option for DNS called the DNS suffix or DNS domain name. This option allows the DNS resolver in your computer to append the DNS suffix to a request. As an example, when you enter http://www in a web browsers and the client is configured with a DNS suffix of sybex.com, the DNS resolver will try to resolve the FQDN of www.sybex.com. We can configure many other DHCP options for the client, but the router, DNS server, and DNS suffix options are the most important. I will cover DNS in more detail in this chapter.

The Internet Assigned Numbers Authority (IANA) provides a complete list of DHCP options for reference at https://www.iana.org/assignments/ bootp-dhcp-parameters/bootp-dhcp-parameters.xhtml. The client must understand how to use the various options.

Lease Time/TTL

A DHCP lease is a period of time the IP address given out by the DHCP server is good for. Both the server and the client keep track of the lease time. The server does not keep track if the IP address is in use; it only knows that the lease has been granted for a time period. When the time period has expired or the lease is manually deleted, the IP address can be served to another computer. A DHCP lease should never be manually deleted from the server, unless you know it is no longer in use by the client.

After the initial DHCP DORA process, the server does not communicate with the client in reference to the DHCP lease period. It is the responsibility of the client to renew its lease. I will use the default lease cycle for a Windows DHCP server of 8 days for the following explanation of the DHCP lease life cycle in Figure 1.85. When the lease is granted to the client, the lease timer is started. At 50 percent of the lease (the fourth day), the client is responsible for renewing its lease with the DHCP server via a DHCP Request packet. If successful, the lease time is restarted for 8 days. If the DHCP server does not acknowledge the lease, the client will wait until 87.5 percent of the lease cycle (the seventh day), where it will send a DHCP Request to any server in hopes of "rebinding" the lease to another server. If a DHCP does not acknowledge the rebind request, at 100 percent (the eighth day) of the lease, the client must release the IP address. The client will continue with the DHCP DORA process to obtain another IP address from any responding server.

FIGURE 1.85   The DHCP client lease life cycle

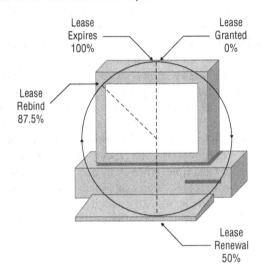

DHCP Relay/IP Helper

As I discussed earlier in this section, the DHCP DORA process is dependent on broadcasts for a client to obtain a DHCP assigned address. As you learned in the section "Name of Section," routers stop broadcasts. This presents a problem when we want to centrally manage DHCP from one point for all routed subnets. Luckily there is a fix for this problem: we can use an IP helper statement on a router or a DHCP relay agent.

We configure an IP helper on a router interface to intercept broadcasts for DHCP and forward them directly to the configured DHCP server IP address. In Figure 1.86 we see a network that is segmented with a router. The router will listen for DHCP Discover packets and forward them directly through unicast to the DHCP server. The DHCP server will send a unicast DHCP Offer packet back to the router, where the router will forward it back to the client. This process continues until the DORA process is complete.

A DHCP relay agent is a configured service on a server that intercepts broadcasts for DHCP and forwards them directly to the configured DHCP server IP address. In Figure 1.87 we see a network configured like the one in Figure 1.86. The DHCP relay agent operates identically to an IP helper on a router. The difference is that it is a service on a server. If this was a branch office and the router didn't support IP helper configuration, a local file or print server could be configured as a DHCP relay agent.

FIGURE 1.86   An example of a network router configured with an IP helper

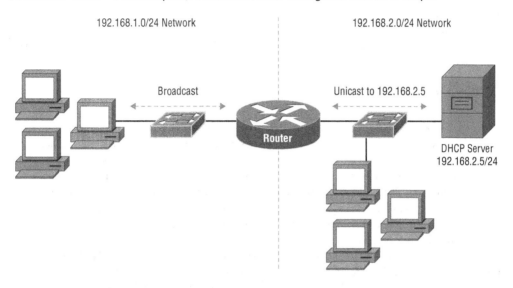

FIGURE 1.87   An example of a DHCP relay agent configured on a server

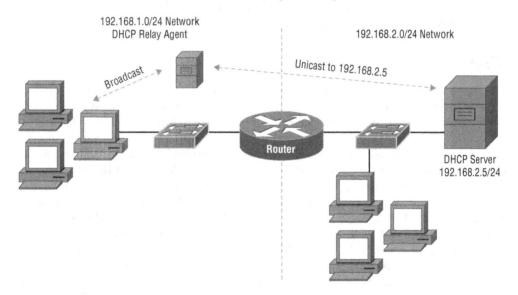

You may be wondering how the DHCP server knows which scope to serve the remote subnet when an IP helper or DHCP relay agent is used. The answer is the GIADDR (Gateway Interface Address) field of the DHCP packet is used when an IP helper or DHCP

relay agent is present. The GIADDR field is filled with the IP address of either the IP helper interface or the DHCP relay agent IP address in which the broadcast was heard on. It is the router or DHCP relay agent's responsibility to complete the GIADDR field. When the DHCP server receives the unicast packet from the DHCP relay agent, the scope to be served from is matched against the GIADDR IP address and the proper subnet scope is served.

NTP

Network Time Protocol (NTP) is a network protocol that is optimized for synchronizing clocks between hosts over the Internet. NTP uses a hierarchy of precision clocks called stratums.

A stratum 0 is the highest precision clock; it is generally an atomic cesium or rubidium clock. A stratum 1 is a host system that derives its clock from a stratum 0. A stratum 2 is a host system that derives its clock from a stratum 1 and so on. The highest stratum (lowest precision) is a stratum 15; a stratum 16 means that the host system's clock is not synchronized.

Because there is a round-trip delay in requesting time over the Internet, NTP uses an algorithm for calculating the precise time accounting for this delay. With the expansive growth of cloud computing, NTP is becoming an extremely important protocol for synchronization of time among computer systems. When virtual machines (VMs) run on a hypervisor, the clocks in the VMs are emulated and drift quickly over time. NTP prevents these emulated clocks from large time skews that could affect client access.

IPAM

IP Address Management (IPAM) is another essential service used for the planning, tracking, and management of IP address space. Internet Service Providers has used commercial IPAM applications for years because of the scarcity of IPv4 addresses. With the release of Microsoft Server 2012, Microsoft included an IPAM service as part of the operating system, and it has become a vital service for internal networks as well. IPAM allows us to track individual IP addresses, ranges of IP addresses and CIDR blocks of IP addresses.

Most internal and external IPAM services should have a direct integration to DNS and DHCP. This allows for the control of DHCP directly from IPAM and also enables monitor and tracking with DNS integration. Microsoft's implementation allows for direct integration of both DHCP and DNS so that both services can be controlled from IPAM directly. Microsoft also has several other unique features like host and user tracking by IP address.

IPAM can be used in a variety of ways; the most common is that we can use IPAM to quickly look at the available IP address space for expansion of the network. This allows us to plan network resources for future expansion as well. We can then track the IP address throughout its life cycle. This tracking is done because each IP address has firewall rules and certain DNS entries that should be removed after the IP address/application server has been decommissioned. This prevents future application services from having exploitable exposure that they should not normally have.

Exam Essentials

Understand what the various DNS resource records are and how they are used.   The A record or host record is used for FQDN-to–IP address resolution. The AAAA record (quad A) is used for FQDN-to–IPv6 address resolution. TXT records are used for various purposes, where text should be returned when a record is queried. SRV records, called service locator records, are used for host lookup of a service on the network, such as LDAP or SIP servers. MX records, called mail exchanger records, are used for lookup of a destination mail server. CNAME, or canonical name records, allow for a FQDN to be mapped to another FQDN that has an A record for resolution. NS records or name server records are used by the DNS servers to define who can have a copy of the DNS zone file. SOA records, or start of authority records, are used to define the parameters of a zone file, such as the primary DNS server, refresh intervals, and TTL. PTR records, or pointer records, are used solely for reverse DNS queries. The PTR record allows for IP address–to-FQDN lookups. Dynamic DNS is the process in which a host will register its A record and PTR record, with the forward zone and reverse zone, respectively.

Understand the differences and considerations between external DNS and internal DNS. External DNS is used for resolution of public IP addresses for services published externally on the Internet. Internal DNS is used for resolution of private IP addresses for services published internally on the network.

Understand how third-party and cloud provided DNS is commonly used.   Third-party DNS servers are often used when you register a domain name with a registrar. The registrar often offers this service as part of the registration of the domain name.

Understand the hierarchy of DNS systems.   DNS is a decentralized distributed database of databases, where all resolution starts at the root or far right of an FQDN. Primary DNS servers own the editable copy of the DNS zone file. Secondary DNS servers contain the copy of a particular DNS zone file, but the copy is read-only. Forwarding DNS servers may not contain any zone files, but they allow DNS requests to be forwarded to another DNS server such as an ISP; these servers often cache the queries as well.

Understand the difference between forward and reverse zone lookups.   Reverse zone lookups allow for IP address to FQDN resolution using PTR records. Forward zone lookups allow for all other name resolution, such as FQDN-to–IP address lookups, TXT lookups, and so on. You should review the structure of a zone file for both forward and reverse zones.

Understand the various components of DHCP.   DHCP MAC reservations allow for a host to be treated like a DHCP client, yet always retain the same IP address. The DHCP pool is the range of servable IP addresses that can be allocated via DHCP. IP address exclusions allow us to exclude a range from the DHCP pool for statically assigned hosts such as servers. Scope options are additional parameters that can be supplied along with the IP address and subnet mask from DHCP pools.

Understand the DHCP lease process. The lease time of the IP address is always the client's responsibility to renew. DHCP clients renew the lease at 50 percent of the lease cycle. If the original server does not respond, then at 7/8ths of the lease cycle the client will send DHCP discover packets to all listening servers in hopes of a new lease. If this does not occur, then at the end of the lease cycle the client must release the IP address.

Understand how an IP helper and DHCP relays work. An IP helper is a process on a router interface. The IP helper intercepts DHCP broadcast messages and sends them via unicast to a defined remote DHCP server. A DHCP relay performs the same service as a IP helper and is often a server on the immediate network that is configured to intercept DHCP broadcasts and send them as unicast to the remote DHCP server.

Understand how NTP is used and how it operates. Network Time Protocol (NTP) is used to synchronize time between hosts on the Internet. NTP uses a series of stratum levels; lower is more precise and higher is less precise.

Understand how IPAM is used in networks. IP address management (IPAM) is used for the planning, tracking, and management of IP addresses over their life cycle in the network. IPAM often allows for integration between DHCP and DNS so that these systems can be managed directly from IPAM. IPAM lets us have one spot where all IP address resources reside and can be controlled.

Review Questions

1. You need to provide text console–based access to a server for administration. Which protocol will provide encrypted text console based access for the server?

    A. Telnet

    B. RDP

    C. SSH

    D. SFTP

2. Which protocol is built into Microsoft servers for remote access purposes?

    A. SNMP

    B. LDAP

    C. Telnet

    D. RDP

3. Which transport layer protocol provides assured delivery and retransmission of segments lost in transmission?

    A. ICMP

    B. UDP

    C. IP

    D. TCP

4. You cannot reach a particular destination network and believe that one of the connecting networks are down. Which utility will allow you to examine the path packets are taking?

    A. ping

    B. tracert

    C. NDP

    D. ICMP

5. Which layer of the OSI does encryption and decryption occur on?

    A. Application

    B. Presentation

    C. Session

    D. Transport

6. Several of your users are complaining that the network slows down several times a day. You recently added a large number of clients to the immediate network. What should be done to reduce the impact of the additional hosts?

    A. Create a single broadcast domain.

    B. Create a single collision domain.

    C. Create several broadcast domains.

    D. Assign static IP addresses to all computers.

7. What is the normal maximum transmission unit (MTU) size for an Ethernet network?

   A. 1500 bytes

   B. 1548 bytes

   C. 9000 bytes

   D. 1648 bytes

8. You had captured network traffic with a network capture utility. Several of the MAC addresses are FF:FF:FF:FF:FF:FF. What could these packets be?

   A. ICMP traffic

   B. Broadcast traffic

   C. Multicast traffic

   D. IGMP traffic

9. You need to trunk two switches from two different vendors together. Which trunking protocol should you use?

   A. ISL

   B. 802.1D

   C. 802.1Q

   D. 802.1w

10. When calculating Spanning Tree Protocol (STP), which switch will always become the root bridge?

   A. The switch with the highest priority

   B. The switch with the highest MAC address

   C. The switch with the lowest MAC address

   D. The switch with the lowest priority

11. You have recently deployed several POE security cameras on a switch. You had chosen the switch because it met the power requirements of the cameras. However, several ports will not power up and you have now discovered that you are drawing too much power. Which option will quickly rectify the problem?

   A. Purchase cameras with a lower power requirement.

   B. Purchase a new switch that can provide more power.

   C. Turn on POE+ support on the switch.

   D. Turn on LLDP on the switch.

12. Which routing type is best implemented in stub networks?

   A. Default routing

   B. RIP routing

   C. Static routing

   D. Dynamic routing

13. You are obtaining another Internet provider for your company's connectivity to the Internet. You want to make sure that if there is a failure, the routing protocol will advertise your company's IP addresses and fail over. Which routing protocol should you use?

    A. RIPv2

    B. EIGRP

    C. OSPF

    D. BGP

14. Which IPv6 address is not a valid address?

    A. 2001:db8:f::0000:1e2:2c0:2

    B. 2001:0db8:0:0:0:8d8:242:1

    C. 2001:0db8::10e:0:12

    D. 2001:0db8:45::10a::12

15. Which of these IPv6 addresses is a multicast address?

    A. fe80:4e56:e423:0001:0045:a0aa:eb7c:9850

    B. fc05:b44e:ce5d:1e67:73e5:7a3e:a86c:8a35

    C. ff03:0340:508e:e0ee:e2be:3cec:abd8:e24b

    D. 2004:ef5c:ecec:3a5c:3e0c:0bce:234c:ffe2

16. Which quality of service (QoS) method is used at layer 2 of the OSI?

    A. 802.1Q

    B. ToS

    C. Diffserv

    D. CoS

17. You have two different routers in your network, each by a different vendor. You need to provide high availability for the default gateway in your networks. What should you implement to provide high availability in the event of a router going down for maintenance?

    A. RSTP

    B. VRRP

    C. HSRP

    D. VLSM

18. Which of the following IP and CIDR mask combinations is not valid for IP addressing of a host computer?

    A. 192.168.20.37/28

    B. 208.44.26.128/25

    C. 187.54.22.72/29

    D. 213.45.6.255/22

19. You have been called to troubleshoot a computer that cannot reach the server. You perform an `ipconfig /all` on the computer and see the following information. What is the problem?

```
Ethernet adapter Local Area Connection:

Connection-specific DNS Suffix  . :
Description . . . . . . . . . . . : Intel(R) PRO/1000 MT Network Connection
Physical Address. . . . . . . . . : 00-0C-29-39-6C-E3
DHCP Enabled. . . . . . . . . . . : Yes
Autoconfiguration Enabled . . . . : Yes
Link-local IPv6 Address . . . . . : fe80::bc82:6ccb:a1e1:32f6%11(Preferred)
Autoconfiguration IPv4 Address. . : 169.254.50.246(Preferred)
Subnet Mask . . . . . . . . . . . : 255.255.0.0
Default Gateway . . . . . . . . . :
DHCPv6 IAID . . . . . . . . . . . : 234884137
DHCPv6 Client DUID. . . . . . . . : 00-01-00-01-15-91-63-B7-00-0C-29-39-6C-E3

DNS Servers . . . . . . . . . . . : fec0:0:0:ffff::1%1
fec0:0:0:ffff::2%1
fec0:0:0:ffff::3%1
NetBIOS over Tcpip. . . . . . . . : Enabled
```

   A. Nothing; the computer is using IPv6 addressing.

   B. The IP address is not in the same subnet as the server.

   C. The DNS servers are IPv6 and you are configured for IPv4.

   D. The DHCP server is unavailable or not functioning.

20. Which Internet of Things (IoT) wireless connectivity operates on the 900 MHz ISM band?

   A. ANT+

   B. Z-wave

   C. Bluetooth

   D. NFC

21. Which wireless standard first introduced channel bonding?

   A. 802.11n

   B. 802.11ac

   C. 802.11g

   D. 802.11a

22. Which cellular standard was developed by the European Telecommunications Standards Institute (ETSI)?

  A. TDMA

  B. CDMA

  C. GSM

  D. LTE/4G

23. Which three wireless channels on 2.4 GHz wireless are nonoverlapping?

  A. 1, 3, and 9

  B. 1, 9, and 11

  C. 1, 6, and 11

  D. 1, 6, and 12

24. Hosting a disaster recovery (DR) site on Microsoft Azure is an example of which National Institute of Standards and Technology (NIST) type of cloud service?

  A. IaaS

  B. DRaaS

  C. PaaS

  D. SaaS

25. You need to make sure that a printer is configured with the same IP address every time it is turned on. However, the printer is too troublesome to configure a static IP address. What can be done to achieve the goal?

  A. Configure an A record for the printer in DNS.

  B. Configure a DHCP exclusion for the printer.

  C. Configure a DHCP reservation for the printer.

  D. Configure a PTR record for the printer in DNS.

Chapter

2

Domain 2.0: Infrastructure

THE FOLLOWING COMPTIA NETWORK+ OBJECTIVES ARE COVERED IN THIS CHAPTER:

✓ **2.1 Given a scenario, deploy the appropriate cabling solution.**

- Media types
  - Copper
    - UTP
    - STP
    - Coaxial
  - Fiber
    - Single-mode
    - Multimode
- Plenum vs. PVC
- Connector types
  - Copper
    - RJ-45
    - RJ-11
    - BNC
    - DB-9
    - DB-25
    - F-type
  - Fiber
    - LC
    - ST

- SC
  - APC
  - UPC
  - MTRJ
- Transceivers
  - SFP
  - GBIC
  - SFP+
  - QSFP
  - Characteristics of fiber transceivers
    - Bidirectional
    - Duplex
- Termination points
  - 66 block
  - 110 block
  - Patch panel
  - Fiber distribution panel
- Copper cable standards
  - Cat 3
  - Cat 5
  - Cat 5e
  - Cat 6
  - Cat 6a
  - Cat 7
  - RG-6
  - RG-59
- Copper termination standards
  - TIA/EIA 568A
  - TIA/EIA 568B
  - Crossover
  - Straight-through

- Ethernet deployment standards
    - 100BaseT
    - 1000BaseT
    - 1000BaseLX
    - 1000BaseSX
    - 10GBaseT

✓ **2.2   Given a scenario, determine the appropriate placement of networking devices on a network and install/configure them.**

- Firewall
- Router
- Switch
- Hub
- Bridge
- Modems
- Wireless access point
- Media converter
- Wireless range extender
- VoIP endpoint

✓ **2.3   Explain the purposes and use cases for advanced networking devices.**

- Multilayer switch
- Wireless controller
- Load balancer
- IDS/IPS
- Proxy server
- VPN concentrator
- AAA/RADIUS server
- UTM appliance
- NGFW/Layer 7 firewall
- VoIP PBX

- VoIP gateway
- Content filter

✓ **2.4 Explain the purposes of virtualization and network storage technologies.**

- Virtual networking components
  - Virtual switch
  - Virtual firewall
  - Virtual NIC
  - Virtual router
  - Hypervisor
- Network storage types
  - NAS
  - SAN
- Connection type
  - FCoE
  - Fibre Channel
  - iSCSI
  - InfiniBand
- Jumbo frame

✓ **2.5 Compare and contrast WAN technologies.**

- Service type
  - ISDN
  - T1/T3
  - E1/E3
  - OC-3 – OC-192
  - DSL
  - Metropolitan Ethernet
  - Cable broadband
  - Dial-up
  - PRI

- Transmission mediums
  - Satellite
  - Copper
  - Fiber
  - Wireless
- Characteristics of service
  - MPLS
  - ATM
  - Frame relay
  - PPPoE
  - PPP
  - DMVPN
  - SIP trunk
- Termination
  - Demarcation point
  - CSU/DSU
  - Smart jack

The infrastructure of a city consists of physical structures, facilities, and roads connecting the city. These components all support the city's operation. A network is similar; it requires physical components such as routers, switches, and servers. It also requires the connections inside the network and leading outside the network to the Internet and other networks. This chapter will cover a wide array of networking infrastructure to support your network.

For more detailed information on Domain 2's topics, please see *CompTIA Network+ Study Guide,* 4th ed. (978-1-119-43225-8) or *CompTIA Network+ Deluxe Study Guide,* 4th ed. (978-1-119-43227-2), both published by Sybex.

2.1 Given a scenario, deploy the appropriate cabling solution.

In this section, I will cover the common cabling, connectors, termination points, and wiring specifications involved in connecting a network. Over your career as a network professional, you will need to deploy the proper cabling for many network connectivity scenarios. At the end of this section, you should be able to describe the practical application of the cabling, connectors, termination points, and specifications for a network design.

Media types

When wiring a network, you will have two main media types: copper cabling and fiber-optic cabling. The decision between the two is based on a number of factors that I will detail in the following section. After the selection of the appropriate cable type for the network design, there are several different specifications of these cables that we will cover later in the section.

Copper

As a network professional, you will be responsible for identifying cabling, diagnosing cabling problems, and ordering the proper cabling for the installation required. Coaxial cable is not used for networking anymore, but you should be able to identify and understand its practical application.

UTP

Unshielded twisted-pair (UTP) is the most common cabling for Ethernet networks today, and it is the least expensive option for cabling a network. It is *unshielded* from electromagnetic interference (EMI), so the placement of cables in a network should avoid EMI sources. UTP should always be cabled away from electrical lines and non-network cabling. Because of the lack of shielding, electrical lines can induce erroneous electrical signals if the cables are run in parallel with electrical lines. UTP cable has a PVC or Teflon cable jacket, as shown in Figure 2.1; inside are four pairs of wires (eight conductors). Each of the four pairs have a specific number of twists per inch. I will cover the category specification later in this section that defines speed in relation to the twists and how the pairs are separated.

FIGURE 2.1   A common UTP cable

STP

Shielded twisted-pair (STP) is commonly used in industrial settings, where *electromagnetic interference (EMI)* can induce erroneous data into the cable. STP cables should be used when running network cables around or near large motors, welding equipment, HVAC equipment, high-voltage lighting, and so on. There are several different types of STP cable depending on the severity of EMI. The most common STP cable consists of a PVC or Teflon jacket, as well as a metal weaved shielding that protects the four pairs of twisted wires, as shown in Figure 2.2. Depending on the application, the individual pairs may have foil shielding as well. The cabling is significantly more expensive in price than UTP and more difficult to install because of the Ethernet jack shielding and RJ-45 shielding required.

FIGURE 2.2   A common STP cable

When installing cable in an industrial setting such as a factory where cabling is exposed to vibrations, chemicals, temperature, and EMI, the MICE (Mechanical, Ingress, Climatic, Chemical, and Electromagnetic) classification should be followed. The standard is defined in an ISO/IEC (International Organization for Standardization/International Electrotechnical Commission) publication. It is best to engage an engineer to define the type of cabling to use when in doubt for an industrial setting, because safety can be compromised.

Coaxial

Coaxial cable is no longer used in networks today for Ethernet communications on the local area network (LAN). Coaxial cable, shown in Figure 2.3, is still used for security cameras and broadband cable networks where you may see this cabling. In the datacenter, you can use a connectivity method between servers and switching equipment called Twinax. A *Twinax* cable is a fixed-size coaxial cable with transceivers on each end. It usually comes in lengths of 1 meter, 5 meters, and 10 meters.

FIGURE 2.3   Coax cable elements

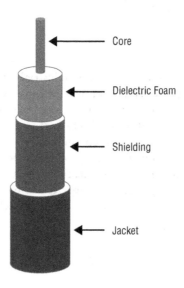

Core

Dielectric Foam

Shielding

Jacket

Stranded vs. Solid Core

Stranded network cabling is used for patch cables such as wiring from the network jack to the computer or wiring from the patch panel to the network switch. Stranded cabling is flexible and used for wiring that requires being moved around often. Stranded cabling should never be used for installs that require wire to be run in a riser, since stranded cabling lacks a strength member. The proper RJ-45 end should be used with stranded network cabling, and the teeth that crimp into the wire should be perfectly straight. Stranded wire also cannot be punched down to a punch panel.

Solid core network cabling is used for permanent installation such as wall wiring from the patch panel to the network jack. It is not flexible like stranded network cabling. The solid core allows for the wire to be punched down to a patch panel or network jack. Solid core wire also can be identified by its strength member inside the jack. The strength member allows for cabling to be run in a riser. The strength member prevents the copper from weighing down the cable when run vertically and stretching the copper conductions. The proper RJ-45 end should be used with solid core, and the teeth that crimp into the wire should be offset on an angle opposing each other. This is done to clench the wire between the angle of the offset inside the RJ-45 end. Both solid and stranded core cables are shown for comparison in Figure 2.4.

FIGURE 2.4 Cross-section of solid core vs. stranded core cables

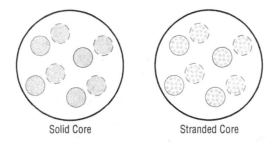

Solid Core   Stranded Core

Fiber

Fiber-optic cable (fiber), shown in Figure 2.5, is often used to transmit high data rates over longer distances than conventional copper cable. It is also used in applications where the EMI is too high for copper cable, such as running cable in the proximity of an electric blast furnace. Fiber-optic cable can also be used for extremely confidential networks, because unless you are spliced in directly, it emits no emissions of RF to eavesdrop on. In the following section, I will discuss the different modes and sizes of fiber, as well as their advantages and disadvantages.

FIGURE 2.5 A typical fiber-optic cable

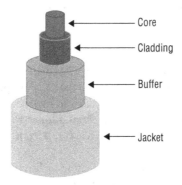

Core

Cladding

Buffer

Jacket

Single-Mode

Single-mode fiber-optic cable (SMF) is used for high-speed and long-distance communications. SMF offers less dispersion of light traveling down the glass fiber, so it is considered a single mode of light when it reaches the destination. It achieves this by using an extremely small core of 8 to 10 microns and precision lasers called transceivers. Normally, SMF is advertised as 9-micron fiber. It should be used in any application that requires 10 Gbps or higher data rates and can span up to 120 kilometers (approximately 75 miles) before it needs to be repeated. It is commonly used in long-distance communications and internal building wiring. It should be used in any new installations to future-proof bandwidth requirements. The standard color of SMF patch cables is yellow, but it is always best to check the cable's numbering. Arguably, it is easier to terminate than other types of fiber cable—since the diameter is so small, a smaller area needs to be polished.

Multimode

Multimode fiber-optic cable (MMF) is used for short to medium distances. MMF disperses light into numerous paths inside the core, which is why it is called multimode. MMF has a maximum speed of 10 Gbps at very short distances and a maximum distance of 3000 feet. It is mainly used for internal building connectivity. MMF is available in both glass core and plastic core, but speed is limited with plastic core. The core size of MMF is 50 microns, it is usually used for Fibre Channel and network connectivity, and the patch cable color is often aqua. MMF is also available in a 62.5-micron core size, and the patch cable color is often orange. See Table 2.1 for details.

TABLE 2.1   Fiber-optic cable specifications

Core size	Fiber type	Max distance	Max speed	Patch cable color
9 microns	SMF	75 miles	Over 400 Gbps	Yellow
50 microns	MMF	3000 feet	10 Gbps	Aqua
62.5 microns	MMF	2000 feet	10 Gbps (under 26 meters)	Orange

PVC vs. Plenum

Polyvinyl chloride (PVC) cable is made with a PVC plastic–jacketed cable and is often used for patch cable, since these are short cables that are in open office spaces. When PVC cabling catches fire, it emits a toxic black smoke and hydrochloric acid that irritates the lungs and eyes. If this concerns you, be aware that a lot of the material in office spaces today are made of PVC because it is inexpensive. It is acceptable for use as patch cables in open air environments.

Plenum cable is made with Teflon-jacketed cable or fire retardant–jacketed cable. It does not emit toxic vapors when burned or heated, and it is more expensive than PVC cables. Plenum cabling should be installed in any circulated airspace such as HVAC duct-ing and returns. It is specified in the National Electric Code (NEC) that is published by the National Fire Protection Association (NFPA). A plenum is defined as any airspace that provides ventilation or air-conditioning. Since this is a loose definition, when in doubt use plenum cabling. You will not want to be responsible for failing a code inspection, because a code inspector defines a cabling passage as an airspace.

Connector types

After the cabling is installed in the network, you will have the task of adding connectors to the cable ends. This is commonly called terminating the ends of the cable. There are two main connector types: copper and fiber-optic. In the following section, I will discuss the advantages of each different connector for the respective connector types.

Copper connectors

Copper connectors are not made out of copper, as their name suggests. They are usually made of a harder metal and copperplated. Copper is soft and can wear over time from connecting and disconnecting the connectors. These connectors allow us to easily con-nect wires between two devices. Without connectors we would be using a screwdriver and screwing down wires to screw terminals, like back in the mainframe days. Connectors serve a second useful purpose: providing an easy diagnostic point for when connectivity is the suspected problem.

RJ-45

The RJ-45 is a connector used for connecting network equipment, such as network switches, routers, and network interface cards (NICs). Today it is a worldwide standard for wired Ethernet connectivity. If you have a wired connection to your computer from a network, it is most likely an RJ-45 connector. The RJ-45 connector has four pairs (eight wires) attached to eight pins, as shown in Figure 2.6. I will cover the TIA/EIA wiring standard for these connectors later in this chapter.

FIGURE 2.6   An RJ-45 connector

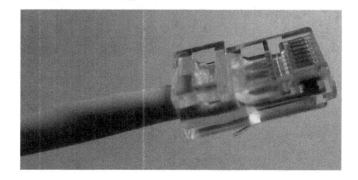

RJ-11

The RJ-11 is a connector used for telephone connection. It is commonly used in the United States and most other countries. If you have a land line telephone, then it is connected to the phone jack with an RJ-11 patch cord. The RJ stands for (Registered Jack) and is designated a *Universal Service Ordering Code (USOC)* of 11. This standard was adopted by Bell Systems from the FCC for customer compliance in connecting phone equipment. The RJ-11 connector has two pairs (four wires) attached to the four pins, as shown in Figure 2.7. There is a primary pair that is green and red, and a secondary pair that is yellow and black. This allows you up to two phone lines on one cable. You will encounter this wiring in networks only if you are making a connection to a fax machine, modem, or DSL modem.

FIGURE 2.7   An RJ-11 connector

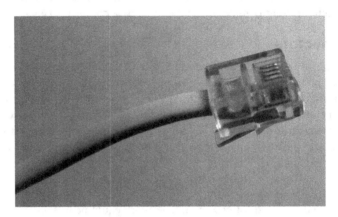

BNC connector

The BNC in *BNC connector* stands for Bayonet Neill-Concelman or British Naval Connector, depending on who you ask. BNC connectors, shown in Figure 2.8, were used in networking for 10Base2 LAN coaxial networks. These connectors are now considered legacy in terms of LAN networking. They are still used for T3 (DS-3) *wide area network (WAN)* connections, radio equipment, and security camera systems that use coax cameras. The connector operates with a slight spring tension when inserted; then you twist it slightly to lock it into place.

FIGURE 2.8   A BNC connector

DB-9

The DB-9 connector is commonly used for RS-232 serial connections. It is part of the family of D-sub connectors that are in the shape of a D, so they can be plugged in only one way. The DB-9, shown in Figure 2.9, has nine wires attached to the connector. They are found on networking equipment for configuration purposes and older computers. In the dialup days, they were used for connecting the computer to a dialup modem. These connectors are gradually being replaced with more modern connectors such as USB. Computers today are no longer manufactured with serial ports; if a DB-9 is required, you must purchase a USB-to–DB-9 (serial) adapter.

FIGURE 2.9   A DB-9 (RS-232) connector

DB-25

The DB-25 connector, shown in Figure 2.10, is also commonly used for RS-232 serial connections. It is part of the family of D-sub connectors. They were commonly used on the modem side of a connection between a computer and modem. They have also been used for printer, scanner, and even SCSI connections in the past. These connectors have been replaced with modern connectors such as USB and today are considered legacy connections. If you need to interface with a DB-25 connector, you must purchase a DB-9–to–DB-25 cable. These conversion cables were very popular and were mainly used for modem connectivity back in the day.

FIGURE 2.10   A DB-25 connector

F-connector

The F-connector is a coaxial connector used with RG-6 or RG-59 cabling, as shown in Figure 2.11. You will commonly see this connector used for cable TV and cable modem connections. Coaxial cabling with F-connectors are also used for *Media over Coax Alliance (MoCA)* networking. This type of networking is typically used by providers to allow networking between set-top boxes (STBs) inside your house or business. It can even be used to transmit data of up to 2.5 Gbps. When using an F-connector, you insert the exposed coaxial core into a female F-connector and then thread it on until it is tight.

FIGURE 2.11 An F-connector

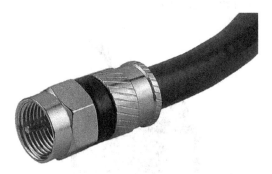

Fiber connectors

There are several different fiber connectors to use in a fiber-optic installation. In this section I will cover the most common fiber connectors used in networks today. Each fiber connector has a benefit or purpose in a fiber-optic installation. It is important to know the visual differences between the fiber connectors and their respective names.

LC

The local connector (LC) resembles an RJ-style connector; it has a spring-loaded detent similar to the RJ connector that allows it to be held in place. The LC connector has become a popular cable connector because of its size; this allows greater density of ports on a switch. The connector is commonly found on MMF and SMF optic cables. The cable cannot be disassembled like the SC connector (see Figure 2.12), so transmit and receive fiber lines cannot be swapped side to side.

FIGURE 2.12 An LC connector

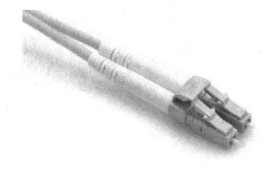

ST

The straight tip (ST) connector, shown in Figure 2.13, was originally designed by AT&T for fiber-optic cables. It is commonly used with single-mode fiber, discussed earlier in this section. The connector is one of the most popular connectors to date with fiber optics for WAN connectivity on SMF. The cable connector can be found in both SMF and MMF cable installations. The cable operates similar to a BNC connector; it is a bayonet-style mechanism that you twist and lock into position. The benefit to this cable is that it will not come loose over time because of the positive locking mechanism.

FIGURE 2.13 An ST connector

SC

The standard connector (SC) connector is a square connector with a floating ferrule that contains the fiber-optic cable, as shown in Figure 2.14. The cable comes with a plastic clip that holds the transmit and receive cables secure for insertion. These clips generally allow you to disassemble the cable ends so transmit and receive can be swapped. The SC connector is often referred to by installers as "Square Charlie," and it's the way I've remembered the shape throughout the years. It can be found in SMF and MMF installations, but it is most popular with MMF installations. The SC connector is larger than most modern connectors, so it is starting to be replaced in new installations. The cable operates with a push-on/pull-off mating mechanism.

FIGURE 2.14 An SC connector

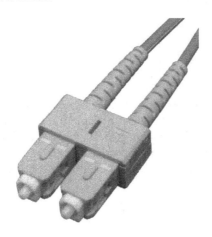

APC vs. UPC

The angled physical contact (APC) and ultra-physical contact (UPC) describe the polished finish on SC connectors. Fiber-optic cable is susceptible to insertion loss—the loss of signal due to the gap between the adjoining optics. Fiber is also susceptible to reflection loss—the loss of signal due to reflection back at the source. Both APC and UPC try to minimize insertion loss with a tight physical contact (PC). UPC cable ends have a dome to the polish to focus light into the center of the core. APC cable ends have an 8-degree angle to combat reflection loss, since any light reflected back from the cable will be at an 8-degree angle. UPC cable ends are blue, and APC cable ends are green. If APC or UPC is used in your network in lieu of the standard PC fiber-optic polished finish, the proper cable ends must be used or additional loss can occur. Most network patch cables will have a UPC finish on them, depicted by the blue cable ends. If the cable end is white, it should be assumed to have a standard PC finish.

MTRJ

The mechanical transfer registered jack (MTRJ), shown in Figure 2.15, is another RJ-style connector that closely resembles an RJ-45 connector. It too contains a transmit-and-receive pair of fiber cables. The RJ-45 style detent locks it into place similar to an Ethernet connector. The connector is also gaining popularity with networking equipment because of its size; it allows greater density of ports on a switch. The connector is commonly found on multimode and single-mode fiber-optic cables. The cable cannot be disassembled like other cables to swap the transmit-and-receive pairs.

FIGURE 2.15 An MTRJ connector

Transceivers

The job of the *fiber-optic transceiver* is to convert between the internal electrical signaling of the network equipment and light. The job of a copper transceiver is to convert between the Ethernet and the internal electrical signaling of the network equipment. Most network cards have a built-in transceiver, but modular network cards and modular networking equipment allow for transceivers to be inserted. The equipment usually has a top speed that cannot be exceeded, but slower transceivers can be inserted to lower monetary costs and design requirements. Transceivers can be used for a wide range of applications such as Fibre Channel, Ethernet, and SONET. Another important factor is distance versus speed versus compatibility of the transceiver. All transceivers require a specific media type for a specific distance.

SFP

The small form-factor pluggable (SFP) transceiver is a hot-swappable module used for both fiber-optic and copper media (see Figure 2.16). Its small design allows for a high density of ports on networking equipment such as network switching. SFPs can be found in both MMF and SMF installations, and they can support up to 1 Gbps of network connectivity. Depending on the SFP chosen for the installation, the speed and distance will vary, according to the vendor's specifications for each model.

FIGURE 2.16 A typical SFP transceiver

GBIC

The Gigabit Interface Converter (GBIC), shown in Figure 2.17, is an older style transceiver used for Gigabit Ethernet and Fibre Channel connectivity. It is a hot-swappable module just like the SFP and can achieve a top speed of 1 Gbps. Because of its size and speed, it has been widely replaced with SFP and SFP+ standards.

FIGURE 2.17 A typical GBIC transceiver

SFP+

The small form-factor pluggable+ (SFP+) transceiver is also a hot-swappable module used for both fiber-optic and copper media. It looks identical to the SFP and is differentiated only by its part number. However, the SFP+ can support speeds of 10 Gbps or higher (up to 400 Gbps). The SFP+ also has the added benefit of providing controller data to the equipment, such as signal loss and TX/RX power. The SFP+ is slowly replacing the SFP because of speed and functionality. Distances will also vary, just like with the SFP specification.

QSFP

The quad small form-factor pluggable (QSFP), shown in Figure 2.18, is another transceiver that is slowly becoming a current standard in switching products. It also allows for hot-swappable operations and is used for high port density on switching equipment because of its size and quad transceiver. The QSFP contains a quad transceiver that allows for 4×1 Gbps, 4×10 Gbps, and 4×28 Gbps (4 Gbps, 40 Gbps, 100 Gbps) operation. The QSFP modules can also be purchased as a fanout cable; this cable separates each transceiver to a separate connection. This is useful when connecting other switches contained in the same rack space. One QSFP transceiver can connect up to four switches at 10 Gbps or higher.

FIGURE 2.18   A QSFP transceiver

Characteristics of fiber transceivers

When choosing a transceiver, you should look up the compatibility matrix of the equipment it is being used in. This compatibility matrix will describe the speeds supported, distances supported, cabling to be used, and the model number of transceiver to be used. Depending on the application of the fiber transceiver, you can buy bidirectional or duplex transceivers. Typically you will find bidirectional transceivers in WAN connectivity scenarios.

Bidirectional

Fiber-optic cable can be expensive to install. It is even more expensive to lease, since it is a reoccurring cost based on scarcity and distance of the connection. Bidirectional transceivers allow the use of a single fiber-optic cable to both transmit and receive data. It is common in WAN scenarios to purchase two fiber strands and use bidirectional transceivers on both. The bidirectional transceivers are usually more expensive than duplex transceivers. This allows for fault-tolerant connection in case a transceiver goes bad on one end.

A bidirectional transceiver operates on two different light wave frequencies. Say Device A is transmitting on 1310 nanometers, and Device B is transmitting on 1490 nanometers. Because of these two different wavelengths, the bidirectional transceivers are purchased as a pair. One transceiver is considered the upstream transceiver, and the other is considered the downstream transceiver. In each of the transceivers, a semi-reflective mirror diverts the incoming transmitted light wave to an optical receiver. The transceivers are using different light wavelengths in opposite directions to communicate on the same strand of fiber-optic cable. In Figure 2.19 you can see how a typical bidirectional transceiver functions internally.

FIGURE 2.19   How bidirectional transceivers work

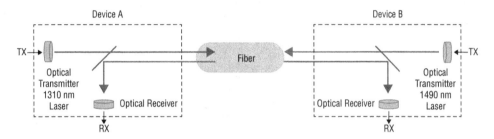

Duplex

Most of the internal fiber-optic cabling you will use inside your network will be a *duplex connection*. The duplex fiber-optic transceiver reserves one fiber-optic strand for transmit and the other for receive per each side of the fiber-optic connection. The fiber-optic strands on the other side of the connection are mapped to the receive and transmit, respectively.

Termination points

Termination points are useful as a diagnostic point or termination of responsibility. When you are dealing with a telco provider, it is usually the 66 block where the service comes into the building. When dealing with a fiber provider, it is the fiber distribution panel. The provider is responsible for a clean, clear signal to that point. It is also useful as a diagnostic point when used internally within your organization.

66 Block

The 66 block, shown in Figure 2.20, is commonly used for analog wiring of telephone equipment. It is main purpose is to supply *Plain Old Telephone System (POTS)* line access to a business or apartment building. Voice providers use the 66 block as a diagnostic point or demarcation point when supplying a dial tone. There are four prongs: the two on the left are connected to each other, and the two on the right are connected to each other. The center prongs have a clip that connects the two sides. Wires are punched down to each of the outer prongs: one to the telephone equipment and one to the dial-tone source. When you are diagnosing a telephone issue, you remove the clips in the middle to isolate the dial-tone source from the telephone equipment. The prongs are also long enough so that a lineworker's handset can clip on for testing dial tone.

FIGURE 2.20   A 66 block panel

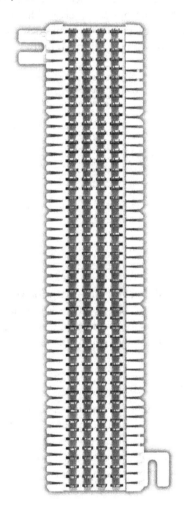

110 Block

The 110 block, shown in Figure 2.21, is commonly used for analog wiring of telephone equipment. These 110 blocks can often be found side by side with wire pairs punched down between them. Often one side will lead back to the *private branch exchange (PBX)* and the other side to the phone equipment; this is called a cross-connect. It is common setup on *in-house* wiring or *on-premise* wiring. The fixed wiring to the phone or PBX is punched down with a tool on the back side of an insert. The wire pairs are then punched down to the front side, which allows for the wire pairs to be removed and re-punched down in a different spot for reconfiguration.

FIGURE 2.21   A 110 block panel

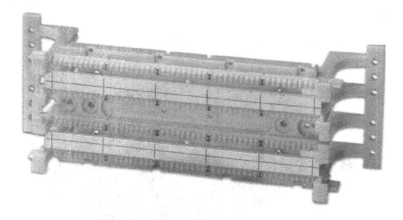

Patch Panel

Patch panels, like the one shown in Figure 2.22, are commonly used in wiring closets as a diagnostic point. The back side of the patch panel is punched down to the network cabling that is installed to the computer terminal RJ-45 jack. The front side of the patch panel is connected with a patch cable to the network switching equipment. This termination point allows for a field technician to check the wiring end-to-end first; then he or she can remove the patch cable on each end and test with a known good cable. This can be done on each end until the problem is isolated.

FIGURE 2.22   A typical patch panel

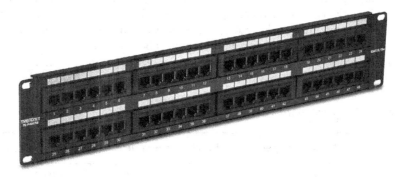

Fiber Distribution Panel

When fiber-optic cabling is installed in your network, it is generally one cable with multiple pairs of fiber. Fiber-optic cable can normally be purchased with 4, 6, 12, and 24 strands in a single cable binding. Fiber distribution panels like the one in Figure 2.23 are used to terminate the individual fragile strands to a common fiber-optic connector. Fiber distribution panels serve two purposes: distributing the individual strands and serving as a diagnostic point for troubleshooting.

FIGURE 2.23   A typical fiber distribution panel

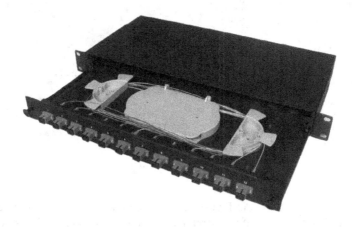

Copper cabling standards

Network cabling has been categorized jointly by the Telecommunications Industry Association (TIA) and the Electronic Industries Alliance (EIA). These standards allows for the proper cabling to be installed as per the specification of a network. The differences between the various categories of network cabling are the number of twists per inch to reduce crosstalk, how the pairs are separated inside the jacket, and the thickness of the conductors. When the pairs are twisted tighter, an electrical balance is created between the wires to reduce noise from other pairs; this noise is called crosstalk. The better they are separated, the less crosstalk you encounter if wires become tangled inside the jacket. A thicker conductor allows for higher frequencies and larger data rates. Table 2.2 shows the maximum speeds for each category of cabling.

TABLE 2.2   Cable categories and speeds

Category	Maximum speed	Maximum distance	Certified frequency
Cat 3	10 Mbps	100 meters	16 MHz
Cat 5	100 Mbps	100 meters	100 MHz

Category	Maximum speed	Maximum distance	Certified frequency
Cat 5e	1 Gbps	100 meters	100 MHz
Cat 6	1 Gbps	100 meters	250 MHz
Cat 6	10 Gbps	55 meters	250 MHz
Cat 6a	10 Gbps	100 meters	500 MHz
Cat 7 (unofficial)	10 Gbps	100 meters	600 MHz

Cat 3

Category 3 cable is classified as a cabling for 10 Mbps networks; it is sometimes referred to as voice-grade cable. It was commonly used for PBX wiring and network wiring. Category 3 cabling is legacy cabling, because there is no difference in price between Cat 3 cabling and Cat 5e cabling. All installations should have at least Cat 5e cabling or higher to future-proof the installation. This includes wiring to be run for PBX voice installations (non-VoIP).

Cat 5

Category 5 cable is classified as a cabling for 100 Mbps networks. It has been superseded by Category 5e cable. Cat 5e cable is classified as a cabling for 1 Gbps networks. There is a nominal price difference between Cat 3, Cat 5, and Cat 5e cable, so all installations should be using Cat 5e or higher.

Cat 6

Category 6 cable is classified as a cabling for 1 Gbps and 10 Gbps networks. This cabling has a maximum distance of 33 to 55 meters for 10 Gbps and a maximum distance of 100 meters for 1 Gbps networks. It should be used in datacenters where the distance is 55 meters (approximately 180 feet) or less when 10 Gbps speeds are required. This cabling has a plastic separator that keeps the four pairs spaced and separated. Most often different RJ-45 ends must be used to accommodate the larger diameter of cable.

Cat 6a

Category 6a cable is also classified as a cabling for 10 Gbps networks. This cabling has a maximum distance of 100 meters. The Category 6a specification will soon become the standard for cabling of 10 Gbps and replace the Category 6 standard. It should be used as cabling for networks as to future-proof installations for 10 Gbps. This cabling has a plastic separator that keeps the four pairs spaced and separated. Most often, different RJ-45 ends must be used to accommodate the larger diameter of cable.

Cat 7

Category 7 cable is not recognized by TIA/EIA as a defined standard and is considered an unofficial standard. It allows for 10 Gbps networks speeds at distances up to 100 meters. The unofficial standard requires GG-45 connectors, which look similar to RJ-45 connectors with the addition of four top connectors on each side of the cable detent. The GG-45 female jack is backward compatible with standard RJ-45 connectors. In years to come we might see this become an official TIA/EIA specification.

> When purchasing the cabling, you will notice an MHz rating on the cable as well as the category. This MHz rating is for certification after installation; specialized equipment called cable certifiers are used to test and certify the cable. The MHz rating is the highest frequency that can be transmitted on the cable before data crosstalk occurs. It is not directly related to the speed at which the network operates. When a cable is certified, it means that it can pass the recommendations of the TIA/EIA or the manufacturer's specifications. Beware of inflated numbers that the manufacturer advertises; cable certifications should always be benchmarked against TIA/EIA specifications. This should be part of the scope of work when contracting a cable installer.

RG-59 and RG-6

RG-59 and RG-6 are both 75-ohm coaxial cable specifications, typically used for security camera and broadband cable installations. RG-59 is thinner in diameter than RG-6 and should not be used for infrastructure wiring. RG-6 has a larger inner core, larger insulator, and better shielding than RG-59. Many suppliers have stopped selling RG-59 or have limited supplies of RG-59, because RG-6 has become a standard in new installations of coaxial cable. The price difference is nominal between the two cables, so bigger is better!

Coaxial cables are constructed of an inner core of copper, an insulator (dielectric foam), a foil shielding, a metal weaved shielding, and a protective jacket. RG-59 and RG-6 are usually terminated (crimped) with either BNC connectors or F-connectors.

Copper termination standards

When terminating the RJ-45 connectors on the ends of a patch cable, use the defined standard of wiring for the RJ-45 connector set forth by the TIA/EIA. The TIA/EIA specification of 568 has published two standards for this wiring that I will cover in the following section. When you are punching down the wires on a patch panel, the manufacturer will often have their own standard coloring code. The proper wiring standard should be used when terminating patch cables or punching down onto a patch panel. If these standards are not used, the network cabling could fail certification or may not work at the speeds expected.

TIA/EIA 568A/B

The TIA/EIA 568A specification was originally created back when 10 Mbps networks were standard. Today all patch cables use the TIA/EIA 568B specification on both ends. However, that doesn't mean that the TIA/EIA 568A specification is obsolete. It is cabled on one end when you need a crossover cable, as I will explain in the following section. Figure 2.24 shows the wiring specification for TIA/EIA 568A and TIA/EIA 568B along with the position of pin 1 through pin 8 on an RJ-45 connector.

FIGURE 2.24   TIA/EIA 568A and 568B wiring standard

EIA/TIA 568A			EIA/TIA 568B	
Position	**Color**		**Position**	**Color**
1	White Green		1	White Orange
2	Green		2	Orange
3	White Orange		3	White Green
4	Blue		4	Blue
5	White Blue		5	White Blue
6	Orange		6	Green
7	White Brown		7	White Brown
8	Brown		8	Brown

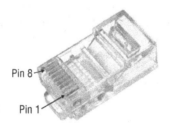

Pin 8
Pin 1

Straight-Through Cables

A network cable that has the TIA/EIA 568B specification terminated on both ends is considered a straight-through network cable. A network cable can have the TIA/EIA 568A specification terminated on both ends and also be considered a straight-through cable. However, the TIA/EIA 568A is deprecated for straight-through cables; it was originally used with Category 3 cable.

As seen in Figure 1.25, the computer expects to transmit data on pins 1 and 2 and receive data on pins 3 and 6. Conversely, the switch expects to transmit data on pins 3 and 6 and receive data on pins 1 and 2. The straight-through cable aligns pins 1 and 2 for transmitting (computer side) to pins 1 and 2 on the adjoining equipment (switch side) for receiving. Pins 3 and 6 are receiving (computer side) from pins 3 and 6 on the adjoining equipment (switch side) for transmitting.

Straight-through cables should be used when you are

- Connecting computers to switches
- Connecting routers to switches
- Connecting computer to hubs

FIGURE 2.25 Straight-through cable wiring

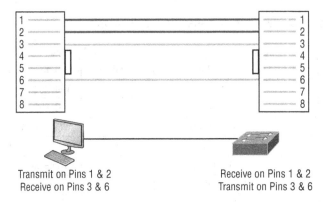

Transmit on Pins 1 & 2
Receive on Pins 3 & 6

Receive on Pins 1 & 2
Transmit on Pins 3 & 6

Crossover Cables

A network cable terminated with the TIA/EIA 568A and TIA/EIA 568B specification is considered a crossover cable. This aligns pins 1 and 2 for transmitting with pins 3 and 6 on the other end for receiving (see Figure 2.26). This is because both switches and/or computers expect a straight-through cable to be attached.

FIGURE 2.26 Crossover cable wiring

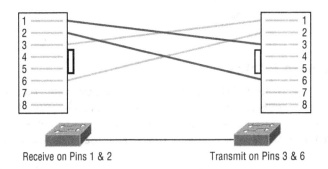

Receive on Pins 1 & 2

Transmit on Pins 3 & 6

On newer switches, a feature called *auto MDI-X (Medium Dependent Interface Crossover)* allows for automatic detection of the transmit and receive pair. The auto MDI-X will auto-crossover the connection when a straight-through cable is present connecting a switch to another switch.

Crossover cable cables should be used when you are

- Connecting switches to switches
- Connecting routers to routers (via Ethernet)
- Connecting computers to computers
- Connecting hubs to hubs
- Connecting hubs to switches

Ethernet deployment standards

Ethernet is based on a set of standards published by the *IEEE 802.3* committee. Over the past three decades, the IEEE has published subcommittee specifications on 802.3 that I will cover in the following section. You should be familiar with these specifications and their respective capabilities.

100BaseTX

The 100BaseTX specification is defined by the IEEE as 802.3u. It is capable of an Ethernet speed of 100 Mbps and is commonly referred to as Fast Ethernet. 100BaseTX uses TIA/EIA Category 5 or higher cabling and uses only two of the four pairs in the cabling. It has a maximum distance limitation of 100 meters (330 feet).

1000BaseT

The 1000BaseT specification is defined by the IEEE as 802.3ab. It is capable of an Ethernet speed of 1 Gbps and is commonly referred to as Gigabit Ethernet. 1000BaseT uses TIA/EIA Category 5e or higher cabling and uses all four pairs in the cabling. It has a maximum distance limitation of 100 meters (330 feet).

1000BaseLX

The 1000BaseLX specification is defined by the IEEE as 802.3z. It is capable of an Ethernet speed of 1 Gbps over 9-micron single-mode fiber with a 1300 nm laser. It is commonly called "long haul" because of the distances it can achieve of up to 10 kilometers (6.2 miles).

1000BaseSX

The 1000BaseSX specification is also defined by the IEEE as 802.3z. It is capable of an Ethernet speed of 1 Gbps over multimode fiber. It is commonly called "short haul" because it is used for short distances. It uses an 850 nm laser with either 62.5-micron or 50-micron fiber-optic cabling. You can use 62.5-micron fiber to achieve a maximum distance of 220 meters. You can use 50-micron fiber to achieve a maximum distance of 550 meters.

10GBaseT

The 10GBaseT specification is defined by the IEEE as 802.3an. It is capable of an Ethernet speed of 10 Gbps and is commonly referred to as 10 Gigabit Ethernet. 10GBaseT uses TIA/EIA Category 6 or higher cabling. Category 6 cable has a maximum distance of 55 meters, and Category 6a cable has a maximum distance limitation of 100 meters (330 feet).

Exam Essentials

Know the types of copper cables.   The most common cables used in networks today are UTP, STP, and coaxial cable. UTP cabling is the most common cable used in networks today. STP cabling is used in networks that have high amounts of EMI from machinery. STP cabling is usually used in industrial Ethernet circumstances and is more expensive than UTP. Coax cable is commonly used for security cameras and broadband cable installations. RG-6 is the most common cable used for coax cabling; it is slightly bigger than RG-59 and provides less signal loss.

Know the types of fiber-optic cable.   There are two main types of fiber-optic cable: single-mode fiber, which is normally 9 microns (yellow patch cables), and multimode fiber, which includes 50 microns (aqua patch cables) and 62.5 microns (orange patch cables). Single-mode fiber can span distances of 75 miles, and multimode fiber can span distances of 3000 feet.

Understand the difference between plenum and non-plenum cable.   PVC is a plastic that when burned can cause irritation in the lungs and eyes. Therefore, it is specified in the electrical and fire code that plenum cable be used in airspace that provides ventilation or air-conditioning. Plenum cable is coated with a fire-retardant coating that is usually Teflon based.

Be familiar with various copper connectors.   Although there are several different types of connectors, RJ-45 connectors are the most common in networks today. Know the physical characteristics of each connector and their application.

Be familiar with the various fiber-optic connectors.   There are many different fiber-optic connectors that provide unique advantages; you should be familiar with these and understand their purpose. Know the physical characteristics of each connector and their design.

Be familiar with the various transceivers.   Most all transceivers are hot swappable. The SFP transceiver has a maximum speed of 1 Gbps. The SFP+ transceiver is slowly replacing the SFP transceiver. The SFP+ can operate at over 10 Gbps up to 400 Gbps. The GBIC transceiver has a maximum speed of 1 Gbps and is an older standard. The QSFP transceiver has a quad transceiver in one module; it can support speeds of 1 Gbps to 100 Gbps. The QSFP transceiver can also be purchased as a fanout cable that can supply four 10 Gbps links switches in the same rack. Bidirectional transceivers can use a single strand of fiber for bidirectional communications. Duplex transceivers use two strands of fiber for communications; one strand is a transmit strand and the other is a receive strand.

Know the various termination points.   A 66 block is generally used by telco providers to create a termination point for POTS lines. A 110 block is generally used with PBX systems and in-house wiring for connecting telephones. A patch panel is used to create a diagnostic point for troubleshooting purposes. Fiber distribution panels are used to separate the strands in a fiber-optic cable; they allow for distribution on signal and serve as a diagnostic point.

Know the categories of UTP cables and their purpose.   Category 5e cable supports a maximum speed of 1 Gbps at 100 meters. Category 6 cable supports a maximum speed of 10 Gbps at 55 meters. Category 6a cable supports a maximum speed of 10 Gbps at 100 meters. Category 7 cable is an unofficial standard that supports a maximum speed of 10 Gbps at 100 meters.

Know the copper termination standards.   The EIA/TIA 568A specification is an older specification for 10 Mbps networks, and EIA/TIA 568B is the current specification for cable termination. When you terminate a cable with 568A and 568B, it creates a crossover cable. Normal patch cables have the 568B specification terminated on both ends.

Know the various Ethernet deployment standards.   You will need to memorize the various standards and their capabilities.

2.2 Given a scenario, determine the appropriate placement of networking devices on a network and install/ configure them.

The various building blocks inside a network perform the vital functions of moving, distributing, protecting, and controlling data. Each of these devices performs specific functions. It is important for you to understand the function of these devices so that you can make an educated decision when implementing them in your network infrastructure. In this section, I will cover the functionality of each device you will commonly find inside a network.

Firewall

Firewalls control and protect data inside the internal network as well as access from outside the internal network. Firewalls can be either a hardware appliance (see Figure 2.27) or a software solution. Since Windows XP SP2, Microsoft has had a built-in firewall. *Linux* has a built-in firewall called IPTables, and macOS has a built-in firewall called the Application Firewall. These OSs or application firewalls can control how applications are allowed to communicate inside our network. However, OS firewalls are not the only software firewalls out there; pfSense, McAfee, Cisco, Barracuda, and many other companies offer software-based firewalls that perform like hardware firewalls. With the ever-growing expansion of virtualization and cloud computing, the list grows daily.

FIGURE 2.27 A typical hardware firewall appliance

The protection functionality of a firewall is synonymous with the term firewall. The definition of firewall is *a wall or partition to inhibit or prevent the spread of fire.* A firewall partitions our network with rules or groups of rules called policies that the administrator configures to prevent unauthorized access to data by filtering access at various levels of the OSI model. The rules in a firewall are configured as condition and action. Conditions can be configured on layer 3 protocols and IP addressing, layer 4 ports and states, and even specific application requests. Actions are triggered when conditions are met. The most common actions are permit traffic, block traffic, and log traffic. More advanced firewalls can slow traffic down when a condition is met. Firewalls can also control packets based on malicious activity such as port scanning or threat detection.

Routers

Routers are the heart of our networks and the Internet. I like to think of them as intelligent pumps, which sort and move data packets to their intended network destination. They perform these routing decisions on the destination IP address of the packet, so they are considered layer 3 (network layer) devices. Figure 2.28 shows a typical router found at the edge of our internal networks today.

FIGURE 2.28 Typical edge router

Another vital function routers perform is the segmentation of broadcast domains. A broadcast domain defines the boundary of the network where a broadcast message can be heard. This is why you get an IP address from your home router and not your neighbor's router. Outside of the DHCP protocol, there are many other useful broadcast-based protocols that require a certain amount of network bandwidth. If we didn't have routers, the Internet would be a very slow and loud shouting match of devices!

Switches

Switches are the main connectivity device within networks today. Switches function at layer 2 (data link layer) of the OSI, which makes them extremely efficient. They do not have the same problems associated with hubs, since they perform two important functions at layer 2: MAC address learning and forward filter decisions based on the MAC addresses learned. These functions are performed by *application-specific integrated circuits (ASICs)*. Figure 2.29 shows a managed switch you will typically find in wiring closets and datacenters; they vary in configuration options and port density. The arrangement and sophistication of ASICs dictates the switching speed and price. Managed switches can also perform a third vital function: loop avoidance through STP (Spanning Tree Protocol), which I will cover in Chapter 4, "Domain 4: Network Security." Managed switches offer several features, most notably VLANs. VLANs allow you to make virtual switches inside the physical switch to segment the network further for security and control of broadcasts. I will also cover VLANs in Chapter 4.

FIGURE 2.29   Typical managed switches

Hubs

Hubs are considered legacy devices and are not currently used in LANs today. However, it is important to understand network hub functionality so that you do not use hubs in lieu of a switch. Hubs function at layer 1 (physical layer) of the OSI model because they are nothing more than multiport repeaters. If you used a four-port hub similar to the one in Figure 2.30 and a device on any of the ports transmitted an Ethernet frame, the frame would be repeated on all the other connected ports. This behavior forces devices that are not directly participating in the exchange of data to listen to the conversation. It may not seem to be a problem, since devices not participating in the exchange of data will just disregard, or more specifically drop, the frames. However, this robs useful bandwidth from those devices not participating in the exchange of data. Although full-duplex hubs can be purchased, they are always referenced as being half-duplex devices. Hubs typically operate at speeds of 10 Mbps or 100 Mbps. Hubs can be useful when you want to capture a conversation between two computers with a packet analyzer, since the frame is repeated to all connected ports. Advanced managed switches now have these capabilities built in.

FIGURE 2.30   Four-port active hub

Bridges

Bridges perform functionality identical to that of switches. They perform address learning and forward filtering decisions based on the MAC address table. They can even use STP. However, bridges have a limited number of ports and are usually software-based switches. They do not have the extremely fast ASICs switches do. They were the very first implementation of switching and still have useful purposes today; most current operating systems support bridging. You can use Microsoft Windows to extend the wireless network to the Ethernet network attached to the Windows computer via bridging. Linux also supports bridging between Ethernet adapters and can even perform STP.

Modems

Modems are considered legacy devices in network architecture today. The analog modem functions by encoding data over telephone lines as audible screeches of chirps and hisses. As a network administrator you will not build this device into your network, unless you need an out-of-band connectivity method for a router or switch—for example, if you were deploying routers across the country and needed to be in two places at once. You could simply dial into one router as you were configuring the local router. Outside of that use case, you might find analog modems in purpose-built equipment like fire panels, alarm systems, and elevator equipment for relaying service-related information. So it is useful to know what you are dealing with.

Wireless access point

A wireless access point (WAP) is a device that extends the wired network to a wireless network. This allows mobile devices, such as laptops, tablets, and specialized wireless-enabled equipment, to access your network infrastructure. Each WAP can be directly wired to your network infrastructure, or WAPs can join other WAPs already wired, creating a wireless mesh. This is useful in designs where cabling back to a switch would cost too much or the distance is too great. Many municipalities use these wireless mesh technologies to add IP cameras to busy intersections. In Figure 2.31 you can see two common configurations of WAPs with internal and external antennas. WAPs are sometimes called autonomous WAPs when they are used without a wireless controller, because they function autonomously of each other. I will cover wireless controllers later in this chapter.

FIGURE 2.31   WAPs with internal and external antennas

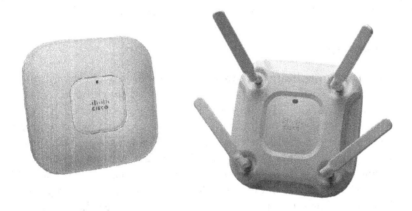

Media Converters

Copper Ethernet has a defined limitation of 100 meters (330 feet), which limits what copper Ethernet can be used for. A common problem is remote locations where you need Ethernet connectivity, such as for a VoIP phone or a security camera, but the distance is over 100 meters. This is where we can benefit from media converters, because they allow us to convert from copper Ethernet to fiber-optic cable back to copper Ethernet again. Media converters and the fiber optics that accompany extending copper Ethernet raise the costs of the project and introduce failure points, so they should be used sparingly.

Wireless range extender

A wireless ranger extender is often referred to as a wireless repeater. It operates by associating to a wireless network and rebroadcasting the SSID. It can be useful in wireless networks that have a dead zone, but a major drawback is that the bandwidth is reduced by 50 percent.

This is because all network communications now must travel two wireless signals to reach the wired network. Wireless range extenders are usually only found in *small office, home office (SOHO)* networks. Larger networks should use wireless LAN controllers, which I will cover in the next section.

VoIP endpoint

A voice-over IP (VoIP) endpoint is any device that connects to a VoIP PBX and is the final destination of a voice call over VoIP. Devices that fall into this category are VoIP phones, VoIP soft phones, SIP-to-PRI gateways, and cordless VoIP phones. Many large networks have a network segment set aside for VoIP endpoints. They are configured with DHCP and a special vendor-specific option that points the VoIP endpoint to an SIP configuration server. The SIP configuration server typically uses the MAC address of the phone to map it to a configuration file. This configuration file is downloaded by the VoIP endpoint and configures the extension number, SIP server address, and many other vendor-specific options.

Exam Essentials

Know the functions and applications of various network devices. Firewalls protect data with condition action-based rules and groups of rules called policies. Firewalls filter data based on these rules at various levels of the OSI model. Routers function at layer 3, performing routing decisions based on destination IP addresses. Routers use routing tables to look up the destination network for routing decisions. Switches perform three important functions: forwarding of filter decisions, MAC address learning, and loop avoidance. Switches function at layer 2, forwarding and filtering frames via the destination MAC addresses. Hubs operate at layer 1 and are nothing more than multiport repeaters. Hubs repeat the data received on one port out all other active ports regardless of destination MAC address. Bridges perform functionality identical to that of switches, but they are usually software implementations of switches and have a limited number of ports. Modems are legacy devices but are still useful for out-of-band management of network equipment. Wireless access points are used to extend a wired infrastructure to a wireless infrastructure for mobile device access. Media converters allow us to extend copper Ethernet past 100 meters by converting it to fiber-optic media. Wireless range extenders are useful for SOHO networks where you need a wireless dead spot covered. A VoIP endpoint is any device that is the final destination of a voice call over VoIP.

2.3 Explain the purposes and use cases for advanced networking devices.

The devices in this section are more advanced than the basic building blocks of the previous section. All of these advanced devices perform a group of functions to move, distribute, protect, or control data. It is important for you to understand the functions of each of these devices. In this section, I will cover their functionality. At the end of this section, you should be able to explain how to implement these devices in your network infrastructure.

Multilayer switch

Routers move data through the process of routing, and switches move data through the process of switching. With switches, we can also create VLANs to segment the network, but you will need a router to route between the segments. So you may be asking yourself, "Why can't we just combine a switch and a router?" Well, we can. The answer is the multilayer switch, sometimes referred to as a layer 3 switch. The multilayer switch was born from the necessity to route VLANs. Every VLAN requires a unique IP subnet, so routing is essential if we want to communicate between VLANs. It seems a waste of equipment, complexity, money, and most importantly latency of the data to send everything to a router from the switch only to come back to the switch. So multilayer switches have a routing function built into them; a virtual interface can be created by the administrator and configured with an IP address. Routers have a fixed number of interfaces, but multilayer switches can create hundreds or thousands of these virtual interfaces. Since a multilayer switch has a router built in, we can segment our network to alleviate the number of broadcasts in each VLAN subnet. This capability increases the usable bandwidth in large networks. I will cover VLANs in Chapter 4.

Wireless controller

When we talk about data and network equipment, there are three main types of data: the control, data, and management planes. These terms are universal with all networking equipment, not just wireless. The control plane is the data that WAPs use to control internal functions, like SSID and channel assignment. The data plane is the data that WAPs move between the wireless clients and the network. The management plane is the management data for configuration and diagnostics. One of the problems with using multiple WAPs in a wireless network is channel assignment, and roaming between WAPs is not coordinated for the client.

We can solve this coordination problem between WAPs by dumbing them down as lightweight access points (LWAPs) and introducing a wireless LAN (WLAN) controller. When a WAP is converted to an LWAP, their autonomous capabilities are surrendered, and all configuration and management is orchestrated by the WLAN controller (see Figure 2.32). Not all WAPs can become an LWAP, and many vendors sell their wireless equipment as autonomous or lightweight and offer conversion between modes. When the WLAN controller is configured with the LWAPs, all of the LWAPs' data planes will flow through the WLAN controller. The controller allows the LWAPs to broadcast the same SSID, but on different channels in each of the wireless cells. The controller also uses 802.11 extensions to communicate with the client, so the client can switch to the new channel based on signal strength. When a WLAN controller is used, generally all of the data on the data plane is also transmitted back to the WLAN controller, where it is switched to the destination client. This allows the WLAN controller to have complete control of the wireless clients and aids in roaming of the wireless clients.

FIGURE 2.32   Wireless LAN controller functionality

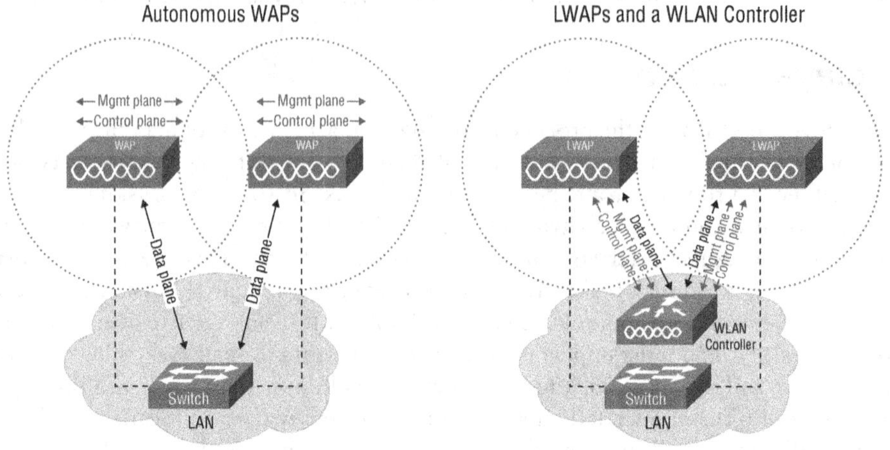

Load balancer

Load balancers allow administrators to distribute the load of requests from users to multiple resources or even multiple locations. Load balancers typically function at layer 4 (transport layer) and layer 3 (network layer), inspecting the transport layer ports and destination IP addresses. (I will cover the OSI in detail in Chapter 5, "Domain 5: Network Troubleshooting and Tools"). The load balancer then makes a decision, based on the load of ongoing requests from other users, to forward the new request to the next available server. Load balancers also function at layer 7 (application layer) for redirection of users to the server with the least amount of load or to the closest server. It is common to find load balancers distributing load to web servers, since websites have static content and they are the perfect candidates for this technology. It is also common to employ geographic load balancers, because applications are now global, and directing a user to the closest server provides the fastest response to the end user. With the expansion of cloud services, geographic load balancing is a popular technology.

Websites are not the only candidate for load balancers. Microsoft Server 2016 has a built-in load balancing mechanism that can be configured for load-balancing DHCP. Load balancers are also used for Terminal Services and virtual desktop servers. They can be found in just about any service that has a stateless request for resources. They can be configured to provide affinity for a server until the user is done with the request. Load balancers can be hardware or software solutions—they are commonly deployed today as software solutions, since virtualization and cloud services have become mainstream for corporate hosting of services.

IDS and IPS

An intrusion detection system (IDS) functions similar to antivirus software. The IDS watches network traffic and differentiates between normal traffic and an attempted intrusion. It performs this function in two ways: signature based or anomaly based. Signature-based detection matches signatures from well-known attacks. These signatures are generally a subscription from the IDS provider, similar to antivirus signatures. The anomaly-based detection method detects abnormal traffic patterns or packets. Each IDS anomaly algorithm is the IDS provider's "special sauce." The most notable function of an IDS is that when it detects an intrusion, it gathers, identifies, and logs the traffic, and then alerts administrators responsible for security. This functionality is useful when you have dedicated security response personnel or need to perform postmortem network analysis to prevent future intrusions.

An intrusion prevention system (IPS) functions similar to an IDS in that they both use signature-based and anomaly-based detection. They are often referred to as intrusion detection and prevention systems. They both gather, identify, and log traffic, and then alert administrators. However, the IPS will try to prevent the intrusion by dropping the packets of the malicious transmission, or it will actively block the offending IP address. Most firewalls today have this functionality built in to avert attacks and intrusions based on signature subscriptions from the provider. This is often part of a maintenance agreement with the provider.

Proxy Servers

Proxy servers are used to proxy a connection from a user to a web application. When we proxy something, we are sending the request to the intermediary (proxy), which fetches the request on behalf of our request and returns the data. Proxies provide an administrator with a single point of egress (*forward proxy* or just proxy) or ingress (*reverse proxy*). This provides not only a layer of protection, but also a way to centrally log access to the data. We can also filter access since the proxy is the single exit point or entry point. When we filter access on a proxy, it becomes the control point—this is how content filters work. (I cover content filters later in this chapter.) The most useful property of a proxy is the caching ability; when we enable caching, this type of proxy is referred to as a *caching proxy*. When we enable caching, we significantly reduce bandwidth consumption and load on web servers we maintain.

In Figure 2.33 you can see a typical internal network on the left and the Internet on the right. When implementing a proxy server, administrators will block clients from directly connecting to web server on the Internet at the router. The clients will be forced to use the proxy server to connect to the web servers on the Internet. When a request is made for a web page, the request will be directed to the proxy server, which will request the page in behalf of the client. When the reply comes back from the Internet web server, it is returned to the proxy server, and the proxy server returns the web reply back to the client. To the left of the proxy server is a caching and filtering (content filter) engine. Proxy servers do not have to use caching engines. However, if they do, we benefit from reduced bandwidth. All of the consecutive requests to the same web page will never generate a request to the Internet until the cache timer expires on the content. We can also employ content filtering that can restrict the user from inappropriate web pages.

FIGURE 2.33   Overview of a proxy server implementation

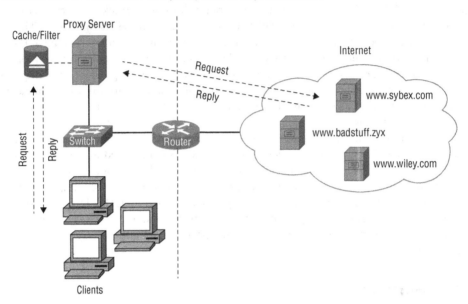

Reverse proxy servers serve clients as well, but in the reverse order of requests. In Figure 2.34 you see the Internet on the left and a private network or cloud service provider on the right. You'll notice the router and switch are only there for connectivity. In this example, a client on the Internet requests a web page from www.wiley.com. However, in lieu of requesting the web page directly from the server, the client sends the request to a reverse proxy. The client doesn't know that the request is being proxied on the backend. This reverse proxy then requests the web page from the actual server(s), and the server responds to the reverse proxy. The reverse proxy then responds back to the client. The benefit of a reverse proxy is caching, for the simple reason of saving CPU cycles to render the page on the actual server. It also reduces the server's load by handling encryption, security certificates, and authentication to enable a single sign-on to access multiple services. Reverse proxies are useful for load balancing when more than one actual server is used. They are also very handy to mitigate denial-of-service (DoS) attacks that create an enormous amount of web page requests, resulting in CPU cycles wasted and denying legitimate users access to the web pages. Reverse proxies are often referred to as server publishing.

FIGURE 2.34   Overview of a reverse proxy server implementation

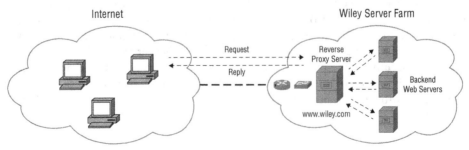

VPN concentrator

A virtual private network (VPN) is an encrypted tunnel across the public Internet or an unsecured network. A VPN concentrator protects data at ingress or egress points in your network. VPN concentrators are normally used for remote access users as a concentrated point into the network through a VPN tunnel. The VPN concentrator is responsible for terminating the encrypted tunnel back to the original unencrypted packets. VPN concentrators function at layer 3 (network layer) by encrypting the original data and encapsulating it inside of various VPN protocols. Common VPN protocols are *Point-to-Point Tunneling Protocol (PPTP), Layer 2 Tunneling Protocol (L2TP)*, or *IPsec*. I will cover these protocols in Chapter 3. VPN concentrators can also create a VPN tunnel between two locations, such as a branch office and the main office. VPN concentrators can be hardware or software. However, for large numbers of users, hardware VPN concentrators are the best option, because they usually have specific hardware for cryptography of data during the encryption and decryption process.

AAA/RADIUS server

The Remote Authentication Dial-In User Service (RADIUS) or Authentication, Authorization, and Accounting (AAA) server has been around since dial-up Internet service providers (ISPs). It was originally used to authenticate subscribers of ISPs for dial-in access entitlement. It's not an obsolete protocol; it is still a viable protocol and has now been adapted to extensible methods of authentication such as *Active Directory (AD)*, *Lightweight Directory Access Protocol (LDAP)*, SQL databases, and countless other mechanisms of authentication. VPN concentrators commonly use RADIUS to authenticate users for connectivity to the network. It is also commonly used to authenticate users and computers to wired and wireless network via the 802.1X protocol. I will cover the 802.1X protocol in Chapter 4.

The AAA/RADIUS server provides three important functionalities; it allows for the authentication of users, the authorization of users, and the accounting of user connections. Authentication and authorization of the user are performed via UDP port 1812. When the AAA/RADIUS server receives the request, it compares the username and password against its authentication directory. If a match is found and the user is authenticated, it then checks rules based on connection type, time of day, groups associated with the user, and so on. If these rules are met, then the user is authorized for the connection. In addition to authentication and authorization, the AAA/RADIUS server provides a mechanism for accounting of users and computers that have connected. It uses UDP port 1813 for accounting purposes.

The user will never directly communicate to the AAA/RADIUS server. Instead, the device authenticating the user will communicate to the server (see Figure 2.35). When an AAA/RADIUS server is used with a network device, the network device is considered to be the client. Between the client (network device) and the radius server, a shared secret or public/private key pair encrypts the conversation and authenticates the network device. The actual client in this process is called the supplicant.

FIGURE 2.35 AAA/RADIUS components

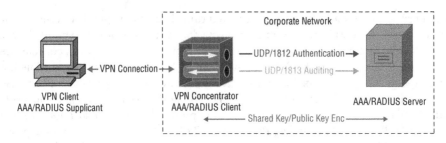

UTM appliance

A unified threat management (UTM) appliance is sometimes also called a unified security management (USM) appliance. The purpose of the UTM is to unify all security-related functions into one management interface and appliance. UTM appliances today combine the functionality of a firewall, IDS/IPS, VPN concentrator, content filter, antispam scanner, load balancer, gateway antivirus scanner, and many other threat- or security-related functions. UTM appliances also help with identity management; they log who accessed what information and where the person accessed it from. Because all of the critical network threat detection is done on one platform, UTM appliances usually offer comprehensive reporting functionality. They are invaluable if your company is bound by a regulatory compliance requirement to provide routine security audits and employ identity controls.

The main disadvantage of UTM appliances is the single point of failure they create. Vendors have you covered on that problem as well—just buy two of them and cluster them together. UTM appliances are often sold as software solutions or hardware solutions, depending on the size of the network and the user base. Also, since many of the services UTM appliances deliver are ever changing, subscriptions are normally sold with the unit to provide updates to antispam controls, gateway antivirus definitions, IDS/IPS signatures, and other features that require constant updates. These subscriptions are often purchased as a maintenance contract for the UTM appliance.

NGFW/Layer 7 firewall

Next-generation firewalls (NGFWs) are layer 7 firewalls that help protect applications by inspecting the layer 7 traffic. Most traditional firewalls inspect traffic at layer 3 (network layer) and layer 4 (transport layer). These inspections of traffic at layers 3 and 4 do not mitigate malicious intent to applications that are allowed past these traditional firewall rules. An example of this is your public mail server; you may have Outlook Web Access (OWA) configured for your users to access mail when they are away from the office. A traditional firewall rule will stop SYN floods and other DoS attacks, but it will not prevent a malicious user from trying to access the Exchange control panel from outside your corporate network. This level of firewalling must be done at layers higher than 3 and 4. This is where an NGFW helps mitigate security problems. We can create a policy that restricts any user who is not on the internal network from accessing the Exchange control panel via the Uniform Resource Locator (URL) for the control panel.

NGFWs do much more than just restrict access based on URLs. Most NGFWs perform something called deep packet inspection (DPI) and use an IPS to mitigate known threats. This can often be tricky when using Secure Socket Layers (SSL) encryption, because everything is encrypted. Most NGFWs allow for the termination of this encryption at the firewall itself so that DPI can be performed. In addition to DPI, NGFWs help with quality of service and bandwidth management at the application level. Many of the features that a UTM appliance provides the NGFW can provide as well.

VoIP PBX

Voice-over IP (VoIP) private branch exchange (PBX) is a private phone system that communicates with VoIP. PBXs have been around for several decades. They provide phone communications using specialized phones often called *time-division multiplexing (TDM) phones*. PBX systems allow for call forwarding from the individual phones, call pickup groups, conference calling, and many other enterprise-type call features. With the expansive adoption of VoIP, the VoIP PBX has become a popular upgrade path that moves away from the vendor lock-in of TDM phone equipment. You will find that VoIP phones and VoIP PBXs offer features that are vendor specific as well. However, with VoIP phone systems we no longer need to maintain a separate wired infrastructure; it is all treated like data. This is a tremendous selling point when you're deciding to convert to a VoIP PBX, since the sunk cost of switching equipment has probably already been made. An added benefit that the VoIP PBX enables is the ability for remote offices to use the same VoIP PBX as the main office for all end-user communications needs. VoIP PBXs can be software or hardware appliances, depending on the number of users and features required.

VoIP PBXs offer all of the features a traditional TDM PBX phone system does. Many other advanced features can be purchased along with the VoIP PBX such as Unified Communications (UC). UC is a collaboration of applications and VoIP services. In business today, information is not bound to a phone call or a voicemail. UC combines VoIP, instant messaging, voicemail, interactive voice response (IVR), and web conferencing, just to name a few. An example of UC is when you dial into your bank and are presented with an IVR requesting your account number and purpose of the call. Your call is routed to an agent, and that agent now has your information on their screen, ready to assist. Microsoft recently purchased Skype as a building platform for UC to replace a prior product called Microsoft Lync. Microsoft is not the only company—Cisco and other phone system providers offer their own version of UC.

VoIP gateway

A VoIP gateway allows a VoIP PBX to interface with an existing PBX or the *Public Switched Telephone Network (PSTN)*. The VoIP gateway is often referred to as a PSTN gateway when describing its functionality. VoIP gateways do not need to be used exclusively with a VoIP PBX. UC platforms such as existing Microsoft Lync or Skype often use a VoIP gateway to interface with the existing TDM PBX (see Figure 2.36). Most TDM PBXs use either ISDN PRI interfaces or T1 interfaces to connect to the PSTN. VoIP gateways can interface with the TDM PBXs as if they were the PSTN. This enables the reuse of a phone system with UC platforms.

FIGURE 2.36   UC platform and VoIP gateway

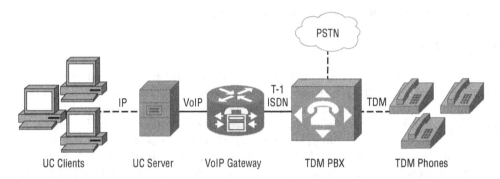

VoIP gateways are also used when you want to convert your TDM PBX to use a VoIP provider to send and receive phone calls (see Figure 2.37). If the PBX is too old, it might not support VoIP directly. A VoIP gateway will act as the PSTN and hand off a T1 of ISDN PRI to the PBX as if it were the PSTN, thus lowering calling costs via VoIP.

FIGURE 2.37   VoIP gateway acting as the PSTN

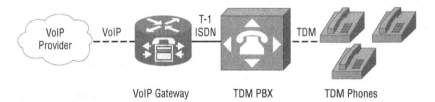

Another common use of the VoIP gateway is to provide a plain old telephone system (POTS) dial tone for fax machines, alarm systems, and so forth. The VoIP gateway can then be used to imitate the PSTN for dial-tone services (see Figure 2.38). The POTS equipment will send and receive phone calls over a VoIP network without ever knowing it is doing so. This strategy helps bridge the gap of technology when transitioning to VoIP.

FIGURE 2.38   VoIP gateway serving POTS

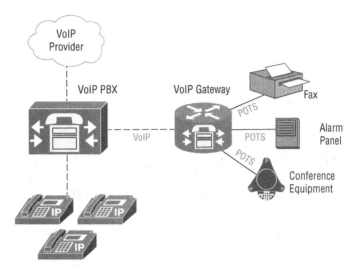

Content filter

Content filters are useful in corporate networks to restrict users from viewing material that is either non-work-related, questionable, or malware. Content filtering is usually dictated by company policy and upper management. The content filter operates at layer 7 (application layer) by watching content and requests from web browsers and other applications. The content filter functions in two ways. The first is content based; when images and text are requested from a website, the content filter can use heuristic rules to filter the content according to administrator-set policies. The second method is URL based, which is much more common since many websites now use SSL (encryption). Content filters are typically purchased with a subscription that provides updates to the categories of material administrators block. Content filters can be hardware solutions or software solutions, although it is common to find them installed as software solutions.

Exam Essentials

Know the functions and application of various advanced network devices.   Multilayer switches are switches and have an embedded router process that allows routing of VLANs through the use of a virtual interface. Wireless controllers are used with lightweight access points. The wireless controller allows for the convergence of the data, control, and management planes. Load balancers distribute the load of applications commonly based on layer 4 and layer 3 traffic. IDS/IPS allows for detection and prevention of common threats via a threat signature. Proxy servers act as an intermediary between the user and the resource. The proxy server fetches content on behalf of user requests. VPN concentrators allow for remote user access via VPN protocols. AAA/RADIUS servers are used for authentication, authorization, and accounting of user access to network resources. UTM appliances have a number of converged services such as IDS/IPS, antispam scanning, identity management, and so on. NGFWs operate by using deep packet inspection to analyze threats via IDS signatures. VoIP PBXs are software or hardware phone solutions that replace traditional phone systems with VoIP phones. VoIP gateways allow for the extension of a VoIP network to a PSTN network. VoIP gateways will also allow for the extension of a PSTN network to a VoIP network. Content filters filter content users request based on heuristic rules or URLs.

2.4 Explain the purposes of virtualization and network storage technologies.

Before virtualization became a mainstream standard, applications had a one-to-one relationship with servers. When a new application was required, we purchased server hardware and installed an operating system along with the application. Many of these applications never use the full resources of the servers they were installed on.

Virtualization solves the problem of acquisition of server hardware and applications not fully utilizing server hardware. Virtualization allows for the partitioning of server hardware with the use of a hypervisor by enabling each virtual machine (VM) to use a slice of the central processing unit (CPU) time and sharing random access memory (RAM). We now have a many-to-one relationship with applications to servers. We can fit many applications (operating systems) onto one physical server called a physical host hardware. Each operating system believes that it is the only process running on the host hardware, thanks to the hypervisor.

Virtual networking components

So far we have covered components that support physical infrastructure. A virtualized infrastructure uses networking components similar to the physical components you have learned about already. You should have a good working knowledge of virtualized networking components, since virtualization is here to stay and is growing rapidly.

Virtual Switch

A *virtual switch* is similar to a physical switch, but it is a built-in component in your hypervisor. It differs in a few respects; the first is the number of ports. On a physical switch, you have a defined number of ports. If you need more ports, you must upgrade the switch or replace it entirely. A virtual switch is scalable compared to its physical counterpart; you can just simply add more ports.

The virtual switch also performs the same functions as a physical switch, with the exception of how the MAC address table is handled. The virtual switch only cares about the MAC addresses of the VMs logically attached. It doesn't care about everything else, since all other MACs can be sorted out after forwarding the frame to a physical switch. When a physical switch doesn't know the port a MAC address is associated with, it floods the frame to all the active ports. Virtual switches don't care about MAC addresses outside of VMs they are responsible for. If the MAC address is unknown, the virtual switch will forward it to a physical switch via the uplink port and allow the physical switch to forward the frame. This is how we can achieve low latency switching on a hypervisor virtual switch.

Virtual Firewall

A *virtual firewall* is similar to a physical firewall. It can be a firewall appliance installed as a virtual machine or a kernel mode process in the hypervisor. When installed as a firewall appliance, it performs the same functions as a traditional firewall. In fact, many of the traditional firewalls today are offered as virtual appliances. When virtualizing a firewall, you gain the fault tolerance of the entire virtualization cluster for the firewall— compared to a physical firewall, where your only option for fault tolerance may be to purchase another unit and cluster it together. As an added benefit, when a firewall is installed as a virtual machine, it can be backed up like any other VM and treated like any other VM.

A virtual firewall can also be used as a hypervisor virtual kernel module. These modules have become popular from the expansion software-defined networking (SDN). Firewall rules can be configured for layer 2 MAC addresses or protocol along with tradition layer 3 and layer 4 rules. Virtual firewall kernel modules use policies to apply to all hosts in the cluster. The important difference between virtual firewall appliances and virtual firewall kernel modules is the traffic never leaves the host when a kernel module is used. Compared to using a virtual firewall appliance, the traffic might need to leave the current host to go to the host that is actively running the virtual firewall appliance.

Virtual NIC

The *virtual network interface card (vNIC)* is just like any other virtualized hardware in the VM. The vNIC is a piece of software that pretends to be physical hardware. It communicates directly between the VM and the virtual switch.

The virtual NIC is usually a generic hardware that is installed in the VM. Examples are DEC 21140 NIC and the Intel E1000 NIC. Some hypervisors also have more advanced cards that support unique features such as VMware's VMXNET3 NIC card. The VMXNET3 NIC can support IPv6 TCP segment offloading (TSO), direct paths into the hypervisor's I/O bus for performance, and 10 Gbps data rates. These virtual NICs require the VMware drivers, since they are not generic hardware presented to the VMs. Hyper-V has a virtual NIC called a synthetic NIC; the NICs allow for similar functionality with features such as IPv6 TSO, single-root I/O virtualization (SR-IOV), direct ties into the Hyper-V VMBus, and 10 Gbps data rates. It too requires the VM to install the guest services software.

Virtual Router

The virtual router is identical to a physical router in just about every respect. It is commonly loaded as a VM appliance to facilitate layer 3 routing. Many companies that sell network hardware have come up with unique features that run on their virtual routing appliances; these features include VPN services, BGP routing, and bandwidth management, among others. The Cisco 1000v is a virtual router that is sold and supported by cloud providers such as Amazon and Microsoft Azure. Juniper also offers a virtual router called the vMX router, and Juniper advertises it as a carrier-grade virtual router.

Hypervisor

The virtual networking components would not be virtualized if it weren't for the *hypervisor*. The hypervisor sits between the hardware or operating system and the VM to allow for resource sharing, time sharing of VMs to the physical hardware, and virtualization of the guest operating systems (VMs). The hardware that the hypervisor is installed on is called the host, and the virtual machines are called guests. There are three different types of hypervisors, as shown in Figure 2.39.

FIGURE 2.39 Hypervisor types

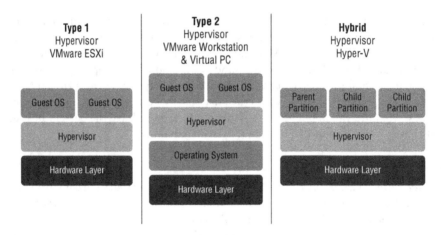

A *Type 1 hypervisor* is software that runs directly on the hardware; its only purpose is to share the hardware among VMs running as the guest operating system. This concept is not as new as you might think. IBM has offered mainframes that perform this partitioning of hardware as early as 1967! Examples of Type 1 hypervisors are Xen/Citrix XenServer, VMware ESXi, and Hyper-V. Although Hyper-V fits into the third category of hypervisors, it is still considered a Type 1 hypervisor.

A *Type 2 hypervisor* is software that runs on the host operating system. It runs as a process in the host operating system. Despite what you may think, Type 2 hypervisors do talk directly to the CPU via Intel VT or AMD-V extensions, depending on which vendor you are using. Memory utilization is similar to CPU utilization, but the host operating system parlays the requests via Direct Memory Access (DMA) calls. All other hardware is proxied through the host operating system. Examples of Type 2 hypervisors are VMware Workstation, VirtualBox, Parallels for macOS, and the open source QEMU.

Hybrid hypervisors are a bit different than Type 1 or Type 2 hypervisors. They function outside of the norm of cloud computing hypervisor models. They require a host operating system but function as a Type 1 hypervisor. As an example, Hyper-V requires the Microsoft operating system to be installed, but the host operating system is a guest called the parent partition. It is treated the same as guest or child partitions, but it is required for management of the hypervisor. Examples of hybrid hypervisors are Linux Kernel–based Virtual Machine (KVM), FreeBSD bhyve (pronounced beehive), and Microsoft Hyper-V.

Network storage types

As you just learned, hypervisors allow resources to be shared among virtual machines. The three main resources shared are compute, network, and storage. Hypervisors share the resources of RAM and CPU, which fall under compute resources. However, hypervisors need storage, and this is where network storage enters the cloud computing model. Two main storage types exist for hypervisors: *network attached storage (NAS)* and *storage area networks (SANs)*. Each type has its own unique benefit to the hypervisor or cluster.

It is important to note that over the past few years a third type of storage called hyper-converged storage has become popular. It is a cross between a SAN and *direct attached storage (DAS)*, and the hypervisor is responsible for the storage. You should expect to see this type of storage become popular in the coming years, because it removes the requirement of external storage.

Although I introduced this section on network storage focused on hypervisors, network storage is not exclusively used for hypervisors. It just seems to be the current trend of the market since virtualization is mainstream. Network storage is also used as storage for Microsoft Exchange, SQL databases, file servers, and many other nonvirtualized applications.

NAS

Network attached storage (NAS) is technically nothing more than a file server. Although I've oversimplified NAS as a file server, the important fact is that NAS serves file-based storage via a filer process. Examples of these filers are *Server Message Blocks (SMB)* and *Network File System (NFS)*. When the hosts read, writes, and deletes files, the commands sent are to a higher-level process such as SMB. SMB is then responsible for performing the commands against a file structure such as NTFS. An important aspect of NAS is that the security for the data is facilitated by the filer process and the filesystem. In other words, the NAS unit is responsible for filing and processing the requests for storage over the existing network.

NAS is commonly used as storage of files in an appliance-based solution. You can find NAS appliances serving files to clients where a server-based file server is administratively too costly, like in a remote office/branch office (ROBO). NAS appliances allow for features like backup and replication that normally require a high level of administration. Because

NAS appliances are purpose built, these functions are easy to set up and maintain for the administrator.

NAS can also be used for hypervisor support, but certain protocols, such as SMB 2.0 or lower, will not handle the requirements of the hypervisor. With the introduction of Hyper-V 2012, SMB 3.1 is now supported and can handle many of the requirements of a hypervisor in respect to storage. NFS is commonly used for Linux NAS storage as a filer protocol.

SAN

A storage area network (SAN) is separated either logically or physically from the local area network (LAN). When we talk about a SAN, we generally refer to the unit itself, but a SAN refers to the entire network for storage. The most dominant SAN technology on the market today is Fibre Channel (FC). Fibre Channel equipment is expensive to purchase and difficult to maintain. It is common to find one admin dedicated to Fibre Channel storage networks in large companies. However, many networks already have datacenter switching in place, so Internet Small Computer System Interface (iSCSI) is becoming popular as a replacement for Fibre Channel. I will cover both Fibre Channel and iSCSI later in this chapter.

SANs perform an important function: they provide block-level storage. Block-level storage is different from file-level storage in that the host connecting to the storage is responsible for storage of information directly to the volume on the SAN. This is coordinated by the use of a special adapter card called the *host bus adapter (HBA)* card when using *Fibre Channel* or the Ethernet card when using *iSCSI*. The hypervisor sends data to the HBA or the iSCSI initiator, which then formats the data to be written or read directly to the *logical unit number (LUN)* in a block format. This gives the host better performance and lower latency to the storage since read and write commands are at a very low level.

SANs perform security of the volume at a hardware layer. In Fibre Channel, zoning is used to partition devices to a LUN. This creates a logical layer of security that prevents one host from accessing a LUN dedicated to another host. In iSCSI, security is performed in the initiator and target as part of the iSCSI protocol. Since block-level storage gives the host hardware-level access, it is important to logically separate out the LUNs on a SAN or data loss could occur.

Storage is a complex part of a hypervisor structure and networks today. The CompTIA Network+ exam covers basic concepts on the subject of storage. If you want to learn more about storage, I recommend *Information Storage and Management: Storing, Managing, and Protecting Digital Information in Classic, Virtualized, and Cloud Environments*, Second Edition (9781118094839), published by Wiley.

Connection type

When you're connecting SANs to your hosts, you can choose from several different connectivity methods. I've covered two of the types of network storage: NAS and SAN. Next I will discuss the four common connection types for SANs: Fibre Channel, iSCSI, FCoE, and InfiniBand. Several others exist, but these are the most common found in storage area networks today.

Fibre Channel

SANs have different requirements than an Ethernet network, such as a lossless connection. Let's first explore potential problems of using a LAN for the storage network. Normal network switching performs a best-effort delivery of data, with the expectation that upper-level protocols will retransmit lost data. This retransmitting of data creates latency for the storage connection. At this point you may expect that data is not lost in transit in this day and age, and you are correct. However, normal switching equipment performs a function called blocking when too much data enters the switching equipment's interface buffer. There are expensive ways to fix this problem, such as nonblocking Ethernet datacenter switching equipment. This is one of the reasons Fibre Channel SANs are a choice for hypervisor clusters—they are designed for storage at wire speeds and lossless in their connections since they handle congestion differently.

The Fibre Channel protocol operates by encapsulating SCSI commands inside the Fibre Channel protocol. The Fibre Channel protocol uses buffer credits to avoid congestion. The buffer credit system allows for the source and destination to agree upon a buffer size. The source and destination use a hardware address called a worldwide name (WWN), similar to a MAC address. WWNs are generally 128 bits or 64 bits, depending on the age of the equipment. Common Fiber Channel speeds are 1, 2, 4, 8, and 16 Gbps.

Fibre Channel SANs also addresses redundancy and fault tolerance. Just as your Ethernet network has redundancy considerations, the Fibre Channel SAN is even more important because if a failure occurs, it will result in loss of data. The host's HBA has two connections, and each is connected to a separate storage switch for redundancy. Each of the storage processors on the Fibre Channel SAN storage unit are then connected to each Fibre Channel switch; this creates a storage fabric. As seen in Figure 2.40, if there is a fault on any storage processor, switch, or connecting lines, the SAN will remain operational.

FIGURE 2.40   A typical storage area network

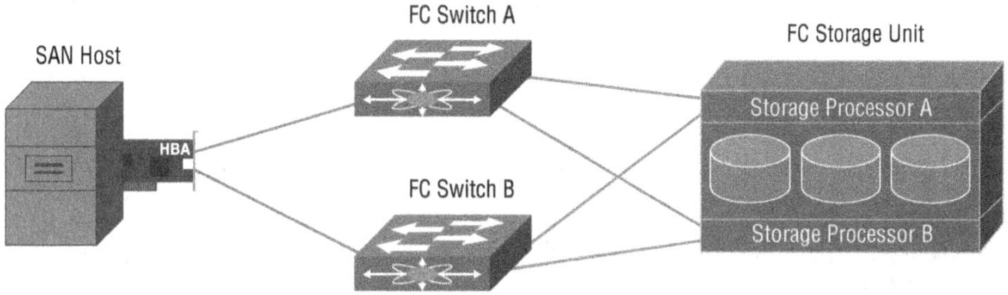

It is important to note that although FC SANs require FC switches and an FC fabric, Fibre Channel can be connected without an FC switch in an arbitrated loop. The arbitrated loop is often used for direct connection of storage equipment that is not shared to other hosts. The Fibre Channel arbitrated loop is often referred to as FC-AL.

FCoE

Fibre Channel over Ethernet (FCoE) is becoming a popular connectivity method for hosts. This technology was developed for datacenters to reduce the complexity of cabling. When you add a new host to your datacenter and you run Fibre Channel, you need two power cables (A side and B side), two Ethernet cables for host communications, and two Fibre Channel connections. FCoE reduces all of the cables (except for power) to two Ethernet cables. We can perform this magic with the help of a special card called a converged network adapter (CNA) and a datacenter switch that is FCoE compliant.

The CNA acts as a Fibre Channel HBA and an Ethernet card. The host addresses both of these functionalities separately, as if you had two separate cards installed. In most cases, the CNA requires two separate drivers as well, one for the FC HBA and one for Ethernet. When Fibre Channel commands are sent to the CNA, it encapsulates the FC data into an Ethernet frame and sends it to the datacenter switch. The datacenter switch then reads the frame and forwards it to the FC switching plane and eventually to the FC storage unit. In Figure 2.41 we see a network with a separate FC network and one with a converged FC network.

FIGURE 2.41   A comparison between separate SAN and network switching vs. a converged FCoE network

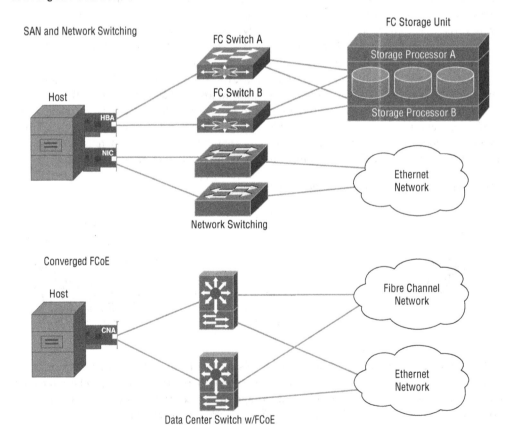

iSCSI

When you implement an iSCSI SAN, you are using Ethernet to transmit data over the existing switching equipment. SCSI commands are encapsulated with TCP/IP headers, typically TCP port 860 and TCP port 3260. These SCSI commands can then be sent over a normal TCP/IP network. The expectation is that you have similar redundancy and the proper data-center switching equipment in place, such as nonblocking Ethernet.

iSCSI is a cheaper alternative to Fibre Channel—that is, if you have the proper equipment in place already. It can deliver faster speeds than Fibre Channel implementations on the market today and uses the open standard of the iSCSI protocol. Typical speeds of iSCSI can range from 1 Gbps to 40 Gbps.

When sharing out a LUN to a host, you will associate the LUN with a target. The iSCSI target listens for requests from iSCSI initiators on the SAN storage device. This iSCSI target is where you implement security via MAC addresses, IP addresses, and a shared key called the Challenge Handshake Authentication Protocol (CHAP).

The initiator is a piece of software on the host operating system that connects to the iSCSI target. The initiator's job is to authenticate to the target, create SCSI commands, and encapsulate them in an IP packet. Most all operating systems today support iSCSI.

InfiniBand

InfiniBand (IB) is a standard high-performance computing network protocol that is used as a SAN connectivity type. It is different from Ethernet, because it was designed to be an extremely low-latency, high-throughput, and lossless connection. It requires an InfiniBand switched fabric dedicated to the SAN similar to Fibre Channel. The major difference is that very few companies produce this high-end switching equipment.

The host units connecting to storage require a host channel adapter (HCA) and the storage unit contains a target channel adapter (TCA). There are several different types of InfiniBand types that are out of the scope of the Network+ exam. The current specification of InfiniBand, called FDR, can deliver speeds of 56 Gbps to the storage target.

Jumbo Frames

Jumbo frames are just that, bigger frames! The maximum size of an Ethernet frame is 1500 bytes, and a jumbo frame is 9000 bytes. iSCSI storage benefits from these jumbo frames. If jumbo frames are used, data is less likely to be fragmented into smaller 1500-byte frames. When packet fragmentation occurs, the higher-level protocol of IP at layer 3 must reassemble the fragments. The reassembly of these fragmented packets causes latency and higher CPU utilization. Latency is the enemy of SANs.

A caveat to jumbo frames is that all the network equipment in the switching path must support this larger framing of data, also called the maximum transmission unit (MTU). If one of the switches doesn't support the jumbo frames MTU and you turn on jumbo frames at each end (initiator and target), you could end up with a performance decrease of up to 30 percent or higher!

Exam Essentials

Know the function and understand the fundamentals of virtual networking components. A virtual switch functions similarly to a physical switch, except for the difference of how the MAC addresses are handled. You can install virtual firewalls as a virtual appliance, and some virtualization software offers a kernel mode firewall in the hypervisor. The virtual NIC is a software emulated generic network card in the guest operating system. Virtual routers are similar to hardware routers; many network equipment manufacturers offer a virtual router. Hypervisors allow the hardware resources to be shared among virtual machines. There are two main types of hypervisors: type 2 hypervisors require a host operating system, and type 1 hypervisors are the host operating system.

Understand the types of network storage. Network attached storage (NAS) is a file-level storage system. NAS requires a higher-level protocol called the filer to process file requests. Storage area networks (SANs) are block-level storage systems. The two main types of SAN are Fibre Channel and iSCSI. SAN storage allows the host to access a LUN directly and read and write at the data block level.

Know the different storage connection types. Fibre Channel normally required dedicated FC switches and was designed for wire speeds and lossless connections for storage. With Fibre Channel over Ethernet, a single Ethernet cable carries both the Ethernet traffic and the Fibre Channel traffic. iSCSI is becoming a popular replacement for Fibre Channel, because existing Ethernet datacenter switching can be used for connectivity. InfiniBand requires a similar fabric as Fibre Channel and was created for high-performance computing.

Know the function of jumbo frames. Jumbo frames allow for larger frames to be send containing 9,000 bytes of data compared to 1,500 bytes in a normal Ethernet frame. This prevents the fragmentation of data at layer 3, which causes high CPU utilization.

2.5 Compare and contrast WAN technologies.

In this section I will cover different types of wide area network (WAN) connectivity technologies. In the real world, the choice of WAN technology is often based on availability rather than functionality and price. Each WAN technology offers a benefit and has different characteristics that I will describe here.

Service type

The service type defines the service from the provider or the type of service. For example, broadband cable is a cable company service type, and DSL is a phone company service type.

There are many different service types well beyond the following list. However, these are the most common service types that you will see for WAN connectivity service offerings.

ISDN

Integrated Services Digital Network (ISDN) is a useful service for voice calls, but not that useful for data. You will probably never use it for data services, and if you run into it, you will probably be migrating away from it. It is a popular connectivity technology for phone systems, like private branch exchanges (PBXs). You may have to interface with a PBX for integrated voice services someday. ISDN is still used today by phone service providers. It is deployed in two different modes: Basic Rate Interface (BRI) and Primary Rate Interface (PRI). PRI, which I will cover later in this section, is the most common implementation.

T1/T3

A *T1*, or tier 1, of service is sometimes referred to as a DS-1, or Digital Service tier 1. You specify the tier of service that you require when ordering service as a T1. The T1 provides 1.544 Mbps of bandwidth.

A T1 is a group of 24 channels of serial data. Think of the T1 as a conveyor belt consistently moving from one location to another. On the conveyor belt there are 24 buckets, and each bucket is a channel of data (DS0). We use a special device called a channel service unit/digital service unit (CSU/DSU) to convert the channels back into a stream of data. I will cover CSU/DSUs later in this section. If each channel is 64 Kbps and we have 24 channels, in total we have 1.544 Mbps of bandwidth. Channels can be used for voice or data. We can even divide T1 so that some of the channels are for the PSTN and some are for data. We can even purchase only a few channels of data; this it is called a fractional T1.

A *T3*, or tier 3, of service is sometimes referred to as a DS-3. It is the next step up from a T1 when you need more bandwidth. You may be wondering what happened to the T2. It existed at one point, but T1 and T3 became the popular ordering standard. A T3 is 28 T1 connections, or 672 DS0 channels, combined together to deliver 44.736 Mbps of bandwidth.

E1/E3

An *E1* is only common in Europe and interconnections to Europe. It too works by channelizing data in 64 Kbps buckets, the same as a T1. However, it has 32 channels. This gives us 32 channels of 64 Kbps, for a total of 2.048 Mbps. An *E3* is the European standard and consists of 16 E1 connections, or 512 DS0s, combined together to deliver 34.368 Mbps of bandwidth.

OC3-OC1920

The *OC* stands for optical carrier, since these services are delivered over fiber-optic cables. They still have channelized data and require a CSU/DSU—it just happens to be delivered over a fiber cable via a SONET ring. An OC1 has a speed of 51.84 Mbps. Unfortunately, there is some overhead in an OC1, which takes usable bandwidth to approximately 50 Mbps. We use the 51.84 Mbps when calculating OC speeds. An OC3 is three OC1s combined together to supply approximately 150 Mbps of bandwidth. An OC12 is 12 OC1s combined together to supply approximately 600 Mbps of bandwidth. You can see how the OCs are calculated. An OC-1920 is 1920 OC1s combined together to supply 100 Gbps, which is currently the top speed of optical carriers.

DSL

Digital Subscriber Line (DSL) uses copper phone lines to transmit data and voice. These lines are already running to your house or business, which is why telephone providers became ISPs. The provider will have a piece of equipment called a DSL Access Multiplexer (DSLAM) at the local central office (CO) where your phone line is wired for dial tone. The DSLAM is between the POTS in the CO and your house or business (premise). The DSLAM communicates with the modem at your premise by using the frequencies above 3400 hertz. The POTS system filters anything above 3400 hertz, which is why music sounds terrible over a phone call. Filters are placed on the existing phones at your premise, so your calls do not interrupt data communications, and your voice calls are not disturbed with the modem's screeching of data. Figure 2.42 shows a typical DSL connection and its various components.

FIGURE 2.42   A DSL network

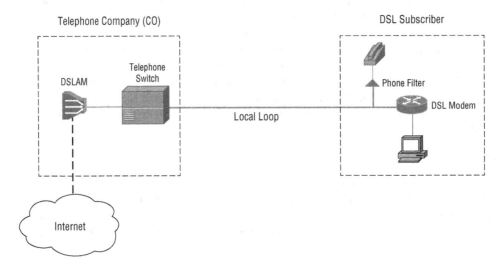

ADSL

Asymmetrical Digital Subscriber Line (ADSL) is the most common DSL offering to home and small business. The download speed is asymmetrical to the upload speed. ADSL has a typical download rate of 10 Mbps and an upload speed of 0.5 Mbps (512 Kbps). The upload speed is usually 1/20th of the download speed. Although this connectivity method has a decent download speed, you will be limited by the upload speed. ADSL is good for users who require Internet access for web surfing, but it is not the ideal technology for hosting services and servers.

SDSL

Symmetrical Digital Subscriber Line (SDSL) is a common DSL offering for small business. The download speed is similar to the upload speed: 1.5 Mbps. SDSL is comparable with T1 leased lines, which is relatively slow for most businesses today. SDSL is cheaper in comparison to leased lines, so for many businesses that do not require high speed, it is a good option.

VDSL

Very-high-bit-rate Digital Subscriber Line (VDSL) is today's replacement for ADSL and SDSL, and it lacks speed. VDSL can supply asymmetrical speeds of 300 Mbps download and 100 Mbps upload, or symmetrical speeds of 100 Mbps download and 100 Mbps upload. Just like ADSL and SDSL, it can handle these data speeds across the same phone lines you use to make phone calls.

Metropolitan Ethernet

Metropolitan Ethernet, sometimes referred to as Metro-E, is an emerging technology that allows service providers to connect campus networks together with layer 2 connectivity. This technology allows for the network over a large area to act like a LAN. The provider achieves this by building Ethernet virtual connections (EVCs) between the campus networks. The customer can purchase point-to-point EVCs between two locations, or multipoint-to-multipoint EVCs between several locations, to create a full meshed network. Metro-E can also provide this connectivity over many different connectivity technologies, such as lease lines, ATM, SONET, and so on. Metro-E is an extremely flexible connectivity technology that is cost effective and easy to configure, since it acts like a giant switch between network campuses.

Broadband cable

Cable companies introduced Internet access on their cable infrastructure over 20 years ago. It was this existing cable infrastructure at the time that allowed cable companies to become ISPs. Today broadband cable is available almost anywhere in metro areas and surrounding suburban areas. Broadband cable operates on a specification called *Data Over Cable Service Interface Specification (DOCSIS)*, through the use of a DOCSIS modem, sometimes referred to as a cable modem. It can typically deliver 300 Mbps download and 100 Mbps upload speeds.

A cable modem communicates over coax lines that are run to your house or business and lead back to a fiber-optic node (see Figure 2.43). The fiber-optic node is a device in your area that converts coax communications to a fiber-optic line that ultimately leads back to the head end. The head end is the cable company's router and distribution of their Internet connection. One disadvantage is the shared coax line that leads back to the fiber node. Congestion and interference on this shared coax line can degrade services and speed for everyone in your service area.

FIGURE 2.43   The broadband cable network

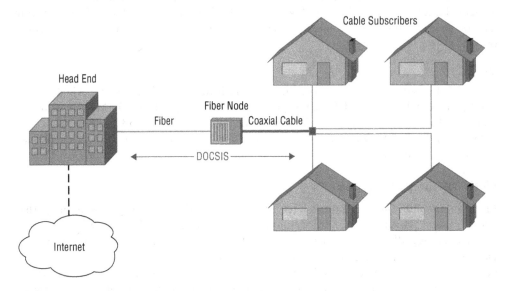

Dialup

Dialup uses modems on the public switched telephone network (PSTN) using a plain old telephone system (POTS) line. It has a maximum theoretical speed of 56 Kbps with the V.92 specification, although North America phone systems limited speeds to 53 Kbps. Dialup is too slow to browse the Web, but it is extremely useful for out-of-band management of routers, switches, and other text-based network devices. All you need is a phone line and you can dial in to the device. You may ask why you need it, if you have an IP address configured on the device. It is often used if the device loses connectivity from the Internet or network and is too far away to drive to. You can just dial in to troubleshoot it. Dialup is a backup control for network outages, since it uses the PSTN network for connectivity.

PRI

Primary Rate Interface (PRI) is an ISDN circuit, and it can be used for voice and data. When you purchase an ISDN circuit, you basically purchase a T1 lease line with ISDN signaling. A T1 has 24 channels of 64 Kbps. The ISDN functions by using one of the channels as a control channel called the D (delta) channel. The other 23 data channels are called the B (bearer) channel; this is sometimes noted in shorthand as 23B + D.

The D channel will control call setup, and the B channels will carry data or voice calls. Twenty-three channels at 64 Kbps is 1,472 Kbps (1.472 Mbps) of bandwidth. This is how ISDN excels when it is used for voice communications, since the D channel communicates call information for the other 23 channels to both ends (provider and PBX). In doing this call setup, it avoids something called call collisions. Call collisions happen when a call is coming in and going out on the same channel. It is a popular technology for voice but not for data.

Transmission mediums

Once you have purchased a WAN technology from a provider, you need to communicate to the provider for the WAN services. WAN providers offer various transmission mediums for the connection. Some providers, depending on service type, will allow the customer to dictate the transmission medium they hand off for the connection.

Satellite

Satellite communications allows unidirectional and bidirectional communications anywhere there is a line of site to the earth's equator. There is a group of satellites about 22,000 miles above the equator in a geosynchronous orbit used for communications. If you have a satellite dish, you are pointed to one of these satellites. In a unidirectional setup, you can receive video, voice, music, and data, but you cannot send information back. Your satellite dish operates in this mode of communications. It is also popular for command and control situations where first responders need to only view camera feeds and data such as weather. In a bidirectional setup, you can also send data back through the use of a *very small aperture terminal (VSAT)*, which is a dish that can transmit and receive data. Although this technology sounds amazing, there are some issues such as the transmission distance and the speed of light at about 186,000 miles per second, which is how fast your transmission travels. There are four transmissions that need to traverse the distance between you and the satellite and the satellite and the provider (see Figure 2.44). You first send your request to the satellite; then the satellite relays it to the provider, the provider replies back to the satellite, and the satellite replies back to you. So although it is a great technology for remote locations, the delay can make real-time protocols such as VoIP very difficult.

FIGURE 2.44 A typical satellite network

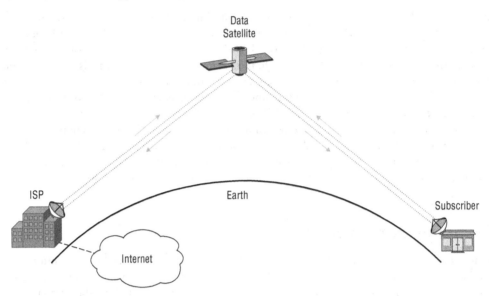

Copper

Copper cable is a popular handoff from the provider when the network equipment is within 100 meters or less from the provider's termination point. The various services that copper is used with include leased lines, broadband cable, DSL, and dialup. Metropolitan Ethernet services can be ordered as either a copper or fiber handoff from the provider. Copper has limited distance and speed, so fiber handoffs from the provider are more common.

Fiber

Fiber-optic cable (fiber) is used to provide extremely fast connectivity for long distances. Typical speeds of 10, 40, and 100 Gbps are transmitted on fiber, but higher speeds can be achieved. Distances will vary with the speed and type of cable being used; the typical range can be 150 meters to 120 kilometers (75 miles).

Fiber comes in two variations from the service provider: lit fiber and dark fiber. Lit fiber, also called managed fiber, is similar to Verizon's FiOS service. The provider is responsible for installing the fiber cable and for the equipment and maintenance on each end. Dark fiber is just a piece of fiber from one location to another, and the customer is responsible for lighting it and maintaining it. Dark fiber is used inside the network campus, and it can also be used for WAN connectivity. Dark fiber is the cheaper option after the upfront cost for equipment. Fiber is used to deliver several of the services covered in this chapter.

Wireless

Wireless transmission mediums are normally used when cabling cannot be accomplished or is too expensive. An example of this is Internet connectivity for ships and planes; other examples are remote locations in mountainous terrains.

Some services are exclusively delivered via wireless. *Worldwide Interoperability for Microwave Access (WiMAX)* is a connectivity technology similar to Wi-Fi in respect to delivering Internet over wireless. It is defined by the IEEE as 802.16 and operates on 2 GHz to 11 GHz and 10 GHz to 66 GHz. It can be used line of sight or non–line of sight when there are obstructions such as trees. The service provider will mount a WiMAX radio on a tower, similar in concept to cellular communications. The WiMAX tower can cover areas as large as 3,000 square miles (a 30-mile radius). This allows rural areas, where running dedicated lines is impossible, to have Internet connectivity. Subscribers need either a WiMAX card in their computer or a WiMAX router to connect to the tower. When WiMAX originally launched, it was capable of delivering speeds of 40 Mbps; it can now deliver speeds up to 1 Gbps. It is commonly used by many cellular providers to backhaul cellular traffic from remote cell towers.

Characteristics of service

Many of the connectivity technologies discussed in this section are dedicated, circuit switched, or packet switched. As you just learned, leased lines are dedicated point-to-point lines. If you put data in one end it comes out the other. In the following section, I will discuss the differences between circuit-switched data and packet-switched data (see Figure 2.45).

FIGURE 2.45   Circuit-switched vs. packet-switched

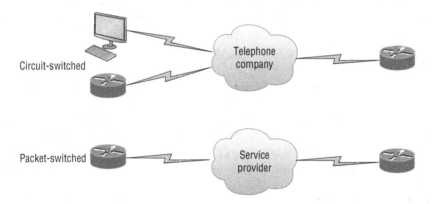

Circuit-switched data is similar to a plain old telephone system (POTS) call. When you pick your handset up and make a call, you create a virtual connection to the other side. During that time nobody can use the connection you have created. This is called the circuit, also referred to as a *switched virtual circuit (SVC)*. When you hang up, the SVC is torn down, and others are allowed to use it again. ISDN is also another type of circuit-switched technology that uses a dedicated channel of the ISDN line to place a call or transmit data (depending on implementation). Both POTS calls and ISDN calls/data use are examples of a dedicated channel on a shared public infrastructure of either the PSTN or public data network.

Packet-switched circuits take data streams and divide them into packets; then the packets are sent through the internetwork. The packets do not necessarily take the same path to the destination; they can take multiple different paths to the same destination. TCP/IP and frame relay are packet-switched technologies. Packet switching is the technology that allows the Internet to work.

MPLS

Multiprotocol Label Switching (MPLS) is an emerging connectivity technology that uses packet-switching technology. It operates by adding MPLS labels to each packet generated from the customer and switching them in the provider's network. This MPLS label allows the MPLS provider to packet-switch the data based on the label and not the layer 3 network addressing. This is why MPLS is considered to work at layer 2.5; it is not a true layer 2 protocol because it is augmented with an MPLS label. It is also not a true layer 3 protocol since the destination IP address is not used for routing decisions. This makes it an extremely efficient protocol for moving data. It is considered a packet-switched technology and can be used across many different types of connectivity technologies, such as SONET, Ethernet, and ATM.

ATM

Asynchronous Transfer Mode (ATM) is a networking technology from the 1980s. It provides high-speed data up to 500 Mbps by breaking data into 53-byte fixed-length cells. Since each cell is the same size, it allows for very efficient transfer of voice, data, and video simultaneously. Since data does not need to be fragmented and reassembled due to varying packet size, ATM can efficiently switch the data. The technology is used by both ISPs and voice providers, but it is slowly being replaced with IP services and MPLS.

Frame Relay

Frame Relay is a type of leased line service over T1 or fractional T1 with a top speed of 1.544 Mbps (see Figure 2.46). Frame relay is deprecated technology, and many service carriers have stopped offering it as a WAN technology. However, you will see it in service since it is most popular with manufacturing, where a very small amount of data needs to be sent and received between many locations. This technology is great for very small bursts of data like 64 Kbps. However, it should not be used if you require constant communication at higher bandwidth.

When you order Frame Relay circuits, you specify the locations that data will be exchanged and the committed information rate (CIR) that you require between the locations. You are charged based on the subscribed CIR, so it is less than a full leased T1 circuit. Frame Relay also shares the same T1 leased line for all the locations mapped to it, so it is cheaper than purchasing point-to-point leased lines for each location. Frame Relay is a packet-switching technology over shared telecommunications switching. This means that although your packets are private, you are sharing time in the telco switch, and if you are over your CIR, the packets can be dropped. The path between the two locations are built as a permanent virtual circuit (PVC) and are assigned a data link connection identifier (DLCI). When sending packets on the Frame Relay network, you encode them with the DLCI, and the packets are switched to the other location via the PVC.

FIGURE 2.46   A typical Frame Relay network

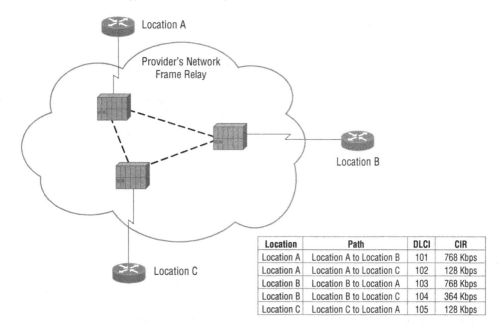

Location	Path	DLCI	CIR
Location A	Location A to Location B	101	768 Kbps
Location A	Location A to Location C	102	128 Kbps
Location B	Location B to Location A	103	768 Kbps
Location B	Location B to Location C	104	364 Kbps
Location C	Location C to Location A	105	128 Kbps

PPP

The *Point-to-Point Protocol (PPP)* is a standard layer 2 protocol used by many different serial point-to-point connectivity technologies. PPP allows multiple protocols to be carried over a logical (IP-to-IP) or physical connection (lease lines). PPP also provides mechanisms for authentication, error checking, header compression, and multilink connectivity. The authentication methods that can be used are Password Authentication Protocol (PAP), Challenge Handshake Authentication Protocol (CHAP), and Extensible Authentication Protocol (EAP). The PPP protocol contains three subprotocols (Figure 2.47) that are used to provide these features. The Network Control Protocol (NCP) allows multiple protocols to be used on a PPP link. The Link Control Protocol (LCP) provides the mechanisms for authentication, compression, error detection, multilink, and PPP callback. As you can see, LCP is the workhorse of the PPP protocol suite. The third protocol is High-Level Data Link Control (HDLC), and its primary responsibility is to frame data to get it from point A to point B.

PPP can be used on a range of different connectivity methods such as POTS modems, leased lines, VPN tunnels, and so forth. It is a very versatile protocol. When we have two leased lines on a router that connect point A to point B, we can use PPP multilink to aggregate them together. For instance, if we had two T1 leased lines at 1.544 Mbps, PPP could aggregate them together with multilink for a combined bandwidth of 3.08 Mbps.

FIGURE 2.47 The PPP protocol suite

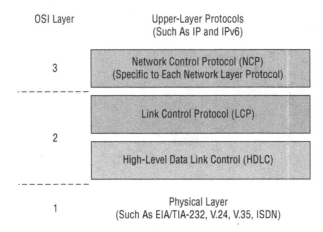

PPPoE

Point-to-Point Protocol over Ethernet (PPPoE) is a protocol widely used with DSL connections. The DSL modem uses the PPPoE protocol to authenticate users on DSL lines. It is also used in wireless provider networks where authentication is required.

PPPoE contains the Point-to-Point Protocol. PPP is used for the framing of data and authentication of the DSL connection, as discussed earlier. PPP was originally designed as a point-to-point protocol for serial lines. With DSL there are multiple lines connected to the DSLAM; this is sometimes referred to as multiple access.

This is where the PPPoE protocol adds some unique features to PPP, such as automatic discovery of the authentication point (DSLAM). It does this via a PPPoE Active Discovery Initiation (PADI) Ethernet frame. The authentication point then responds with a PPPoE Active Discovery Offer (PADO). This frame contains the MAC address of the authentication point, its name, and the name of the service. The client then confirms receipt of the information with a PPPoE Active Discovery Request (PADR), and the authentication point replies with a PPPoE Active Discovery Session-Confirmation (PADS). The PPP protocol can now exchange information for authentication purposes with the authentication point.

DMVPN

Dynamic Multipoint Virtual Private Network (DMVPN) is a protocol that dynamically builds Internet Protocol Security (IPsec) VPN connections between branch offices. DMVPN is mainly supported on Cisco routers and a few other vendors such as Huawei. IPsec by itself is not very scalable because of the complex configuration. However, the DMVPN protocol allows for a scalable mesh topology of IPsec VPN connections.

DMVPN operates in a hub spoke topology to allow the spokes of the hub to communicate directly between each other. The DMVPN operates as a service that runs on VPN routers and VPN concentrators. When a branch location (spoke) needs to communicate with another branch location (spoke), it will contact the main site VPN concentrator (hub). The main site VPN concentrator will communicate the IPsec VPN setup information for the other branch location, and the two branch locations can then securely communicate with each other.

The advantage of allowing communications between the two branch offices directly is a reduction of bandwidth through the main site. VPNs for branch offices normally are initiated from the main site. Traffic would normally traverse the main site when a branch needed to communicate with another branch. However, DMVPN allows for the branches to securely communicate directly between each other, thus saving bandwidth at the main site. In addition, DMVPN lowers the administrative cost of setting up VPN connections between the branch offices.

SIP trunk

A *Session Initiation Protocol (SIP)* trunk is purchased from a SIP provider for connecting VoIP PBXs calls. The SIP trunk is an IP version of a leased line for a PBX, since it allows for connectivity to the PSTN for VoIP. When you purchase a SIP trunk, you also purchase phone numbers for inbound calling that are called direct inward dialing (DID) numbers. Using a SIP trunk lowers operational costs since you are using the Internet as the method of connectivity for phone calls. Not all PBXs can support SIP trunks, so it is common to find older PBXs using a VoIP gateway as an intermediary.

SIP trunks function for both outgoing and incoming phone calls. You register a SIP trunk connection with a username and password via the SIP protocol. When a phone call is placed on a VoIP PBX outbound to the PSTN, the SIP protocol sets up the call on the SIP provider's side, and your VoIP phone uses the Real-time Transport Protocol (RTP) to transmit your voice. When a phone call is placed inbound to the DID registered with the SIP provider, the phone call is passed from the provider's side to the IP address that your VoIP PBX registered during the SIP trunk registration process. The RTP stream is then initiated from the provider's network to your VoIP phone.

There are two ways to set up a SIP trunk. The first, as described earlier, is when your VoIP phone makes the direct connection to the phone provider's VoIP service for RTP. This method reduces CPU utilization on the VoIP PBX, since the RTP is streamed end to end without the use of the VoIP PBX once the call is set up. The second method is to allow the VoIP PBX to proxy the RTP communications; this raises CPU utilization on the VoIP PBX. However, it adds security since all VoIP calls must pass through the VoIP PBX.

Termination

The termination is yet another characteristic of service. It defines the point in a network that a provider terminates their responsibility for their service before it becomes the customer's responsibility. It also defines how the service is handed off to the customer, sometimes referred to as the *handoff*.

Although it is not a formal objective for the CompTIA Network+ exam, you should be aware of how providers hand off services to the customer. Many WAN technologies I discussed in the previous sections can hand off the Internet connection in several different methods to the customer. The most common is Ethernet, but if distance is a factor, then fiber optic maybe specified in the buildout of services. Wireless can also be an option, when wiring is too costly or impossible due to terrain. All of these handoffs are outlined in the buildout of the services from the provider to the customer; it is generally a component of the initial setup costs. However, the buildout costs can sometimes be absorbed into the monthly reoccurring costs of service over the length of the contract for services.

No matter what method is chosen, the other side of the connection containing the customer premise equipment (CPE) is your responsibility. This is the sole function of the termination—it terminates the provider's responsibility for equipment and signaling.

Demarcation point

The *demarcation point,* often referred to as the demarc, is terminology used with lease lines and telephone equipment. Copper phone lines are considered legacy connections today, because of cheaper alternatives from cable providers and fiber to the premise providers. However, back when the phone company ran a copper phone line to your dwelling, you were responsible for all internal wiring. The telephone company would install a box on the outside of your house that would segment your internal wiring from the telephone company's local loop wiring. This box was called the network interface connection (NIC), and it was the demarcation point for the phone company. The phone technician would pull a jumper on the NIC and test the phone connectivity. If it worked fine, then the problem was inside your dwelling and was your responsibility. Of course, they would be happy to fix it for a cost!

Today with many other connectivity options such as broadband cable and fiber to the premise, the demarc has become the equipment that hands off service to the customer. The technician will disconnect the rest of your network and test basic Internet connectivity. Most problems can even be performed from the home office of the provider, since all of the equipment has built-in diagnostics to reduce the number of technicians dispatched.

Leased lines like T1s and ISDN lines have a mechanical jack called an RJ-48X at the patch panel. When the RJ-48 is removed, a shorting block bridges the connection to create a loopback. These mechanical jacks have largely been replaced with a device called a smart jack, which I will cover in the following section.

CSU/DSU

Channel service units/digital service units (CSUs/DSUs) are devices that convert serialized data such as T1 and ISDN to a serial protocol compatible with routers. The CSU/DSU sits between the router and the leased line circuit. In the past it was a separate piece of equipment, but many newer routers have CSUs/DSUs built in.

The CSU/DSU will handle the receipt of clocking data from the data communication equipment (DCE) on the provider's network. The clocking data helps the CSU/DSU convert the channelized data into digital data so that data terminal equipment (DTE) such as a router can understand the data. The CSU/DSU also helps convert data back into serialized data when the router (DTE) sends information on the provider's network (DCE).

The CSU/DSU uses the RJ-48C universal service order code (USOC) to connect to the provider's demarcation point. The CSU/DSU is considered part of the customer premise equipment (CPE), so it is the customer's responsibility. The router side of the CSU/DSU generally has connections for RS-232 or V.35, and in most cases the CSU/DSU is built into the router.

Smart Jack

Smart jacks are normally used with leased line circuits such as T1 and ISDN. The smart jack is a diagnostic point for the provider and is generally the demarcation point. It has largely replaced the RJ-48C electromechanical jacks. Smart jacks allow the provider to convert protocols and framing types from the provider's network. The router still requires a CSU/DSU, but the smart jack can change the framing type the CSU/DSU expects.

The smart jack also offers advanced diagnostic capabilities to the provider. Smart jacks allow the provider to put the circuit into a loopback mode. This loopback mode enables the provider to diagnose signal quality and error rates. The smart jack also offers alarm indication signaling so the provider can determine whether the problem is on their or the customer premise equipment. This alarm indication signaling enables the provider to dispatch technicians when the problem is discovered.

Exam Essentials

Know the various service types of WAN technologies.   ISDN PRI operates on a T1 leased line and reserves one of the 24 channels for call setup. T1 lines are point-to-point serial connections, utilizing 24 DS0 channels and offering a speed of 1.544 Mbps. E1 lines are similar in function to a T1 and are used mainly in Europe using 32 DS0 channels. T3 lines consist of 28 T1 connections and deliver a speed of 44.736 Mbps. E3 lines consist of 16 E1 connections and deliver a speed of 34.368 Mbps. Optic carriers (OCs) are based off an OC1 at around 50 Mbps. ADSL is asymmetrical, which means the download is higher than the upload speed. SDSL is symmetrical, which means download and upload are the same speed. VDSL is asymmetrical but much faster at 300 Mbps download and 100 Mbps upload. Metropolitan-Ethernet is a WAN technology that behaves more like a LAN technology. Broadband cable uses a coaxial network to communicate back to a fiber node that is wired to the head end at the cable company. Dialup is a legacy technology only useful for out-of-band communication when IP services are not available. The maximum speed of dialup is 56 kb/s.

Know the various transmission mediums used with WAN technologies.   Satellite communications allow remote locations to be connected to the Internet via satellite. Copper is used when the customer's equipment is within 100 meters or less from the provider's termination point. Fiber is required when distances are over 100 meters and can span up to 75 miles or more. Fiber can be purchased from a provider as a managed lit service or a dark fiber service in which you must install and manage the equipment on both ends. Wireless transmission mediums are normally used when cabling cannot be accomplished or is too expensive.

Know the various characteristics of WAN technologies. MPLS is a new standard that augments packets with an MPLS label; this label is what switches the packet to the destination. ATM is a legacy technology that switches fixed cells of 53 bytes at 500 Mbps; it is mainly used for service providers as a backbone. Frame Relay is a legacy technology and is being discontinued in many markets. PPP is a standard for point-to-point serial connectivity that provides authentication, compression, error detection, and multilink support. PPPoE is used mainly on DSL connections, and it adds functionality to PPP connections by allowing automatic discover of the authentication point (DSLAM). Dynamic Multipoint Virtual Private Network is a protocol that dynamically builds IPsec VPN connections between branch offices to form a mesh topology. SIP trunks are the IP-based equivalent to PBX lease lines for VoIP PBXs.

Know the various termination points of provider services. The demarcation point is the end of the provider's responsibility. The CSU/DSU converts channelized serial data from the provider's network to digital serial data for the customer premise equipment. The customer premise equipment is usually the customer's router. The smart jack enables the provider to remotely diagnose a leased line connection.

Review Questions

1. You are creating the specifications for a network cabling install. The cabling needs to sustain speeds of 1 Gbps, and the cabling will be installed in the welding area of your plant. What type of cabling should you specify?

    A. Category 5 cable

    B. UTP cable

    C. STP cable

    D. Coaxial cable

2. You are creating the specification for the cabling install between two buildings on your local network campus. You estimate that the buildings will be 2500 feet apart, and you need to supply 40 Gbps network speeds between them. Which cabling type should you specify?

    A. Category 7 cable

    B. Coaxial cable

    C. Multimode fiber-optic cable

    D. Single-mode fiber-optic cable

3. Your building is being renovated, and during the renovation much of the network cabling in the ceiling must be replaced. As the senior network administrator, you are responsible for deciding the cabling to be used. Which network cabling type should you recommend for the new network cabling?

    A. Stranded PVC cabling

    B. Stranded plenum cabling

    C. Solid-core PVC cabling

    D. Solid-core plenum cabling

4. You need to decide which cable connectors to order for a coaxial cable installation at a hotel you administer. The cable installation will provide guests with Internet access over MoCA set-top boxes. Which cable connectors will most likely be used?

    A. F-connectors

    B. BNC connectors

    C. RJ-11 connectors

    D. LC connectors

5. Which fiber-optic cable connector has a similar locking mechanism as a BNC connector?

    A. LC connector

    B. ST connector

    C. SC connector

    D. MTRJ connector

6. You are creating a specification for the equipment to be installed between two buildings that requires 400 Gbps network speeds. Which type of transceiver should you require in your search for the network equipment to support?

   A. SFP transceivers

   B. SFP+ transceivers

   C. QSFP transceivers

   D. GBIC transceivers

7. Your company requires fault-tolerant high-speed network connectivity between two locations. You are working with a dark fiber-optic provider and want to minimize monthly reoccurring costs. What should be ordered to minimize reoccurring costs and maintain the requirements?

   A. Two strands of fiber-optic cable and duplex transceivers

   B. Two strands of fiber-optic cable and bidirectional transceivers

   C. Four strands of fiber-optic cable and duplex transceivers

   D. Four strands of fiber-optic cable and bidirectional transceivers

8. Which termination point allows for easier diagnostics of Ethernet wiring problems to users' computers in your network?

   A. 66-block

   B. 110-block

   C. Patch panels

   D. Fiber-optic distribution panel

9. Your company is creating a new office and you want to future-proof the Ethernet network for 10 Gbps speeds. Which type of cabling should you recommend be installed?

   A. Category 5 cabling

   B. Category 5e cabling

   C. Category 6 cabling

   D. Category 6a cabling

10. Currently your network is running 100 Mbps switching equipment. You need to raise the bandwidth to the desktops to 1 Gbps. You examine the existing cabling and find that Category 5e cable has been installed. What will you recommend to achieve the goal while keeping costs to a minimum?

    A. Replace only the switching equipment.

    B. Replace both the switching equipment and replace the wiring with Category 6a cabling.

    C. Replace both the switching equipment and replace the wiring with Category 7 cabling.

    D. Replace both the switching equipment and replace the wiring with Category 6 cabling.

11. Which cable specification is not recognized by the TIA/EIA standards?

   A. Category 3 cable

   B. Category 6 cable

   C. Category 6a cable

   D. Category 7 cable

12. In which scenarios must you use a crossover Ethernet cable?

   A. Connecting a router to a switch

   B. Connecting a switch to a switch without auto-MDIX

   C. Connecting a switch to a computer

   D. Connecting a switch to a firewall

13. Which IEEE Ethernet specification defines a maximum distance of 550 meters at 1 Gbps?

   A. 1000BaseT

   B. 1000BaseLX

   C. 1000BaseSX

   D. 10GBaseT

14. Which devices provide the lowest latency and highest bandwidth for connectivity?

   A. Hubs

   B. Switches

   C. Bridges

   D. Routers

15. Which networking component allows you to detect and prevent malicious network activity?

   A. Firewall

   B. IDS/IPS

   C. Proxy server

   D. Content filter

16. Which network component will allow a VPN concentrator to authenticate a remote VPN user?

   A. Firewall

   B. Content filter

   C. NGFW/layer 7 firewall

   D. RADIUS server

17. You currently have a PBX that does not support VoIP. Which network component can you use to provide VoIP support to this PBX?

   A. VoIP PBX

   B. VoIP gateway

   C. SIP server

   D. SIP provider

18. Which type of hypervisor allows a virtual machine to directly share the resources of RAM and CPU without the help of the operating system?

   A. Type 1 hypervisor

   B. Type 2 hypervisor

   C. Hybrid hypervisor

   D. All of the above

19. Which storage technology uses dedicated switches to create a storage network for block-level storage?

   A. iSCSI

   B. FCoE

   C. Fibre Channel

   D. NAS

20. You currently use an iSCSI storage unit for your host storage. Recently you suffered a performance problem and found that the CPU utilization on the hosts is higher than expected. What can you do to reduce the CPU utilization while keeping costs low?

   A. Replace the iSCSI storage unit with Fibre Channel.

   B. Implement FCoE as the host access protocol.

   C. Replace the iSCSI storage unit with InfiniBand.

   D. Implement jumbo frames for the iSCSI unit.

21. Which technology uses one channel of 24 channels for call setup?

   A. ISDN

   B. T1 leased line

   C. T3 leased line

   D. E1 leased line

22. You need to provide network connectivity to a remote site on the side of a mountainous terrain. Which technology should you investigate that would cost the least on the initial buildout?

   A. Metropolitan Ethernet

   B. WiMAX

   C. DSL

   D. MPLS

23. You maintain several branch offices that use VPN connectivity to communicate with the main office. You notice that your bandwidth usage has increased at the main office as workers access resources at other branch offices. Which technology might help you lower bandwidth usage at the main office?

A. Frame Relay

B. Metropolitan Ethernet

C. MPLS

D. DMVPN

24. Your company is getting a new DSL Internet circuit. Which protocol will you need to configure to allow it to work?

A. PPP

B. PPPoE

C. DSLAM

D. PADI

25. You are having problems with your ISDN circuit. When the ISDN provider dispatches a technician to your location, where will they perform diagnostic tests when they are on site?

A. Loopback

B. Demarcation point

C. CSU/DSU

D. CPE

Chapter 3

Domain 3.0: Network Operations

THE FOLLOWING COMPTIA NETWORK+ OBJECTIVES ARE COVERED IN THIS CHAPTER:

✓ **3.1 Given a scenario, use appropriate documentation and diagrams to manage the network.**

- Diagram symbols
- Standard operating procedures/work instructions
- Logical vs. physical diagrams
- Rack diagrams
- Change management documentation
- Wiring and port locations
- IDF/MDF documentation
- Labeling
- Network configuration and performance baselines
- Inventory management

✓ **3.2 Compare and contrast business continuity and disaster recovery concepts.**

- Availability concepts
  - Fault tolerance
  - High availability
  - Load balancing
  - NIC teaming
  - Port aggregation
  - Clustering

- Power management
  - Battery backups/UPS
  - Power generators
  - Dual power supplies
  - Redundant circuits
- Recovery
  - Cold sites
  - Warm sites
  - Hot sites
  - Backups
    - Full
    - Differential
    - Incremental
- Snapshots
- MTTR
- MTBF
- SLA requirements

✓ **3.3   Explain common scanning, monitoring and patching processes and summarize their expected outputs.**

- Processes
  - Log reviewing
  - Port scanning
  - Vulnerability scanning
  - Patch management
    - Rollback
  - Reviewing baselines
  - Packet/traffic analysis
- Event management
  - Notifications
  - Alerts
  - SIEM

- SNMP monitors
  - MIB
- Metrics
  - Error rate
  - Utilization
  - Packet drops
  - Bandwidth/throughput

✓ **3.4 Given a scenario, use remote access methods.**

- VPN
  - IPSec
  - SSL/TLS/DTLS
  - Site-to-site
  - Client-to-site
- RDP
- SSH
- VNC
- Telnet
- HTTPS/management URL
- Remote fie access
  - FTP/FTPS
  - SFTP
  - TFTP
- Out-of-band management
  - Modem
  - Console router

✓ **3.5 Identify policies and best practices.**

- Privileged user agreement
- Password policy
- On-boarding/off-boarding procedures
- Licensing restrictions

- International export controls
- Data loss prevention
- Remote access policies
- Incident response policies
- BYOD
- AUP
- NDA
- System life cycle
  - Asset disposal
- Safety procedures and policies

In previous chapters, I discussed the networking concepts that help you understand how a network functions as well as the infrastructure that allows us to build networks from these networking concepts. In this chapter you'll learn how to maintain the infrastructure through the management and planning of daily operations. Regardless if you just built the network or you already have a preestablished network, you need to maintain the network.

The concepts discussed in this chapter help you maintain network operations through documentation, business continuity, disaster recovery, performance, patch management, remote access, policies, and best practices. You must master all of these topics to maintain the network operations of a network.

For more detailed information on Domain 3's topics, please see *CompTIA Network+ Study Guide,* 4th ed. (978-1-119-43225-8) or *CompTIA Network+ Deluxe Study Guide,* 4th ed. (978-1-119-43227-2), both published by Sybex.

3.1 Given a scenario, use appropriate documentation and diagrams to manage the network.

Whether you use a network diagramming application or old-school pen and paper, the underlying principle is documenting your work. To understand how a network or system functions, draw it out. It helps you visually see the flow of information and allows you to create a record for others to use.

Diagramming the network is only a small part. Documentation of key information such as wiring, physical, and logical assets and procedures is a big part of managing the network. If it took some time to obtain the details the first time and you don't write them down, it will take you the same amount of time the next time you need the same information.

Diagram symbols

A large part of becoming a network professional is diagramming the network and processes. However, you must be able to convey ideas with diagram symbols to others in your group as well, either through whiteboarding, documentation, or just plain old pen and pad. In order to document the network and convey these ideas, you should be consistent with the symbols you use in your documentation.

In this section, I will cover the basic symbols that are found in networks and diagrams today. I will detail two types of symbols for each common network device. The first is a scratch symbol that is used when you are whiteboarding or scratching out an idea on paper. The scratch symbol lacks the detail of a finish symbol; its only purpose is to convey an idea or diagram of the network. The second symbol is the finish symbol that is used in reading network diagrams and creating finish documentation.

Hubs

Although networks should not be designed with hubs nowadays, you may still have hubs in your network; hopefully, this is not the case. Hubs are layer 1 devices used for LAN connectivity. The symbol for hubs can be seen in Figure 3.1.

FIGURE 3.1 Hub symbols

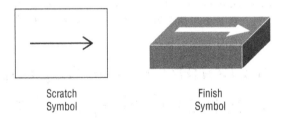

Scratch
Symbol

Finish
Symbol

Switches

Routers are common symbols, as seen in Figure 3.2, that you will use when diagramming the LAN. Switches are layer 2 devices used for LAN connectivity.

FIGURE 3.2 Switch symbols

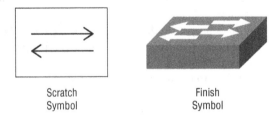

Scratch
Symbol

Finish
Symbol

Routers

Routers are common symbols, as seen in Figure 3.3, that you will use when diagramming the WAN of your network. Routers are layer 3 devices used for WAN connectivity.

FIGURE 3.3   Router symbols

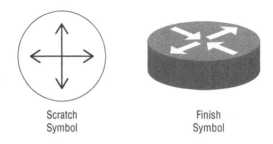

Scratch
Symbol

Finish
Symbol

Firewalls

Firewalls are security devices, and these symbols represent the generic version of a firewall. Each vendor will have unique features that might be detailed in the finish symbol. The scratch symbol should be simple for identification purposes in the diagram, as seen in Figure 3.4. Remember, speed is the critical factor when scratching out a diagram.

FIGURE 3.4   Firewall symbols

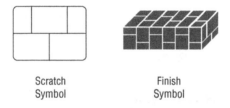

Scratch
Symbol

Finish
Symbol

Wireless Access Points

Wireless access points (WAPs) are symbols used for diagramming of WLANs. Figure 3.5 shows two of the most common scratch symbols and two of the most common finish symbols.

FIGURE 3.5   WAP symbols

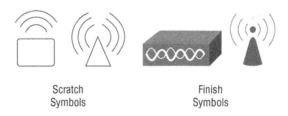

Scratch
Symbols

Finish
Symbols

Clients and Servers

Clients and servers are networking devices, just like firewalls, routers, and switches. You will use the symbols in Figure 3.6 when documenting a client-server process.

FIGURE 3.6   Client and server symbols

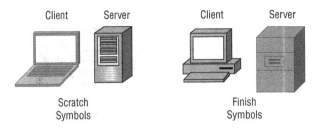

Layer 3 Switches

Layer 3 switches have layer 2 and layer 3 functionality. The symbols in Figure 3.7 are used to diagram a layer 3 switch, often the core of your network.

FIGURE 3.7   Layer 3 multifunction switch symbol

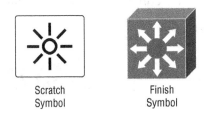

Connection and Network Type Symbols

There are various ways to diagram connections and network types with symbols. As you see in Figure 3.8, an Ethernet symbol is a generic way to diagram an Ethernet network. As you will see in the next section, it is preferable to diagram a switch, but depending on the type of drawing either is acceptable. The WAN connection is diagrammed with a Z shape. A network that is not the focus of the drawing, should be drawn as a cloud. This network shape is not exclusive to WAN diagrams and can be used in LAN diagrams as well.

FIGURE 3.8   Connection and network type symbols

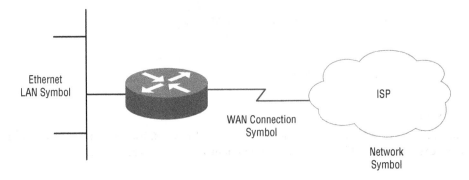

Typical Network Diagram

Figure 3.9 shows a finished diagram of a typical network. As I mentioned in the prior section, the cloud symbol is not exclusive to WAN networks. It can be used for LAN and WLAN networks as well, when you don't need to diagram the individual connections for clients or the detail is not the focus of the drawing.

FIGURE 3.9   Typical network diagram

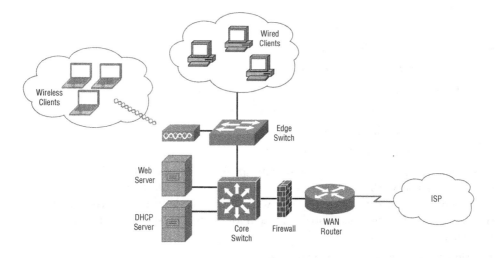

There are several other types of symbols that are out of the scope of this book. This should not be a limiting factor for creating detailed diagrams of the network. Always check the vendor's website for symbol sets, often called network topology icons. A great resource for networking symbols is www.cisco.com/c/en/us/about/brand-center/network-topology-icons.html.

Standard operating procedures/work instructions

Processes, *standard operating procedures (SOPs),* and work instructions are part of documentation process for a *quality management system (QMS).* QMSs are created to meet certain International Organization for Standardization (ISO) requirements. A common ISO certification is ISO9001. When a company is ISO certified, it means that they adhere to strict quality standards for consistent outcomes. There are many information technology ISO standards that your organization can be certified with. You have probably seen these certifications in a sales manual at some point.

A process in a QMS is just that—a process. A process is defined as taking an input and creating an output. Here's an example: the input to the process of decommissioning a server and the output of the process is that the server is wiped clean of corporate information. The process in this example is the decommissioning of a server. (I am oversimplifying the process in this example.) Most processes have an input specification and an output specification.

The SOP in this example outlines how to perform the process of decommissioning of the server. The SOP should clearly explain who and what is responsible and the standard they must achieve for the process. In the example of a decommissioned hard drive, the SOP would define the following:

- Who is responsible for removal of the server from the rack
- Who is responsible for wiping the drives in the server
- What standard the drives should be wiped to
- Who is responsible for removing DNS entries
- Who is responsible for removing firewall rules
- Who is responsible for clearing the BIOS
- In which order the tasks are performed

Several tasks are created from the SOP document. Each task is defined as part of your procedure to achieve the decommissioning of the server. The work instructions serve two primary purposes. The first is to detail how each task should be performed. The exact steps are detailed in the work instructions and for the previous example may include the following:

- How to remove the server from the rack
- How to wipe the drives in the server
- How the drive should be wiped
- How to remove the DNS entries
- How to remove the firewall rules
- How to clear the BIOS

The second purpose of the work instructions is to provide a training process for new employees. The work instructions are a more detailed portion of the procedure, so it becomes a training item for new employees on how to perform their job.

Logical vs. physical diagrams

Before you begin diagramming the network, you must decide what type of drawing you are creating. A *logical diagram* details how a network system operates by showing the flow of information. A *physical diagram* details why a network system operates by showing how the devices are physically connected. An example of a logical diagram appears in Figure 3.10.

FIGURE 3.10 A logical diagram

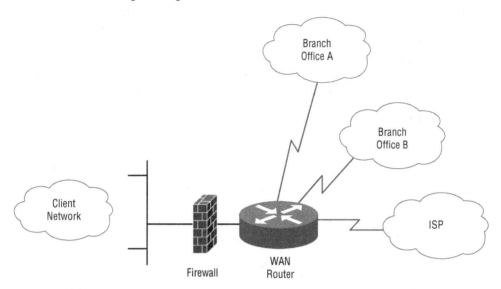

The diagram does not need to be exclusively logical or physical, but the diagram's main purpose should be one type of diagram or the other. Let's suppose you are diagramming your main site in a physical drawing and have several branch sites. The focus of the drawing is the main site; all connections for the main site's network should be detailed. However, the branch sites should only represent a logical connection and should be detailed in a future diagram, as seen in Figure 3.11.

FIGURE 3.11 A physical diagram

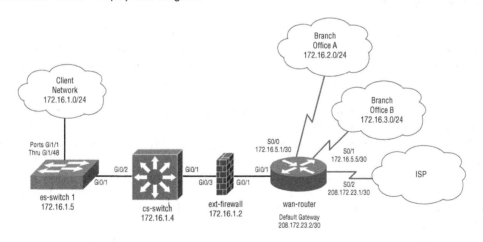

Diagrams do not need to be confined to network topologies. They can also represent ideas and concepts of a system. For example, we can use a logical diagram to detail each abstract layer so that we can easily understand the system as a whole. Figure 3.12 shows a complex SAN and how the disks are allocated to two RAID groups. The RAID groups are then combined, and the usable space is partitioned to LUNs and allocated to systems. Although the concepts in the drawing are out of the scope of this book, the diagram serves as a logical diagram with each layer that makes up the configuration of our SAN.

FIGURE 3.12   A conceptual logical diagram

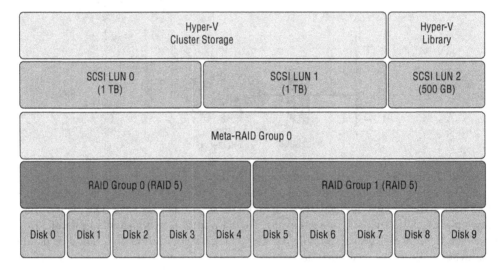

Rack diagrams

Rack diagrams help us to document the configuration of our server racks for three purposes. The first purpose is obvious: being able to locate the servers in the rack. The second purpose is the planning of new server locations. The third purpose is creating a physical diagram to detail how the racks are wired.

A typical server rack is 42 rack units high, and each rack unit is approximately 1.75 inches, for an overall height of about 73.5 inches. The typical rack numbering starts at the bottom of the rack with number 1 and the top of the rack with 42.

When I create this type of documentation, I simply use a Microsoft Excel document and detail each rack unit in the server racks with the server equipment that occupies the rack unit(s). This allows for quick changes when equipment is decommissioned or added and ensures that all administrators can update the documentation. This documentation also helps with planning when a new piece of equipment is ordered and you need to move servers and equipment around.

Many vendors offer Microsoft Visio templates for ongoing management of server racks. These templates allow for a finished diagram of network-server racks in the Visio application. I often use these templates when I am working as a contractor because it provides a finished look to the work being performed or pitched to the customer.

Change management documentation

Change management is a process often found in large corporations, publicly held corporations, and industries such as financial services that have regulatory requirements. The purpose of change management is to standardize the methods and procedures used to handle changes in the company. These changes can be *soft* changes of personnel or processes or *hard* changes of network services.

A change advisory board often meets once a week to discuss changes detailed in the change management documentation. The change advisory board can then evaluate the changes to reduce the impact of the changes on day-to-day operations.

The key to the change management documentation is knowing your audience. The *change advisory board* is often composed of people from the entire organization, not just information technology. Some change advisory boards are strictly IT stakeholders, so you must understand who will review the proposed changes.

The change control form details several pieces of key information:

Item to Be Changed   The item that is being requested for a change. Examples of items are software, hardware, firmware, configuration, or documentation, just to name a few.

Reason   The reason the item is being submitted for a change. Examples are legal, marketing, performance, software bug, or process problem.

Priority   The urgency, or priority, of the change will be documented in this section of the form, although this should also be conveyed in the reason for the change. The priority is often a separate field on the change control form. Examples are emergency, urgent, routine, or a specific date.

Change Description/Plan   The description or plan for the change is documented in this section. For changes in configuration, you would detail the changes to the configuration and why each part of the configuration is being changed. Firmware changes would list the version being upgraded from and the version being upgraded to.

Change Rollback Plan   The rollback plan describes the steps to roll back from a failed primary plan. If it was determined that the primary plan could not be completed, you would implement either an alternate plan or a rollback plan depending on the changes proposed.

Technical Evaluation   In this section of the form, you will document why the primary plan will succeed. The changes should be tested in a lab environment closest to the production environment and documented in this section. When creating the technical evaluation, specific objective goals should be outlined along with the metrics with which they can be measured.

Duration of Changes   Here, you will document the estimated duration the changes will take to be made. Any service outages will be documented in this section.

Each organization is different, and each change management document will be slightly different. However, the sections described here are the most common found on these documents. The change management document must be approved by the majority of change advisory board members or by specific board members.

Wiring and port locations

A tremendous amount of time can be wasted if wiring and port locations are not properly documented. The consequences can be seen each time your network team wastes time chasing down the other end of the cable.

When a building is being constructed, the low-voltage contractor is responsible for the installation and naming scheme of network cabling in the building. The contractor will often use the architect's room numbers as the naming scheme. However, the architect's room numbers will not always match the final room numbers decided by your organization after the building is finished. This is a common problem, and most of the time it cannot be avoided, but it can be documented.

Cabling that is installed after a building is finished is the responsibility of your organization. Some organizations have an internal maintenance department that install required cabling, and some organizations contract this work. Regardless of who provides the labor, a naming scheme should be standardized for your organization and provided before the installation of the cabling is performed. Do not leave it up to the person(s) providing the labor of cable installation—you may find that nothing is documented!

The *American National Standards Institute (ANSI)* and *Telecommunications Industry Association (TIA)* has standardized a generic naming convention for the location of network equipment in the ANSI/TIA-606-B standard. As seen in Figure 3.13, the floor space is divided into quadrants. These quadrants are then numbered on one axis with letters and on the other axis with numbers. So, grid coordinate F07 defines a specific floor space in an office or server room. It is a common practice to label server racks with this naming scheme on the server room floor.

FIGURE 3.13   ANSI/TIA-606-B grid coordinate naming system

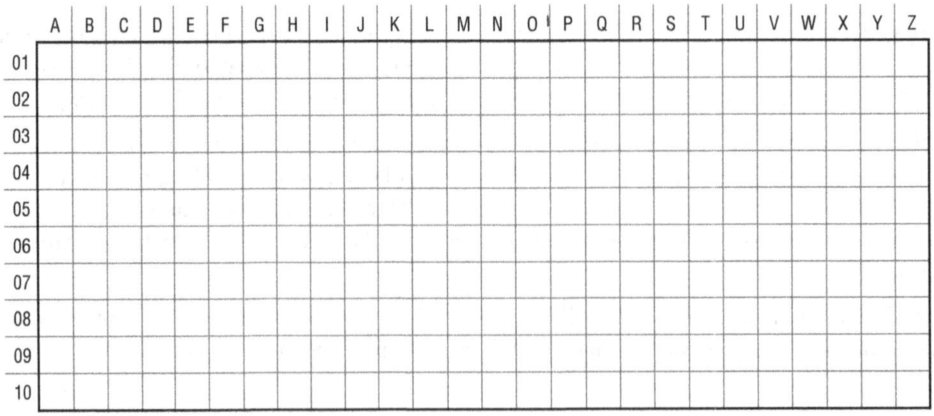

When planning a naming scheme for wiring, you must make it scalable for the entire building. A common naming scheme used internally in buildings looks like this:

Building: E9

Room: 405

Grid coordinates: A05

Patch panel: PP05

Outlet: 01

Using this naming convention, *E9-405-A05-PP05-01* defines a specific location the cable serves, as well as the patch panel that it is terminated on. This naming scheme then becomes the labeling scheme used for the cabling so that your network team never needs to hunt down a cable again.

IDF/MDF documentation

The *intermediate distribution frame (IDF)* and *main distribution frame (MDF)* were terms originally used by telephone providers to describe the distribution of communications. Today, it has become a way of describing the wiring distribution points of our internal networks.

The IDF is the switching closets where cabling is distributed to end client computers. Patch panels are often labeled with the naming scheme adopted by the builder. Often, these numbers do not match the actual room numbers because rooms get renumbered and reconfigured over the years. A document detailing the translation of these room and patch numbers should be kept up to date and available at the IDF locations for network technicians.

The MDF is the central location from which each IDF is supplied network connectivity. The MDF is usually wired to the IDF closets with fiber-optic cabling. Over time the MDF will have several fiber-optic connections, each leading to a different IDF closet. These fiber-optic cables should be documented extensively, because the other end of the fiber-optic cable can be a great deal of distance away.

Labeling

Having documentation is extremely important. However, the documentation might not always be available or easy to find when you need it the most during an outage. Because of these reasons, it is a best practice to always label everything with the designated naming convention.

Labeling for network cabling is produced with printed wraps, as seen in Figure 3.14. These wraps are often printed on plastic-coated protective labels so that they resist damage and do not wear off. Labels can be generated with standard inkjet and laser printers on a sheet when labeling several cables at a time, or they can be generated individually on hand-held labelers.

FIGURE 3.14   Network cable label wrap

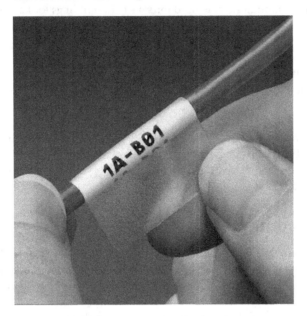

When labeling permanent cabling, use the naming convention explained in the previous section. The label should be clearly marked with the source and destination on both sides. The naming convention used for labeling should be consistent so that the field technician can decipher it.

Network equipment should also be labeled so that field technicians know which server to reboot or which piece of equipment has a fault. The labeling should contain the network name of the device, as well as any key IP address information. I'm sure you would hate to be the technician who took the website down by mistake!

Network configuration and performance baselines

It's important to document the network and its configuration so that you can easily troubleshoot problems when they arise. Examples of these configurations are the installation procedure for software, network wiring diagrams, and so forth. Any system that takes time to install or diagnose should be documented. These documents also serve as a point of diagnostic for others in your group, which relieves the burden of day-to-day operations. The location for these documents should be a shared location that is easily accessible by your team. It should also be secured from people outside of network operations, because these documents will contain sensitive information about your network.

I have been in many network outages where the information about the network was on the network and only on the network. This creates a chicken-and-egg scenario that you don't want to find yourself in during a panic situation. It is a best practice to create hard copies of key information about your network and compile it into a binder. Articles to be included are network diagrams, IP addresses of vital equipment, support numbers, and account information. Back in the mainframe days we called this collection of documents "crash books." If and when the system crashed, it was the first book you would grab.

Unfortunately, not every problem is evident or black and white as a network outage. Performance problems are the toughest and often take a great deal of time to resolve. I will discuss troubleshooting further in Chapter 5, "Domain 5.0: Network Troubleshooting and Tools," but for now we will focus on how documentation can help solve problems quicker. When you experience a performance problem, the first question to come to mind is "How was it performing before?" This is where a performance baseline comes in handy.

The performance baseline should be captured over a period of time that involves normal activity. An example of normal activity is Monday through Sunday during hours of business and inactive times. The best scenario is to constantly monitor and record the performance of selected network services. There are several tools you can use to monitor performance and compile baselines performance of the network. Microsoft includes tool called Performance Monitor that is built into the operating system. Other performance monitoring tools are Multi Router Traffic Grapher (MRTG) and Paessler AG's PRTG, and use Simple Network Management Protocol (SNMP). There are also many different pay-for applications that can monitor performance—too many to mention.

The performance baseline serves two purposes. First, it describes what normal activity looks like and answers the question "How was it performing before?" The second purpose it serves is to validate that you have solved the performance problem.

Sometimes problems are compounded, such as a web server performing poorly and at the same time the SQL database for the web server is performing poorly. These problems can be impossible to solve, because when you implement a solution to the web server, the SQL database is still performing poorly. However, if you had a performance baseline for both the web server and the SQL database, you could visually see if the solution implemented fixed a portion of the system.

Inventory management

Inventory management for IT assets has two specific purposes. The first is the tracing of assets valued by the company. The second is allowing IT to internally account for replacement and upgrades.

Every company has *fixed tangible assets*, such as land, furniture, and equipment. The management of the network equipment is the obvious responsibility of the IT department. When equipment is initially purchased, the accounting department will record it an asset of the company's general ledger.

However, over time the asset will lose its initial value. The accounting department will depreciate the value of asset based on its perceived lifespan. The IT department should work directly with the accounting department when assets are destroyed or no longer function since they will no longer be an asset.

All network equipment should be tracked from the cradle to the grave by the IT department. When equipment enters the company, it should be labeled with an asset tag. This *asset tag* should then be entered into the asset management software. The asset management software is often a module of the accounting package used by the company.

The IT department also uses inventory management to assess upgrades and the replacement of assets. Inventory management is used when a patch or update to firmware needs to be installed. An inventory management system will create a report of how many systems are affected. Another example is a report of all client systems and the amount of RAM for the evaluation of a software upgrade. This type of inventory management is more detailed than a purchasing record. These applications are often internal IT systems that collect data from the operating system through the use of an agent.

Exam Essentials

Know the various diagram symbols used in network drawings.   Two types of symbols are used: scratch symbols and finish symbols. Scratch symbols are used when sketching a diagram to convey an idea to others. Finish symbols are used when finish documentation is prepared. You should be familiar with the common symbols used in both sketches and finish documentation.

Understand how standard operating procedures and work instructions are used.   Standard operating procedure define who is responsible and what they are responsible for in processes in your organization. Work instructions define how to specifically perform tasks required for the standard operating procedures. Process, standard operating procedures, and work instructions are required when a company applies for ISO certification.

Understand the differences between logical and physical diagrams.   Logical diagrams detail how information flows in the network or system. The exact detail of connections between the symbols is less important than why they are connected. Physical diagrams detail how the network or system is actually wired together and operates. Physical diagrams emphasize details of the network.

Understand why we create rack diagrams.   Rack diagrams help us locate the servers in the rack, plan locations of new servers, and detail how the racks are wired. A standard rack is 42 rack units high and each rack unit is 1.75″ high for a total height of 73.5″.

Know what the basic elements of a change management document are and why the document is used.   Change management documentation is used to minimize the impact of day-to-day operations from changes. A change advisory board reviews the changes and signs off on them. A change management request will contain the item to be changed, reason for the change, priority, description/plan, rollback plan, technical evaluation, and duration of the change.

Understand the importance of wiring and port location documentation.   Wiring and port location documentation assist field technicians in locating cabling so that it can be tested or repaired in a timely fashion. Wiring naming schemes help to standardize the description of wiring locations so that a field technician can trace the wire back to the patch panel.

Understand the importance of IDF and MDF documentation.   The intermediate distribution frame (IDF) is the distribution point of cabling for end clients. The IDF patch panels should be documented with a naming scheme to assist field technicians in locating wiring. The main distribution frame (MDF) is the central distribution point for cabling to the IDFs. The cabling that runs between the MDF and IDF is generally fiber-optic cable. It should be well documented to assist in troubleshooting, since fiber-optic cable can travel large distances.

Know the various methods of labeling cables.   Cable labeling can be done with a special printed sheet of plastic labels. This is normally done when a large amount of cabling is being installed. Cable labeling can also be done on a one-off basis using a handheld label printer that prints onto plastic coated labels. Labeling should always define where the location a cable is coming from and going to.

Understand the importance of documenting network configuration and performance baselines.   Network configuration should be documented to help with troubleshooting of network-related problems. The network configuration should be placed in a shared location. Some network configurations should be printed in the event the network is unreachable during a problem. Performance baselines assist in troubleshooting performance problems. The performance baseline establishes a level of normal operations of the network. It is used to validate a problem and assist in validating a solution.

Know the various uses of inventory management.   Inventory management is used for tracking assets from the time they are purchased to the time they are decommissioned or damaged. This tracking process allows the company to use general accounting principles to assess its net worth. Inventory management is also used internally in the IT department to assess upgrades and replacement of assets.

3.2 Compare and contrast business continuity and disaster recovery concepts.

All companies rely on network services in some way for their day-to-day operations. These companies use network services for the storage of internal financial data, communications, client records, and so forth. Many companies such as online retailers and service providers can lose money by the second when there is an outage.

It is your job as a network professional to prevent loss of day-to-day business. The prevention of network impacts is considered business continuity. A simple example is to place your data on a RAID set of hard drives. Your job is also to recover from disasters; this is a reactive process since disaster has already struck. *Disaster recovery* can be as simple as recovering files deleted by accident or it can involve restoration of files because of a virus. In the following section, I will cover many of the concepts that help support *business continuity and disaster recovery (BCDR)*.

Availability concepts

Availability concepts support business continuity and are a preventive measure before failure happens. If you build the network services with resiliency to a failure, you have supported the continuity of your business during minor or major component failures. Each availability concept requires a different degree of cost; therefore, they are often viewed as an insurance policy for your business.

But availability concepts shouldn't just be viewed as an insurance policy. Some availability concepts support the continuity of network services when there are severe loads on the network services. This type of availability allows you to scale out your servers to accommodate the load. However, if this type of availability is not planned, under a severe load you could suffer a failure of the network services.

Fault Tolerance

Fault tolerance is the ability of a system to remain running after a component failure in a system. Redundancy is the key to fault tolerance. When systems are built with redundancy, a component can suffer a failure and an identical component will resume its functionality. Systems should be designed with fault tolerance from the ground up.

When installing the operating system on a hard drive or *Secure Digital (SD) card*, you should mirror the operating system onto an identical device, as seen in Figure 3.15. Mirroring is called Redundant Array of Independent Disks *(RAID) level 1* and supports the fault tolerance of the operating system in the event of a drive or card failure.

FIGURE 3.15   RAID level 1 (mirroring)

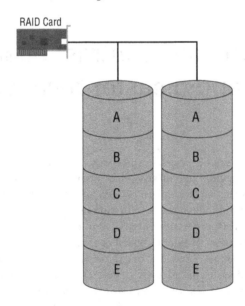

The data drives should be placed on a RAID level as well, but mirroring is too expensive since it requires each drive to be mirrored to an equal size drive. Striping with parity, also called *RAID level 5*, is often used for data drives. RAID level 5 requires three or more drives and operates by slicing the data being written into blocks, as seen in Figure 3.16. The first two drives receive the first two sequential blocks of data, but the third is a parity calculation of the first two blocks of data. The parity information and data blocks will alternate on the drives so that each drive has an equal amount of parity blocks. In the event of failure, a parity block and data block can create the missing block of data. Read performance is enhanced because several blocks (drives) are read at once. However, write performance is decreased because the parity information must be calculated. The calculated overhead of RAID level 5 is 1/N; if three drives are used, then one-third of the capacity is used for parity; if four drives are used, then one-fourth of the capacity is used for parity; and so on.

FIGURE 3.16   RAID level 5 (striping with parity)

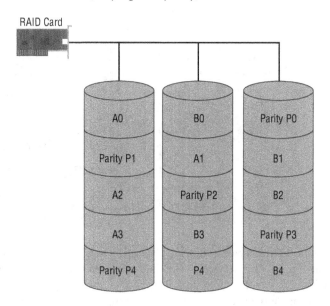

RAID level 5 has its disadvantages. Because of the larger data sets, when a drive fails the other drives must work longer to rebuild the missing drive. This puts the other drives under a severe stress level. If another drive fails during this process, you are at risk of losing your data completely.

Luckily, *RAID level 6* helps ease the burden of large data sets. As seen in Figure 3.17, RAID level 6 achieves this by striping two blocks of parity information with two independent parity schemes, but this requires at least four drives. RAID level 6 allows you to lose a maximum of two drives and not suffer a total loss of data. The first parity block and a block can rebuild the missing block of data. If under a severe load of rebuilding a drive fails, a separate copy of parity has been calculated and can achieve the same goal of rebuilding. The overhead of RAID level 6 is 2/N; if four drives are used; then two-fourths, or one-half, the capacity is for parity; if five drives are used, then two-fifths the capacity is used for parity; and so on.

FIGURE 3.17   RAID level 6 (striping with two parity schemes)

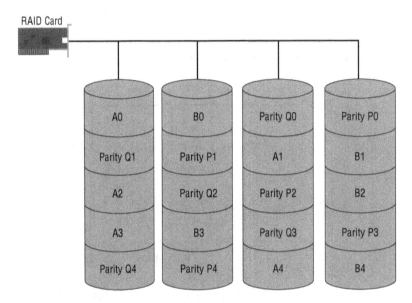

Disks are prone to failure because they have spinning magnetic platters. Disks are not the only thing that can fail in a network—the links between network switches can fail as well. As discussed in Chapter 1, "Domain 1.0 Networking Concepts," we want redundancy of network connections in the event of failure. Spanning Tree Protocol (STP) blocks frames on redundant links so that we don't have broadcast storms and duplicate frames. However, if a link fails STP recalculates and allows frames to be forwarded across the redundant link. We can even bypass entire switches by building redundancy into the network, as seen in Figure 3.18. The distribution layer or core layer can suffer a loss and continue to forward the information. Purchasing redundant switches is costly, but depending on your day-to-day operations and cost, if a failure occurs, the insurance of redundancy might be worth the price.

FIGURE 3.18 Redundancy in a network

Three-Tier Model

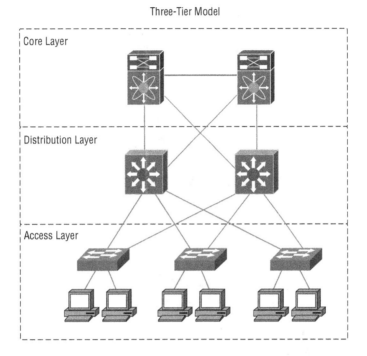

High Availability

Fault tolerance is the redundancy of components to prevent a loss of service in the event of failure. High availability is similar to fault tolerance because it prevents loss in the event of failure. However, the redundant components work together to prevent a failure and allow maintenance in a coordinated system. An example of a high availability system is *first hop redundancy protocols (FHRPs)*, such as *Hot Standby Router Protocol (HSRP)* and *Virtual Router Redundancy Protocol (VRRP)*, discussed in Chapter 1. Both of these protocols offer a highly available default gateway by providing a coordinated virtual router.

Although you could make the case that RAID are highly available systems, RAID systems are made for fault tolerance—when a system, or in this case a hard drive, has failed. Highly available systems generally provide a management interface so that portions of the highly available system can be taken offline for maintenance.

Load Balancing

Load balancing allows requests to an incoming service to be balanced across several servers. Load balancing helps support business continuity by preventing a loss of service from being overwhelmed with requests. A use case for load balancing is a web server with high CPU utilization due to requests. We can add another web server and place a load balancer in front of both web servers. The load balancer will then distribute the load across both web servers. We can even add more web servers as demand increases. When we add servers to satisfy demand, it is called *scaling out*, as seen in Figure 3.19.

FIGURE 3.19 Scaling out a web server

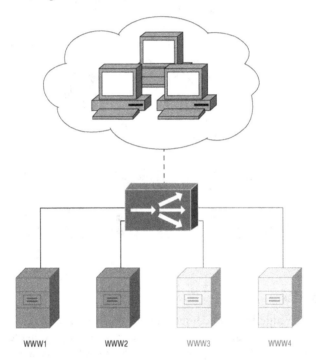

Load balancers can be purchased as hardware appliances, or they can be configured as software services. *Network Load Balancing (NLB)* is a service included in the Microsoft operating system for load balancing of services. HAProxy is a Linux open source solution for load balancing of TCP services.

NIC Teaming

Network interface card (NIC) teaming is a mechanism that allows for multiple network cards to function together to provide aggregation of bandwidth or redundancy of connections. *NIC teaming* can be configured to aggregate the bandwidth of two connections to the switching equipment. In this configuration, a server with two 10 Gbps cards could aggregate bandwidth to 20 Gbps. When NIC teaming is configured for redundancy, as shown in Figure 3.20, if one network card would fail the other card would detect the failure and resume operations for the other failed card. NIC teaming for redundancy often uses a heartbeat between cards to detect a failure. The heartbeat is a broadcast or multicast between the two or more NICs that allows each of the NIC teaming members to monitor each other's connectivity.

FIGURE 3.20   Redundant team of NICs

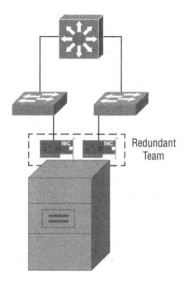

NIC teaming was always a function of the software driver of the network card driver. However, with the introduction of Microsoft Windows Server 2012, Microsoft allows the operating system to team network cards together, even if the software driver never supported the functionality. However, the cards must be of the same speed.

Port Aggregation

Port aggregation is a mechanism for aggregating ports together for increasing bandwidth between switches—say, if you had two switches and needed to provide more bandwidth between the connected switches than the current 1 Gbps link. You could add another 1 Gbps link and aggregate both ports together to provide 2 Gbps of bandwidth, as shown in Figure 3.21. Most switches will allow two to eight links to be aggregated together.

FIGURE 3.21   LACP port aggregation between two switches

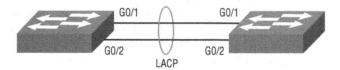

A common protocol used for port aggregation is IEEE 802.3ad *Link Aggregation Control Protocol (LACP)*. LACP is an open standard that will allow aggregation of ports between two different vendors. Another port aggregation protocol is the Cisco proprietary

protocol called *Port Aggregation Protocol (PAgP)*. The PAgP protocol can only be configured on Cisco switches and routers.

Clustering

Clustering provides failover, load balancing, and high availability for the services running on the cluster. *Microsoft Cluster Services (MSCS)* is an example of server clustering in which multiple servers work together to provide high availability of services such as SQL Server.

Server clusters are active-passive clusters that allow only one of the servers at a time, called the active host, to process requests. Servers participating in the cluster have equal access to shared storage where the service is installed. The cluster members monitor each other through the use of a heartbeat. If the active host fails, the passive host becomes the active host serving requests for the service. A failure does not need to occur for a passive host to become the active host. In the event of maintenance, an active host can be placed into maintenance mode. This will allow the active host to close out any current requests and move future requests to the passive host, which will become the active host.

Appliances can also function as clusters to provide failover, load balancing, and high availability of its services. Wireless LAN controllers (WLCs) can generally be placed into a cluster to provide high availability of wireless services. Wireless LAN controllers are just one type of appliance that can provide clustering; there are many others, such as SPAM scanning and datacenter management.

Power Management

Without the proper power management, all of the fault-tolerant and high-availability systems are worthless. Big datacenters like Internet service provider (ISP) co-location facilities often have a person on staff who maintains power management for the facility. However, if you just have a small server farm, you will need to be that person. Over the past 20 years working in a private datacenter, I have learned a lot about power, and I've suffered heartburn from not having the proper power management.

Battery Backup/UPS

An *uninterruptable power supply (UPS)* is a battery backup system that allows for power conditioning during power sags, power surges, and power outages. A UPS should only be used until a power generator can start supplying a steady source of power. For workstations and server installations where backup generators are not available, the UPS allows enough time for systems to gracefully shut down. UPSs are most often used incorrectly as a source of power generation during a power outage. The problem with this scenario is that there is a finite amount of power in the battery system. It may allow you some time to stay running, but if the power is out for too long, the UPS will shut down when the batteries are depleted.

UPS systems should be used to supply power while a power generator is starting up. This protects the equipment during the power sag that a generator creates during its startup after a power outage has triggered it.

There are several types of UPS systems that you may encounter. The main types are as follows:

- A *standby UPS* is the most common UPS that you find under a desk protecting a personal computer. It operates by transferring the load from the AC line to the battery-supplied inverter, and capacitors in the unit help to keep the power sag to a minimum. These units work well, but they are not generally found in server rooms.

- A *line interactive UPS* is commonly used for small server rooms and racks of networking equipment. It operates by supplying power from the AC line to the inverter. When a power failure occurs, the line signals the inverter to draw power from the batteries. This might seem similar to a standby UPS, but the difference is that the load is not shifted. In a standby UPS, the load must shift from AC to a completely different circuit (the inverter), whereas on a line interactive UPS the inverter is always wired to the load but only during the power outage is the inverter running on batteries. This shift in power allows for a much smoother transition of power.

- An *online UPS* is the standard for datacenters. It operates by supplying AC power to a rectifier/charging circuit that maintains a charge for the batteries. The batteries then supply the inverter with a constant DC power source. The inverter converts the DC power source back into an AC power circuit again that supplies the load. The benefit of an online UPS is that the power is constantly supplied from the batteries. When there is a power loss, the unit maintains a constant supply of power to the load. The other benefit is that the online UPS always supplies a perfect AC signal.

Power Generators

Power generators supply power during a power outage. Power generators consist of three major components: fuel, an engine, and a generator. The engine burns the fuel to turn the generator and create power. The three common sources of fuel are natural gas, gasoline, and diesel. Diesel fuel generators are the most common type of generator supplying datacenters around the world.

As mentioned in the previous section, generators require a startup period before they can supply a constant source of electricity. In addition to the startup period, there is also a switchover lag. When a power outage occurs, the transfer switch moves the load from the street power to the generator circuit. UPSs help bridge both the lag and sag in electricity supply during the switchover and startup periods.

Dual-Power Supplies

Power generators and battery UPSs are a requirement to operate during a power outage. However, if a power supply in a piece of network equipment malfunctions, the equipment is dead. With the best support contracts, you could wait up to 4 hours before a new power supply arrives and you are back up and running again. Therefore, dual-power supplies are a requirement if high availability is desired. Fortunately, most networking equipment can be purchased with an optional second power supply. Dual-power supplies operate in a few different ways:

- *Active/passive* dual-power supplies allow only one power supply to supply power at a time. When a power fault occurs, the entire load of the device is shifted to the passive power supply, and then it becomes the active power supply. One problem with active-passive dual-power supplies is that only one power supply operates at a time. If the passive power supply is worn with age and the load is transferred, it has a higher chance of not functioning properly.

- *Load balancing* dual-power supplies allow both power supplies to operate in an active-active configuration. Both power supplies will supply a portion of the power to balance out the load. Load-balancing dual-power supplies have a similar problem as active-passive dual-power supplies, because one will eventually have to carry the entire load.

- *Load-shifting* dual-power supplies are found in servers and datacenter equipment. As power is supplied by one power supply, the load or a portion of the load is slowly transferred to the other power supply and then back again. This method allows for testing of both power supplies, so problems are identified before an actual power outage.

Redundant Circuits

In datacenters each rack is supplied an A and B electric circuit. Each rack will have two power strips, called *power distribution units (PDUs)*. The A PDU supplies the first power supply in a dual-power supply configuration; the B PDU will supply the second power supply. In the event of a problem with one electrical circuit, the second circuit will continue supplying the load. It is also common for each A and B circuit to have separate dedicated UPSs and generators with independent fuel supplies.

Recovery

Recovery is required if you have suffered a disaster. The disaster can be as simple as a file being deleted or as devastating as a tornado. Fortunately, we can plan for recovery in many different ways to speed up recovery.

Cold Sites

A cold site does not describe the temperature as its name might suggest. A cold site is a networked space used after disaster has struck your primary site. Your network team will have to purchase network equipment, since cold sites do not generally contain any equipment. Many ISPs will offer a cold site in the event you actually need one. This is the cheapest of all the disaster recovery plans, because you won't invest in any equipment until after the disaster has struck. The downfall is that it will take time to acquire, set up, and configure the equipment.

Warm Sites

A warm site will contain some network equipment essential to resuming network operations. A warm site can be a dedicated rack in an ISP or even another building that will contain the essential network equipment. The equipment is dedicated to the recovery of operations, so minimal effort will be required. However, manual intervention is required by the network team in a warm site. I've seen many companies use their prior generation of server equipment for a warm disaster recovery site.

Hot Sites

A hot site contains equipment that can resume 100 percent of the primary site's network operations. In addition, it is fully automated, requiring no manual intervention. These disaster recovery strategies are the most expensive to operate and maintain. They require a duplication of the primary site's equipment as well as expensive automation software. However, they will switch operations over with minimal downtime.

Backups

Backups are not just there for disasters. The problem could be as simple as mistakes on the part of the user deleting files. However, backups are typically used for larger problems such as malicious data loss or failures of disk subsystems.

The concept of the *recovery point objective (RPO)* defines the point in time that you can restore to in the event of a disaster. The RPO is often the night before, since backup windows are often scheduled at night. The concept of *recovery time objective (RTO)* defines how fast you can restore the data. The next sections discuss backup methods, some of which can speed up the backing up of data. However, the disadvantage is that these methods will increase the recovery time, as I will explain.

Administrators will adopt a rotation schedule for long-term archiving of data. The most popular backup rotation is *grandfather, father, son (GFS)*. The GFS rotation specifies that the daily backup will be rotated on a *first-in, first-out (FIFO)* basis. One of the daily backups will become the weekly backup on a FIFO basis. And lastly, one of the weekly backups will become the month-end backup. Policies should be created such as retaining 6 daily backups, retaining 4 weekly backups, and retaining 12 monthly backups. As you progress further away from the first six days, the RPO jumps to a weekly basis and then to a monthly basis. However, the benefit is that you can retain data over a longer period of time with the same number of tapes.

Three types of media are commonly used for backups:

- *Disk-to-tape* backups have evolved quite a bit throughout the years. Today, Linear Tape-Open (LTO) technology has become the successor for backups. LTO can provide 6 TB of raw capacity per tape, with plans for 48 TB per tape in the near future. Tapes are portable enough to rotate off-site for safekeeping. However, they require time to record the data, resulting in lengthy backup windows. Restore requires time to tension the tape, locate the data, and restore the data, making the RTO a lengthy process.

- *Disk-to-disk* backups have become a standard in datacenters as well because of the short RTO. They can record the data quicker, thus shortening backup windows. They also do not require tensioning like tapes and seeking for the data like a tape requires. However, the capacity of a disk is much smaller than tapes because the drives remain in the backup unit. Data deduplication can provide a nominal 10:1 compression ratio depending on the data. This means that 10 TBs of data can be compressed on 1 TB of disk storage. So a 10 TB storage unit can potentially back up 100 TBs of data; again, this depends on the types of files you are backing up. The more similar data is, the better the compression ratio. It is important to note that the backup utility in Windows Server only supports disk-to-disk backups. If disk-to-tape is required, third-party software must be purchased. The built-in Windows backup also does not support data deduplication.

- *Disk-to-cloud* is another popular and emerging backup technology. It is often used with disk-to-disk backups to provide an off-site storage location for end-of-week backups or monthly backups. The two disadvantages of disk-to-cloud is the ongoing cost and the lengthy RTO. The advantage is that expensive backup equipment does not need to be purchased along with the ongoing purchase of tapes.

Full

A full backup is just that: a full backup of the entire dataset. A full backup requires the longest windows of all the methods. Therefore, full backups are generally performed on weekends, when we have a lengthy window. All files are backed up regardless of the archive bit state. The archive bit is an attribute of each file; when a file is created or modified, the archive bit is turned on. When a full backup is performed, all of the archive bits are reset on the files in the dataset. This type of backup is not sustainable through the week, because it backs up all the files whether or not they have been modified.

Incremental

An incremental backup is used to speed up backups through the week when backup windows are short. An incremental backup will copy all files with the archive bit set; after the files are backed up, the archive bit will be reset. Only the files that were created and modified from the last full or prior incremental are copied, so backups are small. However, if you need to restore from an incremental, you will need to restore the full as well as all of the incremental backup files up to the RPO required. This type of restore will create a longer RTO, because of the multiple backups that are required.

Differential

A differential backup is also used to speed up backups through the week. It will copy all the files with the archive bit set as well, but it will not reset the archive bit after it has done so. A differential will create a gradually larger backup until a full backup is completed and the archive bits are reset again. This type of backup will have a short RTO than incremental backups, because only the full and the last differential are needed to restore to the RPO required.

Snapshots

Before snapshots, when a user called in and said, "I desperately need this file from 10 a.m.!" all we could say was, "I can restore it from last night at 10 p.m." Unfortunately, this would mean that the user would lose 2 hours or more of valuable work. So snapshots were invented just for this purpose. Starting with Microsoft Windows Server 2003, *New Technology File*

System (NTFS) included a service called the *Volume Snapshot Service (VSS)*. The VSS could snapshot an entire volume in a split second and allow the user to restore files up to the last 64 snapshots. This gives users the ability to restore their own files.

Snapshots do not copy any information; instead, they take a picture of the file and folder structure. When you change or delete a file or folder, it is archived to a protected portion of the operating system, and a pointer is placed into the snapshot. When a user performs a restore for a file or folder from the snapshot, the pointer will direct the restore to the protected storage. This allows up-to-the-minute snapshots with little performance drain on the operating system.

Snapshots are not an exclusive Microsoft technology—Microsoft's implementation is only the most common. The snapshot can also be found on SAN equipment. It is most commonly used for daily backups of data, because a backup can be created from the snapshot. This allows all the files to be backed up at a precise time when the snapshot was taken.

MTTR

The mean time to repair (MTTR) is the measurement of the maintainability for repairable items in a fault-tolerant system. The measurement is generally represented in hours and represents the average time required to repair the failed item.

The MTTR is often found as an article in a maintenance contract for a fault-tolerant system. The MTTR in the contract will define the average time it takes for the vendor to repair the system.

MTBF

The mean time between failures (MTBF) is the average measurement of reliability of a component. You can think of it as the expected life of the component or product. It is commonly found as an advertised specification for hard disks published in hours. A hard disk with a MTBF of 1 million hours based on a specific workload means that a failure could occur after 300,000 hours. However, 300,000 hours is roughly 34 years, and not every hard drive will last that long. That is why this is an average of reliability and not the actual reliability of the component.

SLA requirements

The *service level agreement (SLA)* is an expected level of service that the service provider will adhere to for uptime. The SLA is detailed in the service contract as a percentage of uptime per year; it is often called "the nines." When a service provider exceeds the percentage of uptime defined in the SLA agreement, the provider is in breach of the contract. The contract will often identify what is considered in the SLA requirement as well as the terms if they breach the SLA requirement.

You should be careful with SLAs, because being up 99 percent of the time means the service provider can be down 3 days and 15 hours over the course of a year before breaching the contract. A service provider with 5 nines (99.999 percent) means the service provider can be down 5 minutes and 15 seconds over the course of a year before breaching the contract. Table 3.1 details the different nines of an SLA for uptime.

TABLE 3.1   Uptime for nines of an SLA

SLA %	Downtime per year	Downtime per month	Downtime per day
99% (two nines)	3.65 days	7.2 hours	14.4 minutes
99.9% (three nines)	8.76 hours	43.8 minutes	1.44 minutes
99.99% (four nines)	52.56 minutes	4.38 minutes	8.64 seconds
99.999% (five nines)	5.26 minutes	25.9 seconds	864.3 milliseconds
99.9999% (six nines)	31.5 seconds	2.59 seconds	86.4 milliseconds

Exam Essentials

Understand the concepts of availability for business continuity.   Fault tolerance is the redundancy of components in a system to maintain the system in the event of a failure of one of its components. High availability is similar to fault tolerance because it prevents loss in the event of failure, but the redundant components work together to prevent a failure and allow maintenance in a coordinated system. Load balancing enables the load of a service to be distributed across many identical services. NIC teaming allows bandwidth to be aggregated for the host, or it can create a redundant connection in the event of a connection failure. Port aggregation enables bandwidth to be aggregated between two switches. Clustering provides failover, load balancing, and high availability for the services running on the cluster of hosts.

Understand the concepts for supplying power to network equipment.   Battery backup/uninterruptable power supplies (UPSs) maintain voltage and the quality of the power during a power outage. A stand-by UPS is often found under a desk for an individual PC. A line interactive UPS is often used for small racks of networking equipment, and an online UPS is used for datacenters. Power generators can provide a constant supply of electricity during a power outage with the use of fuel, an engine, and a generator. Dual-power supplies allow power to be fault tolerant at the network device or server level. Redundant circuit are common in datacenters; each rack is supplied with an A circuit and a B circuit. Each of the circuits is plugged into one of the dual-power supplies.

Understand the concepts of recovery for business continuity.   Cold sites do not contain any equipment. Warm sites contain the equipment necessary to run the essential services but not all of the primary site's servers. Hot sites contain the same equipment as the primary site and can operate automatically if the primary site fails.

Understand the concepts of backup systems.   Backups enable minor recovery, such as an accidental deletion of a file, or major recovery, such as in the event of a fire. Disk-to-tape is the traditional backup media, because it can be taken off-site for retention purposes.

Disk-to-disk is used to shorten the backup and restore window (called the recovery time objective [RTO]), by using data deduplication and several disks working together. Disk-to-cloud is an alternative to disk-to-tape that utilizes online storage at service providers. The grandfather, father, son (GFS) media rotation specifies that the daily backup will be rotated on a first-in, first-out (FIFO) basis.

Understand the various backup types.   Full backups copy all the data in a dataset to media and reset the archive bit. Incremental backups copy only the data to media that has the archive bit set; it then resets all of the archive bits. Differential backups copies all the data in the dataset to media that has the archive bit set, but it does not reset the archive bit. Snapshots can create the illusion of an immediate backup by taking a snapshot of the filesystem; then before a file is written to or deleted, the original file is copied to protected storage.

Understand the concepts of availability.   The mean time to repair (MTTR) is the average time required to repair a fault-tolerant system. The mean time between failures (MTBF) is the average measurement of reliability of a component. The service level agreement (SLA) is found in service provider contracts and is an expected level of service that the provider will adhere to for uptime.

3.3 Explain common scanning, monitoring and patching processes and summarize their expected outputs.

Network administrators are responsible for maintaining expected operations of the network and securing its operations. This can be considered the boring part of network administration, but it doesn't have to be. I view this as finding holes and performance problems in the network. It is our job to patch them before someone else finds the issues. In this section, I will discuss several techniques used to identify holes in the network, as well as the remediation.

As network administrators, we also need to understand and manage the tools used to defend the network from active attacks. This might be a little interesting for some, since it requires intervention and not prevention. However, both goals are the same—to keep the network safe!

Processes

There are several processes that a network administrator will use to maintain the operations of a network for both performance and security. These processes can vary depending on the system. The life cycle of these problems are often similar: collect logs, review logs, compare logs to baselines, and take corrective action. This should be a cyclical process so that problems related to performance and security are prevented. However, these processes are often invoked to the reaction of a problem.

Log Reviewing

The optimal strategy for logging is to point all of the logging services to one centralized logging server. This centralized server then collects the logs for all the devices in the network. This creates a central repository of logs for the entire network, but it also creates a massive amount of logs that are collected daily.

When reviewing logs, we must first isolate and drill down to the device we need to focus on. Most log management tools like *Microsoft System Center Operations Manager* and the open source tool Kibana provide drilldown of log data for the system. Once the data is isolated, we must then isolate the normal log data from the abnormal log data so that we can isolate the root cause of the problem or identify the performance problem. This is an art in itself because of the complexity of the data and the problem to be solved. All log reviewing tools have a facility to filter log data—even the built-in *Event Viewer* in the Microsoft operating system has this functionality.

Port Scanning

Port scanning is a method an administrator uses to verify that services are opened on the firewalls protecting the service. Port scanning can also be used to find holes in the network. For example, say you just installed a licensing server. You want to make sure that the licensing daemon (service) is listening on the appropriate port. However, during your port scan, you find that the administrative interface on TCP port 80 is also open to the clients.

The most common port scanning tool used today is the open source *Nmap tool*, shown in Figure 3.22. The tool can be installed on several different operating systems such as Linux, Windows, and macOS. The Nmap tool can perform a number of port scanning functions such as simple TCP/UDP scanning, OS detection, stealth scanning, and many other unique features for auditing your environment.

FIGURE 3.22   Nmap tool example

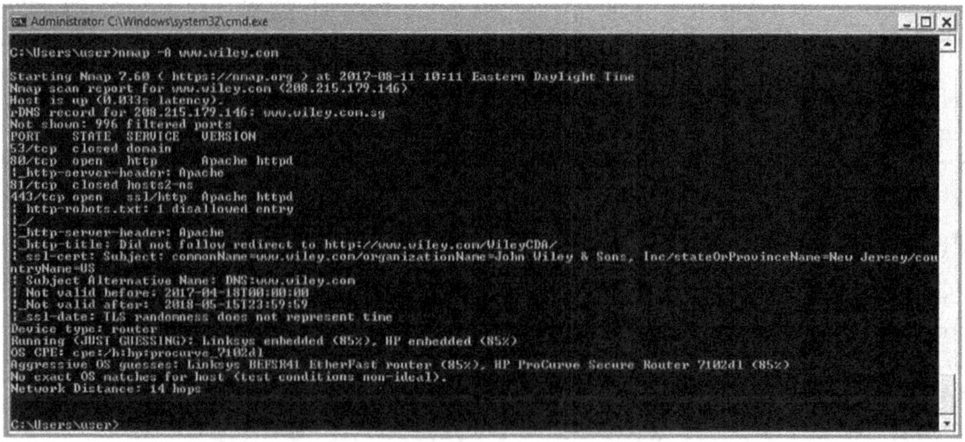

Vulnerability Scanning

Vulnerability scanning can include port scanning. However, having the ability to connect to a service does not mean you can gain access to the service. Vulnerabilities in an operating system can elevate a user's permissions, allow unauthorized access, or allow for the theft of data. So we want to identify vulnerabilities in the operating system and either patch or mitigate them as quickly as possible.

Microsoft created a tool called the Microsoft Baseline Security Analyzer (MBSA) for checking the baseline configuration of its operating systems. The MBSA tool is now deprecated and has largely been replaced by the Microsoft Security Compliance Toolkit (SCT). The SCT allows for a compliance check across the entire enterprise. Both tools are still valuable in a Microsoft-only environment.

Unfortunately, Microsoft operating systems are not the only operating system we must check for vulnerabilities; we must also check network devices for vulnerabilities. The application Nessus has become the de facto standard of network vulnerability scanning in the industry. It identifies vulnerabilities across all network devices and operating systems.

When vulnerability scanning a network with a tool like Nessus that checks for a wide range of vulnerabilities, use caution. When a vulnerability scanner interrogates a network device or operating system, it must partially attack the system to see if it tests positive. This partial attack could crash the operating system or network device. For example, if you're testing for a buffer overflow, the buffer overflow must be tried. If it works, then you have injected garbage test data into the memory of a running device.

Patch Management

After a vulnerability is verified, you must remediate the system(s). Although you could perform this patch management on a manual basis, without an overview of all systems, a manual patch management system is destined to fail. In addition to operating systems and network devices, we must take into consideration the applications that run on the operating systems.

Microsoft Windows Server Update Services (WSUS) is designed to automatically deploy patches, feature updates, driver updates, and security updates to Microsoft operating systems and products. Clients and servers independently assess their Windows Update installations and report back to the WSUS server. The WSUS server can then assess which patches need to be installed on the clients and servers, based on the current patches recommended by Microsoft. The WSUS server provides a graphical reporting, as shown in Figure 3.23. An administrator can then drill down to a host to see which patches are required for the host or which patches are still required. The WSUS server can be configured to synchronize Microsoft's patch catalog each night.

FIGURE 3.23   WSUS computer report

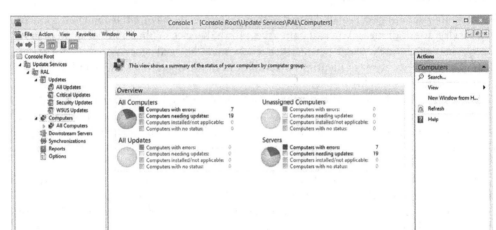

Linux operating systems have their own patch management system. Each distribution of Linux provides a different facility for patch management. However, the Red Hat Linux distribution stands out from the rest with the *Red Hat Subscription Management (RHSM)* portal. This system allows each server to register with the RHSM portal and report its patch status. From the RHSM portal, an administrator can initiate the patching of servers. You can consider this service model as patch management as a service, because you are initiating the patches from Red Hat's cloud service of RHSM.

Applications also need to be patched on a regular basis. Over the past 5 to 10 years we have seen numerous exploits with Oracle Java and Adobe Flash in addition to other applications. Fortunately, we can manage patches for applications as we manage the operating system patches with the use of Microsoft Systems Center Configuration Manager (SCCM). With SCCM, patches are deployed for applications and reporting capabilities similar to WSUS are provided.

Rollback

Although patches in the operating system should always work without a problem, sometimes it is necessary to roll back a patch or installation. If the operating systems are managed with WSUS, then a patch can be approved for removal. When a patch is approved for removal, the patch will be uninstalled on the targeted operating systems. Once this is done, the patch will not be installed if it has not been installed already on other installations.

If patch management is not being utilized, then a patch can be removed manually. In the Windows operating systems, this can be performed by choosing Control Panel ➤ Programs and Features ➤ Installed Updates. In the Result pane, right-click the Windows update and uninstall it manually, as shown in Figure 3.24.

FIGURE 3.24   Manual uninstall of a Windows update

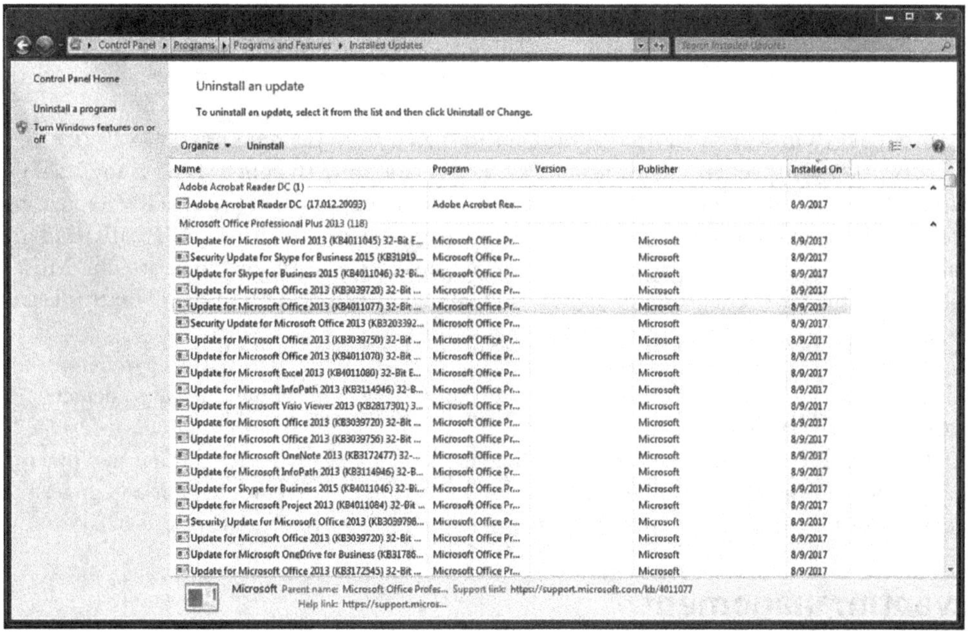

Reviewing Baselines

As discussed earlier, there are two types of baselines you can create: security baselines and performance baselines. When troubleshooting, performance baselines help the network administrator to validate a problem and the solution. A security baseline is a standard of specific patches, security updates, policies, and configuration across systems.

The security baseline should be reviewed periodically to make sure there is compliance across all systems. If a machine does not meet the security baseline, it could be at risk of becoming compromised and should be remediated immediately. There are several automated systems such as SCCM that can automatically alert a network administrator when a system is out of compliance.

If a machine is compromised, the performance can be affected. A typical example is a machine that has not been properly patched and is compromised. The malicious user who compromised the system could spike CPU or network activity. At first this might look like a performance problem, but it is a security problem instead. The security baseline will allow you to verify that a system is secured to the standard your organization has defined. The performance baseline will allow you to verify the system is performing as expected.

Packet/Traffic Analysis

Packet capture utilities such as the open source Wireshark project allow us to capture network traffic at the packet level. Packet captures view the network at a very granular level. You can use this method when diagnosing a network problem because of the depth of detail you can sort through after a capture.

A tool like *Wireshark* will decode the captured data from the data link layer (frame), the network layer (packet), the transport layer (segment), and the upper layers (application data). This decoded data can be useful if you are trying to view what is actually happening at the application layer. For example, Wireshark can be used to capture VoIP calls, and a built-in decoder allows the packet capture to be converted back into a voice stream. Most decoders in the packet capture tool will just create text fields and fill in the data; this leaves the tedious job of searching for the network administrator.

Traffic analysis tools are used to capture packets to deduce traffic patterns in network traffic. These types of systems are common at the ISP level and allow the ISP to detect malicious traffic such as peer-to-peer sharing programs and *distributed denial of service (DDoS)*. The ISP can then react to the malicious traffic by blocking it. ISPs are just one of many types of organizations that use traffic analysis tools—law enforcement and government, for instance, often use these tools to watch patterns in Internet traffic.

Event management

Event management is a core responsibility for the network operations team so that the functionality of the network can be maintained. Automated systems should be used to monitor the performance and uptime of network devices and servers. OpenNMS, Nagios, and PRTG Network Monitor are just a few of popular automated systems; there are many others tools like these on the market. These systems can generate notifications and alerts when systems are performing poorly or not at all. The network administrator can then intervene and repair the fault.

Performance is not the only type of event the network operations team must focus on. Security events need to monitored and acted on when a network or system is being attacked. Tools such as AlienVault Open Source SIEM (OSSIM) can send alerts and notifications to the network administrator or a network security administrator. The responsible team can then take corrective action.

Alerts

Alerts are created when the criteria definition in the event management system is met. If you are monitoring a system's performance in the event management system and the CPU performance crosses the set threshold, an alert would be triggered. When you log into the event management system, you would see the alert. Some event management systems can display a dashboard on a shared monitor for the network operations team to view.

Notifications

Notifications are the programmed events when an alert is triggered. Examples include outputting a log entry, sending an email, or sending a text message. Notifications allow the network administrator to be notified of the event. In large IT organizations, notification escalation is set up to notify on-duty IT staff. If the on-duty IT staff do not respond, the system can engage on-call staff.

SIEM

Security information and event management (SIEM) are software products like AlienVault Open Source SIEM (OSSIM) and are often exclusively used by the security network administrators. SIEM tools combine *security information management (SIM)* and *security event management (SEM)* so that a security problem can be detected and an alert can be generated.

Some business sectors, such as the financial sector and health sectors, are regulated by the government. Because of the regulations on these sectors, security is often a component. When an alert is triggered and a notification is created, the *security operations center (SOC)* is responsible for addressing the problem. The SIEM tools assists the security administrator with a digital record for auditing purposes, as well as recording the outcome to the response of the alert. Depending on the type of business sector, these records may need to be reviewed by the *chief security officer (CSO)*.

SNMP monitors

OpenNMS, Nagios, and PRTG Network Monitor (just to mention a few) can perform basic monitoring of systems with ICMP pings and TCP/IP checks. When a service goes down, these systems create alerts and notifications for network administrator intervention. When these tools use SNMP for monitoring of network devices and servers, we can gain better insight into how the device or server is performing. SNMP monitoring collects statistics from the operating system such as bandwidth, memory, and CPU. We can set thresholds for specific counters, and when a counter crosses the threshold, alerts and notifications are sent to us.

SNMP monitors can also be used for the ongoing collection of statistics from the operating system. This constant recording of statistics creates baselines for comparison over time. It also helps us identify trends and problematic periods of time. As seen in Figure 3.25, around 17:00 hours bandwidth spiked up to 9.2 Mbps. Looking at the weekly graph, these spikes seem normal for brief periods of time.

SNMP monitors, also called *network management stations (NMSs)*, can operate with two basic methods: SNMP get and SNMP trap. An SNMP get is a solicited request to the OS or network device for an *object ID (OID)* value; SNMP gets are considered polling requests. An SNMP trap is unsolicited information from the OS or network device. An SNMP trap is sent when the threshold on the device has been exceeded such as a bandwidth setting or disk space. These SNMP traps can be configured on the SNMP monitor to create alerts and notifications.

FIGURE 3.25   SNMP monitor graph

`Daily' Graph (5 Minute Average)

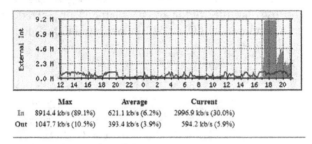

	Max	Average	Current
In	8914.4 kb/s (89.1%)	621.1 kb/s (6.2%)	2996.9 kb/s (30.0%)
Out	1047.7 kb/s (10.5%)	393.4 kb/s (3.9%)	594.2 kb/s (5.9%)

`Weekly' Graph (30 Minute Average)

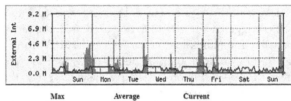

	Max	Average	Current
In	8914.4 kb/s (89.1%)	533.2 kb/s (5.3%)	1658.6 kb/s (16.6%)
Out	1115.5 kb/s (11.2%)	509.7 kb/s (5.1%)	335.2 kb/s (3.4%)

MIB

The *management information base (MIB)* is a database of OIDs published by the vendor of the OS or network device. SNMP monitors require the specific MIB for the device or OS in order to collect statistics. The MIB defines the OID counters, along with the type of data the OID offers for collection.

Metrics

Routing protocols use metrics as a measurement for deciding how to route packets. However, the term *metric* is not solely used with routing protocols; we also use metrics as quantitative measurements for performance.

Any measurement that we capture for network performance can be considered a metric. SNMP monitors collect these metrics when configured with the appropriate MIB and the counters are selected for collection. In addition to the following metrics, many more can be captured for analysis, such as TCP and UDP connections, fragmented packets, latency, and response time, just to name a few. Basically, any measurement defined in the MIB, can be used for network analysis!

Error Rate

The error rate can be captured at layers 2 and 4 for network monitoring and analysis. The error rate is usually a percentage of erroneous frames or segments received. It is important to remember that erroneous frames and segments sent cannot be captured as a metric, because the destination host will not report this information.

When we capture layer 2 (data link) error rate measurements, we are measuring how many frames are received where the cyclical redundancy check (CRC), also called the frame checking sequence (FCS), fails. This is often due to transient interference on the Ethernet wiring or a bad connection on the receive pair. If it is an optical connection and error rates are reported, it can be the result of a dirty optical connection on the receive fiber-optic strand.

It is uncommon to capture layer 4 (transport) error rate measurements. The TCP error rate measurement depicts how many segments are received where the TCP checksum does not validate against the segments payload. It is most common to see these error rates where the sending host is offloading the TCP segments to a network interface card (NIC) for checksum calculation. When the NIC performs this process, it is called the *TCP offload engine (TOE)*. This is often used with iSCSI. Any TCP error observed identifies a problem and should be investigated further.

Utilization

Utilization is a common measurement to capture for network performance. This measurement depicts how much of the bandwidth is being used as a percentage of the connection speed. The measurement is captured for both the incoming and outgoing connections.

Observed high utilization for brief periods of time are expected during peak periods. A high utilization might not be expected in the middle of the day, but during a backup it can be totally normal. However, sustained high utilization rates would suggest connection speeds should be upgraded for the host. Any performance metric that exceeds the baseline should be checked against normal activity.

Utilization can also be used as a metric for CPU and RAM, as well as any other device that has a finite amount of capacity. When utilization is high on a CPU for a network device, such as a router, packet loss can occur.

Packet Drops

Packet drops is a measurement that is detected at the transport layer. It is commonly collected as an incremental counter, but it can also be collected as a percentage of total segments requested for retransmission. When segments are not received and require retransmission, the packet drop counters increase or the percentage increases. High amounts of packet drops can mean that congestion or connectivity issues exist from the sending host.

Packet drops can also be measured by performing a round-trip calculation on ICMP packets; this is also called packet loss. It is commonly collected as a percentage of lost packets against the total number of packets sent. When packet drops are experienced, it means that throughput of the connection has been reduced.

Bandwidth/Throughput

Bandwidth/throughput is another common metric to capture for performance. Although it closely resembles utilization in its definition, bandwidth/throughput is the exact measurement in kilobits per second, megabits per second, gigabits per second, or even terabits per second. Utilization is a percentage of the connection used; both measure the input and output bandwidth.

Observed high bandwidth/throughput for a connection also depicts a problem with the speed of a connection, similar to utilization. However, the bandwidth/throughput measurement shows the exact measurement used for bandwidth. This metric is handy if you are charged over a specific amount of bandwidth for a period of time.

It is common for ISPs to base overages on the 95th percentile of bandwidth used for a 30-day period. The measurements are taken at a specific interval, usually every 5 minutes. The highest 5 percent is removed from the measurements. When the numbers are averaged together, they represent the Internet usage for 95 percent of the time, with an allowed 5 percent burst rate.

Exam Essentials

Understand the processes used to determine security and performance problems. Log reviewing helps derive the root cause of a problem. Port scanning helps administrators verify ports are open in a firewall for a specific service. Nmap is a popular tool for port scanning of hosts and networks. Vulnerability scanning can include port scanning, but it is focused on detecting specific vulnerabilities. Patch management is used after a vulnerability is identified. Baselines should be reviewed for security and performance of network systems. Packet capture utilities such as Wireshark let us review traffic at the packet level. Traffic analysis tools allow the capturing of packets to deduce traffic patterns in network traffic.

Know the key components of an event management system. Event management systems monitor performance, service availability, and security-related events. Alerts are created when a specific set of criteria is met in the event management system. The criteria are often a threshold for a counter, and when it is crossed, the alert is triggered. Notifications are programmatic events, such as an email that is sent when the alert is triggered. Security information and event management (SIEM) systems monitor security-related problems in a network.

Understand how SNMP monitors are used for the collection of statistics. SNMP monitors, sometimes called network management systems (NMSs), are used to collect measurements from operating systems and network devices. SNMP monitors use SNMP get messages to poll the object ID (OID) counters. SNMP traps are set up on the device or operating system and push OID counters measurements when a threshold is met. The management information base (MIB) is a database of OIDs published by the vendor of the operating system or network device.

Know the various metrics used for network performance. Metrics are quantitative measurements from the operating system or network device. The error rate is often captured at layer 2 (data link layer) to identify problems with erroneous frames received by the network device or operating system. Utilization is a percentage of the connection used by network traffic. Packet drops is a measurement at layer 4 (transport layer) as an incremental counter. Packet drops can also be measured at layer 3 (network layer), using ICMP round-trip calculations; this metric is presented as a percentage of loss. Bandwidth/throughput is an exact measurement in bits per second of the bandwidth used for a connection.

3.4 Given a scenario, use remote access methods.

Remote access is implemented to provide access to network systems for end users and administrative personnel at remote locations. Remote access of the network systems can be provided over the public Internet, a local area network, or a wide area network, since it extends the local access of a system. You can be in another room or another country and it is considered remote access, as long you are not at the local mouse and keyboard. We use remote access for a multitude of purposes, such as remote control, remote files access, remote assistance, database access, performance monitoring, and diagnostics. In the following section, I will cover the means of remote access.

VPN

A virtual private network (VPN) extends your company's internal network across the Internet or other unsecured public network. This remote access technology allows clients and branch networks to be connected securely with the company's network privately. There are several different ways a VPN can be used in our network architecture, and we will cover them in the following section. A VPN achieves this private connection across a public network by creating a secure tunnel from end to end, through the process of encryption and encapsulation. The encryption protocols used will vary, and I will cover them in the following section as well. Since a tunnel is created from end to end, your local host becomes part of the company's internal network, along with an IP address that matches the company's internal network. We don't have to be bound to only TCP/IP across a VPN, since this technology can encapsulate any protocol and carry it through the tunnel.

IPsec

The IPsec protocol has been standardized by the *Internet Engineering Task Force (IETF)*. To properly implement IPsec, certificates should be used that make the setup of IPsec difficult for the end user, so it is mainly used for site-to-site VPN tunnels and host-to-host VPN tunnels. Although preshared keys (PSKs) can be used, doing so is not a secure method and should only be used for testing IPsec. When using IPsec for host-to-host communications, it is commonly referred to as transport mode IPsec. When using IPsec for site-to-site communications, it is commonly referred to as tunnel mode IPsec. The IPsec protocol consists of two main mechanisms that provide both integrity of the data and encryption between both hosts:

Authentication Headers (AH) The AH protocol is responsible for providing integrity of the data and verifying the origin of the data. The protocol does so by calculating an integrity check value (ICV). This value is computed using the keys exchanged during IPsec setup between the hosts. The ICV allows the destination to verify that the data has not been altered or manipulated during the transmission process. Since the ICV is computed against the data on the receiving host, we can verify that the message came from the originating host and not a third party. This protocol prevents replay attacks, where a third party intercepts communications and then replays the original packets to further dialogue.

Encapsulating Security Payload (ESP)   The ESP protocol is responsible for the encryption of data and provides confidentiality. ESP also contains an ICV to provide authentication of the originator, but ESP is normally used in conjunction with the AH protocol.

When IPsec establishes a connection, it is established in two phases, as shown in Figure 3.26. Phase one authenticates endpoints and builds a secure channel between the two VPN endpoints using certificates or a preshared key. Phase one also entails negotiating the hashing and encryption policies to be used for AH and ESP in phase two. Phase two is encrypted using the secure channel keys established in phase one. Phase two is responsible for negotiating another set of secure keys used to encrypt data called the Security Association (SA); it is also responsible for rekeying the SA after a period of time or number of packets.

FIGURE 3.26   IPsec tunnel phases

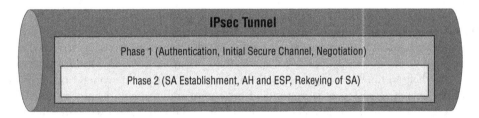

SSL/TLS/DTLS

The Secure Sockets Layer (SSL) VPN protocol has gained popularity over the past decade. Its popularity is mainly due to its use of a common port of TCP 443 and common cryptography of SSL. SSL uses a public-private key pair to create an asymmetrical encryption and authentication of data. It is considered the preferred method of connectivity for client-to-site VPN, since a client exists for almost all operating systems. Its main strength is that it looks like ordinary SSL communications, so most firewalls allow it through by default. With the ever growing popularity of SSL for protecting web communications, it is most likely going to be around forever.

The Transport Layer Security (TLS) and SSL protocol are similar at the cryptographic level. SSL is considered a per-port encryption protocol: if an application connects to a specific port SSL is listening on, then encryption begins. However, TLS differs from SSL because encryption is negotiated via the TLS handshake protocol. TLS is considered a per-protocol encryption protocol because it uses a handshake protocol.

Datagram Transport Layer Security (DTLS) is based on the TLS protocol and provides the same security TLS provides. DTLS is mainly used for UDP encryption of segments and datagrams. As of this writing, TLS 1.2 is considered to be the current secure transport layer security, and SSL 3.0 is considered to be deprecated and insecure.

Site-to-Site VPN

Over the past 10–15 years, using high-bandwidth connections to the Internet has become cheaper than purchasing dedicated leased lines. So companies have opted to install Internet connections at branch offices for Internet usage. These lines can serve a dual purpose: connecting users to the Internet and connecting branch offices together to the main office. However, the Internet is a public network and unsecured, but site-to-site VPN connections can fix that. Companies with multiple locations have reaped the benefits of creating VPN tunnels from site to site over the Internet by ditching their leased lines, installing VPN concentrators at each location, and creating VPN tunnels. Site-to-site VPN is also much more scalable than lease lines, since every location only needs a connection to the Internet and a *VPN concentrator* to be tied together.

Figure 3.27 details two locations tied together with a VPN tunnel. The magic happens all in the VPN concentrator. Since VPN concentrators also have a routing function, when a tunnel is established a route entry is created in the VPN concentrator for the remote network. When traffic is destined for the branch office with a destination network of 10.2.0.0/16, the router encrypts and encapsulates the information as data and sends it to the other side of the tunnel over the Internet. This is similar to a host-to-site VPN, with the difference of the routing being performed in the VPN concentrator. When the packet is received on the other side of the tunnel, the VPN concentrator will decapsulate the data, decrypt the packet, and send the packet to its destination inside the branch network. It is common to find the appliance performing VPN is also the firewall and router. Firewalls today are sold with VPN software built in and licensed accordingly.

FIGURE 3.27   A typical site-to-site VPN

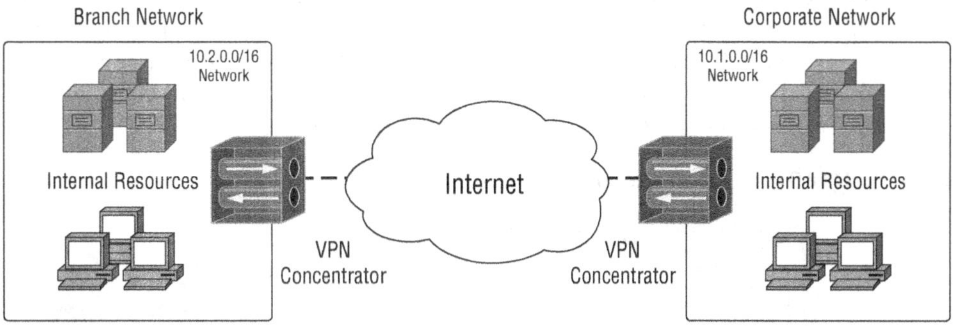

Client-to-Site VPN

Client-to-site VPN connectivity is a remote access strategy for mobile access. It can be used for *telecommuters*, salespeople, partners, and administrative access to the internal network resources. The key concept is that VPN access is granted on an individual or group basis for the mobile users. Using the example in Figure 3.28, you can allow salespeople to connect to the corporate network so they can update sales figures or process orders. This can all be done securely over the Internet while the users are mobile and have access to a network connection.

FIGURE 3.28   A typical host-to-site VPN

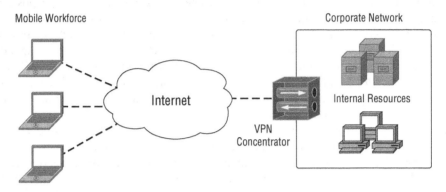

When a client computer establishes a VPN connection, it becomes part of the internal corporate network. This happens by assignment of an IP address from the internal corporate network. In Figure 3.29 you can see a mobile device such as a laptop with a VPN client installed in the operating system. When the connection is established with the VPN concentrator over the Internet, a pseudo network adapter is created by the VPN client. In this example, the pseudo network adapter is assigned an internal IP address of 10.2.2.8/16 from the VPN concentrator. The laptop also has its own IP address of 192.168.1.3/24, which it uses to access the Internet. A routing table entry is created in the operating system for the 10.2.0.0/16 network and through the pseudo network adapter. When traffic is generated for the corporate network, it is sent to the pseudo adapter where it is encrypted and then sent to the physical NIC and sent through the Internet to the VPN concentrator as data. When it arrives at the VPN concentrator, the IP header is stripped from the packet, the data is decrypted, and it is sent to its internal corporate network resource.

FIGURE 3.29   Client-to-site VPN connection

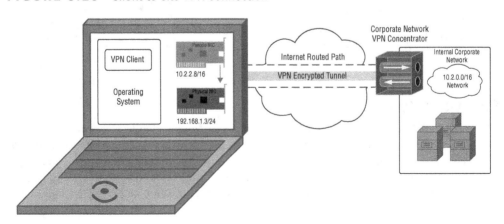

Host-to-Host VPN

We can create VPN tunnels between individual hosts, just like we create VPN tunnels between sites. We build these tunnels for a very different purpose and usually within our own network. You may wonder why we do this if it's inside our network; the answer is security and flexibility. This is commonly done when applications that need to communicate do not support a common network encryption mechanism and the data must be safe from eavesdropping while in transit. These host-to-host VPN tunnels can be created for email and web applications—actually any application at all. A VPN tunnel is formed between the servers at the operating system level. The application does not even know the encryption is being performed as it communicates with the other server. A common protocol for host-to-host VPN is IPsec, and most operating systems support this protocol.

In Figure 3.30 we see a web application and a SQL backend where data is stored. SQL is a clear-text dialogue between the client and server to exchange and transact information. If the web server were to be compromised or another server inside the DMZ were to be compromised, network sniffing could be used to watch these transactions. When we implement a host-to-host VPN tunnel, the data is now encrypted and encapsulated when it is sent between hosts. Similar to host-to-site and site-to-site VPNs, a pseudo network adapter is created inside the operating system. When data is sent from the sending application (web server) to the other host's receiving application (SQL server), it is first sent to this pseudo network adapter to be encrypted, encapsulated, and then sent off to the internal SQL server. When the other host receives the packet, it is decapsulated and decrypted, and the SQL data is sent directly to the receiving application (SQL). The process works both ways as the SQL server sends data back to the web server.

FIGURE 3.30   A typical host-to-host VPN

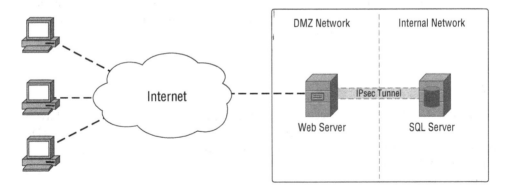

RDP

Remote Desktop Protocol (RDP) is used exclusively with Microsoft operating systems to provide remote access. RDP is used at the remote access protocol and communicates over TCP 3389 to deliver the remote screen and connect the local mouse and keyboard to the RDP session. RDP uses TLS encryption by default.

Microsoft allows one remote user connection or a local connection on desktop operating systems via RDP, but not both. On server operating systems, Microsoft allows two administrative connections that can be a combination of local or remote access, but not to exceed two connections.

Microsoft also uses RDP to deliver user desktops via terminal services. When RDP is used in this fashion, a centralized gateway brokers the connections to each RDP client desktop session. Terminal services requires terminal services licensing for either each user connecting or each desktop served. RDP can also be used to deliver applications to the end users via Microsoft *RemoteApp* on terminal services. When RemoteApp is used, the server still requires a terminal services license. However, just the application is delivered to the user host rather than the entire desktop.

SSH

Secure Shell (SSH) is commonly used for remote access via a text console for Linux and Unix operating systems using TCP port 22. The SSH protocol encrypts all communications between the SSH client and SSH server, which is also called the SSH daemon. SSH uses a public-private key pair to provide authentication between the SSH client and server. SSH can also use a key pair to authenticate users connecting to the SSH server for the session, or a simple username and password can be provided. It is important to understand that both the user and their host computer are authenticated when the user attempts to connect to the server. During the initial connection between the user's host computer and the SSH server, the encryption protocol is negotiated for the user's login.

Beyond logging into a Linux or Unix server for remote access, SSH can provide remote access for applications. Through the use of SSH port forwarding, the application can be directed across the SSH connection to the far end. This allows applications to tunnel through the SSH session. It also encrypts application traffic from the client to the server, because it is carried over the SSH encrypted tunnel. SSH can behave similarly to a VPN connection, but it is more complex to set up than a VPN client.

VNC

Virtual Network Computing (VNC) is a remote control tool for the sharing of desktops. The VNC client normally operates on TCP port 5900. VNC is similar to Microsoft RDP, with the exception that VNC is an open source protocol and allows only one console session on a Microsoft operating system. It supports encryption via plug-ins but is not encrypted by default.

VNC operates in a client and server model. The server install for the host enables remote control of the host, and the client install allows for means to connect to the VNC server. It is normally configured with a simple shared password, but it can also be configured with Windows groups. Several clients that can be used such as RealVNC, TightVNC, and many others, but all of the clients perform in a similar way.

Telnet

Telnet is the original remote access protocol for Linux, Unix, and network device operating systems using TCP port 23. Telnet provides an unencrypted remote text console for remote access purposes. It is not considered secure at all and should not be used because a malicious user can eavesdrop on the session. Many network devices still use Telnet for configuration purposes. However, SSH should be configured and used in lieu of Telnet if it is available.

HTTPS/management URL

Hypertext Transfer Protocol Secure (HTTPS) is a secure version of the Hypertext Transfer Protocol (HTTP) protocol. HTTPS uses SSL/TLS encryption to encrypt the management session. It is commonly used to manage network devices, such as VoIP phones, routers, switch, and firewalls. The use of management URLs with network devices has become very popular, since it allows the management of the device from a simple graphical user interface (GUI) via a standard web browser.

The management uniform resource locator (URL) is the address the network administrator uses to manage the device. An example of a management URL would be `https://192.168.1.1/admin`. However, the vendor might make the management something other than `/admin`, since there is no standard for naming the management URL. When connecting to the management URL, it is often secured with a simple username and password. The username and password combination can be a local user or a centralized authentication system such as Active Directory if it is supported by the device.

Remote file access

Remote file access provides the network administrator with a method to upload and download files from and to network devices and operating systems. Remote file access can be used to upload or download configuration, maintenance files, firmware, or the upgrade of the operating system for a network device. Some remote access tools such as RDP have remote file access built in.

FTP/FTPS

File Transfer Protocol (FTP) is a network protocol used to transfer files between hosts or a host to a network device. FTP uses a client-server relationship, in which the client can send and receive files from the server. It is an aging protocol for the Internet file transfer, but it is still useful for transferring files locally between dissimilar operating systems.

FTP uses a control channel and a data channel, which is why it is losing popularity. FTP operates on a control channel of TCP port 21 to issue commands from the client to the server, such as directory listing, put, and get requests. FTP is not encrypted, so file transfers can be intercepted.

FTP operates in two different modes: active and passive. In active mode, the client sends a request to TCP port 21 on the server along with the information on which port to respond back that is above 1024. The server will then respond to the client from TCP port 20 to the port the client has opened and is awaiting the data. The problem with active mode is that the firewall or NAT between the client and server must forward to the client's awaiting port. Passive mode was created to overcome this problem by instructing the client to connect to a port above 1024 on the server in which the server awaits the initial data transfer. Passive mode allows the client to create a second connection to the server for the data transfer. This overcomes problems with firewalls and NAT processes.

File Transfer Protocol Secure (FTPS) uses the same methods described earlier. FTPS is an extension to FTP in which file transfers are encrypted. FTPS uses Transport Layer Security (TLS) and the Secure Socket Layer (SSL) protocols for encryption. TLS is expected to operate on TCP port 990 for the control channel and TCP port 989 for the data channel. SSL is expected to operate on TCP port 21 for the control channel and TCP port 20 for the data channel, similar to FTP.

SFTP

SSH File Transfer Protocol (SFTP) is quite different from FTP, since it uses SSH as the control and data channel. SFTP is slowly becoming the standard protocol used to transfer files between dissimilar operating systems. SFTP provides the native authentication and encryption of SSH for all communication between the client and server.

SFTP only requires the client to connect to one port for all data transfer, so it is less complicated to troubleshoot from a network perspective. The SFTP client will connect to the SFTP server on TCP port 22, similar to the SSH protocol. A popular client for Microsoft operating systems is WinSCP, which provides a graphical interface. WinSCP can also be used as a command-line tool. On Linux operating systems, the command-line tool scp is used to transfer files to an SFTP server.

TFTP

Trivial File Transfer Protocol (TFTP) is simple file transfer protocol used for transferring files. The TFTP client will request a file transfer to the server on UDP port 69. A popular TFTP client used on Windows operating systems is TFTPd32, which provides a GUI interface.

TFTP does not provide any security or authentication at all. The only security it provides is that you must know the file you are requesting. However, it does not need to because it is mainly used as a maintenance utility. TFTP is often used for upgrading firmware on network devices, such as routers and switches. It is also used for backup and restoring of configuration for these types of network devices. Another common use for TFTP is *preboot execution environment (PXE)* booting. A DHCP option will specify the TFTP server from which the PXE client will obtain the network booted operating system.

Out-of-band management

All enterprise networking devices have data, control, and management planes. The data and control planes service the data flowing through the device. The management plane allows for diagnostic and configuration of the device. Network devices are configured so that the *management plane* is accessible over the *data plane* that the device serves. For example, a router is accessible over the network for which it provides routing. This type of management is considered in-band management.

In-band management of the network device is great when the network device is running and functioning. However, when we have an equipment failure, we need to access the device to check configuration and diagnose the problem. Using the previous example, if an interface on the router goes down, you will lose the ability to manage the device since the management plane is served over the failed data plane. This is where out-of-band management is valuable. Out-of-band management is when the management plane is served out-of-band of the data plane. This allows us to access the equipment independently of the network connections the device is serving. Out-of-band management is also used for security purposes. This prevents a network intruder from accessing key management infrastructure by limiting connectivity to the management infrastructure with a physical connection. Out-of-band management can also be performed via a modem set up for the specific purpose of management.

Modem

Modems are legacy devices but still very valuable to the network administrator. When a WAN goes down, as shown in Figure 3.31, a modem gives console access to the device over the public switched telephone network (PSTN). This connection will have a top speed of 56 Kbps (54 Kbps in North America) on plain old telephone system (POTS) lines. If you are using VoIP lines, the usable speed is far less, but console access is normally 9600 bits per second, so speed is usually not a problem.

FIGURE 3.31   A modem for out-of-band management

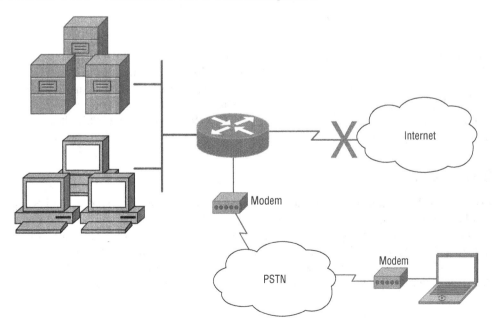

Console Router

The console port, as seen in Figure 3.32, is used to connect either a modem or a serial port for the technician's laptop. The console connection is often an RJ-45 connector terminated to a rollover cable, the other end is either a DB-9 (host) or DB-25 (modem) connector. Both DB-9 and DB-25 connectors are discussed in Chapter 2.

FIGURE 3.32   A router console connection

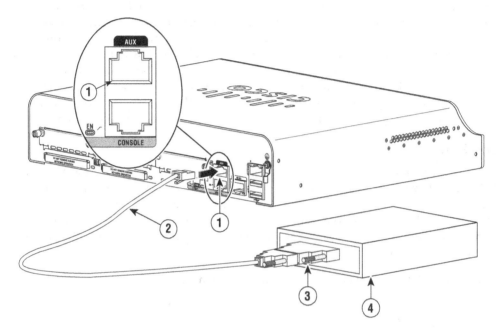

Console connections on routers are valuable to the network administrator, because they allow console command-line interface (CLI) access. The console connection is used by the technician for either out-of-band configuration and diagnostics or initial setup. It is common to ship a router with a modem to a remote site. A network administrator can then dial into the remote site router to set up the other end of a WAN connection. This allows the network administrator to be in two places at once!

Exam Essentials

Understand the various protocols and methods of VPN connectivity.   IPsec is a VPN protocol commonly used for site-to-site and host-to-host VPN connectivity. It is not commonly used for client-to-site VPN because of the complexity of the connection. AH helps validate that the data has not been tampered with in transit and authenticates the sender and receiver. ESP provides the encryption for the data transmitted to prevent eavesdropping. Secure Sockets Layer (SSL) protects data with an asymmetrical public and private key pair.

Transport Layer Security (TLS) negotiates encryption with the TLS handshake protocol. Datagram Transport Layer Security (DTLS) also uses the TLS handshake protocols, but it is used with UDP connections.

Know the various type of VPN connectivity methods.   Site-to-site VPNs allow a remote office to connect to the main office over an Internet connection while protecting the data transmitted over the public Internet. Client-to-site VPNs allow for mobile workers to connect to a main site over the Internet for access to internal resources while protecting data transmitted over the public Internet.

Know the various remote access protocols used for network administration.   Remote Desktop Protocol (RDP) is a Microsoft protocol for remote administration and remote desktop support. Secure Shell (SSH) is a protocol that is commonly used for test console sessions to Linux and Unix operating systems using public-private key pair encryption. Virtual Network Computing (VNC) is a remote control tool for the sharing of a desktops. Telnet is protocol that is commonly used for text console sessions with network devices, and it provides no encryption. Hypertext Transfer Protocol Secure (HTTPS) is a popular method of providing network administrators with a GUI management interface for network devices via a uniform resource locator (URL) address.

Know the various remote file access protocols.   File Transfer Protocol (FTP) is a nonencrypted protocol that allows file transfers between hosts. File Transfer Protocol Secure (FTPS) is an encrypted version of FTP that uses SSL for file transfers. SSH File Transfer Protocol (SFTP) allows for file transfer over the SSH protocol and requires only one port for control and data. Trivial File Transfer Protocol (TFTP) has no security and uses UDP for transferring files.

Understand out-of-band management concepts.   When the management traffic of a device is carried over the same network media that the device serves, the management is considered in-band. With out-of-band, management traffic uses an alternate media that is not served for data purposes by the network device. Modems are a typical out-of-band management device that is used for troubleshooting when a network link fails and in-band management cannot be used.

3.5 Identify policies and best practices.

As network administrators, we can implement hard controls to make sure that users adhere to a specific number of characters in their password or deny users access to certain areas of the network. We must help administer soft controls, or policies, as well. These soft controls should be made in conjunction with your company's legal counsel and human resources (HR) department. Policies are rules and procedures that employees are expected to follow. Best practices are a suggested set of rules that should be followed every time to ensure a positive outcome, such as destruction of hard drive before sending it to the trash.

Privileged user agreement

A privileged user is an individual who has elevated permissions for the administration of computer systems, accounts, data, communications, the processing of data, or any related aspect of the network. Privileged users can affect other individuals in the organization positively or negatively.

When privileged user rights are granted to an administrator, a certain level of trust is bestowed on the individual. The rights granted should not be misused for personal gain or to cause harm to others. A privileged user agreement is normally created in collaboration with the HR department to hold privileged users to a standard of conduct. The underlying thesis of the agreement is that rights will be used only to perform assigned job tasks and duties.

Password policy

As network administrators, we are generally familiar with the hard controls of a password policy. We can require users to change passwords every 90 days and require password complexity, and we can even ensure prior passwords are not reused. However, as we make the password policy more difficult for the user, the users often resort to lax security such as writing down passwords.

The soft controls of a password policy should be drafted between the HR department and the IT department. It should detail the expected conduct by employees and their passwords. The document should outline various expectations such as the following:

- Passwords should never be shared between employees.
- Passwords should never be disclosed to others, including IT employees.
- Passwords should never written down.
- Passwords should not be guessable, such as using the date it was changed (Password-04017).

When developing a password policy for your organization, the sensitivity of the information the users handle should be taken into consideration. The frequency of password changes, password length, and password complexity should be dictated by the sensitivity of information. A user who handles accounts payables should adhere to a stricter password policy than a laborer.

On-boarding/off-boarding procedures

As employees are hired in your organization, a certain amount of initial interaction with IT is required. This interaction is called the on-boarding procedure and is often coordinated with the HR department in your organization. During the on-boarding procedure, the IT representative will help the user log in for the first time and change their password. The password policy is often the first policy discussed with the user. Other policies such as *bring your own device (BYOD)*, *acceptable use policy (AUP)*, and information assurance should also be discussed during the on-boarding procedure. The use of email and files storage and policies should also be covered with the user during the on-boarding process. Each organization will have a different set of criteria that make up the on-boarding procedures.

Eventually, employees will leave your organization. The off-boarding procedure ensures that information access is terminated when the employment of the user is terminated. The off-boarding procedure will be initiated by the HR department and should be immediately performed by the IT department. This process can be automated via the employee management system used by the organization. This procedure can also be manually performed if the employee management system is not automated. However, the procedure must be performed promptly since the access to the company's information systems is the responsibility of the IT department. During the off-boarding procedure, email access or BYOD is removed via the *mobile device management (MDM)* software, the user account is disabled, and IT should make sure that the user is not connected to the IT systems remotely. The off-boarding procedure may also specify that the user assume ownership of the terminated employee's voicemail, email, and files.

Licensing restrictions

Licensing of software is a direct responsibility of the IT department. They should have a detailed account of software purchased, renewal dates of software, and the numbers of users with access to the software.

Software is often purchased either per seat or per user. Software that is purchased per seat is chosen because of shift workers sitting at the same computer. When software is purchased per user, the license can define named users or concurrent users. If software is purchased as a named user, then a license is used and tied to each user using the system. Most software companies will allow a percentage of licenses that can be recycled. If software is purchased as a concurrent license, at any given point in time the number of users accessing the software must not exceed the total number of licenses purchased.

Some software packages require a licensing service to be installed for centralized licensing. The licensing service is typically used for concurrent licensing of software. When the number of concurrent users is exceeded, the software will not activate, and any new users will be denied accessed.

Many software packages require the administrator to track the total number of installs or total number of users accessing the software. This tracking can be automated via license tracking software. When a software package is installed, the administrator will enter it into the license tracking software. An agent on the user's computer will record installation or access to the software. The administrator can then run reports to access compliance of software licensing. These software packages can greatly reduce the expense of a software audit by an outside agency.

International export controls

An export is any product sent from the home country to a foreign destination. An item is "deemed" an export control if it serves as a defense system, national security, foreign policy, or the interest of a country. The item does not need to be a tangible item; it can be software, technology, data, or technical assistance. Many different regulations govern international export controls. A common export control that is highly regulated is the export of encryption devices, such as VPN technology and cryptographic algorithms. These technologies are regulated for export by the Department of Commerce's Bureau of Industry and Security in the United States. If an organization exports data or technology that can be deemed as an export control, the company should have a procedure in place for abiding by the regulations in the home country.

Data loss prevention

When an organization suffers data loss, the information is not lost—it is just out of the control of the organization. Data loss prevention (DLP) is a system used to ensure that end users do not send sensitive and or critical information outside the organization. An example of sensitive information is a Social Security number or the secret sauce recipe for a hamburger chain. The user may not even know they are doing anything wrong in many instances.

DLP systems ensure that data loss will not occur, because the damaging effects can be long term. A common DLP system is an outbound email filter. The email transport filters can sanitize or restrict information such as credit card numbers, Social Security numbers, or any type of data they are programmed to detect. Microsoft Exchange Server allows administrators to create custom DLP policies or use prebuilt DLP policies that ship with Microsoft Exchange. Other systems can classify data based on their sensitivity and restrict users from emailing the information to users outside the company or uploading the information to public cloud services.

DLP systems are efficient at identifying potential data loss and provide a hard control for administrators, but it is best practice to implement soft controls as well by working with the organization's HR department to develop policies and effective training for end users.

Remote access policies

Remote access policies, just like many other policies for organizations, have a soft control and hard control. The soft control for an organization's remote access policy starts with defining who has access and why they have access as it pertains to their job function. The remote access policy can serve as an AUP for accessing the company's data remotely.

Hard controls can be configured in Microsoft Windows Server for remote VPN access. VPN access is controlled via a *Network Policy Server (NPS)*. The NPS can be configured to require security group membership, time of day criteria, and connection type, just to name a few. It is important to note that a freshly installed NPS will not allow connection by default until configured to do so. On Linux and Unix systems, a *Remote Authentication Dial-In User Service (RADIUS)* can control remote access. It is also important to note that the Microsoft NPS functions as a RADIUS server.

Incident response policies

The incident response policy define how a computer incident is handled, such as a security related incident or outage. The policy should focus on the prioritization, communication, and lessons learned so that the *computer incident response team (CIRT)* is prepared for future incidents.

The policy should include the priority of the incident based on the impact to the organizational impact. As an example, a server that is down would have a moderate impact on the organization. In comparison, a workstation that is down would have very little impact on the organization, and the severity would reflect the impact. This prioritization helps the CIRT handle the most severe incidents in a timely manner.

Having a good response plan in place that prioritizes incidents is important. Communications should also be defined in the policy so that the CIRT can effectively relay information to technicians and upper management. During a time of crisis, communications is important to a fast recovery of failed or compromised systems.

The last piece to an incident response policy is the follow-up to the incident with documentation. The CIRT should focus on the lessons learned during the incident. Reflecting back on lessons learned helps the CIRT make better decisions in the future and avoid bad ones from past incidents.

BYOD

The traditional workforce is slowly becoming a mobile workforce, with employees working from home, on the go, and in the office. Mobile devices such as laptops, tablets, and smartphones are used by employees to connect the organization's cloud resources. Bring your own device (BYOD) has been embraced as a strategy by organizations to alleviate the capital expense of equipment by allowing employees to use devices they already own.

Because employees are supplying their own devices, a formal document called the BYOD policy should be drafted. The BYOD policy defines a set of minimum requirements for the devices, such as size and type, operating system, connectivity, antivirus, patches, and many other requirements the organization will deem necessary.

Many organizations use mobile device management (MDM) software that dictates the requirements for the BYOD policy. MDM software helps organizations protect their data on devices that are personally owned by the employees. When employees are terminated or a device is lost, the MDM software allows a secure remote wipe of the company's data on the device. The MDM software can also set policies requiring passwords on the device. All of these requirements should be defined in the organization's BYOD policy.

AUP

There can be many different resources employees use that the organization supplies to conduct its business. An acceptable use policy (AUP) helps protect the organization from employee abuse of these resources. Email is an example of one such resource. It is generally not acceptable for an employee to use an organization's email for religious, political, personal causes, illegal activities, or commercial use outside of the organization's interest.

The AUP should be developed by the organization's legal counsel, HR department, and IT department. The systems that should be included in the AUP are telephone, Internet, email, and subscription services. The AUP might not be exclusive to electronic resources; the organization might also include postage and other nonelectronic resources that could be abused.

NDA

When an organization hires a new employee, the employee may be privilege to certain proprietary information. This information could be a company's secret sauce, passwords to administrative systems, or customer information. A nondisclosure agreement (NDA) legally protects an organization from an employee disclosing this information to a person outside the organization. The NDA is a document that defines the consequences of disclosure by termination and legal recourse. The NDA should be developed by the organization's legal counsel, HR department, and stakeholders of proprietary information in the organization.

System life cycle

The life cycle for IT systems is cyclical and differs slightly depending on the assets. The typical life cycle for IT systems consists of purchasing, deploying, managing, and retiring. Earlier we discussed the asset acquisition process and how it directly relates to inventory management and accounting. When an asset is purchased, the asset becomes an asset to the organization and is depreciated over its useful life in the organization. Once the asset is purchased, the asset is deployed. The deployment phase could involve plugging the equipment into the network and turning it on. Or the deployment phase could involve imaging, configuring, or installing (software assets) the IT system. The management of the system is usually performed directly by the IT department once the system is deployed. However, the management of the system can also involve the end users—for example, in the case of an accounting software package. Eventually all IT systems near their useful life and are retired.

The retirement of IT systems can be done several different ways depending on the type of equipment. End-user computing equipment might be sold for scrap costs, or they could be appropriated elsewhere in the organization. In the case of server and SAN equipment, these systems are usually moved to less critical workloads, such as development or development testing. An organization will commonly have generations of equipment, retiring the prior generation of equipment to another part of the organization. It is also important to note that the retirement process dovetails with the planning and repurchasing process that begins the life cycle again.

Asset Disposal

The last phase of the equipment life cycle is asset disposal. There are two responsibilities of the IT department and the organization pertaining to asset disposal. The first responsibility is to prevent data loss when equipment is disposed of. A procedure should be in place to wipe organization data from systems that are disposed of. The second responsibility is an ethical and legal responsibility to properly dispose of equipment. When an asset is disposed of, there are several environmental issues that can arise from trashing electronic equipment. Often electronics end up in landfills, and depending on the equipment and the local laws, the organization can be liable for fines. When selling equipment for scrap value, the buyer should be able to provide documentation to shield the company from legal ramifications if equipment is dumped.

Safety procedures and policies

Safety procedures and policies protect you from getting injured on the job. They protect the equipment from failure as well. Although you may think that being a network administrator is extremely safe job, you must be vigilant in your actions on the job.

Most datacenters operate on 208-volt alternating current (AC); this voltage or any high voltage can be lethal. When you are servicing equipment, the equipment should always be unplugged from the voltage supply. Most internals of servers and network equipment are low voltage and are user serviceable via field replaceable units (FRUs). Examples of FRUs include memory, CPU, and hard drives. However, power supplies are anything that you are in doubt of and should be avoided. Capacitors can be found in the internals of power supplies and cathode ray tube (CRT) monitors, and these components can store a lethal charge. These circuits require proper discharge procedures or should be avoided.

Your body, clothes, and surfaces can store a lethal charge for electronics. You can see this charge when you skitter across a carpet on a dry day and touch a light switch. Static electricity can kill components without you even knowing. Static electricity is often called the silent killer, because most charges are never seen or heard. A circuit board, such as a RAM stick, can be zapped by just putting it down on a Formica tabletop. Antistatic precautions should always be taken to avoid zapping critical components.

Everything in the datacenter runs on electricity, and although this should be our primary concern, there are more common ways to injure yourself. A standard server is 19 inches wide by about 28 to 36 inches long and can come in 1U, 2U, 4U, and 6U sizes; they can even come in larger sizes. A standard 19-inch 1U server might weigh around 20 to 25 pounds, but 6U servers can weight up to 60 pounds. SAN units that are full of drives can weigh over 100 pounds! You can easily injure your back by lifting one of these pieces of equipment. Many datacenters utilize hydraulic jacks to lift equipment into position and reduce personal injury. Before mounting equipment into the rack, you should have a good understanding of the rail systems so that they are properly secured to the rack and can hold the weight of the equipment. Racks should always be bolted firmly to the floor to prevent tipping hazards, and the heaviest equipment should be mounted on the bottom of the rack.

Every product that is handled or stored by the IT department should have an accompanying *material safety data sheet (MSDS)*. Typical products that have accompanying MSDSs are toner, batteries, cleaning agents, or something exotic like an atomic clock. These sheets should be stored in a central location by the first aid kit. In case of emergency such as eye contact, inhalation, or fire, these sheets provide vital information for first responders.

Fire safety is another important aspect of safety; it is important for human life and the equipment's life as well. We should always be vigilante in cabling and power requirements so that fires do not start. However, if a fire starts in the datacenter, chemicals agents or fire suppression gases are the best choice. Water-based systems can kill all of the datacenter equipment even if it is a localized fire. Fire suppression gases such as FM-200 are used to choke out the fire with minimal harm to other systems, the ozone, and humans. Class C fire extinguishers are used for class C fires, which are defined as electrical. Class C fire extinguishers are normally dry chemical fire extinguishers that disperse monoammonium phosphate, potassium bicarbonate, or potassium chloride, all of which are suitable for putting out class C fires.

A rack unit, which is often referred to as a U, defines the height of network rackable equipment. The rack unit is approximately 1.75 inches, so a 2U server is approximately 3.5 inches high, a 4U server is approximately 7 inches high, and so on.

Exam Essentials

Understand and identify policies and best practices.   A privileged user agreement is used to hold a privileged user to a standard of conduct so that privileges are not abused. A password policy enforces complex passwords of a minimum length.

On-boarding procedures are created for new employees so that a level of IT training and expectations is established. Off-boarding procedures are used to ensure that access for terminated employees is ended at the time they leave the organization. Software licenses are purchased as a per seat license or a per user license, and software can be purchased as permanent licenses or term-based subscriptions. International export controls must be followed if an item is "deemed" an export control and is shipped to a foreign country. Data loss prevention (DLP) systems minimize the risk of data loss, by restricting sensitive information from being moved, viewed, or emailed. Remote access policies defines who has remote access to the organization. Incident response policies help the computer incident response team (CIRT) to react to current incidents and plan for future incidents.

Bring your own device (BYOD) policy defines requirements for employees supplying their own equipment for organizational use. Mobile device management (MDM) software helps minimize an organization's exposure to data loss on BYOD. The acceptable use policy (AUP) helps protect an organization from abuse of organization-owned resources. The non-disclosure agreement (NDA) is an agreement between the organization and the employee when sensitive information proprietary to the company is shared. Safety procedures and policies ensure both the safety of employees and that equipment will not be damaged from improper handling.

Understand the concepts of the equipment life cycle.   The system life cycle is the cyclical process of equipment being purchased, deployed, managed, and retired or replaced. Asset disposal is the retirement phase of the system life cycle. There are ethical and legal responsibilities when disposing of assets.

Review Questions

1. What type of diagram is depicted in the following exhibit?

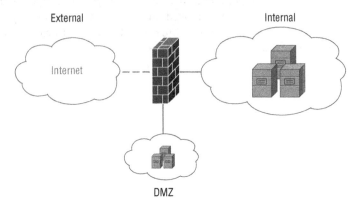

    A. Physical diagram

    B. LAN diagram

    C. Logical diagram

    D. Network schematic

2. When drawing a router on a network diagram, which is correct?

    A. A square with two sets of arrows

    B. A square with one set of arrows

    C. A square with picture inside that looks like the sun

    D. A circle with two sets of arrows perpendicular to each other

3. Which document would you create to detail step-by-step instructions to decommission a server from your network?

    A. ISO document

    B. SOP document

    C. Server policy

    D. Asset destruction

4. Which group of people evaluates changes for the network to reduce the possibility of affecting day-to-day operations?

    A. Network operations

    B. Executive committee

    C. Stakeholders

    D. Change advisory board

5. When labeling cable in a switch closet, which statement is a best practice?

A. The label should have the name of the workstation.

B. The label should be labeled from the least specific to the most specific location.

C. The label should be labeled from the most specific to the least specific location.

D. The label should represent the purpose of the host.

6. Why should performance baselines be captured over a long period of time?

A. To define normal operations and activity

B. To define a historical representation of activity

C. To help validate when a problem is solved

D. All of the above

7. Which type of software helps assist in tracking IT inventory?

A. Asset management software

B. Life-cycle management software

C. Accounting software

D. System upgrade software

8. Configuring a group of disks with RAID level 5 is an example of which availability concept?

A. Fault tolerance

B. High availability

C. Clustering

D. Load balancing

9. You have a high demand of normal requests on the company's web server. Which strategy should be implemented to avoid issues if demand becomes too high?

A. Clustering

B. Port aggregation

C. Fault tolerance

D. Load balancing

10. Which type of recovery is the least expensive to maintain over time?

A. Cold site recovery

B. Warm site recovery

C. Hot site recovery

D. Disaster site recovery

11. A recovery from tape will take 4 hours; what is this an example of?

 A. The recovery point objective (RPO)

 B. The recovery time objective (RTO)

 C. Grandfather, father, son (GFS) rotation

 D. Backup window

12. You are the network administrator for your organization. Backup windows are starting to extend into work shifts. You have been asked to recommend a better strategy; what will speed up backups to shorten the window?

 A. Disk-to-tape backups

 B. Disk-to-disk backups

 C. Full backups

 D. GFS rotations

13. Which backup job will back up files with the archive bit set and then reset the archive bit for the next backup?

 A. Archive backup

 B. Full backup

 C. Differential backup

 D. Incremental backup

14. You are contracting with a new service provider and are reviewing their service level agreement (SLA). The SLA states that their commitment to uptime is 99.99 percent. What is the expected downtime per year?

 A. 3.65 days

 B. 8.76 hours

 C. 52.56 minutes

 D. 5.29 minutes

15. You are the network administrator for your organization. You have been tasked to aggregate bandwidth of two 1 Gbps ports between a Cisco switch and an HP switch. Which protocol should you choose to complete the task?

 A. LACP

 B. 802.1q

 C. PAgP

 D. ISL

16. Which type of uninterruptable power supplies (UPS), often found in datacenters, provides constant power from the battery-powered inverter circuit?

 A. Line interactive UPS

 B. Standby UPS

 C. Online UPS

 D. Failover UPS

17. Which type of backup is used for grandfather, father, son (GFS) rotations?

   A. Copy backup

   B. Full backup

   C. Differential backup

   D. Incremental backup

18. You need to design a patch management strategy for your organization. The majority of your clients are Microsoft Windows clients. What should you recommend as a patch management solution?

   A. NLB

   B. MSCS

   C. MSBA

   D. WSUS

19. You need to capture network packets for analysis of a problem; which tool allows you to capture network packets?

   A. Wireshark

   B. Nmap

   C. SCCM

   D. Event viewer

20. Which high availability protocol is an open standard?

   A. NLB

   B. HSRP

   C. NTFS

   D. VRRP

21. You are using a network management station (NMS) to collect data for network devices. What must be loaded before you can capture data from the network devices via the Simple Network Management Protocol (SNMP)?

   A. OID

   B. MIB

   C. Traps

   D. Gets

22. Which remote access technology uses encryption by default?

   A. Telnet

   B. FTPS

   C. TFTP

   D. SFTP

23. Which policy would you create to define the minimum specification if an employee wanted to use their own device for email?

   A. MDM

   B. AUP

   C. BYOD

   D. NDA

24. A co-worker was replacing a toner cartridge in a printer, and toner has accidentally gotten in his eye. Which document should be consulted for prompt treatment?

   A. MSDS

   B. MSDN

   C. Instructions

   D. Manufacturer's website

25. Which protocol uses a handshake protocol to initiate encryption?

   A. SSL

   B. FTP

   C. TLS

   D. FTPS

Chapter

4

Domain 4.0: Network Security

THE FOLLOWING COMPTIA NETWORK+ OBJECTIVES ARE COVERED IN THIS CHAPTER:

✓ **4.1 Summarize the purposes of physical security devices.**

- Detection
    - Motion detection
    - Video surveillance
    - Asset tracking tags
    - Tamper detection
- Prevention
    - Badges
    - Biometrics
    - Smart cards
    - Key fob
    - Locks

✓ **4.2 Explain authentication and access controls.**

- Authentication, authorization, and accounting
    - RADIUS
    - TACACS+
    - Kerberos
    - Single sign-on
    - Local authentication
    - LDAP
    - Certificates
    - Auditing and logging

- Multifactor authentication
    - Something you know
    - Something you have
    - Something you are
    - Somewhere you are
    - Something you do
- Access control
    - 802.1x
    - NAC
    - Port security
    - MAC filtering
    - Captive portal
    - Access control lists

✓ **4.3   Given a scenario, secure a basic wireless network.**

- WPA
- WPA2
- TKIP-RC4
- CCMP-AES
- Authentication and authorization
    - EAP
        - PEAP
        - EAP-FAST
        - EAP-TLS
    - Shared or open
    - Preshared key
    - MAC filtering
- Geofencing

✓ **4.4 Summarize common networking attacks.**

- DoS
  - Reflective
  - Amplified
  - Distributed
- Social engineering
- Insider threat
- Logic bomb
- Rogue access point
- Evil twin
- War-driving
- Phishing
- Ransomware
- DNS poisoning
- ARP poisoning
- Spoofing
- Deauthentication
- Brute force
- VLAN hopping
- Man-in-the-middle
- Exploits vs. vulnerabilities

✓ **4.5 Given a scenario, implement network device hardening.**

- Changing default credentials
- Avoiding common passwords
- Upgrading firmware
- Patching and updates
- File hashing
- Disabling unnecessary services
- Using secure protocols
- Generating new keys

- Disabling unused ports
    - IP ports
    - Device ports (physical and virtual)

✓ **4.6 Explain common mitigation techniques and their purposes.**

- Signature management
- Device hardening
- Change native VLAN
- Switch port protection
    - Spanning tree
    - Flood guard
    - BPDU Guard
    - Root Guard
    - DHCP snooping
- Network segmentation
    - DMZ
    - VLAN
- Privileged user account
- File integrity monitoring
- Role separation
- Restricting access via ACLs
- Honeypot/honeynet
- Penetration testing

Network security should be the primary focus in the design and operations of your network. We build networks to internally share our organizational information and resources to authorized users. However, we must also protect the information from unauthorized individuals. Many of the unauthorized individuals will be external to the organization and have malicious intent.

In the previous chapters, you learned the fundamental theory of networking. You also learned about the various infrastructure components and how to maintain network operations. In this chapter, you will learn how to secure the network infrastructure.

For more detailed information on Domain 4's topics, please see *CompTIA Network+ Study Guide*, 4th ed. (978-1-119-43225-8) or *CompTIA Network+ Certification Kit*, 5th ed. (978-1-119-43228-9) published by Sybex.

4.1 Summarize the purposes of physical security devices.

Physical security is often taken for granted by network administrators. However, physical security is directly related to network security. As an example, if you went through great lengths to secure your switches and routers with public and private key pairs but did not secure the network closets where they operate, a malicious actor could easily gain access to the switch or router by performing a password reset, which in most cases requires physical access to the device.

It is the network administrator's job to secure physical access for the network equipment. We can perform this duty by either detecting unauthorized access or preventing unauthorized access. Depending on how sensitive the information or system is, we sometimes need to both prevent and detect unauthorized access.

Detection

Detection of physical access lets you know what happened, when it happened, and who did it. The last detail of *who* is often the hardest piece of information to obtain when using detection methods. Detection methods help network administrators resolve and improve physical security problems. Detection can sometimes lead to intervention from the organization's security officers or the local authorities.

Motion Detection

There are several different motion detection types that we can use to detect unauthorized access. *Passive infrared (PIR)* is the most common motion detection used today, mainly because of price. PIR sensors operate by monitoring the measurement of infrared radiation from several zones. In Figure 4.1, you can see the reflective panel that divides the infrared zones. A PIR sensor will always have this grid pattern on the sensor's face.

FIGURE 4.1   A typical PIR sensor

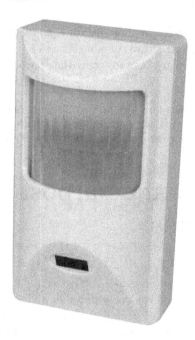

Microwave detectors also look like PIR sensors, but they do not have a reflective panel. Microwave detectors are common in areas where wide coverage is needed. Microwave detectors operate by sending pulses of microwaves out and measuring the microwaves received. These detectors are more expensive than PIR sensors and are susceptible to external interference, but they have a wider area of coverage.

Vibration sensors are another type of sensor used for motion detection. Although you may have seen them in the latest over-the-top heist movie, vibration sensors are really used in physical security systems. They are most often implemented as seismic sensors. They help protect physical security from natural disasters and accidental drilling, or the occasional over-the-top heist.

Video Surveillance

Video surveillance is the backbone of physical security. It is the only detection method that allows an investigator to identify what happened, when it happened, and, most importantly, who made it happened. Two types of cameras can be deployed: fixed and *pan-tilt-zoom (PTZ)*. Fixed cameras are the best choice when recording for surveillance activities. Pan-tilt-zoom (PTZ) cameras allow for 360-degree operations and zooming in on an area. PTZs are most commonly used for intervention, such as covering an area outside during an accident or medical emergency. PTZ cameras are usually deployed for the wrong reasons, mainly because they are cool! PTZs are often put into patrol mode to cover a larger area than a fixed camera can. However, when an incident occurs, they are never pointed in the area you need them! It is always best to use a fixed camera or multiple fixed cameras, unless you need a PTZ for a really good reason. They are usually more expensive and require more maintenance than fixed cameras.

Video surveillance can be deployed in two common media types of coaxial cable and Ethernet. Coaxial cable is used typically in areas where preexisting coaxial lines are in place or distances are too far for typical Ethernet. These systems are called *closed-circuit television (CCTV)*. Coaxial camera systems generally use appliance-like devices for recording of video. These CCTV recorders generally have a finite number of ports for cameras and a finite amount of storage in the form of direct attached storage (DAS).

Ethernet (otherwise known as IP) surveillance is becoming the standard for new installations. Anywhere an Ethernet connection can be installed, a camera can be mounted. Power over Ethernet (POE) allows power to be supplied to the camera, so additional power supplies used with coaxial cameras are not needed. Ethernet also provides the flexibility of virtual local area networks (VLANs) for added security so that the camera network is isolated from operational traffic. IP surveillance uses *network video recorder (NVR)* software to record cameras. Because NVRs are server applications, we can use traditional storage such as network area storage (NAS) or storage area network (SAN) storage. This allows us to treat the video recordings like traditional data.

Coaxial camera networks can be converted to IP surveillance networks with the use of a device called a media converter. These devices look similar to a CCTV recorder. They have a limited number of ports for the coaxial cameras and are generally smaller than the CCTV recorder. This is because they do not have any DAS. The sole purpose of the media converter is to convert the coaxial camera to an Ethernet feed to the NVR.

The use of IP video surveillance allows for a number of higher-end features such as camera-based motion detection, *license plate recognition (LPR)*, and motion fencing. Advanced NVR software allows cameras to send video only when motion is detected at the camera; this saves on storage for periods of nonactivity. LPR is a method of detecting and capturing license plates in which the software converts the plate to a searchable attribute for the event. With motion fencing, an electronic fence can be drawn on the image so that any activity within this region will trigger an alert. Among the many other features are facial recognition and object recognition.

Asset Tracking Tags

Asset tracking tags are used to track, secure, locate, and identify assets for your organization. Asset tracking is widely used in hospitals, because tracking of medical equipment can be critical. In some hospitals, even doctor locations are tracked. Hospital settings are not the only use case for asset tracking; many companies have implemented asset tracking tags for increased productivity. Anyone who has taken on a weekend project and spent more time looking for the tools than performing the task can relate to the problem companies face on a daily basis.

Two main types of asset tracking tags exist: passive and active RFID. The technical operations of both of these technologies are covered in Chapter 5. Passive asset tags require a high-powered transponder to activate the tag via radio frequency (RF)-emitted signals. The passive asset tag will respond to the receiver with the unique ID of the tag that is tied to the asset. Passive asset tags are used to prevent shrinkage of inventory, but they are not practical for tracking and locating assets, mainly because of the limited number of receivers that can be deployed.

Active tracking tags contain a battery-powered transmitter. Active tracking tags come in a variety of deployments, such as traditional 802.11 wireless, Bluetooth, and RFID. Traditional 802.11 asset tracking tags require a powered wireless client, in which a wireless LAN (WLAN) controller can track and triangulate the asset. Bluetooth operates on a similar frequency to 802.11, and many WLAN controllers can track and triangulate Bluetooth active tracking tags as well. Bluetooth is an expensive option for wireless asset tracking, and Bluetooth requires very low power for operations. Triangulation for both traditional wireless and Bluetooth is normally a premium feature on WLAN controllers. RFID asset tracking tags are generally used by dedicated RFID tracking systems and software and require a separate infrastructure from wireless systems. Just like the WLAN controller, RFID systems can triangulate equipment. However, RFID systems can only be used for RFID tags and cannot serve traditional 802.11 wireless clients. Reasons for choosing an RFID tracking systems over an 802.11 wireless tracking systems can be driven by the need of isolation between the current 802.11 wireless system and the asset tracking requirement. Other reasons could be driven by internal politics in your company or the price of adding the functionality to the existing 802.11 wireless system. The reasons for choosing RFID are in isolation of services, chosen by either internal politics or price.

An obvious benefit to asset tracking is locating assets. However, an added benefit is the long-term data captured by these systems. This data can be analyzed for usage and mobility of the assets. From the analysis, an organization can shrink, expand, or redistribute the assets.

Tamper Detection

Tamper detection can indicate that a system is compromised in some way. There are type types of tamper detection: nonelectrical and electrical. Nonelectrical tamper detection consists of a label called a security strip that when peeled off displays a visible mark. Security strips are affixed on a portion of the equipment that would move if it was opened;

therefore, the security tape would need to be peeled off or cut. This type of detection is effective and simple, but it requires intervention by a person to detect the tampering.

Electrical tamper detection is in the form of circuitry in the device and a micro switch. The micro switch is normally mounted on the case, where it makes contact with the case cover. If the case is removed, a tamper is detected on the device, and the operating system will create an SNMP alert. This type of detection is automated and can even generate an email or text message.

Tamper detection does not always need to include the network equipment. The simplest tamper detection is an alarm system. In remote offices where equipment is located, tamper detection can be installed on the door leading to the equipment. If an unauthorized person enters, the alarm can alert the appropriate person(s) to respond.

Prevention

Detection can alert you to physical unauthorized entry into your systems. However, your main duty should be to deter and prevent unauthorized physical access. In the following section I will discuss several tactics to protect physical access from unauthorized persons.

Badges

Identification badges are used to provide proof of access to others. Proper processes and procedures must be in place for a successful implementation of this prevention tactic. Badges are only as good as the enforcement of the badges themselves. In many organizations that implement ID badges, all employees are required to display their ID badge at all times. If an employee is in an area where they are not recognized, other employees are trained to look for the ID badge and take appropriate action if it is not displayed. Many companies have implemented this policy as a personnel safety policy, but it ultimately serves as a physical security protocol.

Biometrics

Biometrics use a metric related to a person's physical body to provide access to a system. Common metrics used are fingerprints, retina, voice, and facial recognition. In recent years several mobile phones have implemented biometrics in the access control of the mobile device. Several manufacturers have adopted fingerprint access control, and some have even adopted facial recognition with the forward-pointing camera.

Biometrics may sound like something out of your favorite spy movie, but it is a valuable tactic for preventing unauthorized access. Fingerprint recognition (Figure 4.2) is the most common biometric used for physical access control. If an electronic badge is used, it can be stolen and used by an unauthorized person for access. However, when biometrics are used only your fingerprint can access the system. I'm sure that you can think of a scene in your favorite spy movie where a fingerprint is stolen and maliciously used, but in real life a passcode is also required. In Chapter 2 I will discuss authentication types in further detail.

FIGURE 4.2   A typical biometric reader

Smartcards

A smartcard is the size of a credit card with an electronically erasable programmable read-only memory (EEPROM) integrated circuit embedded into the card (also called an integrated circuit chip [ICC]). The EEPROM chip is exposed on the face of the card with surface contacts, as shown in Figure 4.3. They are used for physical authentication to electronic systems and access controlled systems. The US military uses smartcards called *Common Access Cards (CACs)* for access to computer systems and physical access controls.

FIGURE 4.3   A typical smartcard

The chip contains a person's private key from their public private key pair and is encrypted with a passphrase or personal identification number (PIN). When the smartcard is inserted into the smartcard reader, the user enters their PIN code and a certificate is validated authenticating the user.

Key Fob

Key fobs are embedded RFID circuits used with physical access control systems (ACSs) that fit on a set of keys, as shown in Figure 4.4. They are often used for access to external and internal doors for buildings. The devices are passive RFID circuits that respond to 125 KHz frequency. I explain RFID circuits in Chapter 1 in further detail. When the ACS authorizes the user for entry, an electronic lock is actuated, and the door can be opened.

FIGURE 4.4   A typical key fob

Locks

The most common physical prevention tactic is the use of locks on doors and equipment. This might mean the installation of a tumbler-style lock for the switching closet or an elaborate electronic combination lock. If a tumbler-style lock is installed, then the appropriate authorized individuals who require access will need a physical key. Using physical keys can become a problem, because you may not have the key with you when you need it the most, or you can lose the key. The key can also be copied and used by unauthorized individuals. Combination locks allow for reprogramming and do not require physical keys, as shown in Figure 4.5. Combination locks for door can be purchased as mechanical or electronic.

FIGURE 4.5   A typical combination door lock

Exam Essentials

Know the various tactics used for the detection of physical security violations.   Motion detection uses passive infrared (PIR) to monitor differences in heat. Microwave motion detection sensors use pulses of microwave and measure the microwaves that bounce back. Vibration sensors detect vibrations and are often deployed as seismic sensors. Video surveillance can be deployed as a coaxial network called closed-circuit television (CCTV) or Ethernet. Asset tracking tags are used to track, secure, locate, and identify assets via software. Tamper detection for network equipment can be specific circuitry that monitors tamper detection or passive stickers that when tampered with display a tamper indication.

Know the various tactics used for the prevention of physical security violations. Badges are used for positive identification of authorized personnel. Biometric use a metric related to a person's physical body to provide access to a system. A smartcard is the size of a credit card and contains an EEPROM storing the private key of the user, which is protected with a passphrase. Key fobs are small devices that fit on a set of keys and contain an RFID circuit. Locks provide physical security with a standard key or a combination lock.

4.2 Explain authentication and access controls.

Several protocols can be used to authenticate a network user. In this section I will discuss the various common protocols used in networks today. You will learn the different factors that are used to authenticate a user and provide multifactor authentication. In addition to authentication and the factors that provide authentication, you will learn about the various network ACSs that restrict access.

Authentication, authorization, and accounting

Authentication, authorization, and accounting (AAA) defines the basics of user administration for access to resources. The AAA system of access is easily explained as a transaction in a physical bank. In Figure 4.6, the customer (user) appears on the far left, and their money (resource) is shown on the far right. In this section I will use the analogy of a bank transaction in which a customer will withdraw money.

FIGURE 4.6   AAA bank analogy

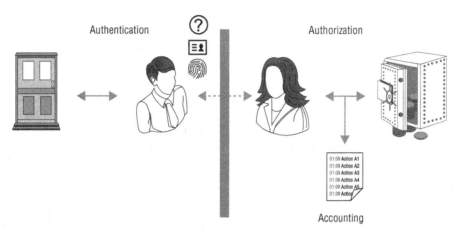

When a user wants to access a resource, they must first provide *authentication* that they are who they say they are. A user can provide authentication credentials using several different factors. The most common authentication factors are something you know (passwords), something you have (smartcard), or something you are (biometrics). I will discuss the various authentication factors in greater detail later in this section. Continuing with the example of a bank, a customer (user) will provide their authentication via their account number (something they know) and identification (something they are). The bank teller can then authenticate they are the person they say they are.

Once the teller has authenticated the customer (user), *authorization* will be checked. In a bank, authorization might be how much money is in your bank account. However, a better example is who can enter the vault and touch the money! I'm sure even if my bank authenticates me, they won't authorize me to count and withdraw my own money. I'm pretty sure that if I tried, I would go to jail and not collect my two hundred dollars. The teller is authorized to touch the money and hand it to you. It is important to note that in this example, the teller is also authenticated when they come into work, although this authentication is less rigorous than your authentication process.

Now that you have been authenticated and authorized to receive your money, an audit trail is created. If you had $400 and withdrew $200, your account would be debited $200. The audit trail in this example is the *accounting* process of the AAA system. Accounting allows us to trust and audit.

In a network system, when a user logs on, they will commonly authenticate with a user-name and password. When the user tries to access the resource, their authorization to the resource will be checked. If they are authorized to access the resource, the accounting of access will be recorded. It is important to note that accounting can record denied access to a resource as well.

RADIUS

Remote Authentication Dial-In User Service (RADIUS) was originally proposed as an Internet Engineering Task Force (IETF) standard. It has become a widely adopted industry standard for authenticating users and computers for network systems. RADIUS creates a common authentication system, which allows for centralized authentication and accounting.

The origins of RADIUS are from the original ISP dial-up days, as its acronym describes. Today, RADIUS is commonly used for authentication of remote access systems, wireless systems, and any network system that requires a common authentication system. RADIUS operates as a client-server protocol. The RADIUS server controls authentication, authorization, and accounting (AAA). The RADIUS client can be wireless access points, a VPN, or 802.1x switches. The RADIUS client will communicate with the RADIUS server via UDP/1812 for authentication and UDP/1813 for accounting. The RADIUS server can be configured with authorization rules that use the connection's attributes. Common attributes are caller IP address, connection type, group association, and the username and password of the user.

TACACS+

Terminal Access Controller Access Control System+ (TACACS+) is a protocol developed by Cisco, from the original dated protocol of TACACS. Although it was developed by Cisco, it was released as an open standard. The protocol is mainly used AAA of routers and switches management access. The TACACS+ protocol is declining in popularity and has largely been replaced with RADIUS.

Kerberos

In Greek mythology, *Kerberos* (Cerberus) is the three-headed hound of Hades that guards the gates of the underworld and prevents the dead from escaping. The Kerberos protocol was developed at the Massachusetts Institute of Technology (MIT) as a secure authentication protocol. It provides strong security for transmitted usernames and passwords via Triple Data Encryption Standard (3DES) and Advanced Encryption Standard (AES) encryption. It was adopted by Microsoft in 2000 as the main authentication protocol for Active Directory.

It's named after a three-headed hound, which describes how it requires a three-way trust to authenticate users or computers. When a service server starts up, it requests a service ticket (proof of authentication) from the authenticating server. A service server can be a file server or email server, and the authentication server can be a Linux/Unix Kerberos server or Microsoft Active Directory server. When the client starts up, it too requests an authentication ticket. When the client accesses the service server, the authentication tickets are exchanged and checked against the authenticating server list. Both the client and service server must trust the same authenticating server for access to be permitted. This completes the three-way trust of client to service server to authenticating server.

Single Sign-On

Single sign-on (SSO) is an aspect of authentication and not a protocol. SSO assists the user logon by allowing the user to authenticate to the first application and then allowing the reuse of credentials for other applications. This way, the user no longer has to enter the same username and password for each application they access.

Each application that participates in SSO requires an SSO agent module. The SSO agent module is responsible for retrieving the authenticating credentials for the user from an SSO policy server. The SSO policy server is can be a *Lightweight Directory Access Protocol (LDAP)* directory or Active Directory Federation Services (ADFS). The protocol *Security Assertion Markup Language (SAML)* is used to exchange credentials; this is considered SAML-based SSO.

Local Authentication

So far we have covered centralized authentication and protocols that support the authentication process. Local authentication is useful when providing access to a small group of people, because each account must be manually created on each device or server to be accessed.

Local authentication is just that—it operates by authenticating the user to a local database contained on the equipment or server. There is no need for protocols, because it's all local and nothing needs to be transmitted over the network. Local authentication is normally used for the management of network devices. It is common to configure network device management to authenticate users from RADIUS or TACACS+, with a fallback to local authentication if the network is down.

LDAP

Lightweight Directory Access Protocol (LDAP) is an open standard directory service protocol originally defined by the IETF. It operates as a client-server protocol used for looking up objects in a directory service and their respective attributes. LDAP was adopted by Microsoft in 2000 for Active Directory lookups of objects on domain controllers.

An LDAP client queries requests to an LDAP server with a specifically formatted uniform resource identifier (URI). The URI will contain the object to search for and the attributes to be retrieved. In addition, filters can be supplied so that only specific objects are searched. LDAP uses a default protocol and port of TCP/389. When SSL is used with LDAP, called LDAPS, the protocol and port of TCP/636 is used.

Certificates

Certificates are a method of using a public key infrastructure (PKI) to validate users and computers. Certificates can also be used to validate the integrity of applications. When using certificates to authenticate a user, the public key of the user's public private key pair is mapped to the user account for the web application. When the user connects to the web application, they provide a certificate created from their private key. The application authenticates the certificate presented using the user's public key, and the result is the authentication of the user to the mapped credentials.

Auditing and Logging

Auditing and logging of user authentication and authorization is the accounting principle of AAA. We always want to trust that our users have the best intentions. This leads us to the mantra of auditing and logging, which is to trust and audit.

Logging of user authentication activity helps us audit who and when our users are accessing the organization's systems. It holds the users accessing the network systems accountable for their actions. We always believe our users have good intentions, but what happens if a user's account is compromised? Reviewing of the log files helps identify failed attempts or successful logins by the bad actor.

Logging of authorization works similar to logging of authentication, with the exception of the amount of data generated. When a user accesses a piece of information that is being audited to create the log event, it generates a log entry. If we are auditing for successful authorization requests, everything a user does could potentially create a log entry. This helps us identify what a user is doing, but it creates a massive amount of data. If we audit only for failures of authorization, it will lower the amount of data collected, but we see only failures and not what the user is accessing. A delicate balance of success auditing and failure auditing must be established. One tactic is to choose carefully what to audit, such as only sensitive information for successful authorization and failed attempts.

Multifactor authentication

All authentication is based on something that you know, have, are, or do, or a location you are in. A common factor of authentication is a password, but passwords can guessed, stolen, or cracked. No one factor is secure by itself, because by themselves they can be compromised easily. A fingerprint can be lifted with tape, a key can be stolen, or a location spoofed.

Multifactor authentication helps solve the problem of a compromised single-factor authentication method by combining the authentication methods. With multifactor authentication, a single-factor will no longer authenticate a user; two or more of the factors discussed in this section are required for authentication. This makes the credentials of the user more complex to compromise.

Something You Know

Computing has used the factor of something a person knows since computer security began. This is commonly in the form of a username and password. We can make passwords more complex by requiring uppercase, lowercase, numeric, and symbol combinations. We can also mandate length of the password and the frequency in which it is changed. However, it is the most common theft of credentials because it can be phished or sniffed with a key logger.

Something You Have

Authentication based on something a person has relates to physical security. When we use a key fob, RFID tag, or magnetic card to enter a building, we are using something we have. An identification badge is something we have, although technically it is also something we are if it has a picture of us on it. Credit cards have long since been something we have to authenticate a transaction. Within the past two decades, it has also become the most thieved credentials. Recently, credit cards have implemented a new authentication method called Europay, MasterCard, and Visa (EMV). EMV will make it harder to steal and duplicate cards. However, if a card is lost, it can still be used by an unscrupulous person because it is something you physically have.

Something You Are

A decade or so ago, authenticating a user based on something they are was science fiction. We now have biometric readers built into our phones for our convenience! All we need to do is place our finger on the reader, speak into the phone, or allow the phone to recognize our face and we are instantly logged in. Computers can be outfitted with fingerprint readers to allow logon of users based on their fingerprint as well. When this technology entered the market, there were various ways to get around it, such as tape-lifting a print, playing back someone's voice, or displaying a picture of a person for the camera. These systems have gotten better since they have entered the market by storing more points of the fingerprint, listening to other aspects of a user's voice, and looking for natural motion in the camera.

Somewhere You Are

A relatively new factor of authentication is based on somewhere you are. With the proliferation of Global Positioning System (GPS) chips, your current location can authenticate you for a system. This is performed by creating authentication rules on the location. GPS sensors are not the only method of obtaining your current location. Geographic IP information queried from *Geo-IP services* can also be used for the authentication process. We can restrict login to a specific IP or geographic location based on the IP address provided.

Something You Do

Another relatively new factor of authentication for network systems is based on something you do. Although it has been used for hundreds of years for documents and contracts, a signature is something that you do and don't even think about how you do it. It is unique to you and only you, because there is a specific way you sign your name. Typing your name into the computer is something you do and don't think about, but there is a slight hesitation that you make without knowing it. Algorithms pick up on this and use the keystrokes as a form of authentication. Arguably, it can be considered biometrics because it is something your brain does without you consciously thinking about it.

Access control

The term *access control* defines the authorization of devices or users on the network or to specific resources in the network. The control can be based on user credentials, IP addresses, MAC addresses, or any variable we configure in an access control rule. In the following section, I will discuss several common access control mechanisms used in networks today.

802.1x

The *802.1x* protocol is used to control access on the internal network, as shown in Figure 4.7. 802.1x commonly uses RADIUS as the authentication server. However, other AAA authentication servers can be used, such as LDAP and TACACS+. 802.1x is used for both wired and wireless network access. When you are using 802.1x with a wired connection, the physical port allows communications of 802.1x credentials. The port will not allow user traffic to be switched until the AAA process is completed and the user or computer is verified. The user's device is called the supplicant, and the port it is plugged into is called the control port, because it controls access to the organization's LAN or resources. The switch that is set up for 802.1x is called the authenticator.

FIGURE 4.7   802.1x switch control

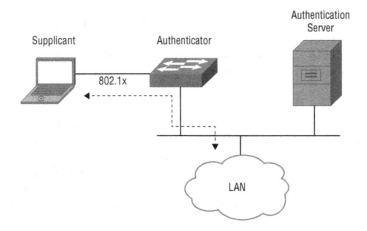

802.1x works with wireless connections, but in lieu of a physical connection an association occurs. When 802.1x is used with wireless, the control port is the port leading back to the network. All 802.1x authentication between the supplicant and the authenticator occurs over the associated connection.

Credentials for the user or computer are encrypted with *Extensible Authentication Protocol (EAP)*, also known as Extensible Authentication Protocol over LAN (EAPOL). Cisco devices use a protocol called *Lightweight Extensible Authentication Protocol (LEAP)*, and Microsoft uses a protocol called *Protected Extensible Authentication Protocol (PEAP)*. I will discuss the various protocols in the next section. Communications between the authenticator and the authentication server are protected with a shared password.

NAC

Although 802.1x can be used by itself for AAA, it is often used in conjunction with a *network access control (NAC)* system. It is often referred to as port-based network access control (PNAC).

As shown in Figure 4.8, NAC agents check the reported health and integrity of the client before allowing it on the network. The NAC agent can check the current patch level of the client, antivirus signature date, and firewall status. The NAC policy is defined by the network administrator. If the client passes the checks, the client is allowed on the network. If the client fails the checks, the client is placed into a remediation network, where the user must remediate the client. It is important to mention that although the figure details a separate NAC server, the NAC and 802.1x are usually the same server.

FIGURE 4.8   NAC and 802.1x

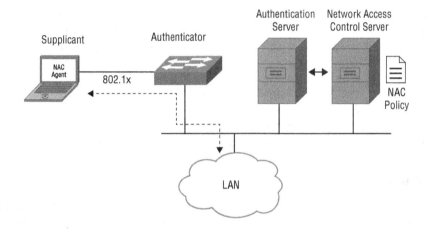

Port Security

Port security is a method of restricting specific MAC addresses or a specific number of MAC addresses on a physical access mode switch port. Port security is supported on many different vendor switches, but I will focus on the Cisco switching platform for this section; all switches support similar port security function. Port security is commonly implemented by the network administrator to mitigate the threat of end users plugging in hub, switches, or wireless access ports (WAPs) to extend switching of a single port.

As covered in Chapter 2, when a switch powers on, a blank table is created in memory called the switching table. When a frame is received on the switch port, the switch records the source MAC address of the frame with the switch port the frame is received on. Each MAC address receives an entry in the switching table for future forward filter decisions. We can restrict how many entries each switch port can record with the following commands on a Cisco switch. In the example port security is configured, and a maximum of one MAC address will be allowed.

```
switch(config)# interface gigabitethernet 0/1
switch(config-if)# switchport port-security
switch(config-if)# switchport port-security maximum 1
```

By using `switchport port-security mac-address sticky`, we can configure the switch to record the first MAC address and limit the port to only that MAC address indefinitely or until an administrator clears it. By default with only the previous commands, the MAC address learned will be cleared after a period of inactivity.

```
switch(config)# interface gigabitethernet 0/1
switch(config-if)# switchport port-security
switch(config-if)# switchport port-security maximum 1
switch(config-if)# switchport port-security mac-address sticky
```

We can also constrain the switch port to a specific MAC address statically. In lieu of the `switchport port-security mac-address sticky` command, we can specify the specific MAC address to limit the switch port to. By configuring the following command, the MAC address will be locked to 0678.e2b3.0a02 for the switch port:

```
switch(config)# interface gigabitethernet 0/1
switch(config-if)# switchport port-security
switch(config-if)# switchport port-security maximum 1
switch(config-if)# switchport port-security mac-address 0678.e2b3.0a02
```

MAC Filtering

MAC filtering is the method of restricting or allowing specific MAC addresses to be forwarded through a switch port on a switch or forwarded though a wireless access point. It is commonly used with wireless LAN controllers (WLCs) to control specific clients by their MAC address. When it is used in conjunction with an 802.1x/NAC solution, the devices can be controlled globally from the authentication server. MAC filtering is a very effective method of security, because of the difficulty an attacker has identifying the specific MAC addresses that are specifically allowed to be forward by the switch or WAP. Switches can be configured to filter specific MAC addresses as well. Port security is considered a form of MAC filtering for switching.

Captive Portal

A *captive portal* is a method of redirecting users who connect to wireless or wired systems to a portal for login or agreement to the acceptable use policy (AUP). Using a captive portal is common for wireless system access. More than likely, if you have stayed in a hotel that offers wireless, you have been redirected to the captive portal to accept the terms. Some hotels require you to purchase the wireless service; this type of service would also redirect you to the portal for login or payment. Captive portals are not exclusively used for hotels; they are also used for corporate access to an organization's wireless system.

A captive portal redirects the user to the captive portal address on the first DNS request the web browser or application initiates. DNS name resolution for all addresses are pointed to the captive portal address, where the user is presented with the login screen. Captive portal systems commonly use a Remote Authentication Dial-In User Service (RADIUS) or Lightweight Directory Access Protocol (LDAP) server when validating credentials for a user.

When configuring the captive portal, we have several different implementations we can use. The two most common implementations are inline and out-of-band. Figure 4.9 details an inline implementation of the captive portal. In order for the client to communicate with the LAN, all traffic must pass through the captive portal. This design is common for small implementations.

FIGURE 4.9   An inline captive portal

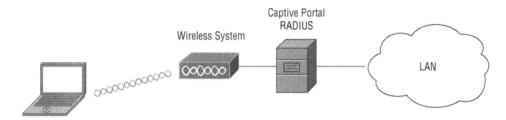

Figure 4.10 shows an out-of-band implementation. When the user first connects to the wireless system, the user is placed into a registration VLAN where the captive portal is the gateway, capturing the user for login. Once the user is authenticated, the RADIUS server directs the switch to change the VLAN for the user. The captive portal is now out-of-band of the user's traffic and the user is solely using the switching network. These implementations commonly use 802.1x for the wireless LAN controller (WLC).

FIGURE 4.10   An out-of-band captive portal

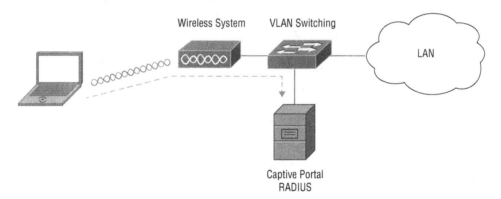

Access Control Lists

Access control lists (ACLs) are used to control traffic and applications on a network. Every network vendor supports a type of ACL method; for the remainder of this section, I will focus on Cisco ACLs.

An ACL method consists of multiple access control entries (ACEs) that are condition actions. Each entry is used to specify the traffic to be controlled. Every vendor will have a different type of control logic. However, understanding the control logic of the ACL system allows you to apply it to any vendor and be able to effectively configure an ACL. The control logic is defined with these simple questions:

- How are the conditions of an ACL evaluated?
- What is the default action if a condition is not met?
- How is the ACL applied to traffic?
- How are conditions edited for an ACL?

Let's explore the control logic for a typical Cisco layer 3 switch or router. The conditions of the ACL are evaluated from top to bottom. If a specific condition is not met for the ACL, the default action is to deny the traffic. Only one ACL can be configured per interface, per protocol, and per direction. When you are editing a traditional standard or extended ACL, the entire ACL must be negated and reentered with the new entry. With traditional ACLs, there is no way to edit a specific ACL on the fly. When editing a named access list, each condition is given a line number that can be referenced so that the specific entry can be edited. For the remainder of this section I will use named access lists to illustrate an applied access list for controlling traffic.

In Figure 4.11 you can see a typical corporate network. There are two different types of workers: HR workers and generic workers. We want to protect the HR web server from access by generic workers.

FIGURE 4.11 A typical corporate network

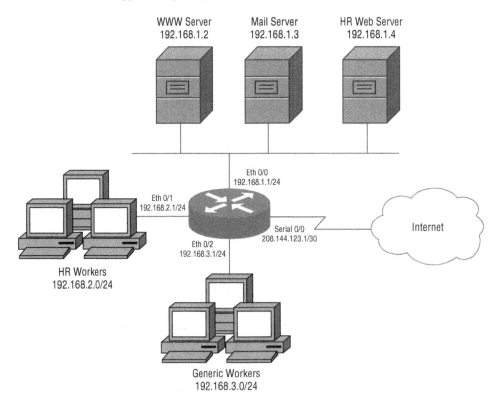

We can protect the HR server by applying an ACL to outgoing traffic for Eth 0/0 and describing the source traffic and destination to be denied. We can also apply an ACL to the incoming interface of Eth 0/2 describing the destination traffic to be denied. For this example, we will build an access list for incoming traffic to Eth 0/2 blocking the destination of the HR server.

```
Router(config)# ip access-list extended block-hrserver
Router(config-ext-nacl)# deny ip any host 192.168.1.4
Router(config-ext-nacl)# permit ip any any
Router(config-ext-nacl)# exit
Router(config)# interface ethernet 0/2
Router(config-if)# ip access-group block-hrserver in
```

This ACL, called block-hrserver, contains two condition action statements. The first denies any source address to the specific destination address of 192.168.1.4. The second allows any source address to any destination address. We then enter the interface of Eth 0/2 and apply the ACL to the inbound direction of the router interface. There rule will protect the HR server from generic worker access, while allowing the generic workers to access all other resources and the Internet.

It is important to note that the focus of this section is to understand how ACLs are used to protect resources. It is not important to understand how to build specific ACLs, since commands will be different from vendor system to vendor system.

Exam Essentials

Understand common authorization, authentication, and accounting systems. Remote Authentication Dial-In User Service (RADIUS) is an industry standard that provides AAA services for users and computers on network equipment. TACACS+ is an AAA protocol developed by Cisco and released as an open standard. Kerberos is an open standard protocol for authenticating users and computers by issuing identity and service tickets. Single sign-on (SSO) allows a user's credentials to be reused for concurrent logins for other applications. Local authentication is performed against a local database of credentials; it is not scalable. Lightweight Directory Access Protocol (LDAP) is an open standard directory service that is used by Microsoft for Active Directory. Certificates are used to authenticate users; the public portion of the public-private key pair is mapped to a user account. The principle of "trust and audit" dictates that logging and auditing should be performed on all user accounts.

Understand the different factors that can be used for multifactor authentication. Multifactor authentication is the process of using two or more factors for authentication. Something you know defines something you know, like a password or personal identification number (PIN). Something you have is a definition of something physically you have that can be used for authentication. Something you are defines biometrics such as fingerprint scans and voice and facial recognition. Somewhere you are is a fairly new authentication method that uses GPS coordinates or an IP to geographic location database. Something you do could be considered a biometric authentication method.

Understand the various access controls that can be used within a network.   802.1x is a control protocol for wired or wireless access, commonly used in conjunction with a RADIUS server for AAA services. Network access control (NAC) works in conjunction with 802.1x by restricting access to a device until it has passed a security posture evaluation by the NAC agent on the device. Port security allows us to restrict the number of devices that can be connected to a switch port. MAC filtering is the method of restricting a specific MAC address or list of MAC addresses. Captive portals redirect the initial request to a portal where the user must log in or accept an agreement; the user is then moved into another VLAN where traffic is switched as normal. Access control lists (ACLs) consist of conditions and actions to control traffic for applications.

4.3 Given a scenario, secure a basic wireless network.

802.11 wireless extends an organization's internal LAN to the outside world via radio frequency (RF). Much care is taken to secure the internal network and the external network via the firewall, but wireless should be equally protected.

Two aspects of wireless should be focused on for security purposes: encryption and authentication/authorization. Encryption of data is important, because wireless can be eavesdropped on and data can be stolen as it is being transmitted. Authentication and authorization are important to keep unauthorized users away from protected portions of your network, which also protects you from theft of services and data.

WPA

Wi-Fi Protected Access (WPA) was standardized by the Wi-Fi Alliance in 2003 in response to the vulnerabilities in *Wired Equivalent Privacy (WEP)*. WPA uses 256-bit keys versus the 64-bit and 128-bit keys WEP used previously. WPA operates in two modes of pre-shared key (PSK), also called personal mode and enterprise mode. PSK is the most common, because it can easily be implemented. Enterprise mode requires a certificate server infrastructure and is also called WPA-802.1x. Enterprise mode uses the 802.1x protocol, RADIUS, and EAP; it is often used in corporate environments.

WPA introduced many improved security features over WEP, such as *message integrity checks (MICs)* that detect packets altered in transit. WPA also introduced *Temporal Key Integrity Protocol (TKIP)*, which uses the RC4 algorithm that provides per-packet keying to prevent eavesdropping on wireless conversations. However, despite the improvements in security, WPA is considered exploitable and is no longer used for wireless security. A common exploit used against WPA is an attack on the helper protocol of Wi-Fi Protected Setup (WPS). WPS is used for consumer ease of setup and should be turned off for security purposes.

WPA2

Wi-Fi Protected Access II (WPA2), also known as 802.11i, is the successor to WPA. WPA was deprecated in 2006, when WPA2 became a wireless security standard. Just like WPA, WPA2 operates in both personal mode (PSK) and enterprise mode.

WPA2 uses the Advanced Encryption Standard (AES) algorithm to protect data. AES is more secure than the RC4 algorithm used with TKIP. WPA2 replaced TKIP with Counter Cipher Mode (CCM) with Block Chaining Message Authentication Code Protocol (CCMP). However, TKIP can be configured as a fallback for WPA backward compatibility. Just like WPA, WPA2 is exploitable if the WPS service is enabled. WPS should be turned off for security purposes, since it is just as exploitable as the WPA version.

TKIP-RC4

Temporal Key Integrity Protocol (TKIP) uses the RC4 encryption algorithm protocol as its cipher. TKIP seeds the RC4 algorithm with a key that is derived from the MAC address and initialization vector. TKIP also works in conjunction with message integrity checks (MICs) to check the integrity of messages received by the access point. The MIC protocol is also called Michael, a 32-bit cyclical redundancy check (CRC). If two CRC MICs fail within 60 seconds, the access point requires TKIP to rekey the RC4 seed value.

CCMP-AES

Counter Cipher Mode with Block Chaining Message Authentication Code Protocol (CCMP) – Advanced Encryption Standard (AES) uses a 128-bit key to seed the AES encryption and a 128-bit cipher block. The prior ciphered text is used to encrypt the next block of text; this type of cipher is called code block chaining (CBC). CCMP-AES also uses a MIC to check the integrity of wireless data received. If the MIC fails, the CCMP-AES rekeys the session.

Authentication and authorization

The ciphering of data and integrity checks of data are important for the confidentiality of the data being transmitted. WPA2 is only exploitable if the attacker is already authorized on the wireless network. It is just as important to secure the network from unauthorized connections as it is to protect the confidentiality of the data being transmitted. This section focuses on the method of securing wireless using authentication and authorization of devices.

EAP

Extensible Authentication Protocol (EAP) is an IETF standard that allows supplicants and authenticators to use various methods of encryption for authentication purposes over 802.1x, as shown in Figure 4.12. These authentication methods are defined by modules that both the supplicant and the authenticator must have in common. These shared modules can be replaced with other modules that expand authentication method functionality, which is why we consider EAP to be extensible. There are many different EAP methods that can be used. I will discuss only the three common EAP methods as per the objectives for this exam.

FIGURE 4.12 Wireless authentication for 802.1x/EAP

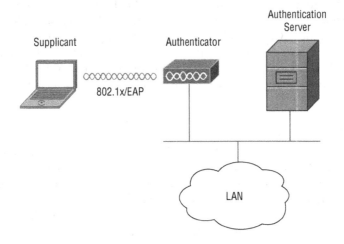

PEAP

Protected Extensible Authentication Protocol (PEAP) was jointly developed by Cisco, Microsoft, and RSA Security. PEAP is used in conjunction with 802.1x authentication systems and provides Transport Layer Security (TLS). TLS protects EAP messages by providing an encrypted tunnel as well as authentication between the host and the authenticating server before credentials are passed. The authenticator will provide the supplicant with a certificate from the authentication server signed by a certificate authority. It is important to note that the supplicant must trust the issuing certificate authority so that the authentication server's certificate is valid.

EAP-FAST

Extensible Authentication Protocol – Flexible Authentication via Secure Tunneling (EAP-FAST) is a Cisco proposed standard to replace the older Cisco proprietary protocol of Lightweight Extensible Authentication Protocol (LEAP). EAP-FAST operates in three phases; the first phase, called Phase 0, is when in-band provision occurs to create a shared secret that will be used for Phase 1 to establish a secure tunnel. Once the second phase called Phase 1 establishes the secure tunnel, then the third phase called Phase 2 allows authentication to occur between the supplicant and authentication server. Because of its use of shared keys, it is faster than PKI for tunnel creation.

EAP-TLS

Extensible Authentication Protocol – Transport Layer Security (EAP-TLS) is an open standard defined by the IETF. Because it is an open standard, many vendor and operating systems support EAP-TLS. EAP-TLS can be deployed with a preshared key (PSK), but it is more common for EAP-TLS to be deployed in conjunction with a certificate authority. When EAP-TLS is deployed in conjunction with a certificate authority, the deployment is more secure because each user or computer is issued an individual certificate. EAP-TLS is the underlying protocol used for WPA-Enterprise mode and WPA2-Enterprise mode. When this protocol is used, EAP transmits the credentials over TLS.

Shared or Open

Shared passphrases are used with Wired Equivalent Privacy (WEP). When WEP is used, it provides 64- or 128-bit encryption via the shared passphrase. The passphrase can easily be cracked with tools like *Aircrack-NG* and is no longer used to secure wireless.

Open security is just that—it is open with no passphrase or authentication protocol. Open security was originally how all wireless access points (WAPs) were shipped to the customer. Open security still has its uses when used in conjunction with guest wireless.

Preshared Key

A preshared key (PSK) is widely used with the wireless protocols WPA and WPA2 personal mode for home wireless applications. A preshared key is a symmetrical encryption, where the key that encrypts the data also decrypts the data. PSK can also be used with other authentication protocols such as EAP-TLS, but PSK is rarely used for EAP-TLS deployments outside of testing.

MAC Filtering

MAC address filtering is used to secure wireless by providing only whitelisted MAC addresses access to the wireless system. It is extremely effective because an attacker will not have knowledge of which MAC addresses are whitelisted. However, there is an administrative burden in entering the MAC addresses to be whitelisted. MAC address filtering is commonly used in wireless deployments that have few clients or static clients that do not change frequently.

Geofencing

Geofencing is a method of controlling mobile devices by their location. Geofencing creates a virtual perimeter around an area with the use of mapping software. The device requires an agent to be installed that reports back the Global Positioning System (GPS) coordinates. When a device is outside of the perimeter, it is considered in violation of compliance and can be applicable to a device wipe to prevent data loss.

Exam Essentials

Know the various methods to protect information transmitted over wireless networks. Wi-Fi Protected Access (WPA) encrypts data using a 256-bit key utilizing the RC4 cipher and can be deployed in personal mode or enterprise mode. Wi-Fi Protected Access II

(WPA2), also known as 802.11i, is a successor to WPA and operates in personal mode or enterprise mode similar to WPA. TKIP-RC4 is the method of encryption for the WPA wireless security protocol. Message integrity checks (MICs) are used in conjunction with TKIP-RC4 to provide rekeying if a cyclical redundancy check (CRC) fails. Counter Cipher Mode with Block Chaining Message Authentication Code Protocol (CCMP-AES) also works in conjunction with MIC to provide encryption with Advanced Encryption Standard (AES) and rekeying if CRC checks fail.

Know the various methods of authentication and authorization for wireless networks. Extensible Authentication Protocol (EAP) is an extensible standard of authenticating users and computers. Protected Extensible Authentication Protocol (PEAP) was developed by Cisco, Microsoft, and RSA Security and provides Transport Layer Security (TLS) via an encrypted tunnel. Extensible Authentication Protocol – Flexible Authentication via Secure Tunneling (EAP-FAST) is a Cisco-proposed replacement to Lightweight Extensible Authentication Protocol (LEAP). Extensible Authentication Protocol – Transport Layer Security (EAP-TLS) is used with WPA2-Enterprise mode to transmit credentials securely. Shared passphrases are used with Wired Equivalent Privacy (WEP) to provide 64- or 128-bit encryption. Open wireless security requires no passphrase or authentication. MAC filtering is a method of whitelisting only allowed devices by their MAC addresses. Geofencing is used in conjunction with mapping software to create a virtual fence to prevent data loss outside of the geofence.

4.4 Summarize common networking attacks.

Networking attacks are the most common type of intrusion for an organization. The actor or actors involved do not need to be in the same vicinity or even the same country as the attack. All network attacks focus on disrupting service, theft of services, theft of data, or direct monetary theft—all of which hurts the organization's reputation and finances. In the following section I will discuss several different types of network attacks.

DoS

A *denial of service (DoS)* is an attack launched to disrupt the service or services a company receives or provides via the Internet. A DoS is executed with an extremely large amount of false requests, whereas the servers cannot fulfill valid requests for clients and employees. There are several different types of DoS attacks that I will discuss in the following section.

Reflective

A reflective DoS is not a direct attack; it requires a third party that will inadvertently execute the DoS. The attacker will send a request to a third-party server and forge the source address of the packet with the victim's IP address. When the third party responds, it responds to the victim. There are two victims in this type of DoS attack; the first is the victim the attack is aimed at, and the second is the third-party server used to carry out lthe attack.

Amplified

An amplified DoS is a variant of a reflective DoS attack. It is carried out by making a small request to the third-party server that yields a larger response to the victim. The most common third-party servers used to carry the attack out are DNS and NTP. As an example, an attacker will request a DNS query for a single hostname that contains 20 aliases while forging the source IP address. The victim is then barraged with the 20 answers from the query.

Distributed

A *distributed denial of service (DDoS)* is becoming the most common type of DoS, because the source of the DoS is varied. It is common for botnets to launch DDoS attacks on organizations.

When a single host is used to create a DoS, it can simply be blocked. However, when traffic is coming from millions of different hosts, it is impossible to isolate the DoS and firewall the source.

Social engineering

Social engineering is the art of extracting vital information from an organization's employee without raising suspicion. Social engineering works because employees often do not know what is sensitive and what is not. When an employee is put into a dilemma, like trying to help a fellow employee, they can disclose sensitive information. The tactics of a social engineering hacker is the "gift of gab."

Insider threat

Often the greatest threats for data loss are from within our own organization. The insider threat can include a disgruntled employee, an employee with criminal intent, or even an employee participating in corporate espionage. These employees have access to sensitive data and can therefore abuse the privileges of access. Logging and auditing is used to control users with access to sensitive data.

Logic bomb

A logic bomb is a piece of code embedded into an application that will cause harmful effects when specific conditions are satisfied. The code can willfully be included in the application or injected into the code by a malicious actor. An example of a logic bomb is a piece of code that will delete files when a specific URL is queried.

Rogue access point

A rogue access point is an access point that has been installed on an organization's LAN by a malicious user or end user. When a WAP is installed without properly implementing security, it opens the organization up to possible data loss or penetration by an attacker. Port security on the local switching equipment is used to mitigate the risk of a rogue access point.

Evil twin

An evil twin attack is a wireless phishing attack in which the attacker sets up a wireless access point to mimic the organization's wireless access points. When a user connects to the evil twin, it allows the attacker to listen in on the user's traffic. Evil twin access points often report a stronger signal to entice the user to connect to the specific access point.

War-driving

War-driving was popular when wireless was first introduced to the market back in 2000. It was used to find open access points for the use of free Internet. It is now used as an attack method for finding misconfigured access points for illegal entry into an organization's network. It is performed with a laptop, GPS sensor, wireless card, and wireless mapping software.

Phishing

Phishing is normally performed via email by an attacker in an effort to gain usernames, passwords, and other *personally identifiable information (PII)*. An attacker will craft an email that looks like an organization's system. The email will generally contain a URL to a compromised web server where the user will be prompted for their information.

Ransomware

Ransomware is malicious software that encrypts files and requests a ransom for decryption of the files. The ransom payment is often requested to be completed to a Bitcoin address, because it is untraceable currency. Ransomware is a current and emerging threat for organizations. Many phishing email campaigns target users in an effort to click and run the ransomware.

DNS poisoning

DNS poisoning is an attack that targets an organization's DNS server. An attacker will attempt to replace valid DNS entries with a compromised server's IP address. The replacement of valid DNS entries is often performed via a DNS exploit or poisoning of DNS cache.

ARP poisoning

ARP poisoning is an attack in which an attacker sends a forged ARP reply to a client to redirect traffic to the attacker's host. The forged ARP reply will contain the MAC address of the attacker's host. The attacker can then use their host as a relay and eavesdrop on the conversation.

Spoofing

Spoofing is performed by an attacker so they can impersonate an IP address of an organization's asset. Spoofing allows the attacker to bypass access control systems and gain access to protected resources on the network. Spoofing is often used in DoS attacks to hide the attacker's IP address.

Deauthentication

The 802.11 wireless protocol contains a method for deauthentication of clients via a deauthentication frame. An attacker can send a deauthentication frame on behalf of the user, which disconnects them from the access point. Attackers will use this method in conjunction with an evil twin attack or in an effort to generate association traffic for purposes of cracking a passphrase.

Brute force

Brute force is a last-ditch effort to crack a passphrase or password. A brute-force system will try every combination of a password until access is granted. A password file is often used to discover common passwords that might be used; this is called a dictionary attack. However, more complex brute-force tools will allow combinations of alpha, numeric, upper- and lowercase, symbols, and hidden characters.

VLAN hopping

VLAN hopping is an attack method in which an attacker switches the VLAN that they are currently assigned to gain access to a system on another VLAN. VLAN hopping allows the attacker to bypass access controls to the protected resource. VLAN hopping is performed by either trunking to a switch by mimicking the Cisco proprietary protocol of *Dynamic Trunking Protocol (DTP)* or double-tagging a frame. When double-tagging is performed, the switch removes the first VLAN tag and forwards the frame. However, when the frame is transmitted on a trunk, the adjacent switch will switch the frame on the VLAN in the second tag.

Man-in-the-middle

Many of the attacks discussed in this section can be used in conjunction with a *man-in-the-middle (MitM)* attack. For example, the evil twin attack allows the attacker to position themselves between the compromised user and the destination server. The attacker can then eavesdrop on a conversation and possibly change information contained in the conversation.

Conventional MitM attacks allow the attacker to impersonate both parties involved in a network conversation. This allows the attacker to eavesdrop and manipulate the conversation without either party knowing.

Exploits vs. vulnerabilities

Exploits and *vulnerabilities* both have the same effect of compromising systems. Vulnerabilities are weaknesses in security for an operating system or network product. Vulnerabilities are the reason we need to constantly patch network systems. Exploits are scripts, code, applications, or techniques used in exploiting the vulnerabilities. Zero-day exploits are exploits in which a system is targeted and no known patch exists to remediate the vulnerability.

Exam Essentials

Know the various networking attacks that are commonly used by attackers.   Denial-of-service (DoS) attacks target organizations in an attempt to disrupt the service or services a company receives or provides via the Internet. A rogue access point is an access point that has been installed on an organization's LAN by a malicious user or end user. An evil twin attack is a wireless phishing attack in which the attacker sets up a wireless access point to mimic the organization's wireless access points. War-driving is an attack method of finding misconfigured access points for illegal entry into an organization's network. DNS poisoning is an attack against an organization's DNS server in an attempt to replace valid entries with compromised server's IP addresses. ARP poisoning is an attack in which an attacker sends a forged ARP reply to a client to redirect traffic to the attacker's host. Spoofing is an attack where the attacker impersonates an IP address of an organizations asset in an attempt to bypass access controls. Deauthentication is an attack that disassociates a client from an access point; it is used in conjunction with other attacks such as the evil twin attack. VLAN hopping is an attack method where the attacker switches VLANs by double-tagging a packet or imitating a switch using the Dynamic Trunking Protocol (DTP). Man-in-the-middle (MitM) attacks allow an attacker to impersonate both parties in an effort to eavesdrop and manipulate the conversation.

Know the various non-networking attacks that are commonly used by attackers.   Social engineering is an attack that is conducted by duping employees into willingly disclosing sensitive information. Insider threats are carried out by a disgruntled employee, an employee with criminal intent, or an employee participating in corporate espionage. Phishing is performed via email in an effort to gain a user's username, password, and other personally identifiable information (PII).

Know the various application-based attacks that are commonly used by attackers. Logic bombs are pieces of code embedded into an application that will cause harmful effect when specific conditions are satisfied. Ransomware is malicious software that encrypts files and requests a ransom for decryption of the files. Brute force is an attempt to guess a password with a dictionary attack in an automated fashion. Vulnerabilities are weaknesses in security of an operating system or network system. An exploit is script, code, or a technique to exploit a vulnerability.

4.5 Given a scenario, implement network device hardening.

When installing an operating system or device in your network, the default configuration out of the box will often be lax in security. This section details many of the common configuration changes that can be implemented to harden the security of operating systems and network devices. I will also cover more advanced methods in hardening operating system and network device security.

Changing default credentials

When installing a network device, the very first thing you must do is log into the device. There is often a standardized default username and password for each vendor or vendor's product line. Most devices make you change the default password upon login to the device.

Changing the default password to a complex password is a good start to hardening the device. However, changing the username will also ensure that a brute-force attack cannot be performed against the default username. There are many different websites dedicated to listing the default credentials for network devices, so it doesn't take tremendous skill to obtain the default username and password of the device.

Avoiding common passwords

Avoiding common passwords is another simple measure to hardening the device or operating system. There are several dictionaries that you can find on the Internet that will include common passwords. Some dictionaries are even collections of compromised passwords that have been made public.

When creating a password, it is always best practice to make the password at least 12 to 18 characters, based on the sensitivity of its use. You should always include symbols, numbers, and upper- and lowercase alpha characters. You should also resist substituting characters for symbols that looks like the character. This substitution is often called "leet speak" and it is in every dictionary downloadable on the Internet. An example of a "leet speak" passwords is *p@$$word*. Another common pitfall in creating passwords is the use of words; passwords should be random and complex. An example of a complex password is *GLtNjXu#W6*qkqGkS$*. You can find random password generators on the Internet, such as https://passwordsgenerator.net/.

Upgrading firmware

When you purchase a network device, you don't know how long it's been sitting on the shelf of a warehouse. In that time several exploits could have been created for vulnerabilities discovered. It is always recommended that a device's *firmware* be upgraded before the device is configured and put into service.

Most hardware vendors will allow downloading of current firmware. However, some vendors require the device be covered under a maintenance contract before firmware can be downloaded. It is also best practice to read through a vendor's changelog to understand the changes that have been made from version to version of firmware.

Patching and updates

When operating systems are installed, they are usually point-in-time snapshots of the current build of the operating system. From the time of the build to the time of install, several vulnerabilities can be published for the operating system. When an operating system is installed, you should patch it before placing it into service. Patches remediate the vulnerabilities found in the operating system and fixed by the vendor. Updates add new features not included with the current build. However, some vendors may include vulnerability patches in updates. Network devices also have patches and updates that should be installed prior to placing them into service.

After the initial installation of the device or operating system and the initial patches and updates are installed, you are not done! Vendors continually release patches and updates to improve security and functionality, usually every month and sometimes outside of the normal release cycle. When patches are released outside of the normal release cycle, they are called out-of-band patches and are often in response to a critical vulnerability.

Microsoft products are patched and updated through the Windows Update functionality of the operating system. However, when an administrator is required to patch and update an entire network, Windows Server Update Services (WSUS) can be implemented. A WSUS server enables the administrator to centrally manage patches and updates. The administrator can also report on which systems still need to be patched or updated. Patch management is discussed in further detail in Chapter 3.

File hashing

A hash is the result of a one-way cryptographic algorithm. The two most common *hash algorithms* are SHA1 and MD5. When a file is processed through a hash algorithm, a unique hexadecimal numeric number is generated. If a single digit of the file is changed, the file hash is changed completely.

File hashing is used to validate that a file is not changed at rest or during the transfer; it is generated at the time of compilation. It is common to see an MD5 hash published with the download of the firmware, operating system, application, or patch. The MD5 is published to the web server, and the link to the download is often another system. This ensures that both systems would need to be compromised if a malicious user changed the file. Once you have downloaded the file, you should run an MD5 hashing tool against it and compare the MD5 hashes. If they are different, then the source file has been compromised in some way and should not be used.

File hashing is also used to verify the integrity of the underlying operating system. Products like Tripwire hash critical files in the operating system that should never change. When the file is changed, the application will alert the administrator of a security-related event. These systems are classified as host-based intrusion detection systems (HIDSs).

Disabling unnecessary services

When services are enabled that are unneeded, it expands the surface area of attack. The surface area of attack is the range of possible exploitable services on an operating system or network device. If an operating system was a house, the entry points would be the doors, windows, and chimney. If we disable services, we remove entry points that can be exploited by attackers.

One of the major design changes to the Microsoft Server operating system was introduced with Windows Server 2008. Starting with Windows 2008, Microsoft disabled all services out of the box, and the firewall was turned on by default. This dramatically reduced the surface area of attack for the operating system compared to prior versions such as Windows 2003 R2.

Linux and Unix have long since used this minimalistic approach to installation. When the Linux/Unix operating systems are installed, no services are installed by default. All functionality must be added via the repository tools such as apt for Ubuntu and Debian and yum for Red Hat–based systems.

Operating systems are not the only network system that contains services; many network devices have services. Network devices are not immune to exploit; therefore, the surface area of attack should be reduced by disabling nonessential services. A typical example is a network printer; printers will often have several protocols enabled for printing, such as Server Message Blocks (SMBs), AppleTalk, Internet Printing Protocol (IPP), and File Transfer Protocol (FTP). Unnecessary protocols and services should be disabled since each one could potentially have a vulnerability.

Using secure protocols

Secure protocols are protocols that provide encryption. Many of the protocols used today by network devices do not provide any encryption. Secure protocols should be used to thwart eavesdropping and manipulation of the network device from an unauthenticated source.

A typical protocol used to manage network devices for firmware upgrades is Trivial File Transfer Protocol (TFTP). TFTP is unencrypted and easily exploitable by way of a man-in-the-middle (MitM) attack, because it uses the UDP protocol. Protocols such as Secure Copy Protocol (SCP) should be used in lieu of older outdated protocols if the device supports it. SCP provides both encryption and authentication.

Telnet is unsecure as well and a worse choice because login credentials are sent in clear text! Telnet is a console-based maintenance protocol that is frequently used by network devices because of its small code footprint. Protocols such as Secure Shell (SSH) should be used if the device supports it. SSH provides both encryption and authentications just like SCP, since SCP is an extension of SSH.

Console-based management protocols such as TFTP and Telnet are not the only protocols immune to insecurity, Hypertext Transfer Protocol (HTTP) is sent in clear text as well. Hypertext Transfer Protocol Secure (HTTPS) should be enabled and used for management of network devices. HTTPS requires a certificate to be installed, but most network devices allow the use of self-signed certificates that are locally managed. HTTPS provides encryption and a minimal layer of authentication for the management endpoint but will thwart an MitM attack.

Generating new keys

Both the Secure Shell (SSH) and Hypertext Transfer Protocol Secure (HTTPS) protocols require public-private key pairs. The key pairs are often generated when the protocols are first enabled. The *modulus* is the length in bits of the encryption key pair. A 512-bit modulus can be cracked within a relatively short period of time. A 2048-bit modulus can take much longer, if it is even possible. The expiry time on the key pairs is directly related to the modulus length. A low-bit modulus key pair will expire sooner than a high-bit modulus key pair, but all key pairs expire at some point. The generation of new keys is required by the network operating system at some point because of the expiration date set on the key pair. Some network operating systems generate the key pair automatically; others require manual intervention.

A generation of new key pairs can also be required if they are compromised. As the administrator you should rekey the system if it is compromised, but the operating system will not care and continue to function as normal.

It is important to note that SSH clients will detect a new key pair upon initial connection after the generation of new keys. The SSH client by default will prompt the user for acceptance of this new key pair. All SSH clients cache the key pairs previously shown in a key chain that is used for future authentication of connections.

Disabling unused ports

A port is considered any interface that serves to connect two host systems together. The port can be an IP port related to TCP or UDP, or it can be a physical port such as a serial or USB port. If the interface allows data to be transferred, then it is considered a port and is a risk to security. In this section, I will cover the most common ports that should be disabled if not needed for hardening of systems.

IP Ports

When we hear the term *port*, it is often associated with TCP/IP ports. Throughout this book you will find protocols that operate on TCP or UDP; these ports are considered well-known ports. A list of the registered ports can be found at https://www.iana.org/assignments/ service-names-port-numbers/service-names-port-numbers.txt. However, this is not a full list because application designers are not required to register the ports the application runs on.

After a system has been installed, it is best practice to disable any TCP/IP port that is not being used for the primary purpose of the network system. This is achieved via host-based firewalls. Microsoft operating systems are proficient at securing the operating system, because starting with Windows Server 2008 the firewall is on by default. Linux systems are also being packaged with firewalls that are enabled by default. Only ports necessary for operations are allowed through the host firewall. When we disable TCP/IP ports, we reduce the surface area of attack of a network system.

Device Ports (Physical and Virtual)

When we disable and/or firewall TCP/IP ports on a network operating system, we prevent remote exploits. However, physical ports are just as susceptible to exploit. If a network device has a serial port, also known as a console port, an attacker could plug in and manipulate the system. Any unused ports on network devices should be either disabled or password protected.

Virtual ports are also susceptible to attacks. Many virtual machine technologies allow for serial ports to be extended to a remote workstation over TCP/IP. These ports generally are just as exploitable as their physical counterparts. If virtual console ports are not required, they should be disabled.

Exam Essentials

Understand the various methods of hardening network systems. Changing default credentials for network systems will thwart brute-force attacks against default usernames. Upgrading firmware ensures that you will have any vulnerabilities patched up to the point of the firmware upgrade. Continual patching and updating of operating systems and network devices ensures that you are protected for any new vulnerabilities as well as newer features. File hashing is used to validate that a downloaded firmware, patch, or application has not been tampered with at rest or in transit to you. File hashing is also used on operating systems to ensure that files have not been replaced by an attacker. Disabling unused services on a network system reduces the area of attack by reducing the number of services that potentially have a vulnerability. The use of secure protocols ensures that eavesdropping of management sessions and manipulation of files in transit do not occur. Generation of new keys is required from time to time, because public-private key pairs have an expiration. Generation of new keys is also required if the keys are compromised in any way. Disabling unused TCP/IP ports and device ports ensures that an attacker cannot take advantage of a vulnerability.

4.6 Explain common mitigation techniques and their purposes.

There are many different threats to a network, as we explored in Chapter 4. I also covered many of the simple implementations to harden a network device, in Chapter 4. There many common security and configuration mistakes that we should also avoid, which could potentially open our defenses to these attacks. In this section, I will focus on common mitigation techniques for security and the proper network function.

Signature management

Public key infrastructure (PKI) is the process of using public-private key pairs for users, computers, and applications. PKI can be used to either encrypt or sign a network transmission, user identity, or applications, as well as serving many other functions. The most important component of PKI is the certificate authority that creates the key pairs and serves the public keys to requestors.

When a user requests a certificate, the certificate authority will calculate a cryptographic key pair. The private key is given to the user and the certificate authority retains the public key. The certificate authority's job is to now to serve the public key to anyone who requests it.

The key pair is used to provide asymmetrical encryption and signing. This means that the public key can encrypt and only the private key of the key pair can decrypt so that only the user can decrypt the data. We can also use the private key to encrypt and the public key to decrypt. In this example, everyone has access to the public key, so everyone can decrypt the data. However, only the user who has the private key can encrypt the message that the public key can decrypt. So this certifies that the message came from the sender and the data is considered signed.

Secure Shell (SSH) uses signatures to authenticate the host you are connecting to and encrypt your session. SSH does not require a certificate authority, because when you initiate a connection for the first time, the SSH agent will receive the public key via SSH. This public key is now stored for the next time you connect to the host. Both the host and the server can now authenticate themselves with the proper signatures.

Secure Shell (SSH) can also use the user's private key to authenticate the user in lieu of a password being entered. In this scenario the server will send a challenge in which the client will decrypt and encrypt using the user's private key. The server will then receive the client's public key and decrypt the signed message; this authenticates the client for login. Using the key pair for login lessens the chance of the username and password becoming compromised.

Device hardening

Device hardening is the action of changing the network device or operating system's defaults to make it more secure. When we install a new device, the first thing we do is change the default passwords and patch the device. This effectively hardens the device from attacks. Other common hardening techniques consist of disabling services and network ports we don't need for the use of the device or operating system. The common hardening techniques are covered in Chapter 4.

Change native VLAN

When data is transmitted on a trunk link that is not tagged with a VLAN ID, the data will default to the native VLAN. The native VLAN is also the VLAN used for switch management. The default native VLAN is VLAN 1 on all unconfigured switches from the factory; it is also the default membership for all ports on an unconfigured switch. This creates a potential security issue; if a new switch is plugged into the network and the default VLAN is not changed on the switch ports, a user will have direct access to the management network.

If the native VLAN is not changed from the default, an attacker can use the native VLAN to launch an attack using the Dynamic Trunking Protocol (DTP) or VLAN hopping attack. A DTP attack is performed by plugging in a rouge Cisco switch to a port that is set to default trunking negotiation. An attacker can then use the untagged packets to move data on the native VLAN of the trunk. A VLAN hopping attack is when the attacker tags the frame twice. The intended VLAN is tagged, then the default VLAN of 1 is tagged. When the switch receives the frame on an access link, the first tag is stripped off and then the frame is switched onto the intended VLAN.

We can mitigate the risk of users being exposed to the management VLAN and VLAN hopping by changing the native VLAN to another VLAN number. It is common to change the native VLAN on trunks to VLAN 999 or another unused VLAN. Then do not use VLAN 1 for any device management and create another VLAN for that purpose.

Switch port protection

The network switches in your network are the easiest attack vector for an intruder with access to a network port. In addition to network intruders, an unwitting user could cause havoc to the entire network by plugging in home equipment and creating a loop. Whether it is malicious intent or an accidental outage, this section covers some of the most common ways to protect switch ports.

Spanning Tree

Spanning tree can create large outages if not properly configured, as you learned in Chapter 1. To find the root bridge, the Spanning Tree Protocol (STP) recalculates the entire switching topology every time a switch or any device is connected to a switch port. During this time, frames are not allowed to pass on the switch port transitioning to an up status. Rapid Spanning Tree Protocol (RSTP) takes a more proactive approach to calculation of the switching topology, so the switch port is turned up quicker.

An attacker can use the STP protocol calculation to redirect traffic through a rouge switch because STP is not authenticated in any way. The root bridge is elected based on the lowest MAC address and the IEEE priority parameter among all switches. An attacker can introduce a switch with an extremely low priority. If the other switches in the network are configured with the default priority, the attacker's switch will become the root bridge.

This type of attack can be mitigated by altering the intended root bridge's priority to zero. It is also best practice to select a backup root bridge and set its priority to 4,096. Every switching vendor supports changing the STP priority parameter. The following command is used to configure VLAN 1 through 3967 on a Cisco switch:

```
SW1#configure terminal
Enter configuration commands, one per line.  End with CNTL/Z.
SW1(config)#spanning-tree vlan 1-3967 priority 0
```

This type of attack can also be mitigated by configuring BPDU Guard and Root Guard on user-facing ports. I will discuss both topics later in this section.

Flood Guard

Switches create a memory-based table that associates the ports and the MAC address on the port. It is called the *content addressable memory (CAM)*, also referred to as the MAC address table. A finite amount of memory is set aside for the CAM. If the CAM is exhausted and the MAC address of the frame to be forwarded is not in the table, the frame will be forwarded to all ports on the switch. An attacker can use a tool called macof that will exhaust the CAM with bogus entries in a matter of minutes. Because the frames will be forwarded to all ports, the attacker can now capture traffic for all hosts.

This type of attack can be mitigated by limiting the number of MAC addresses that can be learned for each port. Port security should be configured for each user-facing port that limits the MAC addresses to two; this allows for a VoIP phone and computer. Each vendor will have an implementation of flood guard. What follows is Cisco's implementation with the port-security commands. I cover port-security further in Chapter 4.

```
SW1(config)# interface gigabitethernet 0/5
SW1(config-if)# switchport port-security
SW1(config-if)# switchport port-security maximum 2
```

BPDU Guard

Bridge Protocol Data Unit (BPDU) Guard is a feature on Cisco switches, but it can also be found on other vendor switches as well. It is configured in conjunction with STP and RSTP on user-facing access ports. It should never be configured on trunk ports between switches.

BPDU Guard will instantly place the switch port into an *err-disable state* if BPDU frames are detected on the port. When a violation occurs, the port is placed into an err-disable state, and administrator intervention is required to reset the port. BPDU Guard is used to prevent STP switching attacks; the commands to configure it on Cisco switches are shown here:

```
SW1(config)# interface gigabitethernet 0/5
SW1(config-if)#spanning-tree bpduguard enable
```

Root Guard

Root Guard is a feature on Cisco switches, and variations can be found on other vendor switches as well. The feature is similar to BPDU Guard because it is configured in conjunction with STP and RSTP on user-facing access ports. It should never be configured on trunk ports between switches, similar to BPDU Guard.

Root Guard will instantly place the switch port into an inconsistent STP state of listening mode if a lower MAC address and priority combination is shown. This lower MAC address and priority combination would otherwise cause an election in which the new switch would win, thus protecting the current root bridge. This will effectively stop the switch port from forwarding any traffic until the BPDUs are no longer received on the switchport for a period of time. Unlike BPDU Guard, the port does not need administrator intervention. Root Guard is also used to prevent STP switching attacks. The commands to configure it on Cisco switches are shown here:

```
SW1(config)# interface gigabitethernet 0/5
SW1(config-if)#spanning-tree guard root
```

DHCP Snooping

An attack called DHCP spoofing is carried out by an attacker running a rouge DHCP server on your LAN. The rouge DHCP server has particular options set such as DNS or the default gateway in an attempt to redirect valid traffic to an exploited website to further compromise the clients. A rouge DHCP server can also be introduced to create interruption of service.

DHCP snooping is a feature on Cisco switches as well as other vendor switches. It prevents a rouge DHCP server, also called a spurious DHCP server, from sending DHCP messages to clients. When DHCP snooping is configured on switches, all switch ports are considered untrusted ports. Only a trusted port can forward DHCP messages; all untrusted ports are filtered for DHCP messages.

Network segmentation

When a network is flat with no segmentation, it is impossible to secure because an intruder has potential access to all hosts and devices. Network segmentation allows for smaller broadcast domains that increases usable bandwidth. We can also implement access control lists (ACLs) between the segments. This directly increases security as well as usable bandwidth.

DMZ

The demilitarized zone (DMZ) is a segment of the network that is both public facing and private facing. Hosts that serve Internet clients are placed in the DMZ. As shown in Figure 4.13, a network segment called the DMZ sits between an external firewall and internal firewall. The external firewall contains ACLs to restrict Internet hosts from accessing services on the server in the DMZ that are not essential for services. The Internal firewall restricts which hosts can talk to internal servers. A typical rule on the external firewall would allow HTTP access for a web server in the DMZ and would restrict all other ports. A typical rule on the internal firewall would allow only the web server to communicate with the SQL backend database in the internal network.

FIGURE 4.13   A typical DMZ with two firewalls

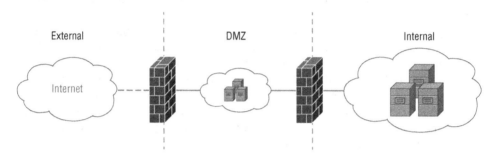

Some DMZ segments are just another interface on a single firewall as shown in Figure 4.14. In this example, the rules for both the external-facing web server and the backend SQL database would be on the same firewall. The benefit of a single firewall is centralized administration of firewall ACLs. Each interface is placed into a trust zone, and the firewall rules allow incoming and outgoing connections.

FIGURE 4.14   A typical DMZ with one firewall

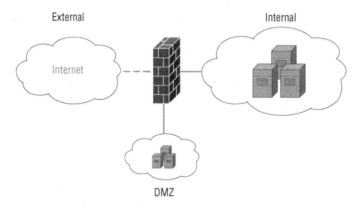

VLAN

A virtual local area network (VLAN) is a logical segmentation of a local area network. The logical segmentation results in subnets and LANs that appear physically separated, as if you had separate switches. When VLANs are used, each VLAN requires a unique IP address network.

The only way for VLANs to communicate with each other is through a router or firewall. This makes the use of VLANs perfect for security. With one switch we can logically segment the network, apply different IP address networks to each segment, and use ACLs to control the flow of information. I discuss VLANs in deeper detail in Chapter 1.

Privileged user account

A privileged user account is an account that has administrative access on a system. When securing a privileged account, you should name the account something other than admin, administrator, or root, since these are common account names for privileged users. It is also important to create a complex password.

The Microsoft Windows operating system as of Windows 2008 has implemented a feature called *User Access Control (UAC)*. Upon logon with a privileged account, the operating system will restrict the use of administrative privileges for the account. A dialog box called the UAC prompt will require the user to click it. This confirms to the operating system that the use of the administrative privilege is acknowledged by the user. macOS has a similar function to the UAC.

File integrity monitoring

Automatic file integrity monitoring has been used since Microsoft Windows Vista and Windows 2008 Server. A process called the *System File Checker (SFC)* runs in the background and checks for the replacement of critical files. When a critical file is changed, the SFC will replace it with a copy of the original file. In Windows XP and Server 2003, the SFC was a manual process that could revert modified files; it is now an integral part of the Windows operating system.

File integrity monitoring is not just a Microsoft feature; it has been used for Linux systems and a range of other operating systems for quite some time. A product called Tripwire creates a hashing table of all the critical files in the operating system. When a critical file is modified that the program is monitoring, it can alert the administrator that a possible intrusion has occurred. These system types are called host-based intrusion detection systems (HIDSs) and are discussed in Chapter 2.

Role separation

Administrative role separation was introduced with Windows Server 2008. Read-only domain controllers (RODCs) allow a normal user to be granted a local administrator role for the server without granting the domain administrator role. The local administrator group permits local logon, server updates, installation of updates, and so forth. Because RODCs are usually at remote offices without network staff, a manager who has been granted a local administrator role can then reboot an RODC or perform critical tasks without having the ability to change network accounts. This is critical if your remote office is more than a few hours away!

Windows Server 2008 introduced role separation, but the concept of role separation was used long before Microsoft released Windows Server 2008. Role separation has been used in the financial sector forever. Auditors do not have any affiliation or operational status of the businesses, which creates a degree of role separation. This type of role separation creates checks and balances. Similar role separation can be found in publicly traded companies with database design. The database administrators (DBAs) often do not audit access records for data—it is done by outside personnel.

Restricting access via ACLs

When the network is segmented, a network router is required for routing between VLANs or physical segments. All packets must pass through the router; therefore, we can implement ACLs on the router to restrict access to services on segments.

Figure 4.15 shows two network segments: one containing clients and another containing network servers. Both network segments are connected via a router, in which an access list is applied to interface Fast Ethernet 0/2 outbound. The ACL permits a host with an IP address of 192.168.1.2 to the web server at an IP address of 192.168.2.2 on TCP port 80. The ACL then denies a host with an IP address of 192.168.1.4 to the web server at an IP address of 192.168.2.2 on TCP port 80. The last statement allows all other communications via TCP/IP.

FIGURE 4.15   An ACL example

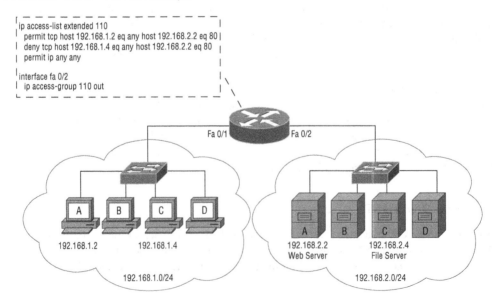

ACLs are used to control traffic to applications by restricting specific conditions, as shown in the previous example. This allows administrators to mitigate the threat of access to a particular service. It is common for ACLs to be used on firewall management IP addresses so that only a specific IP address can manage the firewall. ACLs used in this instance prevent unauthorized access to the device.

Honeypot/honeynet

A honeypot is a physical or virtual host that is set up for the explicit purpose of allowing unauthorized access. The honeypot is a system that is tightly controlled by the administrator, but it allows an attacker to compromise the system so that you can analyze an attacker's efforts. A honeynet is a group of honeypots that work in conjunction to form a network of honeypot systems. This creates a depth of realism for the attacker.

Honeypots are useful for gathering reconnaissance on attackers. They are most notable used to detect spammers and compromised servers that send spam. Honeypot information can be used to tighten firewall rules on the production network by identifying current threats on the honeypot network.

Penetration testing

Penetration testing is the process in which an outside company tries to penetrate your network so that you can learn your network weaknesses and strengthen your defenses. Penetration test firms are contracted by the company to intrude into the network legally. Some firms can be contracted to just scan your external network for vulnerabilities and attempt to exploit the vulnerability. However, some firms can be contracted to test your network vulnerabilities and physical vulnerabilities such as access control systems. When penetration testing is contracted, it is often necessary to avoid warning the internal network security team. This allows a more realistic test of the system because the network security team can react as if it is a real security event.

Exam Essentials

Understand common mitigation techniques for network threats and their purposes. Device hardening is the action of changing the network device or operating system's defaults to make it more secure. Changing the native VLAN thwarts VLAN hopping attacks and the possibility of an end user mistakenly obtaining access to the management network. An attacker can use STP to create an outage or to redirect traffic in an attempt to capture the traffic. Flood Guard prevents a switch from succumbing to content addressable memory (CAM) exhaustion from an attacker using a tool to flood the MAC table. Port security is a flood control used with Cisco switches that restricts a port to a predetermined number of MAC addresses that can be stored in the CAM table. Bridge Protocol Data Unit (BPDU) Guard is a feature on switches that places the port into an err-disabled status if BPDUs are received on the port. Root Guard is another feature that prevents a switch that is plugged into the port protected with Root Guard from becoming an STP root bridge. DHCP snooping is a switching feature that restricts DHCP offer messages from untrusted ports. The only trusted port should be the actual DHCP server. Network segmentation allows for smaller broadcast domains to increase bandwidth and can also be used to provide security between the segments with ACLs. The demilitarized zone (DMZ) is a segment of the network that is both public facing and private facing. VLANs are used to logically segment the network to allow for control via access control lists (ACLs). Honeypots are servers or services that are set up for intruders to exploit so that their techniques can be analyzed.

Understand common mitigation techniques for application threats and their purposes. Private key signatures can be used for authentication purposes with the Secure Shell (SSH) protocol. File integrity monitoring is built into many operating systems. If a critical file has been altered, it will immediately replace the file with a known good file. Administrative role separation was introduced with read-only domain controllers (RODCs). Local administrators can perform administrative tasks on the operating system and do not have to have administrative control of the directory services running on the operating system. Penetration testing is used to identify weaknesses in both network and physical security by a third party so that security can be strengthened.

Review Questions

1. Which motion detection system has a reflective panel to create zones of detection?

   A. Microwave

   B. Vibration

   C. Passive infrared (PIR)

   D. Seismic

2. You need to deploy a surveillance camera in an area that requires you to record the equipment the entire time it has entered your datacenter to the time it is installed. Which type of surveillance camera should you deploy?

   A. CCTV

   B. PTZ

   C. Coaxial

   D. POE

3. You work for a library and require an asset tracking system that is inexpensive and will notify you when equipment leaves the building. Which type of system should you purchase and deploy?

   A. Bluetooth

   B. Passive RFID

   C. 802.11 asset tracking

   D. Active RFID

4. You require a physical security system that authenticates and authorizes employees into an area. Which system should you implement?

   A. Key fobs

   B. ID badges

   C. Biometrics

   D. Combination locks

5. Which is a physical authentication system that requires both a personal identification number (PIN) and the physical card?

   A. Key fobs

   B. Biometrics

   C. RFID

   D. Smart cards

6. Which principle describes the process of verification of a user's identity?

   A. Authentication

   B. Authorization

   C. Accounting

   D. Auditing

7. Which authentication system is an open standard originally proposed by the Internet Engineer Task Force (IETF)?

    A. RADIUS

    B. TACACS+

    C. Kerberos

    D. LDAP

8. Which authentication system can use Advanced Encryption Standard (AES) encryption for encryption of user credentials?

    A. RADIUS

    B. TACACS+

    C. Kerberos

    D. LDAP

9. Which protocol is often used with single sign-on (SSO) to exchange credentials?

    A. LDAP

    B. SAML

    C. ADFS

    D. Kerberos

10. Which principle describes the process of verification of a user's permissions?

    A. Authentication

    B. Authorization

    C. Accounting

    D. Auditing

11. What protocol and port number does LDAP use for directory lookups?

    A. TCP/389

    B. TCP/1812

    C. UDP/389

    D. UDP/1812

12. Which authentication factor is an example of personal human characteristic?

    A. Typing your password

    B. A location you are in

    C. A smartcard and your PIN

    D. Your voice

13. Which authentication factor is an example somewhere you are?

    A. Your IP address

    B. An RFID tag

    C. Your MAC address

    D. Your picture

14. Which Cisco proprietary protocol is used to transmit credentials for 802.1x authentication systems?

   A. LEAP

   B. EAP

   C. PEAP

   D. NAC

15. What is the proper terminology for a switch or wireless access point (WAP), when 802.1x is implemented?

   A. Authenticating server

   B. Authenticator

   C. Supplicant

   D. Authorizer

16. You need to restrict a switch port to a maximum of two devices. What should you implement to guarantee only two devices can communicate on the switch port?

   A. NAC

   B. 802.1x

   C. ACLs

   D. Port security

17. You are implementing a public guest wireless network and require that users accept and acceptable use policy (AUP). What should you implement to accomplish the goal?

   A. ACLs

   B. MAC filtering

   C. Captive portal

   D. 802.1x

18. Which wireless protocol introduced message integrity checks (MIC) and Temporal Key Integrity Protocol (TKIP)?

   A. WPA

   B. WEP

   C. WPA2

   D. CBC

19. You are implementing a wireless network and need to make sure that only hosts that have up-to-date antivirus protection can join. Which technology should you implement?

   A. NAC

   B. 802.1x

   C. EAP-TLS

   D. ACLs

20. Which network attack involves malicious code that is dormant until specific conditions are met?

    A. Evil twin

    B. Logic bomb

    C. Spoofing

    D. Deauthentication

21. Which statement accurately describes an exploit?

    A. A known weakness in the operating system

    B. A configuration that weakens the security of the operating system

    C. A known operating system security flaw

    D. A technique to gain unauthorized access

22. Which algorithm is commonly used with file hashing techniques?

    A. RC4

    B. MD5

    C. HMAC

    D. AES

23. Which attack involves the attacker impersonating both side of a conversation between two hosts?

    A. MitM

    B. Deauthentication

    C. DoS

    D. Spoofing

24. Which console-based management protocol has built-in security?

    A. SSH

    B. SCP

    C. HTTPS

    D. FTP

25. Which mitigation technique is configured on user-facing switch ports to protect the Spanning Tree Protocol (STP)?

    A. Flood guard

    B. Root Guard

    C. DHCP snooping

    D. BPDU Guard

Chapter 5

Domain 5.0 Network Troubleshooting and Tools

✓ **5.2 Given a scenario, use the appropriate tool.**

- Hardware tools
  - Crimper
  - Cable tester
  - Punchdown tool
  - OTDR
  - Light meter
  - Tone generator
  - Loopback adapter
  - Multimeter
  - Spectrum analyzer
- Software tools
  - Packet sniffer
  - Port scanner
  - Protocol analyzer
  - Wi-Fi analyzer
  - Bandwidth speed tester
  - Command line
    - ping
    - tracert, traceroute
    - nslookup
    - ipconfig
    - ipconfig
    - iptables
    - netstat
    - tcpdump
    - pathping
    - nmap
    - route
    - arp
    - dig

✓ **5.3 Given a scenario, troubleshoot common wired connectivity and performance issues.**

- Attenuation
- Latency
- Jitter
- Crosstalk
- EMI
- Open/short
- Incorrect pin-out
- Incorrect cable type
- Bad port
- Transceiver mismatch
- TX/RX reverse
- Duplex/speed mismatch
- Damaged cables
- Bent pins
- Bottlenecks
- VLAN mismatch
- Network connection LED status indicators

✓ **5.4 Given a scenario, troubleshoot common wireless connectivity and performance issues.**

- Reflection
- Refraction
- Absorption
- Latency
- Jitter
- Attenuation
- Incorrect antenna type
- Interference
- Incorrect antenna placement
- Channel overlap
- Overcapacity

- Distance limitations
- Frequency mismatch
- Wrong SSID
- Wrong passphrase
- Security type mismatch
- Power levels
- Signal-to-noise ratio

✓ **5.5 Given a scenario, troubleshoot common network service issues.**

- Names not resolving
- Incorrect gateway
- Incorrect netmask
- Duplicate IP addresses
- Duplicate MAC addresses
- Expired IP address
- Rogue DHCP server
- Untrusted SSL certificate
- Incorrect time
- Exhausted DHCP scope
- Blocked TCP/UDP ports
- Incorrect host-based firewall settings
- Incorrect ACL settings
- Unresponsive service
- Hardware failure

Understanding network concepts, infrastructure, operations, and security help us design networks that are functional and secure. It is assumed that once a network is designed and implemented it operates without any issues forever. Although this is the intended goal, we often run into issues that we must troubleshoot and rectify to regain proper network operations.

So far you've learned about the theories of networking concepts, infrastructure, operations, and security. In this chapter, you will learn how to troubleshoot network issues while applying those theories.

For more detailed information on Domain 5's topics, please see *CompTIA Network+ Study Guide*, 4th ed. (978-1-119-43225-8) or *CompTIA Network+ Certification Kit*, 5th ed. (978-1-119-43228-9) published by Sybex.

5.1 Explain the network troubleshooting methodology.

When a problem arises in the network, we must take an analytical approach to solving it. In this book you are examining the theory of networking, but overall you are learning computer science. Therefore, the scientific method of solving problems is applicable to networking issues you may encounter.

The scientific method for computer science is defined as

- Asking a question or identify the problem
- Researching the problem
- Creating a *hypothesis*
- Testing a solution
- Analysis of the solution
- Conclusion

In the following sections, I will cover network troubleshooting steps. Many of the steps involved will match up to the scientific method described here.

Identify the problem

Identifying the problem is a crucial step. If the problem is not identified correctly, then hours, days, and even months can be wasted focusing on the wrong problem or researching the wrong criteria. Fortunately, some problems are evident and can be reproduced. However, some problems are elusive or intermittent, and these problems are the toughest to identify and solve.

Gather Information

A critical first step is the gathering of information related to the problem. Think of yourself as a detective; you must gather the information that helps reconstruct the problem. As you do, it is important to document your findings. The more complex the problem, the more important it is to document what you learn in this step.

Do not jump to a conclusion as you are gathering information. Jumping to a conclusion will not define the reasons for the problem, and such conclusions will only distract you from the problem. It is best to reserve judgment until the facts are gathered and you can develop a valid hypothesis.

Duplicate the Problem If Possible

Duplicating or reproducing the problem is a component of the identity of the problem. Once you have gathered the information about the problem, you can begin reproducing the problem. The reproduction of the problem can either be live or in a test environment, depending on how disruptive the problem is. It is preferable to reproduce the problem in a test environment so that possible solutions can be tested without affecting others.

When reproducing the problem, be sure to document how the problem is reproduced. Going forward, when and if you need to consult technical support personnel, the documented steps will speed up a solution.

It is extremely efficient when you can reproduce a problem, but sometimes problems are not reproducible. Intermittent problems might not be reproducible and can be the most difficult to solve. Without a clear reproduction of the problem, you can only make a conclusion based on your judgment, and not the facts, of the problem. Using judgment to solve the problem is an educated conclusion or guess. More importantly, if you make an incorrect judgment of the problem and implement a solution that is wrong, it could distract you from the proper solution or make the problem worse. Other problems are not reproducible because of the infrastructure or circumstances required to reproduce them.

Question Users

As part of your detective work in reconstructing the problem, you must interview users who are involved with the problem. The information from users will be biased, so you must be able to read between the lines and ask for exact information. During the interview, users will also try to self-diagnose their problem. Although this information is not always accurate or useful, it does provide their perspective or observation of the problem.

Another pitfall when interviewing users is scope creep. The scope of problem should be maintained during the entire interview process while still listening closely to the user. As an example, suppose you are diagnosing an application freezing up and a user veers from the scope of the problem to tell you that their mouse is also acting weird. The mouse issue might contribute to the perception that the application is freezing up and should be factored into the problem. However, if the user tells you that their CD-ROM is broken, this has nothing to do with the application freezing up and should be treated separately.

When dealing with problems that are either intermittent or not reproducible in a test environment, build a rapport with the users involved. These users will be instrumental in validating that a problem is fixed or that it has occurred again. You may also need to follow up with questions as you formulate a hypothesis of the problem.

Identify Symptoms

During the problem identity process, it is important to identify the symptoms that either cause the problem or are the result of the problem. You must define exactly what the problem affects and under which conditions the symptoms of the problem surface.

I will use the problem of a network slowdown that happens intermittently as an example. One of the symptoms might be that email slows down quite considerably during the slowdown. Another symptom might be that user cloud applications become unresponsive during these times as well. These symptoms might help you determine whether the problem is local to your network or external to your network. In this example, if Internet-connected systems are only affected, then it suggests the problem is outside your network.

Determine If Anything Has Changed

Sometimes problems are a direct result of a change in the network. The change does not need to be a recent one, since some problems only manifest themselves when they are being used and their use may be infrequent. As an example, suppose your firewall rules were cleaned up and a month later your human resources person complains that payroll cannot be uploaded. A firewall rule may have been removed that is creating the connectivity problem. Why a month later? Maybe payroll gets uploaded only once a month.

Some organizations require change management as discussed in Chapter 3. These change management documents might be the best starting point to determine whether anything has changed related to the current problem. Other organizations require the logging of changes to the network to a document called the change log. The change log details what exactly has been changed, when it has been changed, who has made the change, and why the change has been made. If these documents are not used by your organization, then talking among other administrators is advisable. This will help to identify if their changes could be the cause of the current problem.

Approach Multiple Problems Individually

We often get bombarded with problems all at once. When this happens, we often jump to the conclusion there is a central cause. However, problems are often not related to each other, and jumping to a conclusion is casting a judgment on the problem that will waste time. Therefore, each problem should be viewed as a separate problem with no commonality between them.

Each problem should be uniformly approached, and information should be gathered specific to the problem at hand. When interviewing users, focus on the current problem. If the same user has been a part of several problems, you should explain that you want to focus on one problem at a time. This prevents the Chicken Little syndrome of "the sky is falling" that users and network administrators suffer alike. When we look at problems individually, we can form better strategies to solve them individually.

Establish a theory of probable cause

After a problem and its symptoms have been identified, the next step is to form a hypothesis and establish a theory of probable cause. This theory should be based on information gathered and supporting network theory. It is important to note that at this step of troubleshooting, the theory of probable cause could change based on new evidence. It is not uncommon for the first theory of probable cause to be incorrect, especially when all the problem's variables are not well defined.

Question the Obvious

When establishing a theory of probable cause, question everything related to the problem. The most obvious causes can sometimes be overlooked. Although the symptoms might be complex, they do not always describe how complex the cause of the problem is.

As an example, suppose a new VoIP phone system has been installed in your organization. The users complain that they are consistently receiving busy signals when calling others. The most obvious cause is that the other party is actually busy and the new system is leading users to believe the phone is the issue. A theory of probable cause in this example is that they are actually calling a busy phone.

Consider Multiple Approaches

When you establish a theory of probable cause, you shouldn't restrict yourself to one theory. You should practice pitching the symptoms, problem, and your theory to others. This serves two purposes: First, it allows you to articulate the elements of the problem to your peers. They will often ask more questions that you may have not thought of yet or simply overlooked. The second is that others may come up with alternate theories of probable cause to a problem. These alternate theories should be embraced and discussed further with your team.

Although to pitching a problem to others is helpful, it is not always part of the diagnostic process. It is, however, important to keep an open mind and think of other approaches. The more time you invest in the problem, the more you will understand its causes.

Top-to-Bottom/Bottom-to-Top OSI Model

As you are considering different approaches to the problem, compare the OSI layers to the flow of information. Approaching the problem while considering what happens at each layer of the OSI model allows you to trace the process from the key click to the expected outcome. Although what happens in the upper layers of the application, presentation, and session layer is usually unknown to network administrators, you can consult the programmers to validate that these layers are not the root cause of the problem. If the application has been unchanged, most problems will be isolated to the transport, network, data link, and physical layers.

Tracing the information down the originating host's OSI stack, across the network, and up the destination host's OSI stack allows you to understand the flow of information. Problems should be analyzed at each layer down the originating stack and up the destination stack for the potential root cause.

Divide and Conquer

Although examining the data flow at each layer of the OSI is considered a technique to divide and conquer the problem, you should also separate out complex processes. Each separate subprocess should then be tested as a root cause of the problem.

For example, if the problem is a web form that emails from a web page that is not being received, several subprocesses can be divided out of the entire process—subprocesses such as form validation, form submission, server processing of the data, and then emailing of the data. Each one of these subprocesses can be examined individually; for example, "Is a simple email from the server being delivered?" Then you can progress to "Is the form being submitted to email?" Each of these is a theory of probable cause that should be researched separately.

Test the theory to determine the cause

After you have formulated a theory of probable cause, the next logical step is to test your hypothesis. Without a proper test of the theory, you cannot confirm the problem and determine its cause. Tests should be methodically planned out, along with a list of their expected outcomes.

In the earlier example of a web form that emails the contents to a recipient, the theory of probable cause is the web server is not sending emails. A test to confirm this theory is to manually send an email from the web server to a recipient. If it sends the email, the problem is elsewhere; if the email is not sent, then the cause of the problem is found, and your theory is validated.

Once the Theory Is Confirmed, Determine the Next Steps to Resolve the Problem

This task should be simple if you have a solid theory and understanding of the cause. When scientists conduct experiments with the use of the scientific method, there is a preconceived understanding of what the theory represents in relation to the problem. The test of the theory either confirms or negates the theory presented. Once the theory is confirmed, the resolution should be determined to resolve the problem.

In our example of an email *mail transfer agent (MTA)* not sending email to a recipient, we can plan more theories as to why and test them further. A possible resolution might be that the MTA service has stopped and needs to be restarted. The problem might also be more complex and require more testing, but the cause of the problem is now isolated to a system that can be diagnosed further.

If the Theory Is Not Confirmed, Reestablish a New Theory or Escalate

We hope that our theory of probable cause is sound and is confirmed during testing. However, if the test does not confirm the primary theory, then a new theory of probable cause must be established. We should use prior tests to conclude what the problem is not related to. This type of problem solving is known as the process of elimination. It is a relevant problem-solving technique, as long as adequate progress is made during each test.

In our example, if the MTA is operating properly and the test does not confirm the theory of probable cause, then a new theory needs to be established. A new theory might be that the web form is not submitting the web form to the email service. This theory can now be tested, and the MTA system has now been eliminated from the problem as being a possible cause.

At some point in the process, the progress of a problem will cease, and you will need to escalate the problem. Escalation might be in the form of consulting third-party experts or area experts in your organization. In the example, the web form is not submitting email to the email service. The next logical step might be to have a webmaster examine the code and verify that it is properly submitting the form to the email system. We can now state that we have eliminated the email system and provide proof as to why the code might be at fault.

Establish a plan of action to resolve the problem and identify potential effects

The analysis of the solution can be simple or complex. Regardless of how simple the solution seems to be, you should identify its effects. It is frustrating to fix one problem and create several others.

In our example, we determine that DNS is the issue. During our tests, changing the DNS server for the server operating as the MTA fixes the problem. Implementing this change could have zero effect on anything else, or it could potential disrupt all other email services. In this circumstance, further research of the potential problems should be identified and documented.

Implement the solution or escalate as necessary

After we have determined the solution and identified the potential effects, we need to implement the solution. Implementing the solution might be as simple as changing a DNS entry, or it may be as complex as reinstallation of the system. Hopefully, in most cases the solution will be simple and within our control. However, in some instances we may need to escalate the implementation of the solution to a third-party expert or an area expert in our organization.

Verify full system functionality and, if applicable, implement preventive measures

The system functionality should be verified after the solution has been implemented. Outside of the initial system modified, all of the surrounding systems that interact with the modified system should be verified for full functionality.

In the event of a future system failure, preventive measures should be taken. In our example, such a measure might be to save the forms locally to a file or database before transmitting the data via email. This preventive measure would ensure that if the email was to fail again, we still have a copy of the data.

Document findings, actions, and outcomes

The final step of problem solving is the documentation of the findings, actions, and outcomes. Proper documentation is often overlooked and can be a detriment in the future if the same problem arises. Documentation allows us to reflect on the problem so that if we or another technician runs into the same problem in the future we can save time. The actions and outcomes will detail which actions were performed to solve the problem and the specifics of the final solution to the problem.

Exam Essentials

Understand the various techniques for identifying network problems.   You should gather the information about a problem by facts and observation, and avoid jumping to conclusions. When the steps to reproduce a problem have been identified, reproduction of the problem is the next step. Reproduction can be in a test environment or live environment, depending on the requirements of the problem. Questioning users should be done in such a way as to avoid bias to a solution, and the questions should extract factual information. When questioning users, avoid the pitfalls of scope creep, stick to the problem, and build a rapport with the user for future questions. Identifying the symptoms of the problem will help you better understand when the problem is happening. You should review change log records for recent changes in the network as well as change requests to help identify the cause of the problem. As you encounter problems, each problem should be should be approached individually without assuming there is a commonality.

Understand the various techniques for establishing a theory of probable cause.   When establishing a theory of probable cause, question everything related to the problem. Don't restrict yourself to one theory. Listen to what your peers think of the problem and consider multiple approaches. The OSI layers should be compared to the flow of information, and you should consider what happens at each layer of the model. The process that is possibly causing the problem should be separated into smaller subprocesses. Each subprocess should then be tested as a root cause of the problem.

Understand the techniques for testing a theory, implementing a solution, and documenting an outcome for a problem. Tests should be methodically planned out, along with a list of their expected outcomes. The test of the theory either confirms or negates the theory presented. If the test does not confirm the primary theory, then a new theory of probable cause must be established and tested until a theory is confirmed. Following the successful test of a theory that establishes the root cause, the plan of action should be detailed. The plan of action should detail any potential adverse effects that will affect the problem system or supporting systems. After the solution is implemented, the primary system and surrounding systems should be tested for fully functionality. Finally, a synopsis of the problem—all of the symptoms, causes, and fixes—should be documented so that future problems can be solved quickly.

5.2 Given a scenario, use the appropriate tool.

You should have a good understanding of the tools necessary for your day-to-day maintenance, operation, and troubleshooting of the network infrastructure. In this section, I will cover two categories of tools: hardware and software. Both categories are essential for troubleshooting and repairing a network fault. You will find that the software tools are generally used to troubleshoot and that hardware tools are used to troubleshoot and repair. Both are essentials for maintenance and ensuring proper operation of a network.

Hardware tools

As network professionals we use hardware tools to repair and troubleshoot the physical connections in the network. This section covers the most common hardware tools that you will use when diagnosing copper and fiber-optic network cables. In addition, I will discuss testing equipment that is used by network professionals to verify operations.

Cable Crimpers

Cable crimpers, shown in Figure 5.1, are something that all network professionals should have in their toolbox. They are handy for fixing a bad cable end when the detent has broken off and won't stay inserted in the *network interface card (NIC)*. When using a cable crimper for the first time, you may find it a bit awkward, but with a little practice you can crimp a perfect end on the first shot.

FIGURE 5.1   A typical pair of cable crimpers

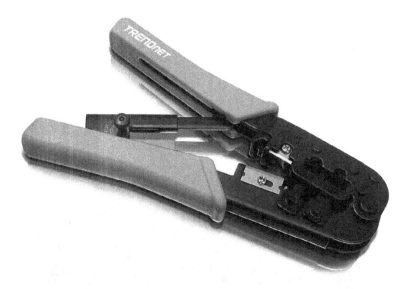

When you need to terminate an *RJ-45* on a network cable, you should first prepare your working area. Have an RJ-45 close by, the crimpers handy, and a wastepaper basket or waste receptacle. Start by cutting the sheath of the cable; give yourself about an inch. Some cable crimpers have a razor blade built in; I often find they cut either too much or too little, so it is best to have a special-purpose tool to score and cut the cable sheath. These tools often are spring loaded with an adjustable razor blade.

After cutting the sheath and pulling off, fan out the pairs so the orange/white orange wires are on the left and the brown/white brown wires are on the right. Next, start untwisting the pairs. Once all of the pairs are untwisted, begin with the arrangement of wires starting left to right: white orange and orange, then white green, then blue, then white blue, then green, and finally white brown and brown. If you need a reminder, print out a wallet card of the EIA/TIA 568B wiring specification and keep it with you.

Next, holding the wire with one hand, wiggle the pairs with the other as you pull on them to straighten them out. Once they are straight, use the razor on the cable crimpers to cut the wires so there is a half inch of wire after the sheath. Then grab the RJ-45 with the connector window facing you (pin 1 is now to the left) and press the RJ-45 end on, making sure the wires are separated in the slot in the connector. Put the connector into the cable crimper, press on the wire until you see the wire cores in the connector end, and then crimp. Practice, practice, practice!

Cable Tester

The *cable tester* is another tool that network professionals should never be without. It is used to check a cable end that has been freshly crimped or to diagnose a patch cable that is suspected to be bad. Cable testers often come in pairs or transmitters and receivers, as shown in Figure 5.2.

FIGURE 5.2 A cable tester pair

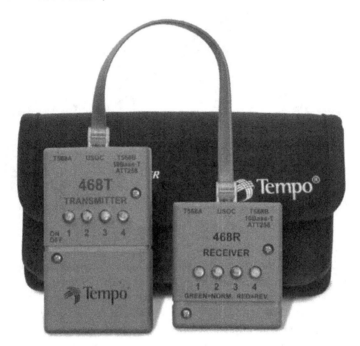

In the previous section, I explained how to terminate an RJ-45 on a network cable. I make it sound easy, but it will take plenty of practice. The cable tester will test each individual wire for any faults or mis-wiring. Most cable testers will sequentially test each pair for the correct continuity and connectivity. Good pairs come back with a green light and red depict a problem.

A *time domain reflectometer (TDR)*, shown in Figure 5.3, is a sophisticated networking tool for troubleshooting wiring. It was once a tool that was out of reach of most networking professionals because of cost. Advanced cable testers now come with this TDR functionality built in for a little higher cost. A TDR allows you to find breaks in cables, bad patch cords, and bad connections, with the added benefit of the location of the problem.

All wires have a reflection of energy. For example, if two people hold a rope tight and you flick one end, the wave created will zip toward the other person and then back to you. Wires work the same way; when a pulse of electric is introduced into them, it reflects back.

The TDR operates by sending low-energy pulses of electricity down the wires and timing when the reflection is detected. Since speed multiplied by time equals distance, we can get an accurate distance of each wire. In a network cable, all eight wires should have the same timing. If one wire is detected before the others, it is shorter than the other, and the problem is revealed. With a little estimating of cable lengths, you can even figure out where the problem is, because the TDR reports back the distances of each wire.

FIGURE 5.3   A time domain reflectometer

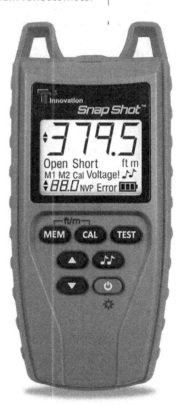

A *cable certifier* does more than just test the cable end wiring; it is used for end-to-end certification of an installation. A cable certifier tests everything from the proper wiring of jacks, patch panels, and all cabling between for the required speed. It operates by sending a signal at the frequency designated by the EIA/TIA categories, as covered Chapter 2. For example, a 1 Gbps category 6a network designates the test frequency of 500 MHz. The signal is introduced to one end of the network and is measured at the other end for loss, accuracy of the signal, and crosstalk. If it passes this test at the designated frequency, then it is certified for 10 Gbps at 100 meters. Figure 5.4 details a typical cable certifier.

FIGURE 5.4 A cable certifier

Punchdown Tool

When you think of a *punchdown tool*, you probably associate it with telephone work. However, in networks we use punchdown tools to punch down wires to patch panels. It is one of those tools right next to my cable crimpers. You can see a typical punchdown tool in Figure 5.5. Cabling on patch panels comes loose sometimes, such as when someone is installing a new network drop and accidentally bumps an existing one loose. Yes, it happens all the time.

FIGURE 5.5 A typical punchdown tool

Punching a wire down on a patch panel takes tremendous force because it clenches the wire and the tire cuts the excess wire off. Thankfully, the punchdown tool has a spring-loaded anvil that releases the force of the spring and does both tasks in a split second. To punch down a wire, first press the wire in the proper slot on the patch panel. Then, put the punchdown tool over the wire and press until you hear it punch the wire down. The die on a punchdown tool has a protruding angled blade on one side. Always make sure you have it pointed toward the excess wire; this is how the excess wire is trimmed, as shown in Figure 5.6.

FIGURE 5.6   A punchdown tool punching a wire into a patch panel

OTDR

An *optical time domain reflectometer (OTDR)* is used for diagnostic and testing of fiber-optic cable. A typical OTDR is shown in Figure 5.7. It has similar functionality to a TDR, but its functionality far surpasses a simple TDR. Fiber-optic cable spans much greater distances than copper Ethernet. It can find breaks in fiber just like a TDR, so the technician can find the location of the fault sometimes spanning up to 75 miles. It does this by pulsing light in a fiber-optic cable and measuring the reflective return of light, which all fiber-optic cable has. It can also measure reflective loss, end-to-end loss, and points of high loss. Most high-end networking equipment today has fiber-optic analysis built in. The OTDR is mainly used by fiber-optic technicians to certify a fiber-optic installation, diagnose problems, and analyze expected loss.

FIGURE 5.7   An optical time domain reflectometer

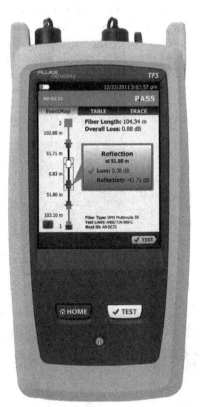

Light Meter

A light meter, also called an *optical power meter (OPM)*, is another tool used for diagnosis and testing of fiber-optic cable. The light meter measures the strength of the light from a reference light source that is paired with the light meter. The light meter also reports the amount of light loss for a fiber-optic cable.

The light meter function is normally built into an OTDR, but it can be purchased as a separate tool. It should also be noted that many small form-factor pluggable (SFP+) transceivers covered in Chapter 2 have a built-in light meter function. In the operating system of the network device, signal strength can be verified with a simple command and without disrupting communications.

Tone Generator

The *tone generator* is used in conjunction with a probe to trace network cables. A typical tone generator and *tracing probe* are shown in Figure 5.8. The tone generator is often integrated into the cable tester, but it can also be purchased as a separate tool. Tone generators can also be purchased for identifying telephone lines.

The tone generator is plugged into the cable connection that needs to be traced. It operates by injecting a warbling electrical tone into the network cable. The electrical tone is very weak, so it does not affect the network equipment it is plugged into. The probe then amplifies the electrical tone into an audible tone. The technique of identifying the wiring is to sweep over the cables with the probe until the faint tone is heard. Then, focus tracing in the area of the faint tone with the probe until the cable is identified by a much stronger tone. The cable tester can then be used to positively identify the cable.

FIGURE 5.8   A tone generator and tracing probe

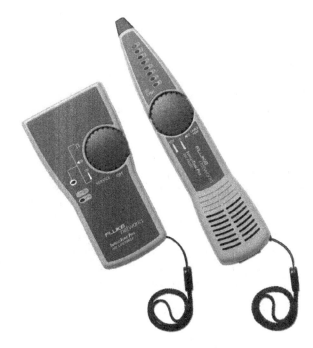

Loopback Adapter

Several different types of loopback adapters are available that you can use in a network. The loopback adapter's job is to redirect transmissions so that the media or connection can be tested. In the following section, I will cover the most common types of loopback adapters that you will use.

Serial

Serial loopback adapters are useful when you are trying to verify the connectivity of a serial adapter. When we plug into equipment and do not get a response back, we need to verify that we have a successful connection. The serial loopback adapter allows proper testing of the connection and lets us verify that we have the correct COM port configured.

The adapter is wired so that the transmit wire is redirected to the receive wire and the receive wire is redirected to the transmit wire. It is placed on the end of the serial adapter; then the terminal emulation program is started and directed to the proper COM port.

If you are able to type characters and they echo back on the screen, your serial port configuration is correct.

Serial WAN

Serial wide area networks (WANs) such as T1 connections often use a loopback adapter to verify wiring. The T1 loopback is wired similarly to the serial loopback; the receive wires and transmit wires are redirected to their respective counterpart. The adapter is often used when working with a T1 provider so that the *customer premise equipment (CPE)* wiring can be verified. The serial WAN loopback provides testing wiring only at the physical layer.

It is important to note that the provider can logically loop back their equipment, and newer transceivers in routers today can provide the same functionality. T1 connections are not the only type of serial WAN connection that use this type of loopback; there are several other types of serial WAN connections such as T3 that can use it as well.

Fiber-Optic

The fiber-optic loopback will be the most common type of loopback you will use. The fiber-optic loopback allows testing of fiber-optic pairs by a single technician and should be an essential piece of equipment in your toolbox. The technician will install the fiber-optic loopback similar to Figure 5.9 on one end of the fiber-optic connection, normally at the patch panel. Then the technician will connect the light meter or OTDR to the other end. This allows the test equipment to test the entire fiber-optic path in one shot.

When testing fiber-optic connections for WAN connectivity, the provider often loops the far-end side of the connection so that the entire path of the connection can be tested with a light meter. The provider often uses a device similar to the one shown in Figure 5.9.

FIGURE 5.9   An LC fiber-optic loopback plug

Multimeter

The *multimeter* is not typically used for testing network connections such as the previously covered equipment. It is used to provide testing of power sources with either the alternating current (AC) mode or the direct current (DC) mode. In Figure 5.10 you can see a typical multimeter.

FIGURE 5.10   A typical multimeter

The operation of the multimeter for testing of high-voltage power at the socket is performed on the AC mode. Multimeters must be set to a specific range for the voltage being tested, such as the range of 0–400 volts for normal AC sockets. This range will cover the typical voltages found in your datacenter of 120v and 208v. It is important to note that every meter will have a different range; 0–400 is only an example range. Some multimeters will range to 20v, 200v, and 1000v; every multimeter is different. Newer multimeters will auto-range so that all you need to do is select the type of measurement. Caution should be taken, since high voltage can be fatal if proper precaution is not taken, as covered in Chapter 3. The multimeter can also be used to test DC power supplies, although normally the voltage being measured is well under 27 volts and these voltages are typically classified as low voltage. Low-voltage DC testing is used with power supplies to confirm that they are supplying the proper voltage for the equipment.

Multimeters are called multimeters because they can also measure continuity and resistance. These functions are handy when you are determining whether a connection is faulty or determining the position of a pair of dry contacts on a relay. The multimeter used in these scenarios is often used with access control system (ACS) troubleshooting.

Spectrum Analyzer

The *spectrum analyzer* is specifically used with wireless communication troubleshooting. The spectrum analyzer allows us to see the radio frequency (RF) spectrum to identify noise and interference with wireless signaling. In Figure 5.11, a sample output from the NETSCOUT AirMagnet displays the 2.4 GHz RF band for 802.11 wireless.

FIGURE 5.11   NETSCOUT AirMagnet spectrum analyzer

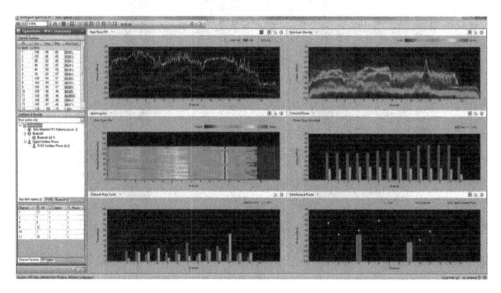

The spectrum analyzer software requires a specialized wireless dongle. This dongle is often connected to the technician's laptop via a USB connection. The dongle allows the software to capture the various RF airspace. Some network device vendors such as Cisco provide software that can connect to the wireless access point and turn it into a spectrum analyzer.

Software tools

Software tools are used to troubleshoot network problems and verify cause and validate effect. In the previous section, you learned about hardware tools that are used to repair network connections. In this section, you will learn about the popular software tools that are used to detect the root cause of problems and troubleshoot networking issues.

Packet Sniffer

Packet sniffers are software-based tools for capturing network traffic. Packet sniffers can be used with wireless and wired network connections to capture packets. An example of a packet sniffer is the open source *Wireshark* packet sniffer and analyzer. Microsoft also offers a free packet sniffer and analyzer called *Microsoft Message Analyzer.*

The packet sniffer by default will be able to capture broadcasts, multicast, or directed traffic only on the host it is installed on. As discussed in Chapter 1, switches will forward frames only to ports that contain the destination host based on the MAC address table. We can configure port mirroring, also discussed in Chapter 1. Port mirroring will allow the port containing the packet sniffer to capture all network frames, mirrored from the other port.

The packet sniffer's ability to capture network traffic is also directly dependent on the NIC. The NIC must support promiscuous mode, which allows the capture of frames with any destination MAC address. Although most newer NICs will allow promiscuous mode, the feature should be checked for the model of NIC with the vendor's specifications.

Port Scanner

Port scanners are used for troubleshooting connectivity issues and security assessments. When the port scanner is used for troubleshooting, the tool will scan the remote server to identify open ports that respond to the tool's requests. This is useful to validate that a server is serving information on the port and a firewall is not blocking the request.

We also use a port scanner to perform a security assessment of our servers. The port scanner verifies the open ports and the ports that are closed (firewalled). This helps reduce the risk that a firewall is misconfigured and allowing unauthorized access to services on the remote server.

There are several different port scanners that can be downloaded for free. The most popular open source port scanner is Nmap. Originally it was compiled for Linux and Unix, but it has since been ported to the Windows platform. Microsoft also offers a free tool called PortQry, which is a command line–based tool similar to Nmap.

Protocol Analyzer

Protocol analyzers decipher frames of data that have been captured with a packet sniffer. Protocol analyzers such as Wireshark and Microsoft Message Analyzer also provide packet sniffing capabilities. The protocol analyzer allows the network administrator to see the details of the data being transmitted or received. This allows the administrator to confirm the data is being transmitted or received correctly or enables the administrator to focus on the problem area.

The protocol analyzer comes preloaded with parsers that help decipher the captured data. The parser is nothing more than a list of protocol numbers that define what protocols are being used from layer 2 through layer 7. Once the protocol is known, the data contained in the rest of the layer can be deciphered and displayed in a readable format.

For example, if a frame is captured with a type field of 0x0806, then the frame is an ARP request and the rest of the data contained within is parsed according to an ARP frame layout. If the type field is 0x0800, then the frame is an IPv4 frame, and the data is parsed according to an IPv4 header layout. The data can be parsed further for the transport and application layers. In effect, the protocol analyzer decapsulates the data captured so it is readable, as shown in Figure 5.12.

FIGURE 5.12   Protocol analyzer of a TCP packet

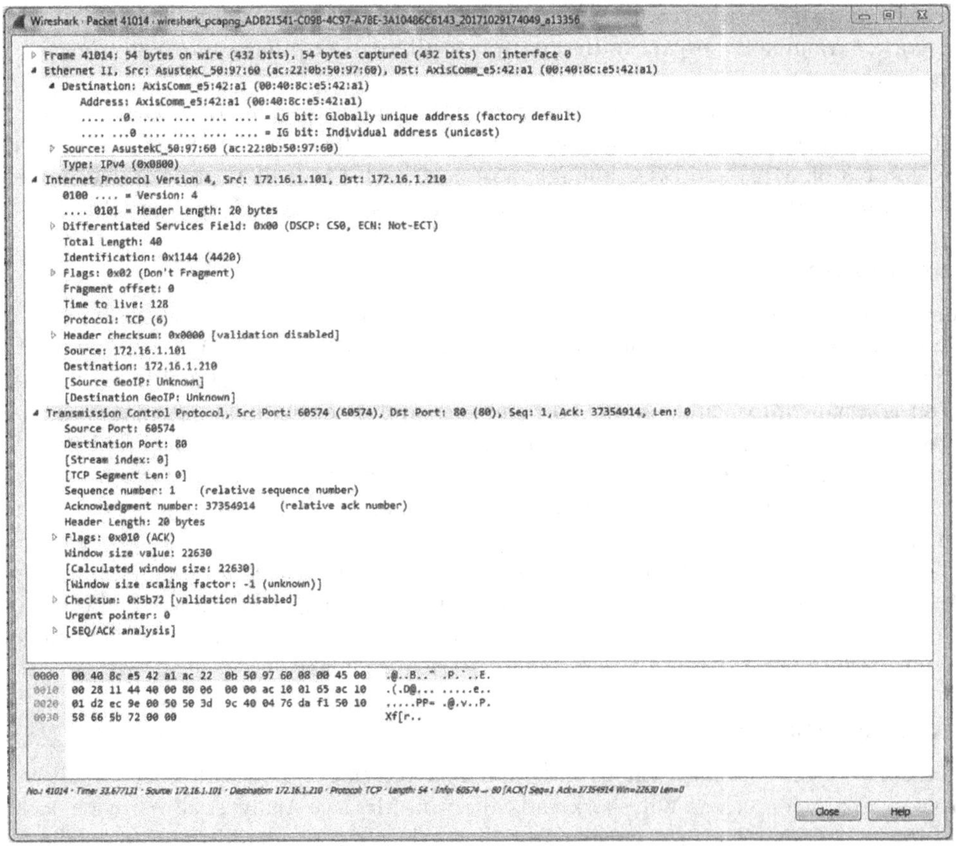

Wi-Fi Analyzer

Wi-Fi analyzers help network administrators identify channel and wireless access point (WAP) problems. The functionality of Wi-Fi analyzers is generally incorporated into spectrum analyzers such as NETSCOUT AirMagnet, discussed in a previous section. However, Wi-Fi analyzers can be used independently and are often free because of the basic functionality they provide. Spectrum analyzers will allow you to see non-Wi-Fi devices utilizing the RF airspace as well as interfering with electronics such as microwave ovens and wireless phones.

A Wi-Fi analyzer will provide power measurements of service set identifiers (SSIDs) and the encryption being used on each SSID. It will also display the channel the SSID is using and the MAC address of the WAP announcing the SSID. This information is useful because it shows the overall RF airspace as a device will see it. Figure 5.13 displays a popular Android phone application called Wifi Analyzer.

FIGURE 5.13   Android Wifi Analyzer

Bandwidth Speed Tester

Public bandwidth speed testers like speedtest.net are public Internet applets that communicate with dedicated Internet servers to determine your download and upload speeds. The inherent problem with these services is that they are being used by countless others and do not report an exact speed. They report the speed at which the server can communicate to you, which may not be the total speed of your connection. They are useful to validate there is a problem with your Internet connectivity.

A more precise method of measuring bandwidth speed is the use of an open source tool called iPerf. It requires a server to be set up to listen for an incoming request from the iPerf client. Many ISPs have an internal iPerf server so that you can test your WAN speed. When the iPerf tool is used, it saturates the entire line to report actual bandwidth speeds. It is also a useful tool for determining how well a firewall can perform under a high-bandwidth load as part of a stress test.

Command Line

On any given day at work, you will always find a command prompt open on one of my many monitors. Using a command line is just faster than a bunch of clicking. Some tools can only be accessed via command line, as you'll see in the next section. These command-line tools allow us to diagnose and troubleshoot network issues.

ping

ping is the most basic troubleshooting command. It uses the Internet Control Message Protocol (ICMP) at layer 3 to verify that a server is reachable. It is also useful for display-ing the round-trip response time to a specific IP address. It is the first command I use when trying to determine if a server is responding. It should be noted that if ICMP is being blocked on the host, it will still respond to application requests but will not respond to the ping command.

In the following example, you see a simple ping to a host in the network. The ping command returns the round-trip time for four ICMP packets. The summary that follows shows the packets sent, packets received, and the percentage of loss. The output will also detail the minimum, maximum, and average round-trip time in milliseconds.

```
C:\Users\Sybex>ping 172.16.1.1

Pinging 172.16.1.1 with 32 bytes of data:
Reply from 172.16.1.1: bytes=32 time<1ms TTL=64
Reply from 172.16.1.1: bytes=32 time<1ms TTL=64
Reply from 172.16.1.1: bytes=32 time<1ms TTL=64
Reply from 172.16.1.1: bytes=32 time<1ms TTL=64

Ping statistics for 172.16.1.1:
    Packets: Sent = 4, Received = 4, Lost = 0 (0% loss),
Approximate round trip times in milli-seconds:
    Minimum = 0ms, Maximum = 0ms, Average = 0ms

C:\Users\Sybex>
```

tracert, traceroute

tracert is another useful ICMP-based command. In Windows, the command is tracert, and in Linux and Unix, the command is traceroute. Both commands perform the same function. For the remainder of this section I will refer to the command as tracert.

The tracert command performs a ping on each hop to a destination IP address. In the following example, it would take 12 hops to reach an IP address of 8.8.8.8 (Google DNS). The round-trip times for each hop are calculated and displayed next to the name resolu-tion for each hop. In Windows the name resolution can be turned off with the -d argument and on Linux/Unix it can be turned off with the -n argument. Turning off name resolu-tion will speed up the output from the command, because no lookup is being performed.

The `tracert` command is used to troubleshoot how packets are reaching the destination IP address by detailing the path the packets will take.

```
C:\Users\Sybex>tracert 8.8.8.8

Tracing route to google-public-dns-a.google.com [8.8.8.8]
over a maximum of 30 hops:

 1   <1 ms   <1 ms   <1 ms  pfSense.sybex.local [172.16.1.1]
 2   20 ms   12 ms   10 ms  96.120.62.213
 3   11 ms   11 ms   11 ms  te-0-4-0-13-sur01.pittsburgh.pa.pitt.comcast.net [68.86.102.61]
 4   12 ms   12 ms   21 ms  te-8-3-ur01.wheeling.wv.pitt.comcast.net [68.86.100.26]
 5   14 ms   11 ms   19 ms  be-11-ar01.mckeesport.pa.pitt.comcast.net [68.86.147.109]
 6   18 ms   19 ms   19 ms  be-7016-cr02.ashburn.va.ibone.comcast.net [68.86.91.25]
 7   17 ms   17 ms   18 ms  hu-0-11-0-2-pe07.ashburn.va.ibone.comcast.net [68.86.83.2]
 8   22 ms   25 ms   17 ms  as4436-1-c.111eighthave.ny.ibone.comcast.net [173.167.57.162]
 9    *       *       *     Request timed out.
10   18 ms   20 ms   19 ms  72.14.233.20
11   17 ms   18 ms   17 ms  209.85.247.207
12   18 ms   25 ms   16 ms  google-public-dns-a.google.com [8.8.8.8]

Trace complete.

C:\Users\Sybex>
```

nslookup

`nslookup` is a command that can be found on both Windows and Linux/Unix operating systems. However, Linux and Unix operating systems favor the `dig` command over `nslookup`. The `nslookup` command stands for name-server lookup and is used to resolve Domain Name Server (DNS) addresses. The command can be used to resolve any type of DNS resource record. It is useful in troubleshooting DNS resolution problems. You can point it to a specific server using the `server=` argument so that you can directly query a specific DNS server.

The command can also be used in either noninteractive command mode or interactive mode. In the next example, the `nslookup` command is used in noninteractive mode to retrieve the MX record for `sybex.com`. I then use it in interactive mode by entering just `nslookup` at a command prompt; then every command thereafter is interactive inside the `nslookup` command.

```
C:\Users\Sybex>nslookup -type=mx sybex.com
Server: pfSense.sybex.local
Address: 172.16.1.1

Non-authoritative answer:
sybex.com    MX preference = 20, mail exchanger = cluster1a.us.messagelabs.com
```

```
sybex.com    MX preference = 10, mail exchanger = cluster1.us.messagelabs.com

C:\Users\Sybex>nslookup
Default Server: pfSense.sybex.local
Address: 172.16.1.1

> set type=mx
> sybex.com
Server: pfSense.sybex.local
Address: 172.16.1.1

Non-authoritative answer:
sybex.com    MX preference = 10, mail exchanger = cluster1.us.messagelabs.com
sybex.com    MX preference = 20, mail exchanger = cluster1a.us.messagelabs.com
>
```

ipconfig

ipconfig is a Windows command used to verify IP address configuration and its associated options. The command also allows control of the DHCP configuration of renewal and release, as well as control of the local DNS cache.

When using the ipconfig command to display the current IP address configuration, you can use either the short or the long mode, as shown in the following code. If you enter the command by itself, the basic information of IP address, subnet mask, and default gateway is displayed. If you add the /all argument, it also displays the MAC address, DHCP status, lease times, DHCP server, and DNS server, in addition to many other configuration options.

```
C:\Users\Sybex>ipconfig

Windows IP Configuration

Ethernet adapter Local Area Connection:

   Connection-specific DNS Suffix . : sybex.local
   Link-local IPv6 Address . . . . . : fe80::bc1e:1758:ba9a:ddf3%11
   IPv4 Address. . . . . . . . . . . : 172.16.1.101
   Subnet Mask . . . . . . . . . . . : 255.240.0.0
   Default Gateway . . . . . . . . . : 172.16.1.1

C:\Users\Sybex>ipconfig /all

Windows IP Configuration

   Host Name . . . . . . . . . . . . : ClientA
   Primary Dns Suffix . . . . . . . :
   Node Type . . . . . . . . . . . . : Hybrid
   IP Routing Enabled. . . . . . . . : No
```

```
    WINS Proxy Enabled. . . . . . . . : No
    DNS Suffix Search List. . . . . . : sybex.local
Ethernet adapter Local Area Connection:

    Connection-specific DNS Suffix  . : sybex.local
    Description . . . . . . . . . . . : Intel(R) 82583V Gigabit Network Connection
    Physical Address. . . . . . . . . : AC-22-0B-50-97-60
    DHCP Enabled. . . . . . . . . . . : Yes
    Autoconfiguration Enabled . . . . : Yes
    Link-local IPv6 Address . . . . . : fe80::bc1e:1758:ba9a:ddf3%11(Preferred)
    IPv4 Address. . . . . . . . . . . : 172.16.1.101(Preferred)
    Subnet Mask . . . . . . . . . . . : 255.240.0.0
    Lease Obtained. . . . . . . . . . : Sunday, October 29, 2017 8:40:20 AM
    Lease Expires . . . . . . . . . . : Sunday, October 29, 2017 11:40:20 PM
    Default Gateway . . . . . . . . . : 172.16.1.1
    DHCP Server . . . . . . . . . . . : 172.16.1.1
    DHCPv6 IAID . . . . . . . . . . . : 246161931
    DHCPv6 Client DUID. . . . . . . . : 00-01-00-01-1A-45-39-41-AC-22-0B-50-97-60
    DNS Servers . . . . . . . . . . . : 172.16.1.1
    NetBIOS over Tcpip. . . . . . . . : Enabled

C:\Users\Sybex>
```

Another common use for the ipconfig command is the release and renew options, used to release the current IP address and obtain a new IP address. When a connection is unplugged and plugged back in, the operating system will automatically release and request a new IP address from the DHCP server. However, if the VLAN is changed, it will not register an unplugged/plugged connection, and ipconfig /release and ipconfig /renew will request a new IP address from the DHCP server.

The ipconfig command can also be used to view and control the local client DNS cache. When the operating system requests a query from the DNS server, the answer is cached locally in memory until the time-to-live (TTL) for the record expires. We can view the local DNS cache with the ipconfig /displaydns command, and we can dump the cache with the ipconfig /flushdns command. The second command is useful if we just change the IP address for a record and want the change to take effect immediately on the local machine. The ipconfig /registerdns command will force the local machine to register its dynamic DNS records with the DNS server.

ifconfig

The ifconfig command is similar to ipconfig, but it's strictly used on Linux and Unix operating systems. It is similar in respect that you can obtain IP address information from the operating system by using the command ifconfig -a:

```
root@sybex:~# ifconfig
eth0    Link encap:Ethernet HWaddr 00:0c:29:e9:08:92
        inet addr:172.16.1.161 Bcast:172.31.255.255 Mask:255.240.0.0
```

```
      inet6 addr: fe80::20c:29ff:fee9:892/64 Scope:Link
      UP BROADCAST RUNNING MULTICAST MTU:1500 Metric:1
      RX packets:141 errors:0 dropped:0 overruns:0 frame:0
      TX packets:92 errors:0 dropped:0 overruns:0 carrier:0
      collisions:0 txqueuelen:1000
      RX bytes:19193 (19.1 KB) TX bytes:11708 (11.7 KB)

lo    Link encap:Local Loopback
      inet addr:127.0.0.1 Mask:255.0.0.0
      inet6 addr: ::1/128 Scope:Host
      UP LOOPBACK RUNNING MTU:65536 Metric:1
      RX packets:0 errors:0 dropped:0 overruns:0 frame:0
      TX packets:0 errors:0 dropped:0 overruns:0 carrier:0
      collisions:0 txqueuelen:0
      RX bytes:0 (0.0 B) TX bytes:0 (0.0 B)

root@sybex:~#
```

The ifconfig command will allow you to do much more than just view the current IP address. Using the command, you can configure an IP address and subnet mask on any available interface. Setting a manual IP address with this command would look like the following. However, this IP address will not be persistent through a reboot. The IP address would need to be configured in the appropriate interface file for the Linux/Unix distribution.

```
root@sybex:~# ifconfig eth0 172.16.1.200 netmask 255.240.0.0
root@sybex:~# ifconfig -a
eth0  Link encap:Ethernet HWaddr 00:0c:29:e9:08:92
      inet addr:172.16.1.200 Bcast:172.31.255.255 Mask:255.240.0.0
      inet6 addr: fe80::20c:29ff:fee9:892/64 Scope:Link
      UP BROADCAST RUNNING MULTICAST MTU:1500 Metric:1
      RX packets:1076 errors:0 dropped:0 overruns:0 frame:0
      TX packets:264 errors:0 dropped:0 overruns:0 carrier:0
      collisions:0 txqueuelen:1000
      RX bytes:94756 (94.7 KB) TX bytes:40618 (40.6 KB)

lo    Link encap:Local Loopback
      inet addr:127.0.0.1 Mask:255.0.0.0
      inet6 addr: ::1/128 Scope:Host
      UP LOOPBACK RUNNING MTU:65536 Metric:1
      RX packets:0 errors:0 dropped:0 overruns:0 frame:0
```

```
        TX packets:0 errors:0 dropped:0 overruns:0 carrier:0
        collisions:0 txqueuelen:0
        RX bytes:0 (0.0 B) TX bytes:0 (0.0 B)

root@sybex:~#
```

In addition to setting an IP address and viewing the IP address configuration, ifconfig allows you to administer an interface to a down status or up status, set the interface into promiscuous mode if the hardware supports it, and change the maximum transmission unit (MTU). It is important to note that any configuration change made with ifconfig is temporary and not persistent, unless it is configured in the appropriate configuration file for the distribution.

iptables

The iptables command allows you to view and edit the iptables firewall that is found on many Linux operating system distributions. The command is useful for checking the iptables firewall for a rule that could be restricting access to an application. As shown here, we use iptables -L to list the current firewall rules configured:

```
root@sybex:~# iptables -L
Chain INPUT (policy DROP)
target    prot opt source          destination
ACCEPT    tcp -- anywhere          anywhere          tcp dpt:ssh
ACCEPT    tcp -- anywhere          anywhere          tcp dpt:smtp
ACCEPT    icmp -- anywhere         anywhere           icmp echo-request

Chain FORWARD (policy ACCEPT)
target    prot opt source          destination

Chain OUTPUT (policy ACCEPT)
target    prot opt source          destination
root@sybex:~#
```

In this example, the INPUT table has several rules configured. The INPUT table also has a default policy of DROP that defines what to do with the traffic if no rule matches. We can change the default policy with the command iptables -P INPUT ACCEPT, which will allow any traffic even if it is not defined in the INPUT table. The command can be handy if we need to troubleshoot a firewall, and it can be reversed with iptables -P INPUT DROP. Using the previous example, if we determined that we need to add a rule for TCP port 80 (HTTP), the following would configure the rule:

```
root@sybex:~# iptables -A INPUT -i eth0 -p tcp --dport 80 -j ACCEPT
```

This command states that we want to append the INPUT table (-A INPUT), for the interface of eth0 (-I eth0), for the protocol of TCP (-p tcp), with a destination port of 80 (--dport 80), and an action of permit the traffic (-j ACCEPT). The command might look intimidating at first, but once you get used to the arguments it's quite easy to write rules. We can even cheat by using the command of `iptables -S` on a system that is already configured, and we can copy the rules, as shown here:

```
root@sybex:~# iptables -S
-P INPUT DROP
-P FORWARD ACCEPT
-P OUTPUT ACCEPT
-A INPUT -p tcp -m tcp --dport 22 -j ACCEPT
-A INPUT -p tcp -m tcp --dport 25 -j ACCEPT
-A INPUT -p icmp -m icmp --icmp-type 8 -j ACCEPT
-A INPUT -p tcp -m tcp --dport 80 -j ACCEPT
root@sybex:~#
```

It is important to note that any rules applied with the `iptables` command are not persistent through a reboot. If you want to save the rules so they survive a reboot, you either need to edit the iptables configuration file directly or save the iptables currently in memory. To save the current iptables in memory, you would use something like `iptables-save > /etc/iptables.rules`. However, you need to know where the operating system is expecting the file to be loaded from. In this example I am using a path of `/etc/iptables.rules`, but ultimately it is up to the administrator and how it was originally configured.

netstat

The netstat command can be found on both Windows and Linux/Unix operating systems. In Windows the command will display all of the current TCP and UDP connections, as well as the state of the TCP connection. The command allows us to view the current bindings of layer 4 communications. This is useful for troubleshooting because it allows us to view the connection to an application. In the following example, we have several established states and one connection that is trying to complete a three-way handshake. The SYN-SENT state tells us that a SYN has been sent to the destination host of 172.16.1.55, but we have not received a response.

```
C:\Users\Sybex>netstat

Active Connections

  Proto Local Address        Foreign Address       State
  TCP   127.0.0.1:443        Wiley:49755        ESTABLISHED
  TCP   127.0.0.1:49755      Wiley:https        ESTABLISHED
  TCP   127.0.0.1:49756      Wiley:49757        ESTABLISHED
  TCP   172.16.1.101:49237   iad23s61-in-f13:https  CLOSE_WAIT
  TCP   172.16.1.101:49238   iad23s60-in-f10:https  CLOSE_WAIT
  TCP   172.16.1.101:50703   172.16.1.161:ssh     ESTABLISHED
  TCP   172.16.1.101:50768   iad23s61-in-f14:https  ESTABLISHED
```

```
TCP  172.16.1.101:50771   iad23s60-in-f14:https  ESTABLISHED
TCP  172.16.1.101:50783   172.16.1.55:ssh        SYN_SENT
TCP  [::1]:8307           Wiley:49762            ESTABLISHED
TCP  [::1]:49762          Wiley:8307             ESTABLISHED
```

```
C:\Users\Sybex>
```

If we use the command `netstat -a`, we will get back all of the connections as well as any ports that are listening. This command helps us verify that the application has requested from the operating system a port to listen for requests on. Up until this point, I have focused on the output for the Windows operating system. Both the Windows and Linux/Unix versions of `netstat` operate the same to this point. In the next example, you see additional information about Unix sockets that is only relevant to Linux/Unix operating systems. A Unix socket is an interprocess communications (IPC) endpoint for the exchange of data on the same host.

```
root@sybex:~# netstat -a
Active Internet connections (servers and established)
Proto Recv-Q Send-Q Local Address       Foreign Address      State
tcp    0      0 localhost:6011    *:*              LISTEN
tcp    0      0 localhost:mysql   *:*              LISTEN
tcp    0      0 *:ssh             *:*           LISTEN
tcp    0     64 172.16.1.161:ssh    172.16.1.101:50703   ESTABLISHED
tcp6   0      0 localhost:6011    [::]:*           LISTEN
tcp6   0      0 [::]:http         [::]:*           LISTEN
tcp6   0      0 [::]:ssh          [::]:*           LISTEN
udp    0      0 *:bootpc          *:*
udp    0      0 *:8398            *:*
udp6   0      0 [::]:12914        [::]:*
Active Unix domain sockets (servers and established)
Proto RefCnt Flags    Type     State     I-Node  Path
unix  2    [ ACC ]   STREAM   LISTENING  11293  /var/run/acpid.socket
unix  2    [ ACC ]   STREAM   LISTENING  8495    /var/run/dbus/system_bus_socket
unix  8    [ ]       DGRAM              8539    /dev/log
unix  2    [ ACC ]   STREAM   LISTENING  1677    @/com/ubuntu/upstart
```

```
[Output cut]
```

The `netstat -ab` command in Windows can help us verify that an application is communicating by displaying the program that has created the binding. We can also use `netstat -ab` to show applications that are listening. In Linux/Unix, the command is `netstat -ap`.

```
C:\Users\Sybex>netstat -ab
```

```
Active Connections
```

```
Proto Local Address     Foreign Address     State
[svchost.exe]
TCP  0.0.0.0:443      Wiley:0           LISTENING
[wmpnetwk.exe]
TCP  0.0.0.0:902      Wiley:0           LISTENING
[svchost.exe]
TCP  0.0.0.0:5357     Wiley:0           LISTENING
[wininit.exe]
TCP  0.0.0.0:49153    Wiley:0           LISTENING
eventlog
[lsass.exe]
TCP  0.0.0.0:49155    Wiley:0           LISTENING
Schedule
[googledrivesync.exe]
TCP  172.16.1.101:49254   qu-in-f125:5222    ESTABLISHED
[googledrivesync.exe]
TCP  172.16.1.101:49256   iad23s58-in-f10:https CLOSE_WAIT
[googledrivesync.exe]
TCP  172.16.1.101:49894   iad30s09-in-f10:https CLOSE_WAIT
[googledrivesync.exe]
TCP  172.16.1.101:50625   qn-in-f188:5228    ESTABLISHED
[chrome.exe]
TCP  172.16.1.101:50632   209.11.111.11:https  ESTABLISHED
[chrome.exe]
TCP  172.16.1.101:50703   172.16.1.161:https   ESTABLISHED
[chrome.exe]
TCP  172.16.1.101:50803   iad23s61-in-f14:https ESTABLISHED
[chrome.exe]
TCP  172.16.1.101:50804   iad23s61-in-f14:https ESTABLISHED

[Output cut]
```

tcpdump

The tcpdump command is available on only Linux and Unix operating systems. The command is used to dump network data to a file or the console of the host you are connected to. It is useful when we want to see the network packets either entering or leaving a host. The tcpdump command that follows will output all of the packets that match the port of SSH on interface eth0:

```
root@sybex:~# tcpdump -s 0 port ssh -i eth0
tcpdump: verbose output suppressed, use -v or -vv for full protocol decode
```

```
listening on eth0, link-type EN10MB (Ethernet), capture size 262144 bytes
22:17:59.829560 IP 172.16.1.161.ssh > 172.16.1.101.50703: Flags [P.], seq
322381889:322382097, ack 106937580, win 326, length 208
22:17:59.829719 IP 172.16.1.101.50703 > 172.16.1.161.ssh: Flags [.], ack 208,
win 16121, length 0
22:17:59.831710 IP 172.16.1.161.ssh > 172.16.1.101.50703: Flags [P.], seq
208:496, ack 1, win 326, length 288
22:17:59.831782 IP 172.16.1.161.ssh > 172.16.1.101.50703: Flags [P.], seq
496:672, ack 1, win 326, length 176
22:17:59.831856 IP 172.16.1.101.50703 > 172.16.1.161.ssh: Flags [.], ack 672,
win 16425, length 0
22:17:59.831863 IP 172.16.1.161.ssh > 172.16.1.101.50703: Flags [P.], seq
672:848, ack 1, win 326, length 176
22:17:59.831922 IP 172.16.1.161.ssh > 172.16.1.101.50703: Flags [P.], seq
848:1120, ack 1, win 326, length 272
```

[Output cut]

The tcpdump command is so versatile that we can even capture traffic into a file and then pull the file up in Wireshark! The command tcpdump -s 0 port ssh -i eth0 -w capture.pcap will save all the packets that match a port of SSH to the file called capture.pcap. We can also omit the filter for SSH and capture any traffic to and from the system. If we wanted to be really creative, we could use ifconfig eth0 promisc to turn on promiscuous mode for the interface and capture any traffic seen by the host.

pathping

The pathping tool is found in Windows and combines the benefits of tracert and ping. The tool can be used to diagnose packet loss or suspected packet loss to a destination website. It is invaluable to network administrators to help prove to their ISP that packet loss is a problem on their network.

The tool will first trace the entire path to a destination IP address or DNS host. Then, each of the hops will be tested with ICMP for packet loss and round-trip time. It easily identifies router hops that are causing the delay or packet loss. The following is an example of a pathping to my provider's DNS server:

```
C:\Users\Sybex>pathping 75.75.75.75

Tracing route to cdns01.comcast.net [75.75.75.75]
over a maximum of 30 hops:
 0 Wiley.sybex.local [172.16.1.101]
 1 pfSense.sybex.local [172.16.1.1]
 2 96.120.62.213
 3 te-0-5-0-12-sur02.pittsburgh.pa.pitt.comcast.net [69.139.166.77]
 4 be-11-ar01.mckeesport.pa.pitt.comcast.net [68.86.147.109]
 5 be-7016-cr02.ashburn.va.ibone.comcast.net [68.86.91.25]
```

```
  6  ae-4-ar01.capitolhghts.md.bad.comcast.net [68.86.90.58]
  7  ur13-d.manassascc.va.bad.comcast.net [68.85.61.242]
  8  dns-sw01.manassascc.va.bad.comcast.net [69.139.214.162]
  9  cdns01.comcast.net [75.75.75.75]

Computing statistics for 225 seconds...
        Source to Here   This Node/Link
Hop RTT   Lost/Sent = Pct Lost/Sent = Pct Address
  0                          Wiley.sybex.local [172.16.1.101]
                   0/ 100 = 0%  |
  1  0ms    0/ 100 = 0%    0/ 100 = 0% pfSense.sybex.local [172.16.1.1]
                   0/ 100 = 0%  |
  2  14ms   0/ 100 = 0%    0/ 100 = 0% 96.120.62.213
                   0/ 100 = 0%  |
  3  15ms   0/ 100 = 0%    0/ 100 = 0% te-0-5-0-12-sur02.pittsburgh.pa.pitt
.comcast.net [69.139.166.77]
                   0/ 100 = 0%  |
  4  15ms   0/ 100 = 0%    0/ 100 = 0% be-11-ar01.mckeesport.pa.pitt.comcast.net
[68.86.147.109]
                   0/ 100 = 0%  |
  5  23ms   0/ 100 = 0%    0/ 100 = 0% be-7016-cr02.ashburn.va.ibone.comcast.net
[68.86.91.25]
                   0/ 100 = 0%  |
  6  23ms   0/ 100 = 0%    0/ 100 = 0% ae-4-ar01.capitolhghts.md.bad.comcast.net
[68.86.90.58]
                   0/ 100 = 0%  |
  7  25ms   0/ 100 = 0%    0/ 100 = 0% ur13-d.manassascc.va.bad.comcast.net
[68.85.61.242]
                   0/ 100 = 0%  |
  8  24ms   0/ 100 = 0%    0/ 100 = 0% dns-sw01.manassascc.va.bad.comcast.net
[69.139.214.162]
                   0/ 100 = 0%  |
  9  23ms   0/ 100 = 0%    0/ 100 = 0% cdns01.comcast.net [75.75.75.75]

Trace complete.

C:\Users\Sybex>
```

nmap

The nmap tool allows us to scan open and closed ports on remote systems for audit purposes. It can be used to validate that the firewall is open to accept requests for an application. The nmap tool is Linux/Unix-based tool that has been ported to Windows.

The nmap tool can scan all ports of a specific host or a range of hosts in the network. This allows for the discovery of a host that might not be known or protected with firewall rules. The nmap tool will also try to negotiate with Transport Layer Security (TLS) in an attempt to discover the encryption key strength being used. In addition to these features, it will try to predict the operating system the remote system is using.

In the following example, the nmap command was run with the -A argument that enables operating system detection, version detection, script scanning, and route tracing.

```
root@sybex:~# nmap -A scanme.nmap.org

Starting Nmap 6.40 ( http://nmap.org ) at 2017-10-31 21:34 EDT
Nmap scan report for scanme.nmap.org (45.33.32.156)
Host is up (0.094s latency).
Not shown: 993 closed ports
PORT    STATE   SERVICE    VERSION
22/tcp  open    ssh       (protocol 2.0)
| ssh-hostkey: 1024 ac:00:a0:1a:82:ff:cc:55:99:dc:67:2b:34:97:6b:75 (DSA)
|  2048 20:3d:2d:44:62:2a:b0:5a:9d:b5:b3:05:14:c2:a6:b2 (RSA)
|_256 96:02:bb:5e:57:54:1c:4e:45:2f:56:4c:4a:24:b2:57 (ECDSA)
25/tcp  filtered smtp
80/tcp  open    http      Apache httpd 2.4.7 ((Ubuntu))
|_http-title: Go ahead and ScanMe!
135/tcp  filtered msrpc
139/tcp  filtered netbios-ssn
445/tcp  filtered microsoft-ds
31337/tcp open    tcpwrapped
1 service unrecognized despite returning data. If you know the service/version,
please submit the following fingerprint at http://www.insecure.org/cgi-bin/
servicefp-submit.cgi :
SF-Port22-TCP:V=6.40%I=7%D=10/31%Time=59F925EF%P=x86_64-pc-linux-gnu%r(NUL
SF:L,2B,"SSH-2\.0-OpenSSH_6\.6\.1p1\x20Ubuntu-2ubuntu2\.8\r\n");
Device type: general purpose|firewall|WAP|terminal
Running (JUST GUESSING): Linux 3.X|2.6.X|2.4.X (92%), IPFire Linux 2.6.X (88%),
IGEL Linux 2.6.X (85%)
OS CPE: cpe:/o:linux:linux_kernel:3 cpe:/o:linux:linux_kernel:2.6 cpe:/
o:ipfire:linux:2.6.32 cpe:/o:linux:linux_kernel:2.4 cpe:/o:igel:linux_kernel:2.6
Aggressive OS guesses: Linux 3.2 - 3.6 (92%), Linux 2.6.32 - 2.6.39 (90%),
Linux 2.6.32 - 3.0 (89%), Linux 3.5 (88%), Linux 2.6.32 (88%), IPFire firewall
2.11 (Linux 2.6.32) (88%), Linux 2.6.15 - 2.6.26 (likely embedded) (86%), Linux
2.6.32 - 2.6.33 (86%), Linux 2.6.32 - 2.6.35 (86%), Linux 2.6.18 (86%)
No exact OS matches for host (test conditions non-ideal).
Network Distance: 12 hops

[Output cut]
```

If we add the -v argument, we will be able to see the progress of nmap as the scan progresses. The problem with scanning a remote host is that closed ports do not always respond as they should, and some operating systems do not respond at all. This lack of response makes it difficult to know whether the service is running, firewalled, or just dead. There are many other arguments that we can include to change the behavior of the scan:

- Use -sN for a NULL scan in which no flags are set in the transport layer header. If the port is closed, then the destination operating system will send back an RST. If the port is open, then nothing is sent back.

- Use -sF for a FIN scan in which the FIN flag is set in attempt to trick the operating system into responding to closed ports with an RST, similar to a NULL scan.

- Use -sX for an Xmas-Tree scan in which the URG, PSH, and FIN flags are set in an attempt to trick the operating system into sending an RST for closed ports.

route

The route command is the Swiss Army knife of commands for viewing and changing the routing table on a host. The tool can be used to check the local host's routing table if it is suspected there is a routing issue. It is important to note that in Windows routing is not enabled, even if two or more network cards are installed. Routing requires the use of the Routing and Remote Access Service (RRAS). In Linux and Unix, the route command has similar features, such as the ability to view and configure the routing table.

In Windows, we can view the routing table by entering the command route print; in Linux or Unix, the command is route -n.

```
C:\Users\Sybex>route print
===========================================================================
Interface List
 11...ac 22 0b 50 96 60 ......Intel(R) 82583V Gigabit Network Connection
  1...........................Software Loopback Interface 1
===========================================================================

IPv4 Route Table
===========================================================================
Active Routes:
Network Destination      Netmask      Gateway     Interface Metric
        0.0.0.0        0.0.0.0    172.16.1.1   172.16.1.101    10
      127.0.0.0      255.0.0.0      On-link      127.0.0.1   306
      127.0.0.1 255.255.255.255      On-link      127.0.0.1   306
127.255.255.255 255.255.255.255      On-link      127.0.0.1   306
     172.16.0.0    255.240.0.0      On-link   172.16.1.101   266
   172.16.1.101 255.255.255.255      On-link   172.16.1.101   266
 172.31.255.255 255.255.255.255      On-link   172.16.1.101   266
      224.0.0.0      240.0.0.0      On-link      127.0.0.1   306
      224.0.0.0      240.0.0.0      On-link   172.16.1.101   266
255.255.255.255 255.255.255.255      On-link      127.0.0.1   306
255.255.255.255 255.255.255.255      On-link   172.16.1.101   266
===========================================================================
```

```
Persistent Routes:
 None

IPv6 Route Table
===========================================================================
Active Routes:
 If Metric Network Destination    Gateway
 1  306 ::1/128           On-link
 11 266 fe80::/64          On-link
 11 266 fe80::bc1e:1758:ba9a:ddf3/128
                On-link
 1  306 ff00::/8          On-link
 11 266 ff00::/8          On-link
===========================================================================
Persistent Routes:
 None

C:\Users\Sybex>
```

In Windows we can add a route with the command

```
route add 10.0.0.0 mask 255.0.0.0 172.16.1.5 metric 5 if 11
```

In the preceding command, the route add command is followed by the network 10.0.0.0 and the subnet mask 255.0.0.0. It is then followed by the gateway address 172.16.1.5, the metric 5, and the interface 11. We can also change and delete routes by specifying the following commands:

```
route change 10.0.0.0 mask 255.0.0.0 172.16.1.10 metric 5 if 11
route delete 10.0.0.0
```

Note that the route add command is not a persistent command. The route will not be preserved over a reboot. Therefore, the -p must be added between the route command and the add argument. The -p will preserve the route and make it persistent across a reboot.

arp

The arp tool can be found in every operating system, even network device operating systems. The tool allows the administrator to observe, delete, and change the *Address Resolution Protocol (ARP)* table in memory. The ARP table consists of the mapping for IP addresses to MAC addresses. The operating system keeps this information cached to speed up the communications process while limiting the number of ARP broadcasts in the network. If the operating system didn't keep this cache, it would need to perform an ARP request for the destination IP address it wants to communicate per frame.

The administrator can view the ARP table in memory for Windows by typing **arp -g** or **arp -a** in Linux/Unix. The arp tool also allows us to flush the table in Windows or Linux/Unix

by typing **arp -d ***. We can also remove a specific entry by typing **arp -d 172.16.1.1**.
In the following example, you will see the ARP table as well as the deletion of a specific entry:

```
C:\Users\Sybex>arp -g

Interface: 172.16.1.101 --- 0xb
  Internet Address      Physical Address    Type
  172.16.1.1        00-15-5d-01-12-0b   dynamic
  172.16.1.5        00-15-5d-01-12-07   dynamic
  172.16.1.10       74-d4-35-03-a6-b9   dynamic
  172.16.1.12       14-dd-a9-92-2f-1c   dynamic
  172.16.1.205      08-10-76-26-32-ec   dynamic
  172.16.1.210      00-40-8c-e5-42-a1   dynamic
  172.31.255.255     ff-ff-ff-ff-ff-ff    static
  224.0.0.22        01-00-5e-00-00-16   static
  224.0.0.251       01-00-5e-00-00-fb   static
  224.0.0.252       01-00-5e-00-00-fc   static
  239.255.255.250     01-00-5e-7f-ff-fa    static
  255.255.255.255     ff-ff-ff-ff-ff-ff    static

C:\Users\Sybex>arp -d 172.16.1.1
C:\Users\Sybex>
```

Notice that some entries have a static type and some have a dynamic type. The dynamic
entries are removed from the ARP table after their TTL has expired. The TTL varies by
operating system; the maximum TTL is around 2 minutes. The static entries will never
be removed unless the host is rebooted or the ARP cache is manually flushed. The arp
tool allows us to map a specific IP address with a specific MAC address. This is sometimes handy with older hardware during the setup process. The command to map an
IP address to MAC address in both Windows and Linux/Unix is arp -s 172.16.1.1
00-15-5d-01-12-0b.

dig

The dig tool is almost identical to the nslookup tool and has become an adopted standard
for name resolution testing on Linux/Unix operating systems. The tool allows us to resolve
any resource record for a given host and direct the query to a specific server.

The command does not offer an interactive mode like the nslookup command. The command by default queries A records for a given host, and the output has debugging turned on
by default.

In the following example, we see a query being performed on the DNS server of 8.8.8.8
for an MX record of sybex.com. The debugging output shows that one query was given,
two answers were retrieved, and nothing was authoritative (not the primary servers). The
output also details the query made and the answers returned.

```
root@Sybex:~# dig @8.8.8.8 mx sybex.com

; <<>> DiG 9.9.5-3ubuntu0.13-Ubuntu <<>> @8.8.8.8 mx sybex.com
```

```
; (1 server found)
;; global options: +cmd
;; Got answer:
;; ->>HEADER<<- opcode: QUERY, status: NOERROR, id: 49694
;; flags: qr rd ra; QUERY: 1, ANSWER: 2, AUTHORITY: 0, ADDITIONAL: 1

;; OPT PSEUDOSECTION:
; EDNS: version: 0, flags:; udp: 512
;; QUESTION SECTION:
;sybex.com.            IN   MX

;; ANSWER SECTION:
sybex.com.       899  IN   MX    10 cluster1.us.messagelabs.com.
sybex.com.       899  IN   MX    20 cluster1a.us.messagelabs.com.

;; Query time: 76 msec
;; SERVER: 8.8.8.8#53(8.8.8.8)
;; WHEN: Wed Nov 01 21:43:32 EDT 2017
;; MSG SIZE rcvd: 104

root@Sybex:~#
```

Exam Essentials

Know the various hardware tools that you will encounter and use daily as a network administrator.   Crimpers are used to crimp RJ-45 ends on network cabling. The cable tester is used to test patch cables and network cabling with male RJ-45 ends. The punch-down tool is used to punch the wire of the network cable into a patch panel or female cable end. The optical time domain reflectometer (OTDR) is used to measure the length of fiber-optic cable and identify breaks in the fiber-optic cable. The light meter allows the administrator to measure the amount of signal loss in a fiber-optic cable. The tone generator is used for locating network cabling with a signal probe. The fiber-optic loopback is used to loop one end of the fiber-optic cable so that testing can be done end-to-end. The multimeter is commonly used to test power at outlets and power supplies and to test continuity in low-voltage wiring circuits. The spectrum analyzer helps the administrator see the radio frequency (RF) spectrum and is often used to diagnose wireless interference problems.

Know the various software tools that you will encounter and use daily as a network administrator.   Packet sniffers are used to collect network frames and packets for analysis and troubleshooting. Port scanners allow an administrator to verify that ports are not being firewalled and that they are open awaiting a request. The protocol analyzer provides an analysis of packet captures and allows the administrator to see the information contained inside the captured data. The Wi-Fi analyzer helps the administrator see the various wireless access points (WAPs), SSIDs, security, the MAC addresses of the WAPs, and the strength of the signal. Bandwidth speed testers are used to view the maximum download speed and maximum upload speed for a given connection.

Know the various command-line tools that you will use daily for troubleshooting. The ping command is used to verify that a host is reachable via layer 3 connectivity. The tracert (Windows) or traceroute (Linux/Unix) command allows us to see the path a packet will follow. The nslookup command helps us test DNS resource records from a specific DNS server. The ipconfig (Windows) or ifconfig (Linux/Unix) command allows us to verify the IP address configuration of the host. The Linux/Unix ifconfig command allows us to configure the IP address/subnet mask, promiscuous mode, and turn the interface up and down. The iptables command allows us to view the Linux iptables firewall as well as configuration of the firewall rules. The netstat command is used to see the port bindings and TCP states on both Windows and Linux/Unix systems. The tcpdump command is a packet sniffer and is used to capture packets from the local host. The pathping command sends multiple ICMP requests to each hop and measures the round-trip time for each hop. The nmap command is a port scanner and helps us determine whether firewall ports are open and the service is awaiting request. The route command is used to configure routes and view the current routing table of the host. The arp tool is used to view and configure the Address Resolution Protocol (ARP) table contained in the host's memory. The dig command is similar to the nslookup command; it allows us to verify name resolution for resource records.

5.3 Given a scenario, troubleshoot common wired connectivity and performance issues.

In this section, I will cover various scenarios that can cause issues in your wired network. I will discuss how these issues can be detected using the tools you learned about in the previous section. I will also cover troubleshooting steps to determine the causes.

Attenuation

The term *attenuation* is often associated with the maximum distance of a network cable. However, the maximum distance of a network cable is normally not susceptible to attenuation. The distances network cables are defined by are related to the time an electrical signal takes to travel down the wire before the frame is removed from the originating host's send buffer.

Coaxial cables are susceptible to attenuation, because an RF signal is transmitted through the cable. As the RF signal resonates down the wire, it dissipates energy; this dissipation of energy is called attenuation. Attenuation in a coaxial cable can cause connectivity and speed issues, because the amount of data is hindered by the error detection. Cable modems' coaxial connections are extremely susceptible to attenuation when cables have a poor signal entering the cable and the cable runs are too long.

Latency

Latency is the measurement of time for data traveling from the source host to the destination host. Latency for network connections is measured in millionths of a second, called milliseconds. When hosts are directly connected, the latency between the connections has sub-millisecond latency. However, as switches are introduced into the network, the forward filter decisions they perform create latency in the switch path. When routers are introduced, latency is increased, because routing decision must be made in the route path. Network address translation (NAT) increases latency of data, since more complex decisions must be made during translation. Each switch, router, and process that the data must traverse to the intended destination will introduce a certain amount of latency.

Latency can measured with the ping, tracert/traceroute, and pingpath commands. The ping command measures round-trip time of a packet in milliseconds. The traceroute command details round-trip time for each hop, and only the highest latency is relevant. The pathping command will also measure round-trip time but over a longer interval.

As a rule of thumb, latency for LAN communications should be under 20 milliseconds. Latency for WAN communications should be under 50 milliseconds for most network destinations. Latency over 100 milliseconds can introduce problems with time-sensitive protocols such as VoIP communications. Latency of over 200 milliseconds can make most network protocols problematic, as 200 milliseconds is 2/10 of a second.

Jitter

Latency is the delay between packets traveling from source to destination, as discussed in the previous section. *Jitter* is the variance between the latency of packets received. Jitter is measured in milliseconds, just like latency.

The latency of packets should be steady to any given host. ICMP tools like ping are usually not used to measure jitter, because ICMP takes lower precedence on routers. UDP is often used to measure jitter, because routers will not mark it with a lower priority. A high jitter measurement in latency can cause problems with time-sensitive protocols like VoIP and video conferencing. A high jitter measurement is anything over 20 to 40 milliseconds. Upward of 100 milliseconds, real-time communications is affected severely.

Crosstalk

Crosstalk is encountered when the signal of one wire induces a signal onto a parallel wire. The wires closely bundled together create induction, which in turn creates interference to each other. The induction effect, called *crosstalk*, can be mitigated by twisting the wires so that they are no longer parallel to each other. The tighter the twists per inch, the better the resistance to crosstalk the wires will have.

The proper use of the network category wiring specs you learned in Chapter 2 combat the phenomenon of crosstalk. The Telecommunications Industry Association (TIA) creates manufacturing specifications that define how many twists per inch are in each of the wire categories.

EMI

Electrical magnetic interference (EMI) is an electrical disturbance in signal quality from a source of electrical or *radio frequency (RF)* signal. EMI is normally generated from outside sources, such as motors, transformers, radio equipment, and many others. However, the phenomenon of crosstalk is actually from EMI. It just happens to be from the electrical signals of the other pairs of wires in the cable.

If the proper category of cabling is used for network speed and transient signals still persist, then EMI could be the cause. EMI is generated by fluorescent lighting, high-voltage wiring that is run parallel with network cabling, or any source of high energy or RF. An amplified cable probe described in the "tone generator" section of Chapter 5 can often be used to identify EMI. However, sometimes you must use a spectrum analyzer to see the EMI. In high-EMI environments such as industrial settings, it is best to run shielded twisted pair (STP) wiring to prevent EMI.

Open/Short

An open connection refers to an open circuit, in which the circuit is not completed or connected. This can be a simple wire that is loose on a patch panel, or it can be a break in a wire. A cable tester is used to determine open connections in a patch cord, patch panel, or any network cabling between the tested points. A multimeter can be used for continuity checks on other wiring such as power cords and serial cables.

A short is just that: a short circuit between two connections. A cable tester can be used to identify shorts in network cabling. Although uncommon in network cabling, a short could be the source of a problem if the wire insulation has been scraped off during installation. A multimeter can also be used for checking shorts in other low-voltage cabling.

Incorrect pin-out

Incorrect pin-out of connectors can also be troublesome for the administrator. A cable should always be tested after a cable end is crimped. The wires are very thin, and the person crimping the cable end must have a great deal of coordination. A cable tester will verify that the cabling has been crimped properly.

Network cables are not the only place that you can find the problem of incorrect pin-out. Serial cables and other low-voltage cables can contain incorrect pin-out problems. Specialized testers are made to check the various cables you may encounter. However, if you have an understanding of the cable pin-out, a multimeter can be used to check continuity between the pins at each end of the cable.

Incorrect cable type

The proper cabling should always be used for the installation of any network and low-voltage or high-voltage application. In networks, if the wrong cabling is used, you may not be able to communicate at the required speeds. In extreme cases, you may not be able to communicate at all. Crosstalk at higher network speeds will increase error rates and create communication problems.

Using the incorrect cable type for coaxial installation can also have dramatic effects on operation. Coaxial cable is rated for both impedance and loss. The impedance of the cable should always match the installation requirements. Impedance is advertised in the form of resistance, such as 50 ohm or 75 ohm. The loss of the cable should match the distance requirements. For example, for a long coaxial cable run RG-6 should be used rather than RG-59, which has significantly more loss.

Other types of low-voltage wiring, such as door lock and card reader wiring, must be of the proper gauge. Most RFID card readers operate on serial connections and have a defined wiring specification. Door locks contain a solenoid that draws a significant amount of amperage to lock and unlock. The proper cable gauge must be used to carry the current, or you could burn out the lock, power supply, and wiring, or it just might not work at all.

High-voltage cabling requires the proper cabling for safety and operations. When installing an electrical circuit, an electrician will take into account the amperage of the circuit, length of the circuit run, and the electrical code so that the proper wiring is used.

Bad port

As a network professional for the past 25 years, I have come across very few bad ports on switches and routers. You should suspect the configuration of the port first and compare it to a known good working port.

However, you may run across a bad port from time to time. When you do, the equipment on which the bad port resides should be replaced so that time is not wasted in the future if the port is used again. In the interim while you are waiting for acquisition of new equipment, the host should be moved to a known good working port to regain operations.

Transceiver mismatch

Transceiver mismatch is not common with Ethernet transceivers because most transceivers auto-negotiate speed and duplex. Also, most Ethernet transceivers are backward compatible with lower speeds. However, most 10 Gbps transceivers are not backward compatible with lower data rates, and some 1 Gbps transceivers are not compatible with lower data rates as well.

Fiber-optical transceivers must be identical on both sides of the fiber-optic cable. The wavelength of the light must match on the transmit side and the receive side, or the link will not turn up. The wavelength of the transceiver is advertised in nanometers. Distance is also a factor; higher-powered transceivers should be matched, or you run the risk of dropping a connection when the loss increases from vibrations of the mating surfaces.

Regardless of the type of transceiver, the specification of the transceivers should be checked against the requirements of the installation. The specifications of the cable should also be checked against the specifications of the transceivers to ensure a proper installation and trouble-free operations.

TX/RX reverse

Ethernet cabling is standardized with the cable end specifications of EIA/TIA 568A/B. Transmit receive reversal is possible if a crossover cable is installed rather than a straight-through cable. Most transceivers will perform automatic medium dependent interface crossover (MDI-X). If a cable is suspected to be a crossover cable, you can test the cable with a cable tester to determine its configuration.

Fiber-optic cable is much more susceptible to TX/RX reversal, because each transceiver has a dedicated transmit optic on the left and a receive optic on the right. If the transmit and receive fiber-optic cable are reversed, the connection will not turn up. All fiber-optic connections must be crossed over on one side, allowing the transmit optic to feed to the receive optic on the other side, as shown in Figure 5.14. It is best practice to always cross the connection at a dedicated patch panel such as your main data frame (MDF). Then instruct the installer at the intermediate data frame (IDF) to connect the cabling as straight-through to the equipment.

FIGURE 5.14   Fiber-optic transceivers

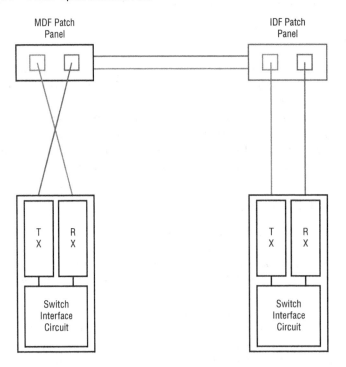

If you are in doubt which cable is which, shine a simple flashlight through the cable. This should always be done from a distance because the cable could be wrong and you could directly look into a laser at the opposite end.

Duplex/speed mismatch

A copper Ethernet connection is either half-duplex or full-duplex. Full-duplex describes that the connection can transmit and receive at the same time. A dedicated pair of wires is set aside for both transmit on one host to receive on the other host. With half-duplex, the connection can transmit only if the other host is not transmitting. A single pair is used for both transmitting and receiving on both hosts, which can cause collisions and reduce the speed by up to 40–60 percent, depending on the amount of traffic.

Auto-negotiation of IEEE 802.3u allows Ethernet 10baseT and 100baseT to auto-negotiate speed and duplex. However, duplex and speed are often set statically on connections to routers and between switches. When this is done, both sides must match. If one side of the connection is set to full-duplex and the other side is set to half-duplex, you will see a high error rate on the full-duplex side and a high collision rate on the half-duplex side. The connection will still function but with severely degraded performance.

A speed mismatch can also occur when the auto-negotiation of speed and duplex is turned off and statically set. However, unlike a duplex mismatch that causes errors and collisions, a speed mismatch will not allow the link to turn up. This is because Ethernet contains a carrier signal that is different between 10baseT, 100baseT, and 1000baseT.

Damaged cables

Cabling can be damaged for a variety of reasons. The cables could be damaged upon installation; it is common for the sheathing on the cable to be burnt off when pulled through tight bends. Cabling can also become damaged when a nail is struck into a wall, piercing the cabling. Other types of cable damage can occur, such as patch cables being run over by chairs and loosened from the cable end.

Damaged cables are can be identified by using a cable tester, which will show you any shorts or open pairs in the wiring. However, sometimes the cabling can become error laden and still work. This can happen if the wiring becomes kinked and the pairs start to separate from the uniform twists per inch inside the cable. A cable certifier can identify a damaged cable of this nature. Once the cable is identified, it should be replaced with an undamaged cable.

Bent pins

Many of the cable connections on networks and computers have pins called male connectors and mating receptacles called female connectors. The pins on the male connector can become damaged or bent when the cable is yanked or inserted improperly.

The bent pin will not always restrict the cable from seating. The only way to check a cable for bent pins is to look at the connector and visually look for a bent pin. Bent pins can often be repaired with very small needle-nose pliers. But if the bent pin is too severely damaged, the connector might need to be replaced.

Bottlenecks

The term *bottleneck* is used to describe a performance problem. Bottlenecks often occur when network traffic or a process slows down at a specific point. The specific point will not have the same capacity as the network traffic or process and is restricted in some way.

An Internet bottleneck can be identified with an Internet bandwidth speed tester. The testing should be done from the trouble area first; then you should move closer to the Internet connection and test again. When you measure a significant increase in bandwidth, the prior component should be suspected as the bottleneck.

Internet slowdowns are not the only type of bottleneck you can diagnose. Any two points in a network, such as the server farm network and the client network, can be tested with a tool called iperf. Unlike with the Internet-based bandwidth testers, you will need to start up an iperf server on one network and then use the iperf client to test on the client network. You will test with the iperf tool similar to an Internet bandwidth speed tester by moving closer to the server until bandwidth measurements increase.

VLAN mismatch

A VLAN mismatch between the switch and the host can occur and is common when new hosts are provisioned. When I describe a VLAN mismatch, I am referring to the access VLAN the switch is configured for or the IP address the host is configured with.

The mismatch can occur with either the host or the switch. The switch may be configured for the wrong VLAN and the host configured for the right VLAN, or the host may be configured for the wrong VLAN and the switch configured for the right VLAN. You will see it both ways and probably experience it firsthand someday.

The symptom is that the host will not be able to communicate with other hosts on the network. The problem occurs because the IP address and default gateway configured on the host will not match the network the VLAN serves. A packet sniffer on the host can capture the ARP broadcasts for the default gateway. This problem can be identified with a packet sniffer, but ultimately you will need to check the configuration on the switch.

Network connection LED status indicators

When an Ethernet link is turned up, the *light-emitting diode (LED)* indicator will light. There is also an activity LED on many Ethernet interfaces that will blink upon activity. Both of these LEDs provide a visual indication that the host is connected and communicating on the network, as shown in Figure 5.15. The link status LED is normally green, and the activity LED is normally yellow.

FIGURE 5.15   A typical Ethernet jack

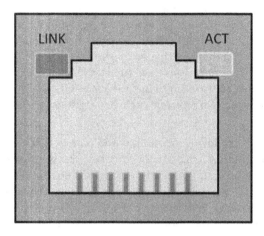

Some LED indicators may be next to the RJ-45 jack; this is common on many network interface card (NIC) expansion cards. In addition, some network indicators may not even be near the RJ-45 jack; they could be on the opposite side of the equipment, which is common on small office, home office (SOHO) switches. Many switch vendors group the indicators together above the ports, to the left of the ports, or to the right of the ports, as shown in Figure 5.16. No matter where the ports are located, every vendor includes a status LED for link status. It is uncommon to see a port without a status indicator.

FIGURE 5.16   A typical Ethernet switch

Exam Essentials

Understand the common scenarios in which wired connectivity and performance issues can arise from physical factors.   Attenuation is common on RF cabling such as coaxial cabling; it is not common in Ethernet networks. Crosstalk happens when the signal from one wire induces erroneous signals into another wire; the twist in each pair counteracts the phenomenon of crosstalk. Electrical magnetic interference (EMI) is generated by radio frequency (RF) devices, large motors, and high-voltage lines and can be counteracted by using shielded twisted pair (STP) wiring. Open conditions in a wire means that a wire is not making a connection, which can happen if a connector comes loose or a wire breaks. A short happens when two wires make a connection; this can happen if the insulation on the wires wears off or a foreign object is run into the wiring. Incorrect pin-out is generally associated with serial cables. The pin-out can be checked with a multimeter. Incorrect cable type can cause all types of problems with network wiring and RF applications. Bad ports on network switches should be identified and the equipment should be replaced so that time is not wasted in the future on diagnosing a bad port. Transceiver mismatch happens when the other transceiver does not offer backward support of the speed or fiber-optic transceivers do not match the expected wavelength on both ends. Fiber-optic cables are also susceptible to the transmit and receive fiber-optic cable being reversed; when this happens, the link will not turn up.

Understand the common scenarios in which wired connectivity and performance issues can arise from network factors. Latency is the delay between two hosts that is introduced with switches, routers, and firewalls and should not exceed 200 milliseconds. Jitter is the variance of latency between several packets and should not exceed 100 milliseconds. Duplex mismatches on Ethernet cabling will cause errors on one side and collisions on the other, but the connection will still operate in the degraded status. Speed mismatches will not allow the link to turn up, because the carrier will be different for each speed. Bottlenecks can be detected on networks using bandwidth speed test applications and a tool called iperf. VLAN mismatches occur when the switch port is set to the wrong VLAN or the host is configured with the IP address and default gateway of the wrong VLAN.

5.4 Given a scenario, troubleshoot common wireless connectivity and performance issues.

In this section, I will cover various scenarios that can cause issues in your wireless network. I will discuss how these issues can be detected using the tools you learned about earlier. I will also cover troubleshooting steps to determine the causes.

Reflection

Reflection is the reaction of RF signals bouncing off a surface. The denser the surface, the more reflection that you will encounter. Metal surfaces cause a high amount of RF reflection. The signals will be reflected back to the transmitter or receiver. High amounts of multipath reflection can degrade the signal because several copies of the signal are offset by microseconds. It is important to note that 802.11ac creates multipath reflection to increase bandwidth and density of a cell. In earlier wireless standards, it will cause performance problems.

Refraction

Refraction is the reaction of the RF signal as it passes through different media. The signal will change in frequency slightly as the medium slows the RF waves down. An example of refraction can clearly be seen with light through a prism; the light is slowed down as it passes through the glass. RF waves produce a similar pattern; it's just not visible to the naked eye.

Refraction should be taken into consideration when planning your wireless deployment. Large glass surfaces and media with a high refractive index should be avoided. Large amounts of refraction will limit the capacity of the wireless access point (WAP) as well as overall performance because of numerous retries. It can even make the WAP negotiate lower data rates.

Absorption

Absorption is the reaction of the RF signal being absorbed into the material upon contact. This is how a microwave oven operates, just with a lot more power. The RF energy is converted into heat and the signal is dissipated. Wireless signals run into the same problems with absorption. Table 5.1 lists common construction materials and their absorption rates. The absorption rate is displayed in *decibels (dB)*.

TABLE 5.1   RF absorption rates by common material

Material	Absorption rate
Drywall	3–5 dB
Glass wall and metal frame	6 dB
Metal door	6–10 dB
Window	3 dB
Concrete wall	6–15 dB
Block wall	4–6 dB

When designing a wireless network, these materials should be taken into account and reflected in your design. It is also important to note that materials can have multiple properties at the same time; for example, glass can both refract and absorb the signal. If the network is already designed and these materials may degrade signal and performance, moving the WAP might mitigate the absorption rate and increase bandwidth.

Latency

Latency is the measurement of time between two points a signal takes to traverse the distance. Latency is measured in milliseconds, similar to a wired connection. It should always be expected that wireless will have a greater latency than a wired connection. Generally the latency is much higher by 20 to 60 milliseconds. Latency will increase slightly as obstacles and distance increase because the signal will need to be resent if the receiver encounters erroneous data.

Another major contributor to high latency is the density of clients and other networking devices in the airspace. Latency will increase because the carrier sense multiple access/collision avoidance (CSMA/CA) contention method uses clear-to-send (CTS) and ready-to-send (RTS) dialogue communications. As the airspace becomes more saturated with devices and clients, it becomes harder to share time on the channel because of the number of CTSs and RTSs seen on the channel.

A wireless analyzer and spectrum analyzer can be used to identify problems on channels. The wireless analyzer will show the broadcasting WAPs, and the spectrum analyzer will help show the utilization of the channel. Moving to a nonoverlapping channel or a different frequency can improve latency considerably.

Jitter

Jitter in wireless networks is the same measurement as in wired networks. Jitter is the measurement of variance between the latency of packets in the wireless network.

Jitter measurements in wireless networks will be higher because latency is expected to vary depending on data transmitted in the RF airspace. Jitter can be high if the variance of latency increases. This can be directly related to varied demand of wireless clients and transient RF signals that require data to be retransmitted.

A wireless analyzer and spectrum analyzer can be used to identify problems on wireless channels. The wireless analyzer can provide data on overlapping WAPs. The spectrum analyzer can provide data on utilization of the channel. Moving clients to a nonoverlapping channel with lower utilization can improve jitter.

Attenuation

Attenuation is also called free space loss; all RFs suffer from attenuation. Attenuation is the loss in the amplitude of a signal as the signal travels further from its source. RF attenuates similar to sound traveling through the air—as you move further from the source, the strength is diminished until you can no longer hear it. Both sound and RF are measured in decibels (dB).

Higher-frequency signals attenuate quicker than lower frequencies. The wireless 5 GHz band is an example of a higher frequency when compared to 2.4 GHz. The 2.4 GHz signals can travel further than 5 GHz signals; thus the lower frequencies attenuate slower.

Wireless signals are measured in dB, and the reading is often labeled as the received signal strength indicator (RSSI). The RSSI is the level of the signal at the receiving point.

802.11 wireless will reduce the speed as the RSSI is reduced to accommodate adequate connectivity. A low RSSI at the WAP means that the clients are too far away or that the antenna should be positioned to allow better sensitivity to the signal.

Incorrect antenna type

The incorrect antenna type can greatly reduce receive and transmit quality of a wireless system. There are several attributes to antennas, such as frequency, radiation pattern, gain, and connectors. Each of these attributes should be researched before purchasing and installing an antenna for wireless operations.

The frequency of the antenna is its most important attribute. If the wrong antenna is purchased and installed, you can even damage wireless equipment. When it comes to antennas, bigger is not always better. The antenna is a piece of wire that is cut to an exact measurement so that it resonates the RF signal at a specific frequency. If the wrong antenna is used, the signals will bounce back and cancel out transmitting signals. This is called standing wave interference (SWI), and it can create connectivity problems. If the *standing wave ratio (SWR)* between transmitting waves and standing waves is too severe, it could damage the transmitter.

Radiation patterns are advertised with the antenna, as discussed in Chapter 1. If the wrong antenna is used to cover an area, the signal will not radiate in the expected pattern to where the clients will be located. There are several aspects of antenna radiation patterns, discussed further in Chapter 1.

The connector is important, but if the wrong connector is purchased, then the antenna will just not fit. It is important to note that most indoor antennas have SMA connectors and most outdoor antennas have N-type connectors that are waterproof. Outdoor antennas also require the proper cabling with the respective connectors.

When researching the proper antenna for a wireless installation, you should always consult the buying guide from the vendor. The buying guide will detail the radiation pattern, signal gain measured in dB, operating frequency, and installation requirements.

Interference

Interference is any signal that interferes with the reception of wireless. The source of interference can be anything, but often it is a device operating on the same frequency of the equipment. Sometimes the interference source doesn't even need to be operating on the primary frequency the interference is observed. The interference can even be caused by other wireless equipment. A spectrum analyzer helps identify interference sources by displaying the spectrum of frequency it is observing.

Common sources of 2.4 GHz interference are Bluetooth, non-Wi-Fi cameras, cordless phones, and microwave ovens. These devices operate closely on the 2.4 GHz frequency. Common sources of 5 GHz interference are radar sources and cordless phones. The 5 GHz frequency band is much cleaner than the 2.4 GHz frequency band, and the radar sources are confined to specific channels of 5 GHz. Both the 2.4 GHz and 5 GHz bands can be checked with a spectrum analyzer for these interfering signals. The technician can then use the spectrum analyzer to locate the source of the interference.

Incorrect antenna placement

The antenna placement of the wireless equipment is a critical part of its installation. The incorrect antenna placement can cause problems such as absorption, reflection, and refraction. The most obvious is the improper coverage of the clients, because of the radiation pattern, as discussed further in Chapter 1.

The initial placement of the antenna might be correct for the coverage. However, office areas are often reconfigured and new obstacles for the wireless signal can be placed in its path. The wireless signal is often the last aspect of construction to be considered, and sometimes it's not even a thought until it becomes a problem. Wireless antenna placement should be documented during the installation and reviewed periodically.

The most common type of antenna used with wireless equipment is the dipole omnidirectional antenna. These antennas are bendable so that the signal can be radiated perpendicular to the equipment, as shown in Figure 5.17. The radiation pattern of an omnidirectional antenna looks like a giant doughnut that radiates around the antenna. Depending on how the WAP is mounted—on a high ceiling or wall, for example—the antennas should be positioned so that the doughnut radiation pattern covers the desired area.

FIGURE 5.17   A typical dipole wireless antenna on a WAP

Channel overlap

In the 2.4 GHz wireless band, only three channels are nonoverlapping, as discussed in Chapter 1. Channels 1, 6, and 11 are nonoverlapping in the 2.4 GHz band. Using these channels ensures that your clients on adjacent channels will not use the bandwidth of the primary channel they are connected on. For example, if you have clients on channel 1, then clients on channel 6 will not interfere with operations on channel 1. However, you cannot control the airspace around you. Other WAPs and clients you don't control can use channels between the nonoverlapping channels, and your WAP will need to abide by the conversations. This in turn will diminish your effective bandwidth.

The good news is that the 5 GHz wireless band has 24 nonoverlapping channels. Each 20 MHz channel is nonoverlapping with the other 23 channels. This ensures that a conversation between a WAP and a client on one channel does not affect another channel. When single 5 GHz channels are used, there is no overlap. Channel bonding was introduced in 802.11n, which means that a WAP can use two adjacent channels and can overlap with a channel your WAP and client are using. 802.11ac introduced high bandwidths by allowing even more channels to be bonded, as discussed in Chapter 1.

Channel overlap has become a problem that can no longer be avoided in wireless networks. Fortunately, WiFi analyzers allow us to see the channels that are not being used by neighboring WAPs. We can switch our WAPs and clients to the unused channels. It doesn't ensure that channel overlap will not occur, but we do have 24 channels to choose from.

Overcapacity

When we think of wireless systems, we often think of how well they work at home. At home we have three to five clients maximum communicating on a WAP. However, in office settings we can easily stretch the capacity of the WAP by having too many clients associated with or moving large amounts of data. When this occurs, we are considered at overcapacity on the wireless cell. The symptoms of overcapacity are low bandwidth, high latency, and client disconnects.

It is important to understand that the bandwidth of a WAP and the 802.11 standard it supports is shared among its associated clients. Therefore, if we have 10 clients on 802.11g running 54 Mbps, each client can theoretically move 5.4 Mbps of data. This statement would be true if everyone was using the channel at the same time. However, that's not the case, so we can fit many more people on a single WAP. The general rule of thumb is 20 to 30 associated clients per WAP. This number is heavily dependent on the data demand of the clients. When planning wireless installations, check with the wireless vendor, who will have a specification for the maximum number of active clients.

When we require higher capacity of clients or higher bandwidth, we can place WAPs closer together and create a dense wireless cell. These installations require a wireless LAN controller (WLC) to coordinate steering of clients to the WAP with the least amount of utilization. The WLC software allows monitoring of channel utilization. A wireless analyzer can also be used to identify utilization problems.

Distance limitations

In wired Ethernet networks, we can guarantee a maximum distance of 100 meters, or 330 feet. In wireless networks, distance is limited by several factors, such as the protocol used, frequency, power level, antenna gain, antenna type, antenna positioning, and building materials, among others. We can easily see that physical factors directly affect our distance from the WAP. Each wireless technology released has effectively increased the distance of wireless access points. In Chapter 1 I discuss wireless protocols and their advertised distances in detail.

As we move further away from the signal source, our data rate is lowered to accommodate retransmits and the longer distance. When we approach the maximum limit, our client will experience disconnects. A wireless analyzer can help identify distance limitations by examining the received signal strength indicator (RSSI). Increasing the power on a WAP does not fix the problem, because the client is still limited in size and power. However, purchasing antennas with higher gain can help with distance limitations.

Frequency mismatch

As I discussed in the previous section on channel overlap, the 2.4 GHz wireless band is limited to three nonoverlapping channels. The 5.0 GHz wireless band has 24 nonoverlapping channels. The 5.0 GHz band is preferred in large wireless deployments, because it simply offers more channels and reduces channel overlap in a coverage area.

However, before you turn off the 2.4 GHz wireless band on your service set identifier (SSID), you must make sure that all clients support it. You are almost guaranteed to have a frequency mismatch between what the client will support and the frequency you want to support. A common practice is to advertise the primary SSID on 5.0 GHz and then create a second SSID that supports the 2.4 GHz band. The 2.4 GHz SSID will often have a 24 on the end to signify the less desirable frequency. For example, your SSID might be SYBEX for 5 GHz and SYBEX24 for 2.4 GHz.

There is no way to avoid frequency mismatch unless you purchase all equipment supporting 5 GHz. In bring your own device (BYOD) deployments, it is impossible to dictate such requirements.

Wrong SSID

When diagnosing wireless client problems, always check the SSID. Users can connect to the wrong SSID, and when this happens, they will be connected to a totally different network. Checking the IP address doesn't always guarantee you'll identify the problem. The other SSID might use an identical IP address scheme. A user doesn't need to intentionally connect to the wrong SSID; the operating system will often prefer a SSID and reconnect when within range.

Wrong passphrase

In the previous section, I discussed a client associating with the wrong SSID. However, sometimes the client will not be able to associate with the correct SSID. Each time we try to connect to the SSID, the connection fails. This is a very common problem when using an SSID that has been configured for *preshared key (PSK)* security. Entering a wrong passphrase will make a client exhibit this symptom during association.

When this occurs, there are some simple steps to troubleshooting. The first troubleshooting step is to verify the passphrase that the SSID is expecting. The second step is to verify that the keyboard is registering the characters properly. You can do so by entering the passphrase in Notepad, copying it, and then pasting it into the SSID passphrase dialog box. Passphrases are case sensitive, and this method allows us to verify the case of each character being typed before we paste it in the dialog box, which is often password masked.

Security type mismatch

A client will exhibit the same symptoms when a security type mismatch exists. The client will not be able to associate with the SSID because the security protocol does not match. Troubleshooting steps to avoid security type mismatch are straightforward. The first step is to verify the wireless security protocol. The next step involves clearing the failed wireless connection, sometimes called forgetting the connection. The last step is to manually set up the new SSID connection with the appropriate security protocol.

Power levels

It is often thought that more is better, except for when it comes to wireless signal power levels. WAPs should be installed relatively close together to provide roaming of clients. When a client moves into the cell, it will connect to the strongest signal. If the power levels are too high on an adjacent WAP, the client might connect to the wrong WAP for its vicinity. Connecting over this perceived longer distance will create latency for the client and could promote disconnects.

The transmitter on a WAP and the installed antennas will always be better than clients' transmit power and antenna. Clients generally choose their signal based on signal strength of the WAP. However, just because the client can hear the WAP doesn't mean they have the power to communicate with it. Therefore, power should always be turned down on the WAP to the minimum level that still allows flawless roaming.

Signal-to-noise ratio

Signal-to-noise ratio (SNR) is used to measure the quality of RF signal against the level of RF noise. Despite its name, it is not a ratio at all. The SNR is the decibel (dB) difference between the measured RF signal and the RF noise floor. For example, if the noise floor was −80 dB and the signal was −60 dB, the SNR would be −20 dB, which is pretty good. The separation of signal to noise should always be at least −20 dB or more. The SNR rule of thumb is the higher, the better.

When the SNR is too low, it means that the RF noise floor and the RF signal are indistinguishable from each other. This causes disconnects to the client and high retries because data will be received with errors. There isn't too much you can do about the noise floor, but a better antenna will raise the signal strength and create further separation. A spectrum analyzer can be used to view the SNR, but many WAPs have this measurement built in.

Exam Essentials

Understand the common scenarios in which wireless connectivity and performance issues can arise from installation problems.   Using the incorrect antenna type in wireless installations can hinder performance and possibly damage the transmitting circuitry in the WAP. The incorrect antenna placement can cause problems such as high absorption, reflection, refraction, and overall poor coverage. Channel overlap diminishes effective bandwidth, because the WAP and client must work around other channels overlapping with the primary channel being used. As a general rule of thumb, WAP capacity should be between 20 and 30 clients.

Understand the common scenarios in which wireless connectivity and performance issue can arise from physical factors.   Reflection is reaction of RF signals bouncing back off solid surfaces. Refraction is the reaction of the RF signal as it passes through different media that can cause performance problems. Absorption is the reaction of RF waves being dissipated into various materials; this can reduce the signal strength. Latency is the measurement of time between two points a signal takes to traverse the distance and is measured in milliseconds. Jitter is the measurement of variance between the latency of packets in the wireless network. Attenuation is the loss in the amplitude of a signal as the signal travels further from its source. Interference is any signal that interferes with the reception of wireless, such as Bluetooth, non-Wi-Fi cameras, cordless phones, radar, and microwave ovens. The signal-to-noise ratio (SNR) is the measurement that reflects the separation between the signal and noise floor.

Understand the common problems associated with wireless connectivity.   A frequency mismatch occurs when the SSID is operating on a frequency the client is not compatible with. If the client connects to the wrong SSID, resources will be unavailable to the client. Using the wrong passphrase will cause the client to continually fail to connect to the SSID. A security type mismatch can also cause continuous failure when connecting to an SSID.

5.5 Given a scenario, troubleshoot common network service issues.

As a network administrator, you will need to identify and solve various problems. In this section, I will cover various scenarios that you will encounter. I will also cover the diagnostic steps used and troubleshooting with the tools discussed in the previous sections.

Names not resolving

We rely heavily on fully qualified domain names (FQDNs) and Domain Name System (DNS) for network communications. FQDNs and DNS also allow for easy reconfiguring of an IP address, and they are easier to remember. www.sybex.com resolves to

208.215.179.132, and www.sybex.com is a lot easier to remember than the IP address. We can also swap out the IP address and you can still reference www.sybex.com to get to it. When an FQDN does not resolve, we simply cannot connect to the destination host. Fortunately, name resolution is simple to diagnose.

To understand the diagnostic process, you need to understand the name resolution process end to end. In Figure 5.18 you see a typical DNS process. On the left we have the client that requires resolution, and at the top we have the Internet DNS servers that contain the authoritative copy of the zone file. All network clients contain a DNS resolver service that is pointed to a DNS server for queries. The DNS resolver also contains a local DNS cache to cache DNS query results. When the DNS resolver does not have the answer for a DNS query, the query will be forwarded to the configured DNS server. In most corporate networks, you will find an internal DNS server, to which all of the clients are pointed for name resolution. This internal DNS server may contain internal DNS zones or caches that take precedence over queries directed to it. If the internal DNS server cannot resolve the answer, it may be configured to query the Internet DNS servers directly using the root zone, or it may forward the request to your ISP's DNS servers. The ISP DNS servers will have a cache and may have local zones configured as well that will take precedence over the query. Ultimately, if the ISP DNS servers cannot answer the query, they will recursively query the Internet DNS servers for the answer. I covered DNS in depth in Chapter 1.

FIGURE 5.18   The DNS query process

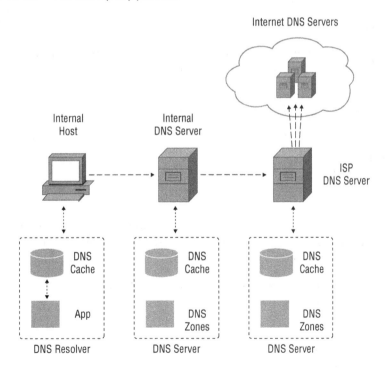

When diagnosing name resolution problems, always verify that the source of your name resolution is returning the proper resource record value and work your way back. You can use nslookup or dig to help verify DNS resolution. Suppose we are having trouble resolving www.sybex.com to the IP address of 208.215.179.132 on the internal host. The sybex.com zone is hosted on an Internet DNS server. Therefore, we will start at the source and check the name servers hosting the sybex.com zone file. We will start by obtaining the SOA record for sybex.com using the nslookup command and querying a public DNS server.

```
C:\Users\Sybex>nslookup -type=soa sybex.com 8.8.8.8
Server: google-public-dns-a.google.com
Address: 8.8.8.8

Non-authoritative answer:
sybex.com
    primary name server = jws-edcp.wiley.com
    responsible mail addr = istech.wiley.com
    serial = 70794
    refresh = 3600 (1 hour)
    retry  = 900 (15 mins)
    expire = 1209600 (14 days)
    default TTL = 3600 (1 hour)

C:\Users\Sybex>
```

We can see that the primary DNS (authoritative) server is jws-edcp.wiley.com, so we will check that next to verify the resource record is correct.

```
C:\Users\Sybex>nslookup -type=a www.sybex.com jws-edcp.wiley.com
Server: jws-edcp.wiley.com
Address: 208.215.179.100

Name:  www.sybex.com
Address: 208.215.179.132

C:\Users\Sybex>
```

We have now confirmed the primary DNS (authoritative) server of jws-edcp.wiley.com is returning the correct IP address for the resource record. We now check our ISP's DNS server to which our internal servers are forwarding requests for resolution.

```
C:\Users\Sybex>nslookup -type=a www.sybex.com 75.75.75.75
Server: cdns01.comcast.net
Address: 75.75.75.75

Non-authoritative answer:
Name:  www.sybex.com
```

```
Address: 208.215.179.132
```

```
C:\Users\Sybex>
```

We have now confirmed that the ISP servers are resolving the record correctly. If a different value was returned than we expected, the record could have been recently changed and still in the ISP's DNS cache. The SOA will define the default TTL that you should wait before checking again. It is also possible for the resource record to have an explicit TTL set. This can be checked by adding -debug to the command string: nslookup -type=a -debug www.sybex.com 75.75.75.75.

Next we check our internal DNS server for the proper name resolution for the resource record.

```
C:\Users\Sybex>nslookup -type=a www.sybex.com 172.16.1.1
Server: pfsense.Sybex.local
Address: 172.16.1.1
```

```
Non-authoritative answer:
Name:  www.sybex.com
Address: 208.215.179.132
```

```
C:\Users\Sybex>
```

We have now confirmed that our internal servers are resolving the record correctly. If a different value was returned than we expected, the record could be cached or a zone file matching sybex.com could be hosted locally. The SOA from the server would verify where the name resolution was answered from. This will guarantee that we are obtaining resolution from the source.

```
C:\Users\Sybex>nslookup -type=soa sybex.com 172.16.1.1
Server: pfsense.Sybex.local
Address: 172.16.1.1
```

```
Non-authoritative answer:
sybex.com
    primary name server = jws-edcp.wiley.com
    responsible mail addr = istech.wiley.com
    serial = 70794
    refresh = 3600 (1 hour)
    retry  = 900 (15 mins)
    expire = 1209600 (14 days)
    default TTL = 3600 (1 hour)
```

```
C:\Users\Sybex>
```

If the problem is not identified, it must be the client cache or perhaps the DNS server the client is configured for name resolution. The `ipconfig` command can be used to check both the resolver configuration and the cache.

```
C:\Users\Sybex>ipconfig /all
[Output cut]

Ethernet adapter Local Area Connection:

   Connection-specific DNS Suffix . : Sybex.local
   Description . . . . . . . . . . . : Intel(R) 82583V Gigabit Network Connection
   Physical Address. . . . . . . . . : AC-22-0B-50-97-60
   DHCP Enabled. . . . . . . . . . . : Yes
   Autoconfiguration Enabled . . . . : Yes
   Link-local IPv6 Address . . . . . : fe80::bc1e:1758:ba9a:ddf3%11(Preferred)
   IPv4 Address. . . . . . . . . . . : 172.16.1.101(Preferred)
   Subnet Mask . . . . . . . . . . . : 255.240.0.0
   Lease Obtained. . . . . . . . . . : Friday, November 10, 2017 7:28:56 AM
   Lease Expires . . . . . . . . . . : Friday, November 10, 2017 11:28:56 AM
   Default Gateway . . . . . . . . . : 172.16.1.1
   DHCP Server . . . . . . . . . . . : 172.16.1.1
   DHCPv6 IAID . . . . . . . . . . . : 246161931
   DHCPv6 Client DUID. . . . . . . . : 00-01-00-01-1A-45-39-41-AC-22-0B-50-97-60
   DNS Servers . . . . . . . . . . . : 172.16.1.1
   NetBIOS over Tcpip. . . . . . . . : Enabled

C:\Users\Sybex>ipconfig /displaydns

Windows IP Configuration

[Output cut]

   www.sybex.com
   ----------------------------------------
   Record Name . . . . . : www.sybex.com
   Record Type . . . . . : 1
   Time To Live . . . . : 895
   Data Length . . . . . : 4
   Section . . . . . . . : Answer
   A (Host) Record . . . : 208.215.179.144

[Output cut]

C:\Users\Sybex>
```

We can see that the wrong IP address is cached on the client. The command `ipconfig /flushdns` will purge all resolver caches on the client. Then the connection should be attempted again, and the command `ipconfig /displaydns` should be used to check for proper resolution of the resource record.

Incorrect gateway

The default gateway in your network is the way out of your immediate network through a router. The gateway is important because it allows you to communicate with other networks, such as other VLANs or the Internet. Think of the gateway as the door that leads out of a room you are in. The door in this analogy is the router, and the room is the immediate network. It is not common to have more than one gateway in a LAN, but you will see this from time to time in networks. It is common to have multiple gateways to the Internet, because this allows for the redundancy of the Internet connection.

If a host is set to the wrong gateway or to a gateway that does not exist, communications to remote networks or the Internet will fail. These problems can be diagnosed with `tracert` on Windows or `traceroute` on Linux/Unix. As shown in the following output, we can see the path the ICMP packets have taken to the destination IP address of 192.168.1.80.

```
C:\Users\Sybex>tracert 192.168.1.80

Tracing route to hostb.Sybex.local [192.168.1.80]
over a maximum of 30 hops:

  1   <1 ms   <1 ms   <1 ms pfsense.Sybex.local [172.16.1.1]
  2    2 ms    3 ms    2 ms int-router.Sybex.local [172.16.2.1]
  3    3 ms    3 ms    2 ms ext-router.Sybex.local [192.168.5.1]
  4    5 ms    7 ms    7 ms hostb.Sybex.local [192.168.1.80]

Trace complete.

C:\Users\Sybex>
```

If an incorrect gateway was configured on any node in the path, we could quickly identify the problem, as shown in the following output. We would then need to check the routing table on the last node that successfully responded, which is 172.16.2.1. You may also see the packet take a path out the wrong gateway, which will also be detailed in the output. The last router that you expected to see in the output should always be checked for the proper route statements to the destination network.

```
C:\Users\Sybex>tracert 192.168.1.80

Tracing route to hostb.Sybex.local [192.168.1.80]
over a maximum of 30 hops:

  1   <1 ms   <1 ms   <1 ms pfsense.Sybex.local [172.16.1.1]
  2    2 ms    3 ms    2 ms int-router.Sybex.local [172.16.2.1]
  3    *       *       *     Request timed out.
  4    *       *       *     Request timed out.
```

```
5    *    *    *    Request timed out.
```

[Output cut]
Trace complete.

C:\Users\Sybex>

Incorrect netmask

The importance of the network mask was covered in Chapter 1. The network mask defines the local host's network ID. The local host also uses its network ID to decide if the packet needs to be routed or locally switched to the destination IP address. The incorrect network mask can create connectivity or performance problems.

In Figure 5.19 you see two /24 networks of 10.1.0.0/24 and 10.1.1.0/24. Each host inside the respective networks has a /24 network mask. However, host A is configured with an incorrect network mask of /16. Everything will work as normal when host A communicates with hosts on its immediate network. However, when host A communicates with host B on the other subnet, host A will match its network ID with the destination network ID and will determine that the host is local; consequently, the information will never make it off the immediate network. The local network ID is derived from the logical ANDing process of the host's IP address and the network mask, which will be 10.1.0.0. The destination IP address will also be ANDed against the host's network mask, which will produce a value of 10.1.0.0. When the two are compared, they will be identical, so the local host will try to deliver it directly via an ARP request, which will never be heard by the remote host B.

FIGURE 5.19   Incorrect /16 netmask in a /24 network

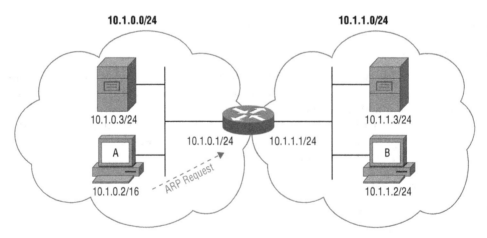

In Figure 5.20 you see two /16 networks of 10.1.0.0/16 and 10.2.0.0/16. In this example, host A is configured with an incorrect network mask of /24. Everything will work normally when host A communicates with host B; the frame will be sent to the router from host A and routed to the remote host B. However, when host A attempts to communicate with the destination server IP address of 10.1.1.3, the frames will first be forwarded to the router, then to the host, and this creates a performance problem. Because host A calculates its immediate network ID as 10.1.0.0 and the destination network of 10.1.1.0, host A will determine the host is remote and forward the frame to the router. When the router receives the frame, it will then attempt to deliver the frame itself. In certain circumstances, the frame might not be delivered at all.

FIGURE 5.20   Incorrect /24 netmask in a /16 network

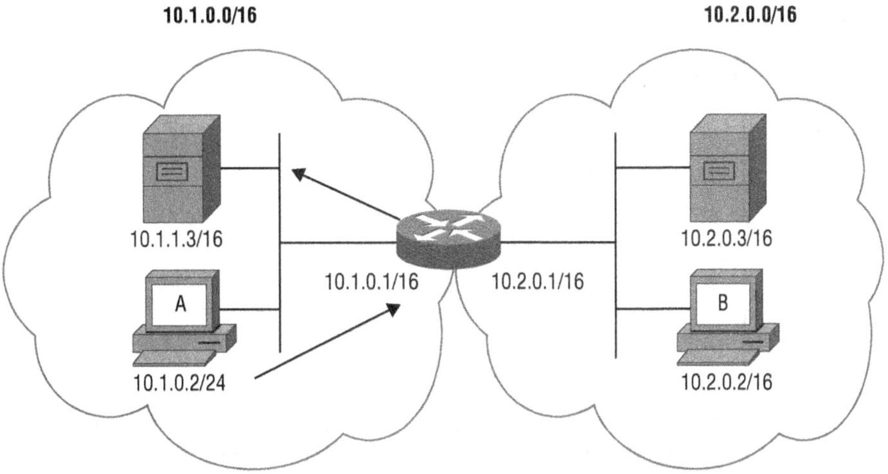

The problems mentioned here can be identified and remedied by using the skills learned in the previous sections. First, we need to diagram the network, as shown in Figure 5.19 and Figure 5.20. Then we should obtain the IP addresses associated with the hosts, along with their subnet mask. We can then identify the problem. The ipconfig command can be used on Windows hosts to obtain the current IP address and subnet mask. In Linux and Unix, the ifconfig command will perform the same function.

```
C:\Users\Sybex>ipconfig

Windows IP Configuration

Ethernet adapter Local Area Connection:

   Connection-specific DNS Suffix . : sybex.local
   Link-local IPv6 Address . . . . . : fe80::bc1e:1758:ba9a:ddf3%11
   IPv4 Address. . . . . . . . . . . : 172.16.1.101
   Subnet Mask . . . . . . . . . . . : 255.240.0.0
   Default Gateway . . . . . . . . . : 172.16.1.1

C:\Users\Sybex>
```

Duplicate IP addresses

Starting with Windows Vista, when the operating system starts up, it will send an ARP request for its configured IP address. If an ARP reply is received, then a message stating a duplicate IP address has been detected will display on the screen. The symptoms of a duplicate IP address on the network will be a loss of connectivity for both hosts sporadically.

Fortunately, with the skills you've learned in this chapter you can identify a host with the duplicate IP address on the network. You must first record the configured IP address using ipconfig.

```
C:\Users\Sybex>ipconfig

Windows IP Configuration

Ethernet adapter Local Area Connection:

   Connection-specific DNS Suffix . : sybex.local
   Link-local IPv6 Address . . . . . : fe80::9e8e:2086:b678:dee3%11
   IPv4 Address. . . . . . . . . . . : 192.168.1.2
   Subnet Mask . . . . . . . . . . . : 255.255.255.0
   Default Gateway . . . . . . . . . : 192.168.1.1

C:\Users\Sybex>
```

Then locate the host by configuring a temporary static IP address on the computer that is not duplicated with any other host and still within the intended network range. You then ping the original IP address; the ping may fail if the firewall is enabled on the remote system. However, this process will allow you to obtain the MAC address via the ARP process. You then use the arp command to obtain the MAC associated with the problematic IP address.

```
C:\Users\Sybex>ping 192.168.1.2

Pinging 192.168.1.2 with 32 bytes of data:
Reply from 192.168.1.2: bytes=32 time<1ms TTL=64
Reply from 192.168.1.2: bytes=32 time<1ms TTL=64
Reply from 192.168.1.2: bytes=32 time<1ms TTL=64
Reply from 192.168.1.2: bytes=32 time<1ms TTL=64

Ping statistics for 192.168.1.2:
   Packets: Sent = 4, Received = 4, Lost = 0 (0% loss),
Approximate round trip times in milli-seconds:
   Minimum = 0ms, Maximum = 0ms, Average = 0ms

C:\Users\Sybex>arp -g

Interface: 192.168.1.5 --- 0xb
  Internet Address    Physical Address    Type
```

```
192.168.1.2        00-15-5d-01-12-0d   dynamic
192.168.1.255      ff-ff-ff-ff-ff-ff    static
224.0.0.22        01-00-5e-00-00-16    static
224.0.0.251       01-00-5e-00-00-fb    static
224.0.0.252       01-00-5e-00-00-fc    static
239.255.255.250    01-00-5e-7f-ff-fa    static
255.255.255.255    ff-ff-ff-ff-ff-ff    static
```

C:\Users\Sybex>

The last step is to connect to the switching equipment and locate the port associated with the MAC address of 00-15-5d-01-12-0d as discovered in the previous step. Most switch operating systems will allow you to show the content addressable memory (CAM) table that is used for forward filter decisions. This allows us to identify the port number the duplicate IP address is occupying by the MAC address recorded in the previous step. If your switch does not support this function, then you will need to visit each computer until you have identified the duplicate IP address.

Duplicate MAC addresses

MAC addresses should always be unique, because each vendor is assigned an organizationally unique identifier (OUI) by the Institute of Electrical and Electronics Engineers (IEEE), and each card produced is given a unique ID. This standard has been adopted to ensure that MAC addresses are globally unique. These concepts were covered in Chapter 1.

Despite these adopted standards, it is still possible to have a duplicate MAC address if the MAC address is statically set. Some NIC firmware allows for manual MAC address configuration. Virtualization platforms also allow for static MAC address assignment, although most virtualization software will not allow a duplicate MAC address to be configured on a virtual machine (VM).

Regardless of how the duplicate MAC address is configured, the symptoms are similar to a duplicate IP address. Sporadic loss of network communication will be observed. These problems are difficult to identify as a duplicate MAC address. Identifying the actual duplicate MAC address is easier than finding a duplicate IP address, because you have the MAC address already. You just need to connect to the switch and find the port that the duplicate MAC address is located on. If it is a VM, the virtualization software will most likely notify you by displaying an error next to the VM, stating that a duplicate MAC address is configured.

Expired IP address

Expired IP addresses are the direct result of Dynamic Host Configuration Protocol (DHCP) failure. The life cycle of DHCP IP address lease was covered in Chapter 1. When the DHCP server allocates an IP address and leases it to the DHCP client, a timer is started on both the server and client. The server's timer for the IP address is used so that the IP address is not allocated for the entire lease period to another host. The client's timer is used for management of the IP address lease. As discussed in Chapter 1 at the 50 percent mark of the lease, the client is responsible for renewing the IP address lease; this resets the timer on the server and client. However, if a DHCP server is not available, then at 87.5 percent, or 7/8ths of the life cycle, the client will try to renew the lease or obtain a new lease with another DHCP server. At the 100 percent mark of the IP address lease, the client must release the IP address as it is expired.

If the IP address is expired, then the client has failed to communicate with the DHCP server at both the 50 percent and the 87.5 percent marks. Therefore, the DHCP services for the LAN are assumed to be down. The ipconfig tool can be used on Windows to verify when the client has obtained an IP address lease and the expiration of the IP address lease. In the following output, we see this client has obtained the IP address at 6 a.m. and the lease will end at 10 a.m. The server is configured to lease IP addresses for 4 hours. Therefore, it is expected that the client renew the IP address lease at 8 a.m., which is 2 hours into the lease.

```
C:\Users\Sybex>ipconfig /all

Windows IP Configuration

Ethernet adapter Local Area Connection:

   Connection-specific DNS Suffix  . : sybex.local
   Description . . . . . . . . . . . : Intel(R) 82583V Gigabit Network Connection
   Physical Address. . . . . . . . . : AC-22-0B-50-97-60
   DHCP Enabled. . . . . . . . . . . : Yes
   Autoconfiguration Enabled . . . . : Yes
   Link-local IPv6 Address . . . . . : fe80::bc1e:1758:ba9a:ddf3%11(Preferred)
   IPv4 Address. . . . . . . . . . . : 172.16.1.101(Preferred)
   Subnet Mask . . . . . . . . . . . : 255.240.0.0
   Lease Obtained. . . . . . . . . . : Saturday, November 11, 2017 6:00:12 AM
   Lease Expires . . . . . . . . . . : Saturday, November 11, 2017 10:00:12 AM
   Default Gateway . . . . . . . . . : 172.16.1.1
   DHCP Server . . . . . . . . . . . : 172.16.1.1
   DHCPv6 IAID . . . . . . . . . . . : 246161931
   DHCPv6 Client DUID. . . . . . . . : 00-01-00-01-1A-45-39-41-AC-22-0B-50-97-60
   DNS Servers . . . . . . . . . . . : 172.16.1.1
   NetBIOS over Tcpip. . . . . . . . : Enabled

C:\Users\Sybex>
```

If the IP address lease expires and the DHCP server is up and operational, then the host and its LAN connection should be checked. A packet capture of the DHCP process from the LAN connection will reveal whether the host is receiving DHCP Offer messages from the DHCP server. If the DHCP discovery, offer, request, and acknowledgment (DORA) process is captured with a tech computer on the LAN connection, then the host is most likely the problem.

Rogue DHCP server

A rogue DHCP server is an unauthorized DHCP server that is serving IP addresses to DHCP clients. A rogue DHCP server can be unbelievably disruptive for a network and its users. The cleanup from a rogue DHCP server is also chaotic. DHCP snooping can prevent a rogue DHCP server from sending DHCP offers to DHCP clients.

However, if DHCP snooping is not turned on to prevent it and you need to track down a rogue DHCP server, it's somewhat simple. The first step is to identify the IP address of the DHCP server; you can do so with the ipconfig utility on an affected client.

```
C:\Users\Sybex>ipconfig /all

Windows IP Configuration

Ethernet adapter Local Area Connection:

   Connection-specific DNS Suffix  . : sybex.local
   Description . . . . . . . . . . . : Intel(R) 82583V Gigabit Network Connection
   Physical Address. . . . . . . . . : AC-22-0B-50-97-60
   DHCP Enabled. . . . . . . . . . . : Yes
   Autoconfiguration Enabled . . . . : Yes
   Link-local IPv6 Address . . . . . : fe80::bc1e:1758:ba9a:ddf3%11(Preferred)
   IPv4 Address. . . . . . . . . . . : 172.16.1.80
   Subnet Mask . . . . . . . . . . . : 255.255.255.0
   Lease Obtained. . . . . . . . . . : Saturday, November 11, 2017 9:30:20 AM
   Lease Expires . . . . . . . . . . : Saturday, November 11, 2017 2:30:20 PM
   Default Gateway . . . . . . . . . : 172.16.1.2
   DHCP Server . . . . . . . . . . . : 172.16.1.50
   DHCPv6 IAID . . . . . . . . . . . : 246161931
   DHCPv6 Client DUID. . . . . . . . : 00-01-00-01-1A-45-39-41-AC-22-0B-50-97-60
   DNS Servers . . . . . . . . . . . : 172.16.1.50
   NetBIOS over Tcpip. . . . . . . . : Enabled

C:\Users\Sybex>
```

The DHCP server that has sent the DHCP offer and DHCP acknowledgment is detailed in the output of the ipconfig /all command. To track it down, we need to cache its MAC address. This is done with ipconfig /release and ipconfig /renew. The process of releasing the IP addresses and requesting a renewal will generate traffic to the DHCP server. We now have a MAC address in the ARP cache that we can use to track down the rogue DHCP with. Now we head to the switch and look at the CAM table. This will show which port on the switch is associated with the MAC address.

```
C:\Users\Sybex>arp -g

Interface: 172.16.1.101 --- 0xb
```

```
Internet Address     Physical Address     Type
172.16.1.1         00-15-5d-01-12-0d    dynamic
172.16.1.50        74-d4-35-03-a6-b9    dynamic
172.31.255.255     ff-ff-ff-ff-ff-ff     static
224.0.0.22         01-00-5e-00-00-16     static
224.0.0.251        01-00-5e-00-00-fb     static
224.0.0.252        01-00-5e-00-00-fc     static
239.255.255.250    01-00-5e-7f-ff-fa     static
255.255.255.255    ff-ff-ff-ff-ff-ff     static
```

`C:\Users\Sybex>`

It is important to note that you can also use a packet capture and analysis to obtain the rogue DHCP server IP address. However, using the `ipconfig` command is much quicker.

Untrusted SSL certificate

When an untrusted SSL certificate is encountered, the web browser will alert you that the SSL certificate is not valid, as shown in Figure 5.21. Every web browser comes with a list of trusted certificate publishers. If a certificate is issued to a website or is not trusted, a warning box will come up preventing you from visiting the site. You can click through the warning prompt and visit the site anyway, but the address bar will still read "Not secure" or display an unlocked lock icon during your visit.

FIGURE 5.21   An untrusted SSL certificate warning

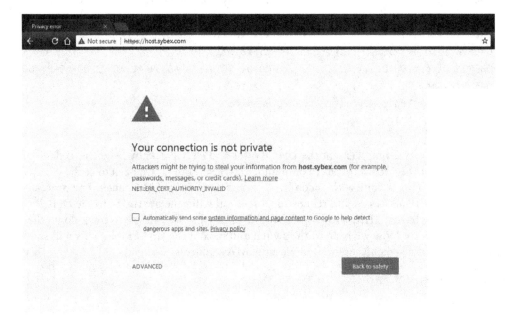

The problem should always be investigated further since information entered in the site could be intercepted if the site was hacked. The first step to diagnose is checking the hostname in the URL. All certificates must match the hostname in the URL that they are issued for. If you tried accessing the site by the IP address, this warning is benign and can be disregarded. However, if you entered the correct hostname, then the certificate should be inspected. Every web browser is different, but every web browser will let you view the certificate, as shown in Figure 5.22.

FIGURE 5.22   A self-signed certificate

In Figure 5.22 we can see that the certificate has been self-signed. This is common when the website is in development, but it is not normal once the website been placed into production. It is also common on network management equipment that allows configuration through a web page. Often the management web page will use a self-signed certificate. For this purpose, the certificate can be imported into your trusted publisher certificate store so that it can be trusted in the future.

Incorrect time

There are many issues that can be resolved by just setting the correct time. When client PCs get old, their BIOS battery that keeps the real time clock (RTC) goes dead or no longer keeps time. When this happens, the date can often get set to January 1, 1900, or a date that isn't in this decade. This will invalidate certificates, because certificates have a valid from and to date. Every SSL-enabled site will display a security warning.

There are also many protocols that are time dependent and will not function if the time is off by even 5 minutes. The Microsoft-adopted protocol of Kerberos is one of them. If the time is off by 5 minutes, you will not be able to authenticate a user account on a domain and get logged in. Normally time is synced via the Network Time Protocol (NTP) from the domain controllers, so the entire network is on the same clock.

Checking the correct time against other hosts in the network that are working fine is the first step to diagnosing incorrect time. The time and date might look fine when you glance down in the lower-left corner of your taskbar. However, the taskbar will not show you the current time zone, also called the time offset. The time might be set correctly if you were in California, but if you are in the Eastern time zone and have it set for the Pacific time zone, you'll be off by 3 hours. The Date and Time dialog box for Windows operating systems is displayed in Figure 5.23

FIGURE 5.23   Windows Date and Time dialog box

Exhausted DHCP scope

A symptom of an exhausted DHCP scope is that clients will not attain their IP address from the DHCP server. Clients will instead autoconfigure a link local address of 169.254.x.x, also called Automatic Private IP Addressing (APIPA).

The first step of diagnosing is with the client. The `ipconfig` utility will display the APIPA address and state that it was configured through autoconfiguration. The client should be checked for the correct VLAN and port configuration.

```
C:\Users\Sybex>ipconfig

Windows IP Configuration

Ethernet adapter Local Area Connection:

   Connection-specific DNS Suffix . :
   Link-local IPv6 Address . . . . . : fe80::bc82:6ccb:a1e1:32f6%11
   Autoconfiguration IPv4 Address. . : 169.254.50.246
   Subnet Mask . . . . . . . . . . . : 255.255.0.0
   Default Gateway . . . . . . . . . :

C:\Users\Sybex>
```

A packet capture and analysis tool can be used to diagnose the problem as well. DCHP discover messages will be seen in the analysis but no DHCP offers from the server. When you determine the problem to be a DHCP server problem and discover the scope is exhausted, you will need to add IP addresses to the range in the DHCP server or release client leases from the clients. Never delete the leases from the server—you will create the problem of duplicate IP addresses if you do so.

Blocked TCP/UDP ports

When TCP and UDP ports are blocked, the symptom can be an unresponsive application. Another symptom might be that features of the application do not function correctly or at all. I have even seen applications crash because the ports are blocked. This can be very frustrating for the network administrator or the people supporting the application.

Most organizations block outbound port connections. This is done to limit the abuse of the Internet but mainly for security reasons. When a new application is installed, the appropriate firewall rules will be configured. The vendor of the application should furnish a document called the firewall rule considerations or specifications.

Blocked outbound ports can be diagnosed by using a port scanner like Nmap to check the destination host ports. This will allow you to see the blocked and permitted ports. A packet capture and analysis tool like Wireshark is also useful to verify that the application is initiating the connection outbound to the destination host. Once the problem is diagnosed as a blocked port, the firewall rules should be checked against the vendor's documentation.

Incorrect host-based firewall settings

When the host-based firewall is incorrectly set, it can affect applications and services the host provides. Similar to perimeter firewalls discussed in the previous section, host-based firewalls must be set up to allow both inbound and outbound ports for the application. When the host-based firewall is incorrectly set, it can affect all clients, if the service or application is accessed by all the clients.

To diagnose incorrect host-based settings, use a port scanner, which will indicate which ports are accessible and which ports are blocked. A packet capture and analysis tool can also be useful to see the incoming requests for the application. If a problem is detected, it is best to consult the vendor's firewall documentation; most application vendors will describe the host-based firewall configuration for their application.

Incorrect ACL settings

Access control lists (ACLs) give us the ability to create security rules for the internal network. We can segregate traffic from client networks and restrict what networks the servers or applications can communicate with. When ACLs are set incorrectly, they can further restrict traffic or allow traffic that is otherwise not intended. Incorrect ACLs settings can restrict applications from communicating, and they can also create security problems. I discussed the use of ACLs for security in Chapter 4.

To diagnose incorrect ACLs, use a port scanner. Run it against the remote services so that you can check the ACLs for proper configuration.

Unresponsive service

An unresponsive service can display the symptoms of ports being blocked. However, firewalls rules and ACL rules should not be suspected unless they have recently changed or the application has been recently updated. The service can become unresponsive for a variety of reasons.

When a service becomes unresponsive and you are positive that it is not fulfilling any new requests, a consideration must be addressed. If you reboot or restart the service, will it affect clients already connected? The netstat utility can help you evaluate this consideration. The utility will allow you to see the current established connections. Ultimately, if the service is unresponsive, it will need to be restarted.

Hardware failure

Eventually everything that spins or is powered breaks. Fortunately, you can plan for these events with redundancy and fault tolerance, as I covered in Chapter 3. Hardware failure is inevitable, but with the proper redundancy the outage can be minimized.

Service contracts on equipment ensure that hardware failures minimize the impact to the network. Contract response time is directly related to the cost of the service contract. Some contracts are designed for a 4-hour turnaround on parts, which is the critical care plan. A 4-hour response time is generally reserved for critical components because of the price. Next business day is the norm for equipment that has redundancy built into it. If one of your dual-power supplies fails, the next business day is more than sufficient.

Exam Essentials

Understand the scenarios and diagnostic process for the common network issues.   Hostnames that do not resolve should be tested from the source to the host having the trouble using the nslookup command. A gateway or network mask incorrectly configured can be diagnosed with the tracert/traceroute command. A duplicate IP address on the network can create intermittent problems for the clients with the duplicate IP addresses. Expired IP addresses are a direct result of a DHCP down or not responding. A rouge DHCP server can be identified by IP address looking at the client's lease. An untrusted SSL certificate should always be investigated since it may be malicious in nature or the host's time is misconfigured. When the DHCP scope has been exhausted and contains no more leases, the client will autoconfigure an APIPA address. A blocked TCP or UDP port can make an application non-responsive. Incorrect host-based firewall settings can make services unavailable for clients. Incorrect ACL settings can prevent applications and services from being reached; they can also prevent security from being properly applied. Hardware failures can be minimized with fault-tolerant systems.

Review Questions

1. Which should you do during the process of identifying the problem?

   A. Duplicate the problem

   B. Establish a plan of action

   C. Question users

   D. Create a hypothesis

2. Which technique is used to determine the root cause of a problem, in which you split a system into smaller subprocesses for examination?

   A. Top-to-bottom OSI analysis

   B. Divide and conquer analysis

   C. Bottom-to-top OSI analysis

   D. Process analysis

3. What is the next step in problem solving once a theory is confirmed?

   A. Create a hypothesis

   B. Consider multiple approaches

   C. Establish a plan of action

   D. Approach multiple problems individually

4. What is the final step in resolving a problem?

   A. Implement a solution

   B. Validate a theory

   C. Establish a plan of action

   D. Document

5. Which tool is used to troubleshoot wiring breaks in network cabling?

   A. OTDR

   B. Tone generator

   C. TDR

   D. Multimeter

6. You need to find a network cable that is not labeled on a wiring panel; which tool should you use to identify the cable?

   A. Cable tester

   B. Tone generator

   C. TDR

   D. Multimeter

7. You are working alone and want to test a fiber-optic cable. Which tool will help you test the fiber-optic cable quickly?

A. OTDR

B. TDR

C. Light meter

D. Loopback adapter

8. Which software tool will allow you check if a web application running on a server is online?

A. ping

B. nslookup

C. tracert/traceroute

D. Port scanner

9. You believe there is problem upstream of your Internet connection and want to gather information to provide the ISP. Which tool will you use to gather statistics?

A. tracert/traceroute

B. pathping

C. nslookup

D. dig

10. Which tool allows examination at the packet level for traffic from an application?

A. Protocol analyzer

B. dig

C. Spectrum analyzer

D. nslookup

11. You need to check the configured MTU on the interface of a Linux host; which command should you use?

A. ipconfig

B. ifconfig

C. mtuconfig

D. iptables

12. You need to check the port an application is listening on; which command should you use to view the information?

A. portqry

B. ifconfig

C. netstat

D. iptables

13. You need to analyze whether an application is responding to a client request; which command will allow you to capture the traffic?

  A. tcpdump

  B. nmap

  C. portqry

  D. netstat

14. Which command will allow you to clear the cached MAC addresses on a host?

  A. arp -g *

  B. ipconfig /flushdns

  C. arp -d *

  D. iptables -f

15. Which describes what happens to a wireless signal as it moves further away from the source?

  A. Increased latency

  B. Increased jitter

  C. Increased attenuation

  D. Decreased reflection

16. You believe there is a break in a fiber-optic cable that spans 5 miles; which tool will help you determine where the cable break cable is?

  A. TDR

  B. OTDR

  C. Cable tester

  D. Cable certifier

17. Which Nmap scan will send an URG, PSH, and FIN flag to trick the operating system to respond with an RST?

  A. Xmas-tree scan

  B. Fin scan

  C. Null scan

  D. UDP scan

18. As routers, switches, and NAT processes are added to a routed switch path, what happens?

  A. Latency increases

  B. Jitter increases

   C. Latency decreases

   D. Jitter decreases

19. Which term describes the phenomenon of a wireless signal changing in frequency as it passes through different materials?

   A. Reflection

   B. Absorption

   C. Attenuation

   D. Refraction

20. You find that a workstation has no connectivity to the network. When you use `ipconfig`, the IP address reports as 169.254.34.22 with a subnet mask of 255.255.0.0. What is the possible problem?

   A. The subnet mask is incorrect.

   B. The IP address is on the wrong subnet.

   C. The gateway address is on the wrong network.

   D. The original IP address has expired.

21. You believe that packets are being routed via the wrong gateway; which tool will allow you to verify the route a packet takes to the destination IP address?

   A. `route print`

   B. `tracert`

   C. `ipconfig`

   D. `dig`

22. You are diagnosing a wireless issue and you believe that the problem is related to RF noise. Which measurement should you focus on to prove your theory?

   A. RSSI

   B. SNR

   C. dB strength

   D. EMI

23. What is the outcome if you have a speed mismatch on a network connection?

   A. Degraded performance

   B. High collision rate

   C. High error rate

   D. No link status

24. You have a high error rate on an interface and believe that crosstalk is to blame. What should be checked to prove your theory?

    A. Network cable specifications

    B. Duplex

    C. Speed

    D. EMI

25. Which command is used to verify the configuration of a host-based firewall on a Linux host?

    A. nmap

    B. iptables

    C. ifconfig

    D. portqry

Appendix

Answers to Review Questions

Chapter 1: Domain 1.0: Networking Concepts

1. C. Secure Shell (SSH) is a cryptographic protocol that provides encrypted text console–based access over an IP network. It is commonly used to securely administer Linux servers. Telnet provides text-based access, but it is in clear text.

2. D. Remote Desktop Protocol (RDP) provides remote access to Microsoft servers for administration of the operating system. The RDP protocol redirects the keyboard, mouse, and monitor to the administrator's computer.

3. D. The Transmission Control Protocol (TCP) provides sequenced and acknowledged segments. Because each segment is sequenced and acknowledged by the receiving computer, any segments lost in the delivery process will be re-requested at this layer.

4. B. The tracert utility will detail the path a packet is taking to get to a destination network. Tracert uses the ICMP protocol to report the path a packet takes to the destination network.

5. B. The presentation layer is responsible for encryption and decryption services. The presentation layer is also responsible for compression and decompression and translation services.

6. C. The addition of the clients added to the immediate network most likely raised the amount of broadcasts in the network. Although you could assign static IP addresses to all computers to reduce DHCP, ARP is still broadcast based. The recommended remedy is to create several broadcast domains with network segmentation.

7. A. The MTU of Ethernet is 1500 bytes, or 1518 bytes if you are including the source MAC address, destination MAC address, type field, and FCS.

8. B. When a broadcast is sent, the destination MAC address will be FF:FF:FF:FF:FF:FF. This destination MAC address tells the switch to forward the traffic to all active ports.

9. C. The 802.1Q protocol is an open standard trunking protocol. Inter-Switch Link (ISL) is another trunking protocol, but it can only be used on Cisco devices. Because your switches are from two different vendors, they are not both Cisco devices; therefore, 802.1Q must be used.

10. D. When calculating STP, the switch with the lowest MAC address will become the root bridge if all of the priorities are set to the default. However, if the priority on a particular switch is lower than the others, it will always become the root bridge.

11. D. Link Layer Discovery Protocol (LLDP) and Cisco Discovery Protocol (CDP) communicate with neighboring devices and exchange power operating conditions. Turning on LLDP will quickly rectify the problem by adjusting power consumption.

12. A. Default routing is best implemented in stub networks, because all networks other than the immediate one are accessed through the default gateway.

13. D. Border Gateway Protocol is used as an external routing protocol for the Internet. When two providers are connected to a single site using BGP, the connection can fail over in the case of one provider suffering an outage.

14. D. The IPv6 address of 2001:0db8:45::102::12 is not a valid IPv6 address. The double colon cannot be used twice in the IPv6 address.

15. C. The IPv6 address of ff03:0340:508e:e0ee:e2be:3cec:abd8:e24b is a multicast address. Multicast addresses always start with FF as the first two digits.

16. D. The Class of Service (CoS) marking is a 3-bit field in the 802.1Q trunk frame. This 3-bit field contains 8 possible queues for QoS at layer 2.

17. B. The Virtual Router Redundancy Protocol (VRRP) is a First Hop Redundancy Protocol (FHRP) used for providing high availability of the default gateway. Because you have two different vendors, you must use VRRP since it is an open standard and Hot Standby Router Protocol (HSRP) is a Cisco proprietary protocol for FHRP.

18. B. The IP address of 208.44.26.128/25 is not a valid IP address. The /25 CIDR mask create two subnets of 208.44.26.0/25 and 208.44.26.128/25. The IP address of 208.44.26.128/25 is the network address of the second subnet and therefore cannot be used for IP addressing.

19. D. The DHCP server is unavailable or not functioning, because the client has obtained APIPA addressing. APIPA addressing also called link-local addressing always starts with 169.254.x.x.

20. B. The Z-wave IoT wireless protocol operates in the United States on 908.42 MHz and in Europe it operates on 868.42 MHz.

21. A. The 802.11n wireless standard introduced channel bonding. The 802.11n standard allows for the bonding of up to two channels to provide a 40 MHz channel.

22. C. The Global System for Mobile Communications (GSM) was developed by the European Telecommunications Standards Institute (ETSI) and is now used globally.

23. C. The 2.4 GHz wireless band has three nonoverlapping channels of 1, 6, and 11. Although they overlap with other channels, these three channels do not overlap between themselves.

24. A. The National Institute of Standards and Technology (NIST) defines three cloud types of: Platform as a Service (PaaS), Software as a Service (SaaS), and Infrastructure as a Service (IaaS). A DR site hosting at a cloud provider is an example of IaaS. Although DRaaS can be used as a term to advertise a type of cloud service, it is not defined by NIST as a type of service.

25. C. A DHCP reservation will allow for the printer to obtain the same IP address every time it is turned on. The DHCP server will serve the same IP address to the printer based on the printer's MAC address in the reservation.

Chapter 2: Domain 2.0: Infrastructure

1. C. The cabling type needs to be STP cable, because there will be a high amount of EMI in the plant area with the welding equipment.

2. D. Although the distance of the cable is below 3000 feet, which would normally necessitate MMF cable, the speed is 40 Gbps and is over the 10 Gbps that MMF cable can provide. So SMF is your only option in this scenario, dictated by speed.

3. D. A renovation is no different than a brand-new building, and fire and electrical code must be followed. You must use plenum-rated cable because it is in a ceiling, which could provide ventilation. Solid-core wiring should be used because it will be a permanent installation.

4. A. The F-connector is used for MoCA set-top boxes and broadband cable boxes. It is the most common cable connector for coaxial cable installations with set-top boxes.

5. B. The straight tip (ST) connector has a similar locking mechanism as the BNC connector. After aligning the fiber-optic tip, a half-turn provides a locking mechanism to engage to secure the cable.

6. B. The SFP+ transceivers can deliver up to 400 Gbps over single-mode fiber-optic cable. The network equipment must be compatible with SFP+ transceivers and be able to deliver the 400 Gbps at the SFP+ port.

7. B. To minimize the monthly reoccurring costs, two strands of fiber-optic should be purchased. The transceivers used on the two strands should be bidirectional transceivers. This will allow each strand to work independently of each other in the event of a failure on one strand. Although four strands with duplex transceivers would achieve fault-tolerance, the monthly reoccurring costs would be double.

8. C. Patch panels are commonly used as diagnostic points for wired Ethernet wiring problems. The patch panel allows for easier diagnostic of these types of problems.

9. D. Category 6a cabling should be specified for the installation. It will allow 10 Gbps speeds at distances of 100 meters. Category 6 cabling will deliver speeds of 10 Gbps but only at distances of 55 meters.

10. A. Category 5e network cable will allow for 1 Gbps speeds at a maximum distance of 100 meters. The only component required to achieve 1 Gbps to the desktops is the switching equipment.

11. D. Category 7 cable is not recognized by the TIA/EIA standards. Although it is being sold at the next-generation of TIA/EIA standards, it has not been officially published as a specification.

12. B. A crossover cable must be used when connecting a switch to a switch when the auto MDI-X mechanism is not available.

13. C. The 1000BaseSX specification defines a maximum distance of 550 meters at 1 Gbps when using 50 micron cable. The SX and LX designations are often used as a mnemonic for short-haul and long-haul, respectively.

14. B. Switches provide the lowest latency with the use of application-specific integrated circuits (ASICs). Hubs are multiport repeaters and diminish usable bandwidth. Bridges are software-based switches and provide higher latency than switches.

15. B. Intrusion detection systems and intrusion prevention systems (IDSs/IPSs) offer detection and prevention of network intrusion of malicious activity.

16. D. RADIUS servers provide authentication, authorization, and accounting for VPN concentrators. They can be coupled to Active Directory or LDAP directory services for user authentication.

17. B. A VoIP gateway can convert a SIP provider's VoIP services to a T1 or ISDN line that the legacy PBX expects. This allows VoIP services to be used with the legacy PBX.

18. A. A type 1 hypervisor allows virtual machines to directly access the resources of the CPU and RAM of the host. Hybrid hypervisors do a similar task, but they require the host operating system for management.

19. C. Fibre Channel uses dedicated Fibre Channel switches to create a storage area network (SAN) for block-level access of an FC storage LUN.

20. D. When jumbo frames are implemented, it changes the MTU of Ethernet from 1500 bytes to 9000 bytes. This reduces the fragmentation of iSCSI layer 3 packets and reduces the CPU utilization on both the host and iSCSI unit.

21. A. An ISDN primary rate leased line uses one of the 24 channels for call setup. The remaining 23 channels are used to place the phone calls.

22. B. WiMAX is a wireless technology sometimes called last mile service. It is mainly used when the cost of the buildout is too expensive due to geographical terrain.

23. D. Although any of these technologies could potentially help reduce bandwidth usage at the main office, you already have a VPN infrastructure in place. DMVPN would allow you to create a mesh VPN and allow branch offices to communicate directly with each other without using bandwidth from the main office.

24. B. DSL providers mainly use the PPPoE protocol to authenticate subscribers and provide DSL modem configuration.

25. B. When the technician is dispatched to your location for diagnostic troubleshooting, they will troubleshoot from the demarcation point back to the provider.

Chapter 3: Domain 3.0: Network Operations

1. C. A logical diagram depicts how a network operates by representing the flows of information.

2. D. A router is commonly drawn as a circle with two sets of arrows perpendicular to each other, depicting a type of crossroads for packets.

3. B. The standard operating procedure document details the step-by-step work instructions necessary to decommission a server.

4. D. The change advisory board reviews changes proposed for the network so that they do not affect day-to-day operations.

5. B. When labeling cable in the switch closet, the label should depict the least specific location, such as a building, to the most specific location, such as the outlet number. Workstation names and purposes can change over time.

6. D. Performance baselines gathered over time help create a historical representation of activity and normal operations. When a server is performing poorly, the baseline can validate both the problem and implemented solution.

7. A. Asset management software assists in tracking IT inventory, such as network equipment and other fixed tangible assets.

8. A. Configuring a group of disks with RAID level 5 striping with parity is an example of fault tolerance, because redundancy of resources is used to ensure operations in the event of failure.

9. D. Load balancing should be implemented with two or more web servers to scale out the servers and lower demand on any one single web server.

10. A. A cold site is the least expensive to maintain over time, because very little or no hardware is at the site. If a disaster occurs, it will take time to acquire hardware and configure.

11. B. The recovery time objective (RTO) is a measurement of how fast you can recover from data loss from backup.

12. B. Disk-to-disk backups will speed up any backup, since the backup is coming off disks and being backed up to disks. Although GFS rotations may speed up end-of-week and end-of-month backups, it is considered a rotation strategy.

13. D. An incremental backup will only back up files that have the archive bit set. After backing up the files, the archive bit is reset for the next backup.

14. C. An SLA of 4 nines is 52.56 minutes per year of expected downtime. This equates to 4.38 minutes per month that the service can be down.

15. A. Link Aggregation Control Protocol (LACP) is an open standard control protocol used for aggregation of ports between non-Cisco switches. Non-Cisco switches will not support the Cisco proprietary protocol of Port Aggregation Protocol (PAgP).

16. C. An online UPS uses the AC power for the rectifier/charging circuit that maintains a charge for the batteries. The batteries then supply the inverter with a constant DC power source. The inverter converts the DC power source back into an AC power circuit again that supplies the load.

17. B. A full backup is used for grandfather, father, son (GFS) rotations. GFS rotations help to maintain a lengthy RPO by keeping fewer backups using daily, weekly, and monthly backups.

18. D. The Microsoft Windows Server Update Services (WSUS) helps facilitate the updating of Microsoft clients and servers.

19. A. Wireshark is a common open source packet capture tool used in networks for analysis of problems.

20. D. Virtual Router Redundancy Protocol (VRRP) is an open standard protocol that is used for high availability of default gateways.

21. B. Before an NMS can collect SNMP statistics, the management information base (MIB) from the manufacturer must be loaded.

22. D. By default the SSH File Transfer Protocol (SFTP) uses public-private key pairs to provide encryption for the remote access session.

23. C. A bring your own device (BYOD) policy defines the minimum specifications for an employee's device used for work-related access. The mobile device management (MDM) software would usually dictate these specifications.

24. A. The material safety data sheet (MSDS) details how materials should be stored, fire safety of materials, and emergency information.

25. C. Transport Layer Security (TLS) uses the TLS handshake protocol to initiate encryption.

Chapter 4: Domain 4.0: Network Security

1. C. Passive infrared (PIR) contains a reflective panel that creates different zones of detection. The reflective panel is distinctive to PIR sensors.

2. B. Pan tilt zoom (PTZ) cameras allow for intervention of a situation. In situations where you must track and record equipment as it is moved, such as in casino environments, PTZ cameras should be used.

3. B. A passive RFID system is inexpensive because the transponder powers the RFID tag. Transponders located at egress points of the library will achieve the requirement.

4. C. Key fobs, ID badges, and combination locks do not provide authentication of employees. Only biometrics will provide a factor of authentication.

5. D. Smart cards are the size of a credit card and contain an integrated circuit chip (ICC). The ICC contains a user's private key that is unlocked with a PIN code.

6. A. Authentication is the process of verification of the user's identify. It can be performed with various factors such as something you know, you are, or have, in addition to other factors.

7. A. Remote Authentication Dial-In User Service (RADIUS) was originally proposed by the IETF and became an open standard for authentication, often used with 802.1x.

8. C. Kerberos is an authentication system that can use Data Encryption Standard (3DES) and Advanced Encryption Standard (AES) encryption for encryption of user credentials. It is exclusively used by Microsoft Active Directory as an authentication protocol.

9. B. Security Assertion Markup Language (SAML) is an open-standard XML-based framework used for transmitting authentication and authorization information of users and computers.

10. B. Authorization is the process of verifying whether a user has permission for a specific action; it is followed by the authentication of the user.

11. A. The protocol of TCP and the port number of 389 is used for LDAP lookups.

12. D. Voice recognition is an example of a personal human characteristic.

13. A. Your IP address is an example of an authentication factor of somewhere you are. Geographical IP lookups via a Geo-IP database helps provide your approximate location.

14. A. Lightweight Extensible Authentication Protocol (LEAP) is a Cisco proprietary protocol that was developed and is used by Cisco devices for authentication via 802.1x.

15. B. A switch or WAP is considered an 802.1x authenticator. The authenticator directly communicates between the supplicant and the authenticating server to relay credentials.

16. D. Port security can restrict a switch port to a specific number of ports configured by the administrator. The specific MAC addresses can be preconfigured or learned dynamically.

17. C. A captive portal will capture the users' first web page request and redirect them to either a login page or AUP.

18. A. Wi-Fi Protected Access (WPA) replaced WEP as a wireless protocol and introduced many new security features, such as MIC and TKIP.

19. A. Network access control (NAC) is used in conjunction with 802.1x and can restrict clients if specific security policies are not met, such as current antivirus and software updates.

20. B. A logic bomb is malicious code that is not activated until specific conditions are met that triggers the code.

21. D. An exploit is a script, code, application, or technique to gain unauthorized access to an operating system through a vulnerability.

22. B. SHA1 and MD5 are two common file hashing algorithms used to validate the integrity of a file.

23. A. A man-in-the-middle attack allows the attacker to impersonate both parties involved in a network conversation.

24. A. Secure Shell (SSH) negotiates encryption when a connection is made. SSH is used a replacement for the unencrypted Telnet protocol.

25. D. Bridge Protocol Data Unit (BPDU) Guard is configured on user-facing switchports to protect the STP protocol from being attacked. If another switch is connected to a switch port protected with BPDU Guard and BPDUs are received, the switch port is placed into an err-disable state.

Chapter 5: Domain 5.0 Network Troubleshooting and Tools

1. **A, C.** During the identification of a problem, you should question users and try to duplicate the problem.

2. **B.** The divide and conquer analysis technique is used to divide complex processes into small subprocesses that are easier to analyze.

3. **C.** After a theory or hypothesis is confirmed, you should establish a plan of action to resolve the problem.

4. **D.** The documentation of the finding, actions, and outcomes is the final step in the resolution of a problem. It allows us to solve future problems more quickly.

5. **C.** A time domain reflectometer is a tool that sends electronic pulses of energy down a wire and reads the time their reflection comes back. A calculation is made to determine the length of the cable.

6. **B.** A tone generator is used in conjunction with a tracing probe to identify network cables. It operates by injecting a warbling tone into the cable so that the tracing probe can amplify the signal audibly.

7. **D.** Although you could use a light meter to test the fiber-optic cable, you would need to move the source over to the other fiber strand. A loopback adapter will allow you to test the cable with one test of both strands.

8. **D.** A port scanner will allow you to check if an application is accepting connections. The port will return an open status, and most port scanners will check for an HTTP response. The ping utility will only check if the server is online.

9. **B.** The pathping tool will perform a traceroute to the destination address. It will then check each hop with a number of ICMP packets and return statistics on each hop.

10. **A.** A protocol analyzer will allow us to inspect packet levels of traffic that is captured from an application.

11. **B.** The ifconfig command will allow you to inspect the MTU on the interface of a Linux host. It will also allow you to change the MTU temporarily.

12. **C.** The netstat command will allow you to see layer 4 binding between applications and the TCP/UDP ports. On Windows, the netstat -ab command will display listening ports. On Linux/Unix, the netstat -ap command will perform the same function.

13. **A.** The tcpdump command will allow packet capture of an interface. When run on the server the application is responding on, tcpdump can capture the response of the application for further analysis.

14. C. The arp command allows you to manipulate the MAC address cache of a host. When you issue the arp -d * command, you will clear all MAC address entries in the ARP cache.

15. C. The attenuation of the signal increases as the signal moves further away from the source. Attenuation is the gradual absorption of a signal's energy in the air.

16. B. An optical time-domain reflectometer (OTDR) sends a pulse of light down the fiber-optic cable and measures the time and reflection strength. This measurement will determine where a break occurs in the fiber-optic cable.

17. A. The Xmas-tree scan will send the URG, PSH, and FIN flags in the TCP header to trick the operating system into sending back an RST for closed ports.

18. A. Latency is the measurement of delay between the source and destination. As components such as switches, routers, and NAT processes are added, latency is increased because of the lookups and forwarding.

19. D. As a wireless signal passes through different materials, the signal will slow down and change in frequency. This phenomenon is called refraction, similar to a prism and light.

20. D. The 169.254.x.x prefix is an Automatic Private IP Addressing (APIPA) IP address, also called a link local address. The presence of this address means that either the original DHCP address has expired or the DHCP server is unavailable.

21. B. The tracert command will allow you to see the path an IP packet takes to the destination. The Linux/Unix command is traceroute.

22. B. Wireless access point (WAP) diagnostics and spectrum analyzers will display RSSI and SNR. The signal-to-noise ratio is the separation of signal to floor noise measured in decibels (dB). The SNR will prove the theory of excess RF noise compared to the originating signal.

23. D. If there is a speed mismatch between the two connection devices, you will have no link status, because the carrier signal is different.

24. A. Crosstalk happens when the electrical signals on one wire induces erroneous signals on another wire. The correct category cable specifications are defined by the Telecommunications Industry Association (TIA).

25. B. The iptables command allows configuration and inspection of the host-based firewall in many Linux distributions.

Index

Note to the Reader: Throughout this index **boldfaced** page numbers indicate primary discussions of a topic. *Italicized* page numbers indicate illustrations.

O

S

Z

Save $100 on the Sybex Security+ SY0-501 Exam Review Course

Enter code **SECURITYVIP** at checkout on **www.sybex.com/go/securityplusfreetrial**

ABOUT THE COURSE

Based on CompTIA Authorized content, this detailed course has everything you need to prepare for the CompTIA Security+ SY0-501 Exam. Fully aligned to the exam objectives with practical examples that illustrate how these processes play out in real-world scenarios, allowing you to immediately translate essential concepts to on-the-job application. You'll learn how to handle threats, attacks, and vulnerabilities using industry-standard tools and technologies, while understanding the role of architecture and design.

This course includes:

- **Video Lectures & Slides** with over 13 hours of high quality, instructional video.

- **Interactive Test Bank** with over 650 practice questions. Practice questions help you identify where further review is needed. Get more than 90% of the answers correct, and you're ready to take the exam.

- Two 90 question **Mock Exams** allow you to simulate the actual exam before the big day.

- 120 **Electronic Flashcards** to reinforce learning and last-minute prep before the exam.

- **Key Term Glossary** in PDF format gives you instant access to all key terms to ensure you are fully prepared.

- The **Exam Planner** allows you to set your exam date and receive a tailored lesson plan with corresponding assignments for each day.

- The **Mobile App** allows you to stream or download all videos, review questions, and flash cards on-the-go.

- 25 hours of **Virtual Labs** allow for practicing skills in a safe and secure virtual environment.

- The **Partner Until You Pass** guarantee means you receive access to your course until you pass, even if your 12 month subscription is over.

Save $100 on the Sybex's PMP® Exam Review Course

Enter code **PMPVIP** at checkout on **www.efficientlearning.com/PMP**

18-468707